The Cistercian Order in Medieval Europe

GIVEN TO THE
PORTLAND PUBLIC LIBRARY
BY THE
JAMES A. HEALY FUND

The Medieval World

Series editor: Julia Smith, The University of Glasgow

Alfred the Great
Richard Abels

Christian–Jewish Relations, 1000–1300
Anna Sapir Abulafia

The Western Mediterranean Kingdoms
David Abulafia

The Fourth Crusade
Michael Angold

The Cathars
Malcolm Barber

The Godwins
Frank Barlow

Philip Augustus
Jim Bradbury

Disunited Kingdoms
Michael Brown

Violence in Medieval Europe
Warren Brown

Medieval Canon Law
J.A. Brundage

Crime in Medieval Europe
Trevor Dean

Charles I of Anjou
Jean Dunbabin

The Age of Charles Martel
Paul Fouracre

Margery Kempe
A.E. Goodman

Edward the Black Prince
David Green

Bastard Feudalism
M. Hicks

The Formation of English Common Law
John Hudson

The Mongols and the West
Peter Jackson

Europe's Barbarians, AD 200–600
Edward James

Cnut
K. Lawson

The Age of Robert Guiscard
Graham Loud

The English Church, 940–1154
H.R. Loyn

Justinian
John Moorhead

Ambrose
John Moorhead

The Devil's World
Andrew P. Roach

The Reign of Richard Lionheart
Ralph Turner/Richard Heiser

The Welsh Princes
Roger Turvey

English Noblewomen in the Late Middle Ages
J. Ward

The Cistercian Order in Medieval Europe
1090–1500

Emilia Jamroziak

London and New York

First published 2013
by Routledge
2 Park Square, Milton Park, Abingdon, Oxon OX14 4RN

and by Routledge
711 Third Avenue, New York, NY 10017

Routledge is an imprint of the Taylor & Francis Group, an informa business

© 2013 Emilia Jamroziak

The right of Emilia Jamroziak to be identified as author of this work has been asserted by her in accordance with sections 77 and 78 of the Copyright, Designs and Patents Act 1988.

All rights reserved. No part of this book may be reprinted or reproduced or utilised in any form or by any electronic, mechanical, or other means, now known or hereafter invented, including photocopying and recording, or in any information storage or retrieval system, without permission in writing from the publishers.

Trademark notice: Product or corporate names may be trademarks or registered trademarks, and are used only for identification and explanation without intent to infringe.

British Library Cataloguing in Publication Data
A catalogue record for this book is available from the British Library

Library of Congress Cataloging in Publication Data
A catalog record for this book has been requested

ISBN: 978-0-415-73638-1 (hbk)
ISBN: 978-1-405-85864-9 (pbk)

Typeset in Galliard
by Graphicraft Limited, Hong Kong

Printed and bound by CPI Group (UK) Ltd, Croydon, CR0 4YY

CONTENTS

	ACKNOWLEDGEMENTS	vi
	INTRODUCTION	1
chapter one	ORIGINS: IDEAS, MYTHS AND INTERPRETATIONS	13
chapter two	THE FIRST MULTINATIONAL? HOW THE CISTERCIAN ORDER SPREAD ACROSS EUROPE	43
chapter three	CISTERCIAN COMMUNITIES AND THE LAY WORLD	92
chapter four	CISTERCIAN NUNS: THE ROLE OF WOMEN IN THE ORDER	124
chapter five	VISUAL CULTURE OF CISTERCIAN COMMUNITIES	156
chapter six	ECONOMY: NOT JUST SHEEP AND GRAIN	183
chapter seven	INTELLECTUAL HORIZONS: WRITING, PREACHING AND CISTERCIAN SPIRITUALITY	208
chapter eight	WAS THERE A CRISIS OF THE CISTERCIAN ORDER IN THE LATER MIDDLE AGES?	238
	CONCLUSION	285
	GLOSSARY	292
	INDEX	298

ACKNOWLEDGEMENTS

First of all I would like to thank Prof. Julia Smith for asking me to write this book for the Medieval World series. It has been a great pleasure to work on this volume and survey such a wide area of medieval Cistercian history. Her comments, suggestions and criticism have been invaluable in the process of improving drafts; she is an exceptional book-series editor and therefore it is particularly sad that this is the final volume in the Medieval World series. The anonymous reader was particularly generous with her advice and comments helping me to improve the text considerably.

The great part of the work on *The Cistercian Order* was conducted during research leave in the academic year 2008–2009, granted and financed by the School of History and the Faculty of Arts, University of Leeds. During that time I benefited from the funding of the Leeds–Copenhagen co-operation fund which enabled me to spend a very productive time in the Latin and Greek library of the Saxo Institute. I would like to thank Profs Christian Troelsgaard and Karsten Friis-Jensen, Mette Birkedal Bruun and Dr Mia Münster-Swendsen for their hospitality and advice. The discussion with Prof. Brian Patrick McGuire of Roskilde University at the early stages of this project reassured me that I was on the 'right track'.

However, the present book would be much poorer if not for the fellowship at the FOVOG in May–June 2009. The wonderful library, discussions with and advice of Prof. Gert Melville, Dr Anne Müller and Dr Jörg Sonntag and lunchtime companionship of Prof. Timothy Johnson, Gerd Jäkel and Tobias Tanneberger enriched my understanding of monastic history. My thanks go to all members of the FOVOG.

In addition, the kind hospitality of Prof. Katariina Mustakallio, the Director of the Institutum Romanum Finlandiae, allowed me to enjoy the riches of the Librairie Française de Rome. I have also benefited from the feedback and comments from those who listened to my presentations on various aspects of this project at the International Medieval Congresses in Leeds, 'Passages' conferences in Tampere, 'Art and Ritual in Late Medieval and Early Modern Northern and Central Europe' conference in Tallinn, 'The Prelate in Late Medieval and Reformation England' conference in Liverpool, and the 'European history 1150–1550' seminar at the Institute of Historical Research in November 2008: all have been very important in the process of shaping up the book.

ACKNOWLEDGEMENTS

I would like to thank Mike Spence and Richard Thomason, whose PhD projects on Cistercian intellectual and material culture I have had the pleasure to supervise for the last few years, and which have helped me to understand white monks in Yorkshire in new ways.

Finally, I would like to thank my medievalist colleagues at Leeds – Axel Müller, Iona McCleery, Melanie Brunner and Richard Morris – for always being so supportive.

Publisher's acknowledgements

We are grateful to the following for permission to reproduce copyright material:

Tables on pages 56 and 62 and map on pp. 70–71 from Terryl Kinder, *Cistercian Europe: Architecture of Contemplation* published jointly 2002 by Cistercian Publications, Kalamazoo MI and by William B. Eerdmans Publishing Co,. English edition © 2002 William B.Eerdmans Publishing Co.

In some instances we have been unable to trace the owners of copyright material and would appreciate any information that would enable us to do so.

INTRODUCTION

The Cistercian Order was one of the most successful trans-European organisations of the middle ages. Its model of spirituality not only drew men and women into joining the Order but attracted support from lay patrons and benefactors. The medieval history of the Cistercians reflects many of the key social, cultural and religious trends of the central and later middle ages. It was not a story of birth, growth and decline of the Order, but one of change, development and continuity.

The present study has a number of central themes that provide an interpretative framework. First, and ever-present from the start, was the concept of reform and renewal, aspiring to recreate the original ideal of coenobitic monasticism through a return to the perfect form of observance. Second, the myths about the origins of the Order were handed down within individual communities and by the Order as a whole in foundation narratives, in institutional histories and in 'hybrid' forms of record keeping, in which thinking about the past was intertwined with the current pragmatic needs. Third, the filiation with its regional, international and cross-border links between Cistercian abbeys facilitated communications and the transfer of information and ideas in the Order and influenced career structures within the monastic communities. The fourth theme is the Order's engagement with the lay world – patrons, benefactors, neighbours, and rural and urban communities. Finally, there was the development tension between the universal (trans-European) structures of the Order and the particular local and regional aspirations of the individual houses.

The present study is neither a compendium of knowledge about the medieval Order, nor a comprehensive account of individual monastic foundations, but an interpretation of the development of the Cistercian movement up to the Reformation. It is organised partly chronologically and partly thematically, to show the most important characteristics of, and developments in, the Cistercian Order in the middle ages. It is not simply a 'history from above', i.e. from the perspective of the international structures of the Order, but one that combines its account of the Order as a trans-European organisation with regional history and 'non-standard' examples of Cistercian practice with a discussion of the trans-European organisation of the Order. The examples of monastic activity are from the broadest possible geographical areas, ranging (with some bias towards the northern part of the continent) from East-Central Europe and Scandinavia to the edges of Latin Christendom in the Holy Land, Greece and Iberian peninsula.

Cistercian History and Modern Scholarship

Writing about the history of the Cistercians is as old as the Order itself; the roots of its historiography go back to studies by Cistercian monks themselves, seeking to understand and commemorate their own past, and to early ecclesiastical historians active during the Counter-Reformation.[1] Many key Cistercian sources, notably monastic chronicles and charters of individual abbeys, were published in the nineteenth and early twentieth centuries and became vital sources for generations of medieval historians.[2]

In the modern Anglophone world, the most influential interpretation of the history of the Cistercian Order is *The Cistercians: Ideals and Reality* (1977) by Louis Lekai, a Hungarian Cistercian monk who emigrated to the USA in 1947 and eventually became a professor in Texas and prior of Our Lady of Dallas.[3] According to Lekai, the 'ideal' – the original body of ideas and practices developed and codified in the early twelfth century – remained the guiding principle for all the Cistercian houses throughout their history. As the Cistercian network developed, this 'ideal' came under increasing pressure from the grubby reality of the lay world. However, in his interpretation, the numerous cases of broken rules or regulations did not indicate, as yet, the symptoms of decline: the speed of the growth and geographical spread of the Order demanded a flexible approach, and without it the Order would never have succeeded in accomplishing what it did. Symptoms of degeneration, according to Lekai, began to appear after 1300 and were seen in the sharp decline in the number of new foundations and chronic financial problems of many houses.[4] Although his interpretation is far from simplistic, it still includes the concept of 'decline'; and it has remained so influential interpretation precisely because it treats the whole of medieval Cistercian history in terms of one defining criterion which can be applied to the entire Order as well as individual communities: how far they remained true to the original ideal of the Order. A cruder version of this model based on the notion of a Cistercian 'Golden Age' in the twelfth century, and the subsequent 'decline and corruption' brought by growing wealth and departure from the original austerity, has been the staple of popular interpretations of Cistercian history and still looms large in non-academic histories, both of the Order and individual houses.

Immensely influential in England has been the work of Dom David Knowles, a Benedictine monk, educated and ordained at Downside Abbey

INTRODUCTION

and Regius Professor at Cambridge (1954–1963), who produced a monumental three-volume history of religious orders (including the Cistercians) in England from the tenth century to the Dissolution (1948–1959), as well as a single-volume survey (1963). This was not only the first modern examination of monasticism in pre-Reformation England, but an extremely eloquent presentation of the 'golden age and decline' paradigm. His approach to post-twelfth century contemplative monasticism was highly judgemental and tested the quality of monastic life according to the strictness of its adherence to the rule and standards of the founders. As these, in his view, were both clearly defined and static, his account of late medieval English monasticism was distinctly negative – perhaps one reason why this field still remains relatively underexplored.[5]

Whilst Lekai and Knowles – being monks themselves – were fully aware of the central role of spirituality in Cistercian history, the development of economic history in the mid-twentieth century introduced a very different perspective. The innovative organisation and material success of the Cistercians invited much comparison with modern economic and social developments. For economic historians it became tempting to see the medieval Cistercian Order as a rationally designed machine run by entrepreneurs, a precursor of modern business organisations, partly because this neatly explains its success and partly because such an interpretation was more palatable to an audience that found it difficult to see religion as providing an adequate explanation for such complex and lasting structures. For them, the Cistercian approach to labour was a rational work ethic, and increased efficiency combined with the prohibition of luxury could be used to explain the white monks' economic success.[6] Some economic historians – notably Richard Roehl and Jean Gimpel – were propounding such view in the 1970s, but they have been revived more recently in the very tellingly entitled *Sacred Trust: The Medieval Church as an Economic Firm*, written by a group of American economists.[7] Such views are, of course, totally unhistorical and completely overlook the core religious reasons for the existence of the Cistercian houses; but like the 'Golden Age and decline' interpretation they offer a strong model that explains the entirety of medieval history of the white monks. Although both these interpretations have been challenged in the last few decades, no other single interpretational structure has emerged, and modern scholarship is focused on change and adaptability as the key feature of the medieval Cistercian experience.

An important factor shaping recent perspectives on the history of the white monks has been a series of anniversaries that gave a major impetus to new studies, albeit sometimes aggravating the neglect of other areas: the 800th anniversary of Bernard of Clairvaux's death in 1953,[8] the 900th anniversary of his birth in 1990 and the 900th anniversary of the establishment of the Order in 1998 stimulated research and resulted in a number of conferences and publications, both academic and popular, on the early history of the Order; but the period after 1300 was left largely unexplored.[9]

The anniversaries did, however, produce a number of prestigious exhibitions illustrating the visual heritage of the Cistercians and covering the whole medieval and post-medieval period, of which the most important was the Aachen exhibition of 1980.[10] The title of the accompanying catalogue volume, *Ordensleben zwischen Ideal und Wirklichkeit*, edited by the Nestor of German monastic scholarship, Kaspar Elm, and containing contributions from leading German historians, is reminiscent of Lekai's paradigm. As a major systematic overview of the main aspects of the history of the Order it remains a much-cited reference work. On the whole, however, many works of the 1990s made more effort to break away from the dichotomy of the 'ideal' juxtaposed with the 'reality', and from writing in terms of 'demythologisation' of the Order's history and 'uncovering the reality' (which is, ultimately, only a variation on the 'decline' theme).[11]

It was not only memorable anniversaries that prompted research; developments in other academic areas have recently opened up new avenues. One important strand in Cistercian scholarship reflects the changes in the focus of medieval archaeology, which, as it moves away from simply studying the chronological stratification of the remnants of buildings, has more to say about the physical context in which Cistercian communities lived and how that changed over time, about changes in usage of space, the ecological context of human activities, and a wide range of medical and cultural evidence from burial sites.[12] Similarly, art history has shifted its focus from the stylistic and chronological evaluation of Cistercian architecture towards questions about Cistercian religiosity, especially the role of devotional imagery in the Cistercian churches. Matthias Untermann's major study *Forma Ordinis* (2001) has re-examined the development of Cistercian architecture in the middle ages, paying far more attention to the functions of spaces and changes linked to the use of buildings.[13] Recent work of art historians on the furnishings in Cistercian churches, devotional objects, reliquaries and burials is particularly important for our understanding of the development of monastic attitudes towards lay piety, spirituality and commemoration in the high and later middle ages.[14]

Historical studies of the Cistercian Order written by members of the community have, not surprisingly, a very specific tone; they have a stake in what constitutes the Cistercian tradition, hence their perspective and focus tend to be different from those of the lay scholars, and even sympathetic scholars who are not monks or nuns themselves find themselves particularly drawn towards early Cistercian history, perhaps because it is more 'charged', and involves a small number of rather striking individuals and powerful ideological messages. The social realities of the established monastic life in the later middle ages, by contrast, can hardly generate the same intensity of emotional response. Research by present-day Cistercians, especially their editing of important primary sources, has done much for a wider understanding of Cistercian history.[15] The Cistercian Publications publishing house, which since the 1960s has been producing (primarily by and for Cistercian monks and nuns) translations of key spiritual and legal texts, has extended its offerings to academic texts and has published a number of monographs and miscellanies on various aspects of Cistercian history.

Heiligenkreuz Abbey in Austria is an important centre for Cistercian studies in the German-speaking world, and there are many German regional studies and monographs on individual abbies that are particularly relevant to the debates about the international dimension versus the local context in the development of the Order. The rethinking of the role of women in Cistercian monasticism has also been much advanced by German and Swiss scholars.[16] On the whole there has been relatively little dialogue between scholarship in different languages, which contributes to fragmentation within Cistercian studies. Even the revival of interest in early Cistercian history has been to some degree at the expense of the neglected later middle ages. To modern observers, there seems to be little connection between the twelfth and fifteenth centuries, and a perplexing lack of clarity about how the Cistercian movement of the high middle ages was connected to that of the late middle ages; but these are lacunae that will have to be filled if we are finally to move away from juxtaposition of 'Golden Age' and 'decline'.

The Roots of the Cistercian Movement

Recent scholarship, which has placed the Cistercians firmly within the wider context of the early twelfth-century reform movement, tends to blur the lines between Cistercians and other groups seeking new forms of monastic life.[17] True, a large body of ideas, influences and solutions were shared between the white monks, their predecessors and their contemporaries: they were all highly critical of the mainstream monasticism of the day, which they saw as 'corrupt', and afflicted by wealth and unreflecting liturgical routines. As regards ideas, the desire to reject the 'corrupting bonds' of the world came into eleventh-century thinking from the much older eremitic tradition of attempting to 'imitate Christ in poverty', and this concept of voluntary poverty was common to Cistercians and other groups.[18] The concept of *Vita Apostolica* was at the centre of all reform movements. It was the practice of a penitential life of poverty, simplicity and spirituality, which was believed to be the path taken by the early church. Ultimately, when hermits had organised themselves into groups on cenobitic lines, the communal prevailed; but elements of the eremitic model survived, for example in Carthusian communities, which were organised as groups of individual hermitages. Many emerging reformed groups adopted existing rules – St Benedict's (for monks) and St Augustine's (for the canons); but while traditional Benedictine monasticism was centred on praying for the salvation of the laity and interceding for their aristocratic benefactors, the new monastic movements laid more stress on spirituality and the importance of an individual monk's salvation. The reform movements deemed prayer, meditation and the practice of penance and mortification to be more important than the advancement of learned theology; and following in the steps of John Cassian (a fifth-century 'Desert Father') held it 'more important to cure one's own ills than to be concerned with the troubles of others'.[19]

In respect of organisation, the reform movements tended to form groupings of linked communities rather than traditional independent houses. This had already begun in the tenth century with the formation of the congregation of Cluny. In the eleventh century, within the new monastic movements, individual houses no longer 'stood alone', but were formally linked to the central 'mother houses' overseeing dependent monasteries.

The growing Cistercian movement was influenced particularly strongly by the Camaldoli, which also followed – very strictly – the Rule of Benedict. Its founder, St Romuald (d. 1027), drew his inspiration from the writings of the ancient Desert Fathers who emphasised absolute poverty, solitude and silence. The first Camaldoli community, founded in 1012 near Arezzo, in the Apennine mountains of northern Italy, was a collection of separate cells and a central oratory, a model followed by all other communities in this congregation. The Camaldolian lifestyle was extremely austere with extensive fasting, a strict vegetarian diet, simple habits and a timetable in which communal Divine Office and individual spiritual readings and prayers were interspersed with manual work. The spread of the Camaldoli movement, both through Romuald's reforms of existing Benedictine monasteries and through his establishing new communities, was to serve as a model for the Cistercians in expanding their network.[20]

Another eremitic-cenobitic group that made an impact on the founders of the Cistercian movement was the Carthusians, founded by St Bruno of Cologne (d. 1101), who, like Romuald, craved solitude and established his community in the remote, inhospitable location of the Grande Chartreuse in the French Alps. The Carthusians followed a very strict rule that combined a communal liturgy with a life of silence, physical work, extreme austerity, poverty and prayer. The community assembled only once a week, for mass on Sundays; otherwise the monks lived solitary lives in individual huts with little gardens located within the monastic precinct. Carthusian communities also included lay brothers (*conversi*) who lived in different accommodation, and whose role was to till the fields and attend to the practical needs of the monastic economy, so that the monks could pursue their contemplative life. A similar model of lay brotherhood was adopted by the Cistercians.[21]

Many of the reformers were contemporaries who knew each other and conducted a regular correspondence. Bernard of Clairvaux travelled to La Chartreuse in 1123 and exchanged letters with Abbot Guido I (d. 1136). Guido's ideas about the centrality of charity in a monastic community and the importance of loving one's neighbour clearly influenced Bernard of Clairvaux and later writers.[22] 'For both Guido and Bernard, the law of charity demanded action, and the idea of the contemplative life as being life of indolent inactivity is . . . nonsensical.[23]

The same characteristics of simplicity, poverty and eremitic elements were common to other eleventh-century monastic groups, which in time became religious congregations: the Vallombrosans had many similarities to the Cameldoli movement, but, unlike St Romuald's group, admitted lay brothers and had an elected abbot-general. Their founder, John Gualbert (d. 1073), tried unsuccessfully to reform his own Benedictine monastery of San Miniato and, having abandoned it for a Cameldolian community, eventually established a new, and successful, monastery at Vallombrosa (Tuscany) in the 1030s.[24] The Grandmontines who emerged at the end of the eleventh century were modelled on the Carthusians, with various borrowings from Cameldoli and Augustianans: extreme poverty, the rejection of various forms of property and a harsh, austere monastic life spent in silence and seclusion with little sustenance. They did enjoy the patronage of both Angevin King Henry II and Louis VII of France and were particularly successful in Aquitaine, Anjou and Normandy.[25]

As Bede Lackner has pointed out, however, all these similarities between the various eleventh-century monastic movements were not a product of any organisational connections between them, but 'grew out of the contemporary milieu'.[26] Nor can one identify any direct brain behind the process by which reform movements such as Sacro Eremo di Camaldoli and Grande Chartreuse gradually evolved into organised communities, effective centres of reform and eventually the headquarters of the new Orders.[27]

The 'Traditional Account' of Cistercian Origins

It would perhaps be well to outline here the simple, linear narrative of the early development of the Cistercian Order that has traditionally held sway – particularly as the next chapter is concerned to show how recent historiography has challenged this narrative. Traditionally, the history of the Order begins in 1098, when Robert of Molesme and a group of fellow monks rejected the 'corrupt' Benedictine model in which monks lived in comfort and luxury, churches were opulent and days were spent on mechanical prayers for the benefactors, and left the abbey of Molesme to establish a new community where they could live according to the monastic ideal. The community they established at Cîteaux near Dijon grew very fast, with new entrants joining in large numbers. Once the number of monks became large enough, Cîteaux sent out groups of them to establish new abbeys. In 1100, during the tenure of Alberic, the second abbot of Cîteaux, the Cistercians received their first papal privilege. A few years later, the first 'official constitution', *Carta Caritatis* (Charter of Love), drafted by Abbot Stephen Harding (1109–1134), and approved by the pope in 1119, set out the structure of the Order, standardising the organisation of individual abbeys and regulating the relationship between them. This understanding of the 'monastic constitution' led some historians to think in terms of a fully formed Cistercian Order already in the early 1130s; and to assume that the General Chapter (an annual meeting of all abbots from the Order) met regularly from 1133/34 onwards. According to the traditional account, the most important turning point in the early history of the Order came with the entry of Bernard of Clairvaux to the Cistercian family in 1113. He is not only credited with 'rescuing' the Cistercian Order, but with driving forward its geographic expansion and establishing its prominence. As the network stretched out ever further, however, the original strictness of practice became strained and eroded, and the wealth accumulated by Cistercian monasteries both from generous donations from patrons and benefactors, and from their own remarkably effective economic planning, corrupted the communities of white monks.

Although such accounts have been rightly criticised as too simplistic, they still dominate popular notions of Cistercian history. The black-and-white image of the perfect austerity of the early generations being overtaken by the corruption of the later Cistercians is difficult to get away from. It is unhistorical, and it is the purpose of this study to argue for a fundamental revision of our understanding of Cistercian history between *c.* 1100 and *c.* 1500. There is no one interpretation that can encompass its development, but the following chapters will attempt to show how

INTRODUCTION

the Cistercian Order's response to social, economic and political changes allowed it to survive, and sometimes flourish, for centuries. Whilst change is one important element of the story, a deep sense of continuity, and of what differentiated the white monks from other religious orders, both in their own eyes and those of their contemporaries, is central to this book.

Advice on Further Reading

Readers looking for literature in English on specific aspects of Cistercian history can expect very uneven coverage. On Cistercian material culture the best starting point is Terryl Kinder's excellent *Cistercian Europe: The Architecture of Solitude* (2002), which explains the meanings and uses of different spaces in the Cistercian houses, and includes illustrations from Cistercian sites all over Europe. Medieval Cistercian nuns are still waiting for a systematic overview and the history of the Cistercian economy is available only in outdated works. There is a brief account of the Cistercians in *Medieval Monasticism: Forms of Religious Life in Western Europe in the Middle Ages* by C.H. Lawrence (3rd ed. 2001), which is the standard account of the subject for undergraduate audiences but also rather outdated. Readers will find an excellent explanation of the Cistercian experience of daily life in Janet Burton and Julie Kerr, *The Cistercians in the Middle Ages* (2011), with a detailed and persuasive account of how Cistercian houses functioned internally and how they interacted with the outside world in the high middle ages. Finally, the new *Cambridge Companion to the Cistercian Order* edited by Mette Bruun (2012) gives the most up-to-date introduction to all major aspects of Cistercian history and religious mentality and a new succinct account of medieval and post-medieval history of the Order.[28]

Notes

1. Ángel Manrique, *Cisterciensium seu verius Ecclesiasticorum Annalium a condito Cistercio tomus primus(-quartus)*, Series abbatum ecclesiæ Palaciolensis in veteri Castella a centum fere annis continuæ sedis Reformatorum Obseruantiæ Hispaniæ etc., 4 vols. (Lyon: Sumpt. hæred. G. Boissat, & Laurent. Anisson, 1642–1659); Manoel Dos Santos, O. Cist., *Alcobaca illustrada: noticias e historia dos mosteyros et monges insignes Cistercienses da Congregaçam de Santa Maria de Alcobaça* (Coimbra: s.n., 1710–1714); Crisóstomo Henríquez, *Fasciculus Sanctorum Ordinis Cisterciensis: complectens Cisterciensium Ascetarum præclarrissima gesta; huius ordinis exordium, incrementum, progressum, præcipuarum Abbatiarum per vniuersum orbem fundationes, ordinum militarum origines, liber primus; accessit huic novissimae editioni Vita B. Famiani Coloniensis* (Cologne: Ex officina Choliniana, sumptibus

Petri Cholini, 1631); Gaspar Jongelincx, *Purpura divi Bernardi, repræsentans elogia et insignia gentilitia, tum pontificum, tum cardinalium: nec non archiepiscoporum, et episcoporum qui assumpti ex ordine Cistertiensi in sacra Romana ecclesia floruerunt* (Cologne: Henrici Krafft, 1644); Gaspar Jongelincx, *Notitia Abbatiarum Ordinis Cistertiensis per orbem universum: libros X complexa* (Cologne: s.n., 1640); Charles de Visch, *Bibliotheca scriptorum Sacri Ordinis Cisterciensis* (Douai, 1649; Cologne: Apud Ioannem Busæum Bibliopolam, 1656); Dom Pierre Le Nain, *Essai de l'histoire de l'ordre de Cîteaux*, 9 vols. (Paris: chez François Muguet, 1699).

2. They are far too numerous to list them all, but Cistercian sources have been published in all key series of medieval source editions initiated in the nineteenth century: Monumenta Germaniae Historica, The Rolls Series, Fontes Rerum Austriacarum, Scriptores Rerum Danicarum and many other national source editions.

3. Bibliographia Cisterciensis, http://www.zisterzienserlexikon.de/wiki/Lekai ,_Louis (accessed 14 September 2012).

4. Louis Lekai, 'Ideals and Reality in Early Cistercian Life and Legislation', in *The New Monastery: Texts and Studies on the Earliest Cistercians*, ed. E. Rozanne Elder (Kalmazoo, MI: Cistercian Publications, 1998), pp. 23–26.

5. David Knowles, *The Religious Orders in England*, 3 vols. (Cambridge: Cambridge University Press, 1948–1959); David Knowles, *The Monastic Order in England: A History of its Development from the Times of St. Dunstan to the Fourth Lateran Council, 940–1216* (Cambridge: Cambridge University Press, 1963).

6. Alfred Kieser, *Von askietischen zu industriellen Bravourstücken. Die Organisation der Wirtschaft im Kloster des Mittelalters* (Mannheim: Universität Mannheim, 1984), p. 58.

7. Richard Roehl, 'Plan and Reality in a Medieval Monastic Economy: The Cistercians', *Studies in Medieval and Renaissance History* 9 (1972), pp. 83–113; Jean Gimpel, *La révolution industrielle du Moyen Age* (Paris: Editions du Seuil, 1975); English edition: Jean Gimpel, *The Medieval Machine: The Industrial Revolution of the Middle Ages* (New York: Penguin, 1976), pp. 3–5; *Sacred Trust: The Medieval Church as an Economic Firm*, ed. Robert B. Ekelund et al. (New York and Oxford: Oxford University Press, 1996), pp. 42–59.

8. Jean Leclercq, *Recueil d'études sur Saint Bernard et ses écrits*, vols. 1–3 (Rome: Edizioni di Storia e Letteratura, 1962–1969); *Bernard de Clairvaux*, Commission d'histoire de l'Orde de Cîteaux, Villème centenaire de la mort de Saint-Bernard (Paris: Aiguebelle, 1953); *Mélanges Saint Bernard XXIVème Congrèse de l'Association bourguignonne des Sociétés* (Dijon: St. Trouve chez M. l'abbé Marilier, 1953); *Bernhard von Clairvaux: Mönch und Mystiker*, ed. Joseph Lortz, Internationaler Bernhardkongress, Veröffentlichungen des Instituts für europäische Geschichte Mainz 6 (Wiesbaden: Franz Steiner Verlag, 1955).

9. A volume resulting from a conference held in Martiano-Latiano-Lecce in 1991, commemorating the 900th anniversary of Bernard's birth, focused solely on the Italian monasteries: *I Cistercensi nel Mezzogiorno Medioevale*.

INTRODUCTION

Atti del Convegno internationale di studio in occasione del IX centenario della nascita di Bernardo di Clairvaux, ed. Hubert Houben and Benedetto Vetere (Lecce: Congedo, 1994). Other conferences held in the late 1990s attempted a systematic survey of the geographic and historical development of the Order. One of them, held at Dijon in September 1998, posed the question of the diversity and unity of the Cistercian Order between the twelfth and eighteenth centuries. Many of the articles in the volume resulting from this conference addressed the formation of different filiation networks from the 'proto-abbacies' and within particular regions, whilst others traced different socio-cultural conditions and how the leadership of particular abbots and abbesses influenced the peculiar paths of local Cistercian developments. However, as the volume shows, many historians still find it difficult to stop assessing 'signs of loyalty to the Cistercian ideal' and to give up the search for symptoms of decline. Marie-Madeleine de Cevins, 'Les Implantations Cisterciennes en Hongrie Médiévale: un réseau?', in *Unanimité et diversité cisterciennes: filiations, réseaux, relectures du XIIe au XVIIe siècle: actes du quatrième colloque international du CERCOR, Dijon, 23–25 septembre 1998*, ed. Nicole Bouter (Saint-Etienne: Publications de l'Université de Saint-Etienne, 2000), p. 477. Other anniversary conferences had an explicitly celebratory character, reflecting on the role of Cistercian tradition in the modern world, such as the conference held in May 1998 at the abbey of Morimond. *Convegno Celebrativo per il XI centenario della Fondazione di Cîteaux 1098–1998: Cîteaux 98: Cantieri di Ideali per Un'identitá culturale Europea*, ed. Giuseppe Ligto and Sandrina Bandera (Morimondo: Fundazione Abbatia Sancte Marie de Morimondo, 2002).

10. *Saint Bernard et le monde cistercien: exposition à la Conciergerie de Paris, 18 décembre 1990–28 février 1991* (Paris: CNMHS, 1990); *Die Geschichte der Zisterzienser: Bilder und Texte der Ausstellung 'Die Zisterzienser: Ordensleben zwischen Ideal und Wirklichkeit'. Eine Ausstellung des Landschaftsverbandes Rheinland, Rheinisches Museumsamt, Brauweiler, Aachen, 3 Juli–28 Sept. 1980*, ed. Peter Joerissen and H.J. Roth (Bonn: Rheinland-Verlag, 1980).
11. Kaspar Elm, 'Mythos oder Realität: Fragenstellungen und Ergebnisse der Zisterzienserforschung?', in *Unanimité et diversité*, p. 45.
12. Good examples of such studies are by architectural historians Peter Fergusson and Stuart Harrison, *Rievaulx Abbey: Community, Architecture, Memory* (New Haven, CT: Yale University Press, 1999) and the volume by archaeologists Roberta Gilchrist and Barney Sloane, *Requiem: The Medieval Monastic Cemetery in Britain* (London: Museum of London Archaeology Service, 2005).
13. Matthias Untermann, *Forma Ordinis. Die Mittelalterliche Baukunst der Zisterzienser* (Berlin: Deutscher Kunstverlag, 2001).
14. In particular the work of Petra Janke, Christina Kratzke, Annegret Laabs and Jens Rüffer.
15. Most noteworthy among these monk-scholars are Chrysogonus Waddell of Gethsemani Abbey in Kentucky, editor and translator of sources and leading specialist in the history of liturgy; Michael Casey of Tarrawarra Abbey in Australia, who specialises in the history of Cistercian spirituality; and Conrad

Greenia of Mepkin Abbey in Southern Carolina, a translator of many works of St Bernard and other early Cistercian texts.
16. Elke Disselbeck-Tewes, *Frauen in der Kirche: das Leben der Frauen in den mittelalterlichen Zisterzienserklöstern Fürstenberg, Graefenthal und Schledenhorst* (Cologne: Böhlau, 1989); Anja Ostrowitzki, *Die Ausbreitung der Zisterzienserinnen im Erzbistum Köln* (Cologne: Böhlau, 1993); Friederike Warnatsch-Gleich, *Herrschaft und Frömmigkeit: Zisterzienserinnen im Hochmittelalter* (Berlin: Lukas, 2005); Brigitte Degler-Spengler, 'The Incorporation of Cistercian Nuns into the Order in the Twelfth and Thirteenth Century', in *Hidden Springs: Cistercian Monastic Women*, ed. John A. Nichols (Kalamazoo, MI: Cistercian Publications, 1995), vol. 1, pp. 85–134; Brigitte Degler-Spengler, 'Die Zisterzienserinnen in der Schweiz', *Cistercienser Chronik* 94 (1987), pp. 124–132; Brigitte Degler-Spengler, 'Zisterzienserorden und Frauenklöster. Anmerkungen zur Forschungsproblematik', in *Die Zisterzienser: Ordensleben zwischen Ideal und Wirklichkeit*, ed. Kaspar Elm (Cologne: Rheinland-Verlag, 1980), pp. 213–220.
17. Marta Newman, 'Stephen Harding and the Creation of the Cistercian Community', *Revue Bénédictine* 107 (1997), p. 307, n. 3.
18. Bede K. Lackner, *The Eleventh-Century Background of Cîteaux* (Spencer, MA: Cistercian Publications, 1972), p. 149.
19. Lackner, *The Eleventh-Century Background*, p. 142.
20. Lackner, *The Eleventh-Century Background*, pp. 170–176.
21. Lackner, *The Eleventh-Century Background*, pp. 203–214.
22. David N. Bell, 'The Carthusian Connection: Guigo of La Chartreuse and the Origins of Cistercian Spirituality', *Cistercian Studies Quarterly* 27 (1992), pp. 52, 60–62.
23. Bell, 'The Carthusian Connection', p. 61.
24. Jean-Baptiste Van Damme, *The Three Founders of Cîteaux: Robert of Molesme, Alberic, Stephen Harding*, trans. Nicholas Grove and Christian Carr (Kalamazoo, MI: Cistercian Publications, 1998), pp. 14–15.
25. Carole A. Hutchison, *The Hermit Monks of Grandmont* (Kalamazoo, MI: Cistercian Publications, 1989).
26. Lackner, *The Eleventh-Century Background*, p. 215.
27. Lackner, *The Eleventh-Century Background*, p. 213.
28. Terryl Kinder, *Cistercian Europe: Architecture of Contemplation* (Kalamazoo, MI: Cistercian Publications, 2002); C.H. Lawrence, *Medieval Monasticism: Forms of Religious Life in Western Europe in the Middle Ages*, 3rd ed. (Harlow: Longman, 2001); Janet Burton and Julie Kerr, *The Cistercians in the Middle Ages* (Woodbridge: The Boydell Press, 2011); *Cambridge Companion to the Cistercian Order*, ed. Mette Birkedal Bruun (Cambridge: Cambridge University Press, 2012).

chapter 1

ORIGINS: IDEAS, MYTHS AND INTERPRETATIONS

The history of the Cistercian order is one of continuous evolution and change. As an order, its structure and organisation did not appear overnight, nor was it the creation of one charismatic individual. It came into being as the result of a longer process in which both its ideals and its practical structures were modified and new members joined and became integrated into it.[1] Before the structure of the Cistercian order developed there was what may be called a Cistercian movement, which was itself part of the wider eleventh-century reform movement described in the introduction. This chapter will first focus on the development of the Cistercian movement in the first half of the twelfth century when it was not yet a fully formed order. Absolutely essential for any study of the origins of the Cistercian movement are the early normative and narrative texts; as to the nature, dating and composition of which, and hence their implications for the interpretation of early Cistercian history, modern historians continue to disagree. The focus then shifts to the role of Bernard of Clairvaux as an early leader of the Cistercian family: although he was undoubtedly a very significant figure in Cistercian history, his activities in the monastic world and beyond were in the long term less significant for the later history of the order than his legend has been. Whilst attention will be duly paid here to Bernard's role as Cistercian leader, charismatic preacher and church reformer, his legend and its function will be revisited several times in later chapters.

The Early Years of the Cistercian Movement

The received narrative of the story of the foundation of Cîteaux begins in March 1098 with the departure of Robert of Molesme (d. 1111) and a group of followers from his Benedictine home monastery in Molesme (Burgundy) to create the 'New Monastery'. They arrived at their destination of Cîteaux, a secluded spot in the wilderness near Dijon, on 21 March, the feast of St Benedict. The land was given to the monks by Odo I, duke of Burgundy, previously held by his vassal Viscount Raynald of Beaune, free from any feudal obligations.[2] We will never know if this, like many later events in the early history of the Cistercians, happened exactly in this way, as our knowledge is based on the 'founding myth' of the order, the creation of four succeeding generations of Cistercian monks, none of whom of course were eyewitnesses.[3]

Certainly it will be more fruitful to consider what seemed significant to twelfth-century and later generations of monks in their own past, and what they handed down to their successors, rather than trying to establish a definitive 'true' account. Later generations of monks needed to have a model of the 'perfect' origins of the movement in its simplicity and purity as a guide for individual monks and communities on how to follow the path of the charismatic founders. For a long time historians tried to see the accounts of the early years as describing the actual conditions of the first generation of Cistercians and to contrast their idealised origins with the failure of later generations to live up to them – an approach that is particularly striking in the 'ideal and reality' model examined in the Introduction.

The topos of striving for perfection and rejecting the 'substandard' monastic practices of the day underlines the story of Robert of Molesme's departure for Cîteaux. It was important for the growing Cistercian movement to establish a separate identity from its predecessors, especially since the new movement had not formulated a new monastic rule as a 'founding document', but followed the traditional Rule of Benedict. Not that the breakaway group left Molesme Abbey because it was corrupt or in decay; on the contrary, Molesme, founded in 1100, had grown very quickly, with over 40 dependent priories, all Cluniac houses, and was closely connected with the local aristocratic families. It was simply that Robert and those who left Molesme with him had decided to abandon the traditional Cluniac custom and follow reform practice as embodying far better the authentic spirit of the Rule of Benedict. Even so, it is clear from some of Robert's initial decisions that the form that any new monastic observance would eventually take was not yet definitively established: Robert had taken with him liturgical books so that the new community could continue the practices of the old house. The devotion to the Virgin Mary typical of Cistercians, whose every house was dedicated to her, could be argued to be a tradition inherited from Molesme, which was also dedicated to Mary. Moreover, Robert accepted a gift of land with two serfs, so the idea that the monks should work on their own land, with their own hands, had not yet been formulated.[4]

When in 1090 the abbot of Molesme, angered by Robert's unauthorised departure and the setting up of a new community, got Pope Urban II to order him back to Molesme, Robert, under pressure from the papal legate and the bishop of Langres, returned.[5] Having returned to his old community he became an abbot there, reforming it according to the Cistercian *ordo*.[6] The headship of Cîteaux then passed (until 1108) to Alberic, who despite holding the abbatial office at a critical juncture after the departure of Robert, has been accorded a very minor role in the Cistercian historical tradition. He was an effective administrator who acquired further land donations for his monastery and secured an important privilege from Pope Paschal II, stating that 'This abbey shall be particularly sheltered under the protection of the Apostolic See, saving the canonical reverence due to the diocese of Chalon'.[7] Alberic was, of course, much overshadowed by the next abbot of Cîteaux, Stephen Harding, who came to be seen as one of the central figures of the early history of the Cistercian movement. Originally from England, he was a child oblate in Sherborne (a monastic cathedral community), studied in France and, after pilgrimage to Rome, entered the Benedictine Abbey in Molesme.[8] In 1098 Stephen was one of the 21 monks who left with Abbot Robert for the new monastery, where he played a key role in establishing the early organisational structures of the new movement. By 1113 the number of recruits to the Cistercian project had grown sufficiently for a new house to be established at La Ferté, 10 miles south of Cîteaux.

Stephen's leadership was distinctively different from that of his predecessors and from that of the even more famous Bernard at Clairvaux. At first he was concerned with devising a strict observance for the Cîteaux community, but as the Cistercian movement expanded, Stephen became preoccupied with uniformity and correctness of practice across a whole developing network of Cistercian communities. Initially, his writings had emphasised the authority of the abbot, but as the Cistercian movement expanded, the concept of unity became more central to many of Abbot Stephen's activities: while uniformity of observance was the thread binding increasingly geographically dispersed communities together, one of Stephen's key projects was a new edition of the Bible, the text of which was to be as trustworthy as possible – to which end the abbot even consulted Hebrew scholars. Another of his important projects was the selection of hymns for a new hymnal: as the Rule of Benedict mentioned the hymns of St Ambrose of Milan, Stephen chose them for use by the Cistercian communities; and as he was convinced that the hymns sung in contemporary Milan were closest to the original sources, he ordered copies of them for Cîteaux. A similar principle was used in creating the authoritative Cistercian antiphonary. For chanting, the community of

Cîteaux used the two oldest copies from Metz, which were believed to contain original Gregorian chants.[9] This attention to the accuracy and uniformity of liturgical books remained important throughout Cistercian history and was to be a significant feature of the late medieval reforms (described in chapter 8).

For the most part, therefore, from the very beginning Cistercian monks did not invent a new monastic rule, but adopted the same core values and prescriptions for monastic life as other contemporary Benedictine houses – communal prayers, fasting, vigils, study of the scriptures, voluntary poverty, permanent membership of one monastic community (*stabilitas*), obedience to the abbot, and engagement with manual labour. The core practices and spirituality of the Cistercians – charity, prayer, asceticism, poverty, simplicity, separation from the world, devotion to Christ and Mary – were not unique, but part of a much wider and older tradition going back to the Desert Fathers. What was new in the Cistercian approach was linking it to their own environment.[10] Much of the Cistercian programme of 'going back to the roots' was well within the reforming tradition of the eleventh century, but Cistercians were also most emphatic that this should be grounded in the interpretative framework of the Rule of Benedict, which differentiated the Cistercians from other monastic reform movements of the era.[11] At the same time the strict, even literal observance of the Rule of Benedict differentiated the Cistercians from their Benedictine predecessors and contemporaries. This was clear to contemporary observers, such as Orderic Vitalis, himself a Benedictine monk, who said in his chronicle that the monks who follow Robert of Molesme observe the Rule of Benedict just as strictly as the Jews observe the Law of Moses.[12] The Rule was at the very heart of the early documents of the Cistercian movement. Whilst 'black monks' (a colloquial name for Benedictine monks derived from the colour of their habits) had 'diluted' it with various collections of regulations and prescriptions specific to different houses (customaries), the Cistercian 'white monks', with their undyed woollen habits, insisted on the strict and literal observance of the Rule in each and every monastery belonging to their family.

Before there was a Cistercian order, there was a Cistercian *ordo*, that is a Cistercian way of monastic life, liturgy and a wider ethos governing relationships within each community and between the abbeys; Bernard of Clairvaux considered himself to belong to 'a shared and customary way of life'.[13] He used different Latin words to describe the Cistercian family – *ordo, consuetude, institutio* and *religio*.[14] When he described the unity of the Cistercian communities he emphasised the distinct identity of the Cistercians. The general term *ordo* in classical Latin denoted class rank or condition. Bernard's writing refers to 'our order' and describes the first Christian community in Jerusalem as an *ordo*.[15] In one of his letters addressed to the monks of Aulps (1138) Bernard gave a clear definition of what constituted 'our order':

> Our order is the lowering of self. It is humility, voluntary poverty, obedience, peace, joy in the Holy Spirit. Our order means being under the master, under the abbot, under the Rule, discipline. Our order means study in silence, exercising oneself in fasting, vigils, prayers, manual labour, and above all things, maintaining a more exalted way of life, which is charity. Thus in these ways we get better from one day to the next and in these very [observances] persevere until the last day.[16]

It was this monastic observance, peculiar to the white monks, that differentiated the Cistercians from other religious houses.

The ethos of the Cistercian movement focused on personal and communal devotions and the life of poverty and simplicity. On the individual level, poverty was emphasised by a number of practices framing the daily life of the monks: as a sign of conversion, all novices entering a Cistercian monastery had to voluntarily reject wealth and the temporal concerns of the material world; and in matters of clothing they discarded fine materials and elaborate styles. The monastic virtue of humility was symbolised by a simplified monastic habit of unbleached wool in a grey-white colour and a black, cross-like cowl. The Cistercian monastic diet, both a means of mortifying the body and a symbol of humility, was very simple, with no meat – fish was the only animal protein allowed – and based on coarse bread with bran, vegetables and wine diluted with water. Spices and honey, considered highly desirable luxuries by their contemporaries, were also rejected in favour of plain food.[17]

Parallel with the rejection of wealth was the elevation of manual labour, which played a far greater role in the daily routine of the Cistercian monks than in that of the Benedictines. Physical work involved not only the monks but, even more, a new group within the communities of white monks – the lay brothers. The institution of the lay brothers (*conversi*) was part of a much wider trend towards closer association between lay people and monastic communities prevalent among reformed monastic groups.[18] Historians disagree as to why the Cistercians adopted the institution of the lay brothers, the most popular view being that it was essential if the communities of white monks were to maintain their self-sufficiency, and dispense with income from tithes, rents and any other forms of revenue that would entangle them in the obligations of manorial lordship. For the peasants, unable to enter Benedictine communities, which continued to be aristocratic establishments, admission into the lay brotherhood offered a unique possibility of a religious vocation with some liturgical duties and a share in the spiritual benefits of monastic life, whilst providing a workforce for the economic operations of the abbey. For the rest, the Cistercians retained the core assumption of their Benedictine predecessors that their economic foundations rested on communal property ownership; while the belief in the redemptive power of monks' prayers continued to attract benefactors, who gave grants of land in exchange for such intercessory services.[19] Hence, while individual monks were poor and owned no property, the abbeys were able to accumulate significant landed properties, which supported all the functions of the monastic houses.

Another example of the Cistercians' rejection of commitments to the lay world was their refusal to undertake pastoral work outside the monastery. Initially, very few Cistercian monks had been ordained as priests because their chief role had been to focus on the salvation of their own souls. The desire for priestly ordination was seen as an expression of vanity and a General Chapter regulation of 1192 tried to limit the aspirations of monks to holy orders to preserve their humility – clearly, the assumption was that it was only the abbot who required priestly ordination. This idea is reinforced by the early depictions of Bernard of Clairvaux as a priest; one such example, an illuminated manuscript of his *Vita Prima* from Zwettl Abbey (*c.* 1175), represents him with a saint's halo performing a mass.[20] Not that the rejection of the world indicated a desire on the part of the Cistercians to separate themselves completely from all external concerns. It was rather an attempt to draw a clear line between the roles of the secular clergy and the monks.[21] It has long been the tradition in the Cistercian historiography to see a practical application of the concept of the rejection of the world in the ideal Cistercian monastery location: in the wilderness, far removed from human settlements. This was regarded as the hallmark of a 'true' Cistercian community, and historians have tended to see any divergence from it as deviation or even corruption. More recently, a different view has started to emerge: that the idea of going into the desert and completely rejecting the world was not a particularly prominent theme in the early Cistercian texts, nor was it particularly emphasised by Bernard of Clairvaux. Indeed, traditionally the desert had been associated with the solitary life of hermits, whereas the Cistercians emphasised the community above the individual; and Bernard himself had regarded the solitude of hermits, free from the control and guidance of the abbot, as a potentially spiritual danger and did not want his monks to abandon coenobitic life for eremitic solitude.[22]

In fact, as Benedicta Ward has pointed out, the concept of a desert as an especially Cistercian environment was only a gradual development in the second and third generation of Cistercian monks that was projected back in time by Cistercian monks seeking to justify and defend their interpretation of monasticism by inventing for it an ancient and venerable tradition. Hence 'desert' was primarily a symbolic concept rather than a reference to some practical reality. Other historians have suggested that the emergence of the ideology of solitude as separation from the world was linked in part to Cistercian claims to exemption from the payment of tithes. What is particularly significant in the Cistercian texts discussing solitude and the desert are the direct references to the treasured 'monastic heritage' of the Desert Fathers in Egypt and Palestine. William of St Thierry, for example, a Benedictine monk writing *c.* 1145–1148 about his own experience of Cistercian life, used the image of the desert in describing his first visit to Clairvaux: 'Wherever I turned my eye in wonder, it was as I saw a new heaven and a new earth, and the ancient tracks of the ancient monks of Egypt our fathers'.[23]

What emerges from these debates is the long-term influence of early notions about the Cistercian life on the Order's subsequent generations. Even so, when the early Cistercians wrote about desert, solitude and simplicity they were not consciously devising a blueprint or prescribing where and how the communities of white monks should live. These early years saw the emergence of a powerful tradition of what constitutes 'Cistercianness' – a set of ideas, concepts and images that influenced the formation of the order and continued to be rehearsed and reinvented by the Cistercian monks throughout the middle ages. Yet it was a far more amorphous body of ideas than many historians have claimed and it cannot serve as a benchmark to assess how faithfully and precisely any community followed the Cistercian ideal. There never was a precise definition of what constituted a suitable location for a monastery, or any fixed set of regulations determining how accommodating white monks should be towards the expectations and wishes of their benefactors. Moreover, even such normative and narrative texts as existed were to undergo significant changes in the course of twelfth century.

The Early Cistercian Texts

Our knowledge of the early development of the Cistercian Order and the development of the structures of the order is based on a number of key texts that formed the ideological backbone of the movement and provided a major source of shared identity, inspiration and myth making for communities of white monks throughout the medieval period and beyond. The early history of the movement and the core ideas of what constituted Cistercian life are all recorded in these early narrative texts, whose function was both to describe the structural developments of the

Order, and to commemorate those prominent individuals whom subsequent generations of white monks came to venerate as founding fathers. Many of these texts were written and amended over decades, others were the work of particular individuals. What is particularly important is that through an extended process of copying, reading and commentary they came to define the Cistercian identity.

Scholars have tried to establish the chronology of the early development – still one of the most contested issues in Cistercian historiography – by focusing on the dating of these texts and the interrelationship between them, but it is unlikely that a definitive answer will ever be found. The *Carta Caritatis*, for example, has often been described as the Cistercian constitution, but this term is misleading.[24] The text exists in three versions: *prior*, *summa* and *posterior*. The oldest of them, *Carta Caritatis Prior* belonged to the early Cîteaux tradition and was confirmed by a bull of Pope Calixtus II in 1119 addressed to Abbot Stephen Harding and his brothers in all the monasteries following the same Cistercian custom (*ordo*). It safeguarded the authority of Cîteaux and applied the ideas of the Rule to the inter-relationships between the different monasteries belonging to the Cistercian family, endorsing the hierarchical order between mother and daughter houses and the supervisory role of the father-abbot. The version known as *Summa Cartae Caritatis*, which is an abridged version of the older text with verbal amendments and some changes to the order of the prescriptions, which Waddell has dated to the abbacy of Raynard de Bar (1133/34–1150). The youngest of the texts, *Carta Caritatis Posterior*, a collective work of several abbots and extensively edited over decades, was confirmed by no fewer than four popes from Eugenius III (1 August 1152) to Alexander III (5 August 1165).[25]

In all its versions, nevertheless, the *Carta Caritatis* insisted on absolute uniformity of observance in all Cistercian monasteries and regulated the relationships between them.[26] Abbots were entrusted with the central responsibility, as leaders of their communities, of guiding the monks on the path to salvation. The spirit of charity was to prevail, not only in individual monasteries, but in relations between them. This was the cement that held together all the Cistercian communities, newly established foundations and those pre-existing monasteries. Whilst they were all independent from the mother house in material terms, they all followed the same customs, liturgy and readings, and, in particular, were all guided by the Rule of Benedict.[27]

The annual meeting (*capitulum*), described in the *Cartae Caritatis*, grew out of the informal meetings of the abbots from Cistercian houses held at Cîteaux and became, in time, a central element of the Order.

Such meetings, not yet named the General Chapter, took place during Bernard of Clairvaux's lifetime and were mentioned by his contemporaries. *Summa Carta Caritatis* uses the words *conventus* and *capitulum* interchangeably to describe the meetings of abbots at Cîteaux.[28] Later, Abbot Peter the Venerable of Cluny referred to such a gathering in one of his letters, and in his *Vita Prima* of Bernard, William of St Thierry mentioned that various abbots had attended a 'Cistercian chapter' at Cîteaux (*capitulum cisterciense*), taking place in the 1120s.[29]

Exordium Cistercii, a relatively brief narrative text describing the departure of Robert and his fellow monks from Molesme and the establishment of the new community, has been called a practical 'manual for instruction of novices', but this idea has now been largely discarded.[30] Several scholars have dated it to 1123/24, but the most recent edition by Chrysogonus Waddell attributes it to the early phase of the abbacy of Raynard of Cîteaux (?1134–1150). Waddell, who prepared a new edition in 1999, linked its creation to the reform of Cistercian liturgical customary, the *Ecclesiastica Officia* (see below), since *Exordium Cistercii* has frequently functioned as a historical introduction to the copies of Cistercian customaries.[31]

The *Exordium Parvum*, a complex, patchwork text describing the early history of Cîteaux combined with copies of official letters and documents, focuses on the development of the 'founding myth'. Its dating and authorship has been much debated, but traditionally it has been ascribed to Abbot Stephen Harding. The new critical edition assigns only some parts of the text (the prologue, chapters 1–2 and chapters 4–14) to Abbot Stephen, dating them to *c.* 1112/13 and suggesting that they were intended as a guide for new recruits to the Cistercian communities. Before 1147 the text underwent major modifications and additions by Abbot Raynard of Cîteaux. It was a complex, polemical document, composed from different types of text – legal documents, letters and narrative fragments – and its aim was to defend the origins of Cîteaux against critics of the new monastic movement. Traditionally, historians have seen in *Exordium Parvum* the founding principle of the Cistercian economy because it prohibits the holding of revenues from churches, altars, burials, tithes, mills and serfs; and have characterised any later deviations in economic practice as 'corruption'. Why such interpretations are questionable will be explained in chapter 6.

Although the Rule of Benedict was at the centre of Cistercian life, it was not detailed enough to provide a guide to all the functions of the monastic community. Whilst Benedictine communities had customaries – providing detailed regulations of monastic life – the *Ecclesiastica Officia*, the first version of which was created during the abbacy of Stephen Harding after 1119, played a similar role for the Cistercians. An important addition to the rather general prescriptions stipulated in the rule, it provided detailed guidance on all aspects of the life of monks: liturgy, organisation of the monasteries, structure of the monastic offices, daily routines, meals, hospitality and many others. The *Ecclesiastica Officia* was in fact not simply a collection of legal rules, but a reworking of the Rule of Benedict for an organisation that extended beyond a single monastery.[32]

Similarly, *Usus Conversorum* was designated to regulate all aspects of the lives of the lay brothers and their role within the monastic community, stipulating much reduced liturgical obligations for the lay brothers, their daily work schedules, accommodation, food and clothing and matters of discipline. It continued to evolve from some unknown point – Waddell suggested the early 1120s, soon after the first version of the *Ecclesiastica Officia* – until 1183, when the first surviving manuscript was created. By 1202 *Usus Conversorum* had become redundant, legislation concerning the lay brothers having been codified by the General Chapter, and further codifications followed in 1237 and 1257.[33]

Such documents were essential for maintaining uniformity of practice. The performance of rituals, the speed of chanting, the precise wording of the prayers, the order and composition of processions, even if seemingly insignificant to an outside observer, identified those involved as members of the community. Several of the early surviving manuscripts of the *Ecclesiastica Officia* contain, at the front, copies of *Exordium Cistercii*, *Exordium Parvum* and *Carta Caritatis*, in which narratives of the origins of the Cistercian movement served as an introduction or historical background to the usages, explaining and justifying various practices and forms of monastic observance. Many Cistercian texts contain, alongside normative documents and historical narratives, supplementary material pertaining only to one particular monastery or region.[34] For example, a thirteenth-century manuscript from Heiligenkreuz Abbey consists of *Exordium Parvum* followed by *Carta Caritatis Posterior*, then *De forma visitationis* (rules governing visitations); then, after a letter of Pope Honorius III (1216–1227) to Cistercian abbots in Bohemia, there follow the *Ecclesiastica Officia* and 89 statutes (*institutiones*) of the General Chapter before the manuscript ends with *Usus Conversorum*, the Rule of Benedict and four privileges of Pope Honorius III.[35]

The fact that historians disagree over the exact dating of the early Cistercian documents does not invalidate their conclusions as why they were created. These documents were all essential steps in the transformation of a religious movement into a well-organised order. With the passage of time and strengthening of Cistercian organisational structures and institutional confidence, different types of text appeared. For the early generations of the Cistercian monks it was a matter of defending their 'experiment' from its critics – hence the need to rewrite the early account and redefine its legal basis. By the end of the twelfth century the monks were more concerned to assert their distinct identity, as manifested by the *Exordium Parvum*, whilst by the time of the canonisation of Robert of Molesme, in 1220, all the controversies surrounding the early Cistercian movement had ceased, and self-confidence prevailed.[36]

Chronologically, the last of these founding texts was the *Exordium Magnum Cisterciense*, the work of the monk Conrad of Eberbach who gathered documentary material and oral history during his stay at Clairvaux, began writing between 1177 and 1193 and completed his project at Eberbach Abbey between 1206 and 1221. The period of its composition coincided with the codification of the legal texts by the Order and Conrad's reflections on the historical narrative and the constitutional compilations and revisions stimulated each other. *Exordium Magnum Cisterciense* presented the foundation of Cîteaux and its remarkable growth as part of a linear history of Christian monasticism stretching from the Apostles, through the Desert Fathers, St Benedict and his Rule, to the immediate predecessors and contemporaries of the Cistercian movement, especially the Cluniac monasteries. In short, the *Exordium Magnum Cisterciense*, extolling the Cistercian movement, was thus described as the embodiment of the true and original spirit of monastic life, constituting an impressive attempt to legitimise the success of the Order in historical terms.[37] For example, Conrad of Eberbach cited, among other letters, all the early papal and episcopal privileges of the Order, incorporating them into the historical narrative, whilst numerous accounts of miracles and visions enacted and experienced by the early leaders and Cistercian monks were marshalled to validate the Order's claim to be the rightful heirs of the apostolic succession. Indeed, one of the main concerns of the *Exordium Magnum Cisterciense* was to show that Bernard of Clairvaux provided a central inspiration for the Cistercian reform spirit and that this spirit had continued into Conrad's generation.[38]

The most important documentary evidence of the growing formalisation of Cistercian structures and of the formation of an organised Order requiring frequent codifications of practices is to be found in the *Instituta* and the *Capitula*. The *Instituta Generalis Capituli apud Cistercium* is a collection of updated and revised statutes from *c.* 1147, which had been subject to various revisions by the early 1180s. The *Capitula*, almost a decade younger (*c.* 1135/36), contains a series of statute-texts arranged in thematic order. The oldest continuous records of the annual General Chapter run from 1157 to 1161[39] and the first formal codification of the General Chapter statutes was promulgated in 1202.⁴⁰ For a long time historians used the early normative texts to reconstruct the formation of the Order and to trace the development of specific practices in the Cistercian movement. The difficulty with this approach is that the original texts were altered by later generations of monks retelling the history of the movement to reflect their own contemporary concerns and can no longer be taken as reflecting a simple chronological development. Even the *Instituta*, as Constance Bouchard has demonstrated very persuasively, were neither a reflection of the actual practice of the Cistercian monks of the first generation nor even a prescription for the second or later generations, but rather an image of an idealised past that never existed.⁴¹

In fact, many of the assumptions of generations of historians are directly linked to the nature of the source editions. The chronology of the Cistercian order given in the edition of the statutes of the General Chapter by Canivez, who dated the oldest section to 1134, created an artificial run of Cistercian statutes from the 1130s, 1140s and 1150s. Canivez amalgamated texts originating from different periods up to the mid-twelfth century and divided them up into annual 'sections'. Yet these artificially created early statutes, the products of different decades, cannot possibly be a reflection of the order's alleged 'ideal'. Jean-Baptiste Auberger was one of the earliest voices to emphasise that the early statutes could not be dated to 1134; and more recently, Waddell, with his own edition of all the twelfth-century statutes on the basis of a far greater number of manuscripts than his predecessor, showed that they were continually revised and edited, making it impossible to fix a single date for their creation.

In the most radical reinterpretation of these texts Constance Berman has argued, using a rather controversial methodology – by identifying a large number of papal confirmation documents as forgeries – that the first collection of Cistercian statutes was assembled only *c.* 1160, that *Exordium Cistercii* also dates from that decade, and *Exordium Parvum* and *Carta Caritatis Prior* only a decade earlier. According to her, the Cistercian Order as such did not come into being before the 1160s or even 1170s, before which only a 'proto-order' existed, of individual, unconnected monasteries that had adopted the Cistercian *ordo*. Berman stresses that the expansion of the proto-order was primarily a process of absorbing existing communities which then adopted Cistercian customs; and that the 'apostolic gestation' process, with Cistercian abbeys sending out monks to found new daughter houses, was not a significant phenomenon in the early period.⁴²

This interpretation of the early history of the Cistercians has been much criticised by other historians, particularly Chrysogonus Waddell.⁴³

Certainly, his opposition to the re-dating of the key texts solely on the basis of problematic manuscript evidence is based on sound methodological principles. As a result, however, he rejected out of hand Berman's broader conclusions about a more gradual development of the Cistercian order. Other scholars, by contrast, notably Martha Newman and Brian Patrick McGuire, who acknowledge the weaknesses of Berman's methodology, nevertheless welcome her fundamental reappraisal of the origins of such a complex institution as the Cistercian Order.[44]

Creation of Cistercian Identity

Why are these texts still central to present-day debates about the history of the Cistercian movement? The twelfth-century Cistercians have been described as a 'textual community' in which monks right across the Order read the same texts that shaped their common understanding.[45] These included key biblical passages such as the Song of Songs, together with *Carta Caritatis* and other works of Cistercian history described above. Like any new religious movement, the Cistercians needed to set themselves apart from their predecessors, while yet emphasising their high spiritual credentials as part of an exalted tradition. The rules of medieval rhetoric pertaining to reform and change were always focused on an ideal past and proclaimed a return to the sources, especially the spirit and practice of the age of the Apostles and the early church. Hence 'new' meant, rather, a 'renewal' in the sense of a return to a perfect past; and it inevitably entailed a degree of blackening of the image of immediate predecessors and contemporaries, who had allegedly failed to adhere to the true monastic observance – notably the Cluniacs and the Benedictine community of Molesme. The assumption behind this thinking is that reform cannot take place without a crisis manifested by corruption.

Bernard of Clairvaux personally knew little about Cluny, having formed his ideas about this particular Benedictine movement on the basis of stories of William of St Thierry, who had been disappointed by the Cluniacs' unwillingness to adopt Cistercian customs and urged Bernard to speak out against Cluny observance.[46] Bernard was nevertheless convinced that the Cistercian interpretation of monasticism was far holier and more authentic than the Cluniacs or, indeed, any other tradition; and in his supremely skilful polemic, *Apologia ad Guillelmum*, he not only attacked the customs of Cluny for their 'excesses', but also propounded the idea of a separate Cistercian identity.[47] He had recourse to similar themes and techniques in a letter to Abbot Richard of Fountains, the leader of a breakaway group from the Benedictine abbey of St Mary's in

York. On this occasion Bernard described the transition from the old tradition to the new movement in decidedly graphic terms:

> Your progress from good to better is no less wonderful, no less gratifying than a conversion from evil to good ... The merest prudence demanded that you should rise above the meritocracy which is so near to apostasy and leave behind you that tepidity which God vomits from his mouth.[48]

Not that the case of Fountains was something artificially conjured up by Bernard of Clairvaux so much as a particular expression of a general trend towards greater austerity in monastic observance – in which respect the aims of the breakaway monks were broadly those of the Cistercian *ordo* itself; and it was this congruency that was being utilised by Bernard.[49]

Even so, the cases of Benedictine monks becoming Cistercians had high propaganda value as embodying the desire to be part of a stricter and more spiritual version of monastic observance. There were important individual cases, such as the highly educated Benedictine monk, William of St Thierry (d. *c.* 1148), who became a Cistercian in his later life; a number of individuals surrounding Bernard of Clairvaux, including one of his secretaries, Nicholas of Clairvaux; and Idung of Prüfening, a former Cluniac monk and the author of highly polemical work criticising his old affiliation and praising the superiority of life under Cistercian observance.[50] Cases of conversion in the opposite direction, that is of Cistercian monks leaving their communities to join the 'softer' Benedictine path, were very much disliked and discouraged by the Cistercian leadership. When a certain Robert, a relative of Bernard himself, left Clairvaux to join Cluny in 1125, his abbot and kinsman sent him a powerfully worded letter:

> Look into your heart: consider your intention: take your counsel with the truth: let your conscience answer for you why you have left, why you have deserted your order, your brothers, your place, and me, who is your relation in flesh and even more so in spirit.[51]

He went on to accuse Robert of deserting the Cistercians because the proper observance of monastic life was too hard for him: 'You [Robert] are afraid of vigils and fasts, as well as of manual labour'[52] – in Bernard's eyes, it was the weakness of the individual, not the manner of the Cistercian observance, which was the problem.

Much as the ideological positing of the Cistercians in opposition to the Benedictines might sometimes cause problems, it remained vital for the Cistercian movement to cultivate friends within the traditional structures of the church, among the higher church authorities, and especially the papacy, which could protect the Order from attacks from many resentful parties. It was not an accident that the privilege granted to Cîteaux by Pope Paschal in *c.* 1100 and a number of charters of the local bishop, Walter of Châlon, the Papal Legate Hugh Archbishop of Lyons and two cardinals, John and Benedict, were copied in the *Exordium Parvum* to provide a shield against any attempts by the community of Molesme to bring the new monastery under its authority.[53]

If episcopal support was crucial for the survival and establishment of the emergent new community and the growing Cistercian family, it remained an important aspect of the Cistercian engagement in the wider church arena throughout the twelfth and thirteenth centuries. Connections to the key decision makers, especially in the early period, secured important privileges, setting the Order apart from other monastic structures and giving the white monks many advantages over the Benedictine communities. Unlike the Benedictines, communities of white monks were not subject to bishops' visitation and were free from obligatory attendance at the diocesan synods; and they also enjoyed the freedom to elect their abbots.[54] The privilege of exemption from the payment of tithes on all Cistercian lands, which they received from Pope Innocent II in 1132, was approved by the Council of Pisa in 1135; and it was in vain that Abbot Peter the Venerable of Cluny protested against it.[55] True, the secular church's attitude to Cistercian exemption from the payment of tithes changed in the second half of the twelfth century: the stubborn refusal of the Cistercian monasteries to pay tithes despite growing pressure from the bishops became a highly contested issue; while for a time the papacy supported the continuation of Cistercian exemption, and used it to gain the Order's support in other matters. But papal policy was not consistent: in 1155 Pope Hadrian IV decreed that Cistercians were free from the payments only on *novalia*, that is lands that had never been cultivated before. His successor, Pope Alexander III, who needed Cistercian support in his struggles against a series of anti-popes, reversed this limitation on the exemption, but in time it became difficult to defend the privilege. Church reformers were turning increasingly towards improving provision for the laity at the parochial level, and the bishops' displeasure focused on lay ownership of churches and exemption from monastic tithes. When addressing the General Chapter in *c.* 1180 Archbishop Richard of Canterbury complained of the financial losses incurred by his church owing to the Cistercian exemption from tithe payment.[56] Whereupon, spurred on by the persistent conflicts between individual monasteries and bishops, the General Chapter decreed in 1180 a ban on any further purchases of land, except in remote areas that were thus free from pre-existing tithe obligations. In 1215 the Fourth Lateran Council endorsed this policy, confining exemption from tithe payment on any new acquisition (even if the monks cultivated it themselves) to land classified as *novalia*.[57]

Bernard of Clairvaux: Abbot, Politician and Saint

Bernard of Clairvaux occupied a central place in the historical memory of the Cistercian order. As an embodiment of the monastic tradition he overshadowed all the other early leaders of the movement, but its striking success in the first half of the twelfth century should not be solely credited to him. What gave Bernard such a prominent position in the history of the Order was his legacy in terms of both a large textual corpus and a vast network of personal connections. The first collection of Bernard's letters was created during his lifetime by Geoffrey of Auxerre and the author personally influenced the selection, removing the examples he considered to be substandard in style and clarity.[58] Bernard of Clairvaux belonged to many ecclesiastical 'friendship networks' that gave him access to the most influential and powerful men of his time; and his fervent 'Cistercian propaganda' campaigns – letters sent widely to various lay rulers – were instrumental in setting up new monasteries and expanding this network of connections to the very frontiers of Latin Europe.[59]

Born in 1090, Bernard came from a lesser noble family centred on Fontaines castle near Dijon, and acquired a level of learning that destined him for an ecclesiastical career. He did not, however, follow a conventional path: when, in 1113, at the age of 22, he entered Cîteaux Abbey he persuaded a group of some 30 relatives and friends to join a reformed group. His family connections were useful in expanding the Cistercian movement, and in 1115 Bernard was sent to establish a new community in Clairvaux in Champagne. Subsequent narratives of the order's origins present him as 'the rescuer of the Cîteaux experiment', but in fact Bernard appeared only after the foundation of La Ferté Abbey in southern Burgundy, when the movement was clearly gaining in strength.[60] Undoubtedly – and admittedly this was important at this early stage – Bernard was very good at gaining the support of people who became ardent believers in the Cistercian project: for example, Bishop William of Champeaux, Guerric of Igny who came to Cîteaux in 1123, and a leading theologian, William of St Thierry. Of course, the dissemination of texts was essential for securing support among the ecclesiastical elites, and Bernard's spiritual writings started to appear as early as *c.* 1119 (less than five years after he became abbot), and to circulate increasingly widely as manuscript copies propagating further reform ideas, passed between monastic communities in the Cistercian network.[61]

The strength of the personal bonds between the Cistercians and many of their ecclesiastical supporters was reinforced by the idea of charity and worked as a powerful tool for resolving conflicts and cementing friendships. In his overarching aspiration to reform the church and spread monasticism, Bernard liked to classify people as potential allies or enemies and Clairvaux attracted many visitors coming to meet him and observe the Cistercian experiment. These included churchmen from the very frontiers of Christian Europe, such as Archbishop Malachy of Armagh or Archbishop Eskil of Lund – in Bernard's eyes a model bishop – who asked Clairvaux to train monks in the Cistercian observance to send to their respective provinces.[62] Such people were crucial allies of Bernard in turning the Cistercians into a trans-European movement connected by the shared *ordo*, beyond the collection of local groups of reform-minded communities.

The quality of church leaders was central to Bernard's ideas about the church – in his view, already during his lifetime, Cistercian monks as exponents of the moral aspects of church reform were directly involved in the episcopal elections, writing and preaching about the virtues of ideal prelates, and criticising what they regarded as low standards of morality;[63] and certainly Bernard himself believed that bishops should be examples to those around them, and that it was essential for the monks to intervene in clerical matters outside the walls of their monastery in situations when the well-being and unity of the church was under threat.[64] In short, he had a clear concept of the Cistercian monastery as 'a training ground for a reformed clergy' and the abbey of Clairvaux became a 'magnet' for influential churchmen from across Europe who wanted to 'retire' to this spiritual centre and even be buried in this spiritually and symbolically powerful space.[65]

If Bernard's letters were for historians a valuable source for reconstructing networks, spanning the lay and ecclesiastical worlds, they were for him a practical tool for recruiting new supporters for his various projects. Among their clerical recipients were supporters of the monastic reform movement from all over north-western Europe, from Burgundy through Champagne to Flanders. Although not Cistercians themselves, they shared Bernard's ideas of reform and joined with him in spreading them – both at a local level and in more far-reaching campaigns in which he was involved. One Benedictine abbot, Alvisius of Anchin, for example, supported Bernard in his campaign against Peter Abelard and in the preparations for the Second Crusade, whilst, another, Abbot Geoffrey of S-Médard (Soissons), later bishop of Châlons-sur-Marne, was an important member and, along with Bernard, a key supporter of Pope Innocent II during the schism of 1130. Indeed, in the first half of the twelfth century the Cistercians' promotion of reform ideas was very dependent on their network of sympathetic bishops – a network that was markedly strengthened when a significant number of Cistercian monks became bishops.[66] After the first such appointment in 1126, by 1160 more than 50 Cistercian monks had been installed in episcopal positions, including 10 cardinals and a pope.[67] In their high posts they continued to associate themselves with the ethos of the white monks, and often actively supported the Order, while Cistercian regulations allowed them to have monks and *conversi* (lay brothers) as companions, which reinforced their ties with the monastic life.[68] Indeed, the degree of co-operation between Cistercians and prelates was unprecedented compared both with that which had previously existed between bishops and Benedictine monks and that which was later developed between bishops and mendicants. This could have been due to the fact that the white monks claimed no responsibility for the salvation of the laity and therefore did not challenge episcopal authority;[69] at any rate, the mutual appeal was often so strong that some of these prelate supporters of the Cistercians retired to Cistercian monasteries in their old age to become monks themselves.[70]

Bernard's strategy within the Cistercian family, one of personal interventions in the affairs of various Cistercian houses, showed just what he understood the key ideas of the *ordo* to be. His response to Abbot Arnold of Morimond's proposal to accompany his monks to the Holy Land in the 1120s testified to the importance of connections within the Cistercian family based on the concepts of chains of command, obedience and responsibility. In Bernard's eyes, being a Cistercian was a distinct way of life and all members should obey the same way of life. In his view, Arnold's superior, the abbot of Cîteaux, ought to be aware of what was happening in Morimond Abbey and intervene if necessary, but as father-abbot appeared not to know about Arnold's eccentric idea, Bernard decided to intervene himself, writing to Arnold to say that his departure for the Holy Land would greatly undermine the rule of stability and, indeed, cause a scandal. He pointed to Morimond's responsibility towards its new 'daughters' (Bellevaux in 1119/20, La Crête 1121, Altenkamp in 1123), for which the care they deserved could not be provided if Arnold and his monks went to the Holy Land. Moreover, by deciding to move his community from Morimond, Arnold was ignoring the advice of his fellow abbots and disregarding the authority of his superior, the father-abbot of Cîteaux. When Arnold ignored this advice, the exasperated Bernard appealed to the Pope Calixtus II to use his authority to save the reputation and unity of the Cistercian movement, and asked Archbishop Bruno of Cologne, too, to exercise his authority over Arnold's followers in his diocese.⁷¹ In the end Bernard got his way and the monks stayed in Morimond.

Bernard also came forward as an authority to pronounce on several other controversies of the day that were quite unconnected with the growing Cistercian movement. Together with William of St Thierry, for example, he was instrumental in the condemnation of Abelard's teaching. Bishop Matthew of Kraków asked him for a theological refutation of the Orthodox Church, and Peter the Venerable for a refutation of the Muslim faith, although he refused to get involved in the controversy surrounding the Eucharist and the validity of sacraments administered by simoniacs.⁷² Through such writings, Bernard's influence reached well beyond the Cistercian family, becoming a staple of every monastic library. Indeed, thanks to his iconic status, many other works were to be incorrectly attributed to him: in a list of the manuscripts in over 180 monastic libraries in England and southern Scotland compiled by English Franciscans from Oxford in the second half of the thirteenth century, no fewer than 51 works were attributed to Bernard of Clairvaux, but only 60 per cent of them were authentic.⁷³

Overall, indeed, Bernard's most significant activity related to matters ranging far beyond the world of the Cistercians. Between the early 1130s and the late 1140s he was largely an absentee abbot of Clairvaux. It is assumed that Bernard refused a number of high ecclesiastical appointments in favour of retaining his position, which gave him far greater opportunity to influence.⁷⁴ As G.R. Evans put it, 'wherever the Church intervened or became caught up in politics, he was liable to find himself involved'.⁷⁵ His ability to influence and appeal to the laity is clear from the letters that he sent to European rulers describing the ideal of the Christian prince – who defended the church, respected the clergy, refrained from appropriating monastic property or interfering in episcopal elections and, of course, supported the Cistercians. One such letter was carried by a group of white monks headed by William, an Englishman, to the court of King Henry I and urged him to support a new Cistercian foundation in his kingdom.⁷⁶ Nor, on the other hand, did Bernard hesitate to castigate the actions of powerful men when he disapproved of them. Regardless of the subject, his letters projected a strong voice of authority.⁷⁷

In his various political involvements Bernard never failed to use the situation to further the growing Cistercian movement and to expand the network of monasteries; and throughout his lifetime Cistercians had particularly good connections with the papal curia. These they exploited, not only to advance their reform agenda, but also to secure privileges for their developing order and expand the Cistercian monastic network. In political terms, probably Bernard's most important undertaking was connected with the papal schism of 1130–1139 when Bernard's support for Innocent II was certainly a significant factor in Innocent's eventual success. For example, several Cistercian houses were set up in strategic locations in the central parts of Italy during the schism – notably Fossanova (1135) on the Via Appia and Casamari on the Via Latina (1140), both on the southern frontier of the area controlled by Pope Innocent II.[78] Meanwhile, there was a new Cistercian foundation, Sambucina Abbey in Calabria, in the area of Innocent II's enemy, Roger of Sicily – the key supporter of Pope Anacletus – with whom Bernard also managed to maintain a useful connection.[79] Eventually, Bernard persuaded the kings of England and France to support Innocent and was present at all key councils at the time, where he persuaded a number of powerful bishops to do the same, and even attempted to win over Roger of Sicily. Not surprisingly, after the end of the schism Bernard continued to act as an influential adviser, and even representative, of Innocent II.[80]

The intimacy between the Cistercians and the papacy reached its apogee during the papacy of Eugenius III (1145–1153), who, as Bernard Paganelli from Pisa, had started his ecclesiastical career as a Cistercian monk at Clairvaux. Under the direction of Bernard himself, he became the founding abbot of the new Cistercian abbey near Farfa in 1138, which was transferred two years later to Tre Fontane (SS. Vincenzo e Anastasio monastery) near Rome.[81] Elected pope in 1145, Eugenius is often described as the 'first Cistercian pope'; and following the election, in a letter to his former monk and friend, Bernard of Clairvaux expressed his delight that 'his son Bernard [Paganelli] has been promoted to be his father'.[82] Between 1149 and 1153 Bernard went on to prepare a work of advice to the pope (*De consideratione ad Eugenium Papam* in five volumes) on the major issue of ecclesiastical politics and the temporal and spiritual role of the pope;[83] and in his correspondence with him Bernard was particularly outspoken in his comments on various papal actions, frequently linked to appointments that the Cistercian leader wanted to influence.[84]

It was not long before Bernard and Eugenius were involved in a joined enterprise: the call for a new crusade. Pope Eugenius delegated the preaching for this second crusade to the Cistercians; and Bernard of Clairvaux himself inaugurated the campaign at Easter 1146, by preaching at a great assembly at Vézelay in central France in the presence of King Louis VII and a gathering of nobility and knights.[85] While Bernard's involvement in the crusade propaganda accorded with the pope's plans, it also served Bernard's own aims of increasing recruitment to the

Cistercian communities.[86] Following preaching campaigns in the autumn of 1146, Bernard moved his attention from the county of Flanders to the Rhineland and the territory of the German king Conrad III, which proved a rich source of recruits. Indeed the role of Bernard and his fellow Cistercian abbots was so significant that after the initial papal initiative to call the crusade it was not Pope Eugenius III but Bernard who directed and organised the propaganda campaign – leading some historians to go so far as to call the second crusade Bernard's.[87] While Bernard was also an exponent of the idea of crusading, not only in the Holy Land, but among the remaining pagans of north-eastern Europe, his followers went on to lend their support, particularly as preachers for the Third and Fourth Crusades.[88] Cistercian involvement is also evident in the contemporary narrative sources, one of the most important chroniclers of the Second Crusade being a Cistercian monk, Bishop Otto of Freising.

One of the most lasting legacies of Bernard's influence on the crusading movement was the creation of a new type of religious order, the Templars, who combined military activity with elements of Cistercian spirituality. The first master of the Templars was a relative of Bernard, Hugh of Payns. From the Council of Troyes in 1128, when the Order's first rule was established, Bernard was directly involvement with it, publicising it in both ecclesiastical and political circles. In a treatise that he wrote for the Knights Templar, Bernard explained their dual nature – metaphysical and literal knighthood defending the faith and the faithful. These knights were knights of a new kind, based on the Cistercian model: converted to the service of Christ, rejecting the worldly trappings of knightly status and embracing spirituality. Not that Bernard was advocating war as a positive human activity – he was vehemently opposed to the killing of fellow Christians – but a holy war, authorised by the ecclesiastical authorities, preferably the pope, against the 'enemies of Christ' was an exception.[89]

Naturally, the failure of the Second Crusade was a significant blow to the prestige of the Cistercian movement; and both Bernard of Clairvaux, and the Templars, regarded as jointly responsible for the military failure, came in for a good deal of criticism.[90] For the Cistercians, try as they might to play down Bernard's involvement, all this was a serious embarrassment at a time when their campaign for his canonisation was getting under way.[91] Clearly, it was of great importance to the movement that its founding father should be counted among the saints. It would be recognition of the spiritual validity of the Cistercian experiment, a further stamp of approval from the pope and a focus for liturgical celebrations in the Order. The canonisation would also enhance the status of Clairvaux Abbey by giving it possession of the relics of its own saint.

Already from 1159, two decades before the successful canonisation, the houses of Clairvaux filiation were celebrating the Office of the Dead in Bernard's memory.[92]

A spell of good relations between Pope Alexander III (1159–1181) and the Cistercians provided a group of abbots and bishops who were former Cistercian monks with an opportunity to lodge a request for canonisation, but the preparation for Bernard's elevation went back several years. The creation of a very extensive *Vita Prima* had already been initiated in Bernard's lifetime, the first book being written by William of St Thierry and containing material gathered by Geoffrey of Auxerre, Bernard's principal secretary from 1140. The *Vita* was completed after Bernard's death by the Benedictine Abbot Ernauld of Boneval (second book) and Geoffrey of Auxerre (third to fifth). In 1163, however, despite the pro-Cistercian stance of the pope, the Council of Tours rejected the request for canonisation; but the Cistercians did not give up and a revised text of the *Vita* was soon completed. That brought the manuscript closer to the required standard, especially with regard to the validity of the miracles. Some stories of healing were removed and in others names of witnesses still alive were removed, so they could not be called to testify, and certain details such as locations were deliberately obscured. Clearly, Alain of Auxerre (d. 1185), who made the revisions, was very careful to get rid of anything that could jeopardise the chances of canonisation; and this strategy worked and the positive decision was promulgated by Pope Alexander III on 18 January 1174.[93]

Conclusions

As emphasised earlier, the Cistercian movement was one of many groups that emerged in the late eleventh century in the search for an authentic monastic life embodying the ideal of the *Vita Apostolica*. For many decades, the movement was just that – a growing collection of various communities following Cistercian customs and practices and connected through charismatic leaders and friendship networks, but only slowly developing formal structures such as the meeting of the General Chapter. The Cistercian 'experiment' was an effective combination of established tradition and new organisational developments. As Lekai observed, the early Cistercians:

> succeeded not because they fashioned their lives according to the Rule, but because they managed to combine the viable elements of the Rule with Gregorian ideals, calling for greater austerity, greater independence from feudal structures, for monks to be clearly set apart from the rest of society, while protected everywhere by an effective centralised monastic government.[94]

ORIGINS: IDEAS, MYTHS AND INTERPRETATIONS

The rapid growth of the monastic family of Cîteaux in the twelfth century was described in the Cistercian texts as the product of a period of enthusiasm, with new recruits joining in great numbers. By the end of the century it had been mythologised:

> Literary works from the late twelfth century that praised the first decades of the Cistercian expansion characterize the second period, when the monks were more concerned with consolidating material and legal gains than in living the life itself.[95]

As the movement slowly turned into the Order and became increasingly institutionalised it became important to link these practical developments to the spiritual heritage for the guidance of subsequent generations of monks.

In the early history of the Cistercians a number of charismatic leaders became very important not just for the contemporaries, but, as founding fathers and examples, for later generations of the monks. Among them, the central place is occupied by Bernard of Clairvaux, whose truly iconic role has a significance well beyond the realm of monastic history. For many historians he was one of the central figures of his age, influencing politics in almost all areas in the first half of that century. As David Knowles has said of him:

> it is difficult to name any other saint in the history of the church whose influence, both on the public life of an epoch and on the conscience of a multitude of individuals, was during his lifetime so profound and so persuasive.[96]

More recently, however, the centrality of Bernard to the history of age – even to the narrower history of the Cistercian Order – has been questioned. Of course he was important, but it is vital to distinguish between the historical Bernard and the later legend developed by the Cistercians. According to Paschal Phillips, the fact that Bernard was less well known to his contemporaries than had been assumed is just one more indication of the over-estimation of his role. Indeed, the interpretation of the public role of Bernard can be seen as 'a subconscious transfer of modern mass media celebrity process'.[97] True, contemporary chronicles show little awareness of Bernard and his public profile, whilst other figures, later completely side-lined, were – even in field of Cistercian history – more famous than Bernard during their lifetimes. This includes, for example, Peter of Tarentaise (d. 1174), one of only three formally canonised medieval Cistercian monks. His career, spanning an abbacy and then the office of bishop, was similar to that of Bernard in respect of extensive travels on various missions; and he was also famous for performing miracles.[98]

In short, although Bernard, tireless networker, politician and Cistercian leader, was of great important in ensuring that the growing Cistercian movement gained the support of key figures in the church and a supply of potential founders in many regions of Europe, the creation of the Cistercian Order and the spread of the new foundations was not solely his own work. While historians debate his role in various episodes of twelfth-century history, it remains important as far as the history of the Cistercian Order is concerned to study Bernard's image and the changes it underwent throughout the medieval period. For after all, it was his legacy that continued to influence what Cistercians believed to be the spirit of their organisation and that remained an important point of reference for future generations.

Notes

1. Jean Leclercq, 'A Sociological Approach to the History of a Religious Order', in *The Cistercian Spirit: A Symposium in Memory of Thomas Merton*, ed. M. Basil Pennington (Shannon: Irish University Press, 1970), pp. 134–136.
2. Jean-Baptiste Van Damme, *The Three Founders of Cîteaux, Robert of Molesme, Alberic, Stephen Harding*, trans. Nicholas Groves and Christian Carr; adapted and arranged Bede K. Lackner (Kalamazoo, MI: Cistercian Publications, 1998), pp. 41–42.
3. Brian Patrick McGuire, 'Was Alberic the Real Founder of Cîteaux?', *Cistercian Studies Quarterly* 34:2 (1999), p. 139.
4. Martha Newman, *The Boundaries of Charity: Cistercian Culture and Ecclesiastical Reform 1098–1180* (Stanford, CA: Stanford University Press, 1996), p. 46; Van Damme, *The Three Founders*, p. 22.
5. *Les plus anciens textes de Cîteaux*, ed. Jean de la Croix Bouton and Jean-Baptiste Van Damme, Cîteaux: Commentarii Cistercienses. Studia et Documenta 2 (Achel: Abbaye cistercienne, 1974), p. 63.
6. Van Damme, *The Three Founders*, pp. 51–52.
7. Van Damme, *The Three Founders*, pp. 55–67.
8. H.E.J. Cowdrey, 'Stephen Harding', in *Oxford Dictionary of National Biography: From the Earliest Times to the Year 2000*, ed. H.C.G. Matthew and Brian Harrison (Oxford: Oxford University Press, 2004); Van Damme, *The Three Founders*, pp. 71–128.
9. H.E.J. Cowdrey, '"Quidam Frater Stephanus Nomine, Anglicus Natione": The English Background of Stephen Harding', *Revue Bénédictine* 101 (1991), pp. 322–324; Martha G. Newman, 'Stephen Harding and the Creation of the Cistercian Community', *Revue Bénédictine* 107 (1997), p. 131; Bede K. Lackner, 'The Liturgy of Early Cîteaux', in *Studies in Medieval Cistercian History presented to Jeremiah F. O'Sullivan* (Shannon: Irish University Press, 1971), pp. 6–8.
10. Jean Leclercq, François Vandenbroucke and Louis Bouyer, *The Spirituality of the Middle Ages*, trans. from the French by the Benedictines of Holme

Eden Abbey, Carlisle (London: Burnes & Oates, 1968), p. 218; Louis Lekai, *The Cistercians: Ideals and Reality* (Kent, OH: Kent State University Press, 1977), p. 29.
11. Louis J. Lekai, 'The Early Cistercians and the Rule of Benedict', *Mittellateinisches Jahrbuch* 17 (1982), p. 97, n. 6.
12. Orderic Vitalis, *Ecclesiastical History of Orderic Vitalis*, ed. Margery Chibnall, 6 vols. (Oxford: Clarendon, 1969–1980), vol. 4, p. 322.
13. Brian Patrick McGuire, 'Bernard's Concept of a Cistercian Order', *Cîteaux: Commentarii Cistercienses* 54 (2003), p. 230.
14. McGuire, 'Bernard's Concept of a Cistercian Order', p. 247.
15. McGuire, 'Bernard's Concept of a Cistercian Order', p. 235 n. 20, p. 236.
16. *The Letters of St. Bernard of Clairvaux*, ed. Bruno Scott James (London: Burns & Oates, 1953), no. 151; *Sancti Bernardi Opera*, vol. 7, ed. J. Leclercq, C.H. Talbot and H.M. Rochais (Rome: Editiones Cistercienses, 1957–1977), p. 340; quoted in McGuire, 'Bernard's Concept of a Cistercian Order', p. 238.
17. Bede K. Lackner, 'The Monastic Life According to Saint Bernard', in *Studies in Medieval Cistercian History*, vol. 2, ed. John R. Sommerfeldt (Kalamazoo, MI: Cistercian Publications, 1976), pp. 53–58; Gregor Müller, 'Von täglichen Brote', *Cisterzienser Chronik* 8 (1896), pp. 278–280, 306–313.
18. Kassius Hallinger, 'Woher kommen die Laienbrüder?', *Analecta Ordinis Cisterciensis* 12 (1956), pp. 1–104.
19. Newman, *The Boundaries of Charity*, p. 71.
20. *Twelfth-century Statutes from the Cistercian General Chapter: Latin text with English notes and commentary*, ed. Chrysogonus Waddell (Brecht: Cîteaux, 2002), 1192: 14, pp. 241–242; James France, *Medieval Images of Saint Bernard of Clairvaux* (Kalamazoo, MI: Cistercian Publications, 2007), p. 72.
21. Lackner, 'The Monastic Life', p. 59; Newman, *The Boundaries of Charity*, p. 2.
22. Thomas Renna, 'The Wilderness and the Cistercians', *Cistercian Studies Quarterly* 30 (1995), p. 185.
23. Benedicta Ward, 'The Desert Myth. Reflections on the Desert Ideal in Early Cistercian Monasticism', in *One Yet Two: Monastic Tradition East and West*, ed. M. Basil Pennington (Kalamazoo, MI: Cistercian Publications, 1976), pp. 183–199; Michael Casey, '*In communi vita fratrum*: St Bernard's Teaching on Cenobitic Solitude', *Analecta Cisterciensia* 46 (1990), p. 257; William of St Thierry, 'From the *Vita Prima*', in *The Cistercian World: Monastic Writings of the Twelfth Century*, ed. and trans. Pauline Matarasso (London: Penguin, 1993), p. 31; Christopher Holdsworth, 'The Past and Monastic Debate in the Time of Bernard of Clairvaux', in *The Church Retrospective*, ed. R.N. Swanson (Woodbridge: Boydell Press for the Ecclesiastical History Society, 1997), p. 112.
24. Jean-Berthold Mahn, *L'ordre cistercien et son gouvernement des origins au milieu du XIIIe siècle (1098–1265)* (Paris: E. de Boccard, 1945), pp. 60–70; C.H. Lawrence, *Medieval Monasticism: Forms of Religious Life in Western Europe in the Middle Ages* (London: Longman, 1989), pp. 186–192.

25. Brian Patrick McGuire, 'Who Founded the Order of Cîteaux?', in *The Joy of Learning and the Love of God: Studies in Honour of Jean Leclercq*, ed. E. Rozanne Elder (Kalamazoo, MI: Cistercian Publications, 1995), pp. 394–395; *Narrative and Legislative Texts from Early Cîteaux: Latin Text in Dual Edition with English Translation and Notes*, ed. Chrysogonus Waddell (Brecht: Cîteaux, Commentarii Cistercienses, 1999), pp. 261–273, 371–380.
26. Lekai, 'The Early Cistercians, p. 98.
27. 'Carta Caritatis', in *Narrative and Legislative Texts*, ed. Waddell, pp. 277–388.
28. 'Summa carta caritatis', in *Narrative and Legislative Texts*, ed. Waddell, pp. 183–184.
29. *The Letters of Peter the Venerable*, ed. Giles Constable (Cambridge, MA: Harvard University Press, 1967), vol. 1, p. 366; *Vita prima Sancti Bernardi Claraevallis Abbatis: liber primus*, ed. Paul Verdeyen (Turnhout: Brepols, 2011), 7.32; McGuire, 'Bernard's Concept of a Cistercian Order', pp. 245–247.
30. *Narrative and Legislative Texts*, p. 139; Van Damme, *The Three Founders*, p. 114.
31. *Narrative and Legislative Texts*, pp. 147–161.
32. McGuire, 'Who Founded the Order of Cîteaux?', pp. 394–397; *Les Ecclesiastica Officia Cisterciens du XIIème Siècle. Texte latin selon les manuscripts édités de Trente 1711, Ljubljana 31 et Dijon 114, version française, annexe liturgique, notes, index et tables*, ed. Danièle Choisselet and Placide Vernet (Reiningue: La Documentation Cistercienne, 1989), pp. 49–50.
33. *Cistercian Lay Brothers. Twelfth-Century Usages with Related Texts. Latin Text with Concordance of Latin Terms, English Translations and Notes*, ed. Chrysogonus Waddell (Brecht: Cîteaux: Commentarii Cistercienses, 2000), pp. 21–22.
34. Chrysogonus Waddell, 'The *Exordium Cistercii* and the *Summa Cartae Caritatis*: A Discussion Continued', in *Cistercian Ideals and Reality*, ed. John R. Sommerfeldt (Kalamazoo, MI: Cistercian Publications, 1978), pp. 37–38.
35. *Narrative and Legislative Texts*, pp. 39–40.
36. McGuire, 'Was Alberic the Real Founder of Cîteaux?', pp. 140, 152, 154.
37. Brian Patrick McGuire, *The Difficult Saint: Bernard of Clairvaux and His Tradition* (Kalamazoo, MI: Cistercian Publications, 1991), p. 290; *Narrative and Legislative Texts*, pp. 299–300.
38. The new edition: *Exordivm Magnvm Cisterciense sive Narratio de Initio Cisterciensis Ordinis*, ed. Bruno Griesser, Corpus Christianorum Continuatio Mediaevalis 138 (Turnhout: Brepols, 1994), and translation: *The Great Beginning of Cîteaux: A Narrative of the Beginning of the Cistercian Order – the Exordium Magnum of Conrad of Eberbach*, ed. E. Rozanne Elder, trans. Benedicta Ward and Paul Savage (Collegeville, MN: Liturgical Press, 2012); *The Foundation History of the Abbeys of Byland and Jervaulx*, ed. Janet Burton, Borthwick Texts and Studies 35 (York: Borthwick Publications, 2006), p. xxx; Brian Patrick McGuire, 'The First Cistercian Renewal and a Changing Image of Saint Bernard', *Cistercian Studies Quarterly* 24 (1989), pp. 25–49.

39. Waddell, 'The *Exordium Parvum* and the *Summa Cartae Caritatis*', p. 34; *Twelfth-Century Statutes*, p. 25.
40. *La codification cistercienne de 1202 et son évolution ultérieure*, ed. Bernard Lucet (Rome: Editiones Cistercienses, 1964).
41. Constance Bouchard, 'Cistercian Ideals Versus Reality: 1134 Reconsidered', *Cîteaux: Commentarii Cistercienses* 39 (1988), p. 217; Chrysogonus Waddell, 'The Cistercian Institutions and their Early Evolution: Granges, Economy, Lay Brothers', in *L'espace cistercien*, ed. Léon Pressouyre (Paris: Comité des travaux historiques et scientifiques, 1994), p. 28.
42. *Statuta capitulorum generalium ordinis Cisterciensis ab anno 1116 ad annum 1786*, ed. Joseph Canivez, 8 vols (Louvain: Bureaux de la Revue, 1933–1941); Jean-Baptiste Auberger, *L'unamité cistercienne primitive: myth ou réalité?* (Achel: Cîteaux, Studia et Documenta, 1986); *Twelfth-Century Statutes*; Constance Hoffman Berman, *The Cistercian Evolution: The Invention of a Religious Order in Twelfth-Century Europe* (Philadelphia, PA: University of Pennsylvania Press, 2000), pp. 46–92, 86–92, 151–160, appendix 1.
43. Chrysogonus Waddell, 'The Myth of Cistercian Origins: C.H. Berman and the Manuscript Sources', *Cîteaux: Commentari Cistercienses* 51 (2000), pp. 299–386.
44. Martha Newman, 'Review of Constance Berman, *The Cistercian Evolution: The Invention of a Religious Order in Twelfth-Century Europe*', *The Catholic Historical Review* 87 (2001), pp. 315–316; Brian Patrick McGuire, 'Charity and Unanimity: The Invention of the Cistercian Order, A Review Article', *Cîteaux: Commentari Cistercienses* 51 (2000), pp. 285–297.
45. Brian Stock, *Implications of Literacy: Written Language and Models of Interpretation in the Eleventh and Twelfth Century* (Princeton, NJ: Princeton University Press, 1983), p. 405.
46. Adriaan H. Bredero, 'William of Saint Thierry at the Crossroads of the Monastic Currents of his Time', in *William, Abbot of St Thierry: A Colloquium at the Abbey of St Thierry*, trans. Jerry Carfantan (Kalamazoo, MI: Cistercian Publications, 1987), p. 115.
47. McGuire, 'Bernard's Concept of a Cistercian Order', pp. 232–236; Michael Casey, 'Reading Saint Bernard: The Man, the Medium, the Message', in *Companion to Bernard of Clairvaux McGuire*, ed. Brian Patrick McGuire (Leiden and Boston: Brill, 2011), p. 67.
48. Eugene Goodrich, 'The Limits of Friendship. A Disagreement between Saint Bernard and Peter the Venerable on the Role of Charity in Dispensation from the Rule', *Cistercian Studies Quarterly* 16 (1981), p. 95; *The Letters of St. Bernard of Clairvaux*, no. 171.
49. McGuire, 'Bernard's Concept of a Cistercian Order', p. 238; Berman, *The Cistercian Evolution*, p. 100.
50. Idung of Prüfening, *Cistercians and Cluniacs: The Case for Cîteaux*, ed. and trans. Jeremiah F. O'Sullivan (Kalamazoo, MI: Cistercian Studies, 1977).
51. *The Letters of St. Bernard of Clairvaux*, no. 1, p. 9.
52. *The Letters of St. Bernard of Clairvaux*, no. 1, p. 12.
53. *Narrative and Legislative Texts*, pp. 236–237, 247–251; McGuire, 'Was Alberic the Real Founder of Cîteaux?', pp. 142–143.

54. Friedrich Pfurtscheller, *Die Privilegierung des Zisterzienserordens im Rahmen der allgemeinen Schutz- und Exemtionsgeschichte vom Anfang bis zur Bulle 'Parvus Fons' (1265)* (Frankfurt a.M.: Peter Lang, 1972), pp. 87–107.
55. Adriaan H. Bredero, 'Saint Bernard in his Relations with Peter the Venerable', in *Bernardus Magister: Papers Presented at the Nonacentenary Celebration of the Birth of Saint Bernard of Clairvaux, Kalamazoo, Michigan*, ed. John R. Sommerfeldt (Kalamazoo, MI: Cistercian Publications, 1992), p. 325.
56. Giles Constable, *Monastic Tithes from the Origins to the Twelfth Century* (Cambridge: Cambridge University Press, 1964), pp. 220–242; *Patrologia Latina*, ed. Jacques-Paul Migne (Paris, 1904), vol. 207, cols. 252–255.
57. *Twelfth-Century Statutes* 1180: 1, p. 86; *Decrees of the Ecumenical Councils*, ed. Norman P. Tanner (London: Sheed & Ward, 1990), vol. 1, p. 260.
58. Jean Leclercq, 'Introduction', in *Sancti Bernardi Opera*, vol. 7, ed. Jean Leclerq and H. Rochais (Rome: Editiones Cistercienses, 1974), pp. ix–xvi.
59. For a revisionist view on the role of Bernard of Clairvaux, see Paschal Phillips, 'The Presence – and Absence – of Bernard of Clairvaux in the Twelfth-Century Chronicles', in *Bernardus Magister*, pp. 35–53 (esp. p. 51).
60. McGuire, 'Was Alberic the Real Founder Cîteaux?', p. 152.
61. Christopher Holdsworth, 'Bernard of Clairvaux and European Spirituality', in *The Birth of Identities: Denmark and Europe in the Middle Ages*, ed. Brian Patrick McGuire (Copenhagen: C.A. Ritzel Publishers, 1996), pp. 51, 61.
62. Bernard of Clairvaux, 'The Life of Saint Malachy', in *The Life and Death of Saint Malachy the Irishman*, ed., trans. and annotated Robert T. Meyer (Kalamazoo, MI: Cistercian Publications, 1978), p. 50.
63. Gillian R. Evans, *Bernard of Clairvaux* (Oxford: Oxford University Press, 2000), pp. 94–95.
64. Evans, *Bernard of Clairvaux*, pp. 94–95; Thomas J. Renna, 'Abelard versus Bernard: An Event in Monastic History', *Cîteaux: Commentarii Cistercienses* 27 (1976), pp. 192–193.
65. McGuire, *The Difficult Saint*, pp. 96–97, 104, 132. For example of Malachy, Bernard of Clairvaulx, 'Sermon on Passing of Saint Malachy the Bishop', in *The Life and Death of Saint Malachy*, p. 97.
66. Julian Haseldine, 'Friends, Friendship and Networks in the Letters of Bernard of Clairvaux', *Cîteaux: Commentarii Cistercienses* 57 (2006), pp. 253–254, 272.
67. Newman, *The Boundaries of Charity*, p. 2.
68. *Twelfth-Century Statutes*, 1185: 1.
69. Newman, *The Boundaries of Charity*, p. 12.
70. For example, former archbishop of Lyon Jean de Belesmes (1181–1193) who retired to Clairvaux. *Twelfth-Century Statutes*, 1197: 55.
71. McGuire, 'Bernard's Concept of a Cistercian Order', pp. 227–229; Immo Eberl, *Die Zisterzienser: Geschichte eines europäischen Ordens* (Ostfildern: J. Thorbecke, 2002), pp. 94–99; Alice Chapman, 'Authority and Power in the Writings of St Bernard', *Cîteaux: Commentarii Cistercienses* 54 (2003), pp. 218–219.

72. Jean Leclercq, 'Towards a Sociological Interpretation of the Various Saint Bernards', in *Bernardus Magister*, pp. 24–25. There is a large literature devoted to the conflict between Bernard and Abelard and specific context of this clash, see especially recent works by Constant Mews.
73. David N. Bell, 'The Cistercian Authors in the *Registrum Librorum Anglie*', in *Erudition at God's Service*, ed. John R. Sommerfeldt, Studies in Medieval Cistercian History 11 (Kalamazoo, MI: Cistercian Publications, 1987), pp. 297–303.
74. Michael Casey, 'Bernard of Clairvaux: The Face Behind the Persona', *Cistercian Studies Quarterly* 27:2 (1992), p. 140.
75. Evans, *Bernard of Clairvaux*, p. 20.
76. William O. Paulsell, 'Saint Bernard on the Duties of the Christian Prince', in *Studies in Medieval Cistercian History*, vol. 2, ed. John R. Sommerfeldt (Kalamazoo, MI: Cistercian Publications, 1976), pp. 64–69; Janet Burton, 'Foundation of the British Cistercian Houses', in *Cistercian Art and Architecture in the British Isles*, ed. Christopher Norton and David Park (Cambridge: Cambridge University Press, 1986), p. 26.
77. Eugene Goodrich, 'The Reliability of the *Vita Prima S. Bernardi*: The Image of Bernard in Book I of the Vita Prima and his Own Letters: A Comparison', *Analecta Cisterciensia* 43 (1987), p. 167.
78. Brenda Bolton, 'Innocent III: Studies on Papal Authority and Pastoral Care', in her *Innocent III: Studies on Papal Authority and Pastoral Care* (Aldershot: Ashgate Variorum, 1995), II, p. 11.
79. Adriaan H. Bredero, 'St Bernard and the Historians', in *Saint Bernard of Clairvaux: Studies Commemorating the Eighth Centenary of His Canonization*, ed. M. Basil Pennington (Kalamazoo, MI: Cistercian Publications, 1977), p. 58, n. 120.
80. Evans, *Bernard of Clairvaux*, pp. 12–16.
81. Peter Dinzelbacher, *Bernhard von Clairvaux: Leben und Werk des berühmten Zisterziensers* (Darmstadt: Primus, 1998), p. 209.
82. *The Letters of St. Bernard of Clairvaux*, no. 205.
83. Bernard of Clairvaulx, *Five Book on Consideration: Advice to a Pope*, ed. and trans. John D. Anderson and Elizabeth T. Kennan (Kalamazoo, MI: Cistercian Publications, 1976).
84. Goodrich, 'The Reliability of the *Vita Prima*', pp. 176–177.
85. *The Second Crusade: Scope and Consequences*, ed. Jonathan Philips and Martin Hoch (Manchester: Manchester University Press, 2001), p. 3.
86. Rudolf Hiestand, 'The Papacy and the Second Crusade', in *The Second Crusade*, p. 37.
87. Hiestand, 'The Papacy and the Second Crusade', p. 37.
88. Iben Fonnesberg Schmidt, 'Pope Alexander III (1159–1181) and the Baltic Crusades', in *Medieval History Writing and Crusading Ideology*, ed. Tuomas M.S. Lehtonen and Kurt Villads Jensen with Janne Malkki and Katja Ritari, Studia Fennica Historica 6 (Helsinki: Finnish Literature Society, 2005), p. 251; Thomas Renna, 'Early Cistercian Attitudes towards War', *Cîteaux: Commentarii Cistercienses* 31 (1980), p. 127.

89. Evans, *Bernard of Clairvaux*, p. 169; Michaela Diers, *Bernhard von Clairvaux: Elitäre Frömmigkeit und begnadetes Wirken* (Münster: Aschendorff, 1991), p. 355; Renna, 'Early Cistercian Attitudes', p. 128; Bernard of Clairvaux, 'De Laude Novae Militae', *Sancti Bernardi Opera*, ed. Jean LeClercq and H. Rochair (Rome: Editiones Cistercienses, 1963) vol. 3, pp. 213–239.
90. Giles Constable, 'Introduction', in *The Second Crusade and the Cistercians*, ed. Michael Gervers (New York: St Martin's Press, 1992), p. xxi.
91. Hans-Dietrich Kahl, 'Crusade Eschatology as Seen by St Bernard in the Years 1146 to 1148', in *The Second Crusade*, p. 35.
92. *Twelfth-Century Statutes*, 1159: 7.
93. Adriaan Bredero, 'The Canonization of Bernard of Clairvaux', in *Saint Bernard of Clairvaux. Studies Commemorating the Eighth Centenary of His Canonization*, ed. M.B. Pennington (Kalamazoo, MI: Cistercian Publications, 1977), pp. 84–89.
94. Lekai, 'The Early Cistercians', p. 102.
95. Patrick Brian McGuire, *Brother and Lover: Aelred of Rievaulx* (New York: Crossroad, 1994), p. 57.
96. David Knowles, *The Monastic Order in England* (Cambridge: Cambridge University Press, 1941), p. 217.
97. Phillips, 'The Presence – and Absence', p. 37.
98. Phillips, 'The Presence – and Absence', pp. 49–50.

chapter 2

THE FIRST MULTINATIONAL? HOW THE CISTERCIAN ORDER SPREAD ACROSS EUROPE

The rapid growth of the Cistercian order coincided with the great expansion of Latin Europe – eastwards beyond the Elba and along the Baltic coast; to the west and south through the *Reconquista* in Spain and the crusades in the Middle East; and with the cultural and religious integration of Europe's northern periphery – Scandinavia, Scotland and Ireland. The lesser nobility, knights and peasants were attracted by the availability of land and the prospect of accelerated social advancement. Moved from densely populated western territories to the eastern frontier, these areas offered great opportunities for the Cistercian Order too, as the first truly trans-regional order, with a durable structure connecting individual monasteries scattered throughout Latin Christendom.[1]

This chapter will examine how the pan-European structures were organised, how the individual houses were interconnected to form a large network, and how the organisation of each community was designed to be both self-contained and a part of the filiation network. It will be also demonstrated that the process in which individual houses came into being became fairly standardised, with uniformity of observance being a hallmark of Cistercian monasticism.

The Organisation of the Cistercian Order

In the early decades of the formation of the Cistercian movement, as we saw in chapter 1, papal support was crucial, and became formalised in a series of papal privileges and exemptions which gave the Cistercians a degree of freedom from the powers of the secular church that their Benedictine predecessors had never enjoyed.

Central to the Cistercian organisation – and to its success as a large trans-European organisation – was the General Chapter, the highest authority within the Order, which in the early years of its formation functioned more as 'a working-group concerned with moral progress than a legislative assembly'.² It did not have legislative power in the modern sense and its composition was initially restricted to houses relatively near Cîteaux; and the development of Cistercian administrative procedures was a gradual process stretching over decades.³ The general aims of the governing body were initially defined in the *Carta Caritatis* as controlling proper observance of the Rule, making decisions, preserving good relations between the abbots and providing the members with the opportunity to 'discuss the salvation of their own souls'.⁴ Only later, from the early thirteenth century onwards, did the General Chapter became more focused on formulating rules and regulations rather than simply discussing individual cases – by which time, in creating procedures and establishing legal formulations and an effective bureaucracy, the white monks were in line with many other church institutions of the day.⁵

In recording information on the decisions and pronouncements of the General Chapter, the statutes followed a strict formula. In their developed form from the late twelfth century onwards, the meetings of the General Chapter were devoted to issues affecting all or many abbeys, as well as to conflict between different Cistercian houses, matters of poor discipline in specific houses and individual cases. The statutes of the General Chapter are central to our understanding of the working of the order, the relationships between different houses, the geographical spread of the new foundations, the concerns of the abbots and their responses to threats and opportunities in a changing world.

Meetings always took place in mid-September, after the harvest and before winter conditions made travel difficult. In the early thirteenth century a set of norms was established defining the format of the meetings, which lasted five days, with 'business matters' being interspersed with masses, prayers, readings from martyrologies, the Rule, *Carta Caritatis* and sermons.⁶ Although the General Chapter was theoretically a gathering of all abbots, it was always in practice a selection of those eligible to attend. The abbots of French houses were far better represented than those from distant northern and north-eastern Europe – for example, from as early as 1179, or shortly before, the Scottish abbots were obliged to attend every fourth year, as were abbots from Ireland after 1190.⁷ A careful watch was kept on the attendance of abbots from afar, and the abbots of La Ferté, Pontigny, Clairvaux and Morimond were obliged in 1199 to report during their yearly visitation to Cîteaux which particular abbey of their filiations was due to attend and in which year. The precise regulations concerning exemptions were first codified in 1202, and again in 1237 and 1257. An extended list was included in the *Libellus antiquarum definitionum* in 1289, which stated that the abbots from Ireland, Scotland, Sicily, Galicia and Portugal could attend every fourth year, whilst the most distant houses in Syria and Cyprus were only obliged to do so every seventh year. Abbots from Norway and Livonia in the north, and from Greece in the south, attended every fifth year; while the obligation to attend every third year applied in a wider-ranging group of regions – Hungary, Leon, Castile, Frisia and Styria – and biennial attendance was demanded of abbots from Aragon, Navarre and Catalonia. The co-ordination of attendance from within particular regions and kingdoms was organised in such a way as to ensure that two abbots from each region were in attendance to guarantee that the decisions of the General Chapter were transmitted to the rest.[8]

The journey to Cîteaux Abbey was long and sometimes dangerous and a number of Cistercian chronicles recorded the deaths of abbots travelling to and from meetings of the General Chapter, whose records on absenteeism sometimes provide an explanation for a particular abbot's failure to attend. According to the *Chronicle of Melrose* in Scotland, Abbot Alexander of Deer died on his way to the General Chapter in 1222 and Abbot Geoffrey of Dundrennan died on the way back. When in 1197, however, the abbots of the Hungarian monasteries failed to appear at Cîteaux because they had been attacked, wounded and robbed en route, the General Chapter seems to have taken a decidedly sceptical view of their story, reprimanding them and ordered them to show up without fail next year.[9] Of course, travel was expensive and often uncomfortable; and the hospitality of Cistercian abbots along the way could leave something to be desired: in 1197 the abbot of Fontmorigny in central France, who had refused to provide his guests with wine at their midday meal, was reprimanded, along with his fellow abbot of Aubepierre, for failing to give adequate hospitality to abbots travelling to the General Chapter meeting.[10]

The preparation of the agenda for the annual meetings of the General Chapter was the responsibility of an executive committee known as *definitores* – appointed after 1197 by the abbot of Cîteaux and the proto-abbots (abbots of the four oldest monasteries) – which obviously became a very powerful body. In the 1260s, however, simmering conflict within this group gave rise to an open dispute and a crisis of authority at the centre of the Order. Pope Clement IV took an active interest in finding a solution, which came in the shape of the bull *Parvus fons* in 1265 (commonly known as *Clementina*). This reconstituted the *definitores* group so as to establish a better balance between the appointees of the abbot of Cîteaux and those of the proto-abbots, who also joined it as *ex officio* members, while at the same time the limiting the powers of the abbots vis-à-vis the General Chapter (for more details about this reform see chapter 8).

Even so, although in theory all abbots were equal, the position of the abbot of Cîteaux remained special as the head of the mother house of the whole order and from 1221 Cîteaux also became the central archive of the Order and repository for all the documents pertaining to the Order as a whole (but not to individual houses).[11] In addition to the statutes of the General Chapter, for example, the Order also produced several codifications of its own regulations: the *Libelli definitionum* of 1202, 1220, 1237, 1257, and 1288/89, the *Libellus antiquarum definitionum* in 1316 and the new *Libellus novellarum definitionum* of 1350.

In addition to record keeping and the promulgation of rules, however, the General Chapter also served as the financial office of the Order. From 1235 it was regularly organising the annual collection of taxes from all the abbeys belonging to the Order. In each region one abbey was responsible for gathering funds and transmitting them to the centre. This taxation was necessary for running the central organisation of the Order, especially the meetings of the General Chapter, which routinely involved several hundreds of participants with their entourages demanding vast supplies of food and drink, tableware and cutlery, parchment (and later paper), ink, sealing wax and candles, to say nothing of additional staff in the kitchens, stables and elsewhere. In the fourteenth century funds earmarked for the General Chapter were also spent on the Order's representatives at the Avignon court, papal taxations and university fees for Cistercian monks studying for degrees. These sums were collected and recorded by the officials known as *receptores*, usually abbots of French houses, and their records of who paid and who owed what were duly sent to Cîteaux. With the growth of the Cistercian network it was not easy to collect all the payments due and many monasteries accumulated large debts to the General Chapter of the Order; while problems over the enforcement of payments were compounded by a lack of consistency in record keeping, with some payments being wrongly assigned. During the General Chapter of 1340, for example, one of the *receptores*, Abbot Pierre of Clairefontaine, noted receipts of payments from 'several foreign abbots whose names he does not know. They will receive receipts as soon as the *receptores* know their names'; and in 1343 he recorded a receipt of over £10 'from someone'. Between 1337 and 1347 the Order made an effort – with some success – to enforce the back-payments and to reach out to the most remote houses in Scandinavia, central-eastern Europe, Portugal and Greece. Even so, the financial difficulties of the Cistercian Order, aggravated by its ineffective taxation system, were to became a major issue in the later middle ages (see chapter 8).[12]

In the general context of Benedictine monasticism the emergence of the General Chapter as a central governing body was a great innovation. Although the abbot was the unchallenged authority within each monastic house, the establishment of the General Chapter made it possible to investigate and depose abbots for mismanagement, financial abuses and other offences.[13] The statutes offer a wealth of evidence on the kind of transgressions of which the abbots and members of their communities were accused, ranging from financial mismanagement and improper behaviour to lapses from Cistercian customs in liturgy, living arrangements, food and relations with the outside world. The General Chapter of 1215, for example, heard that Abbot Hugh of Beaulieu Abbey was eating and drinking with noble lay visitors in a manner not befitting a monastic setting. His grandiose style extended to eating from silver plates and keeping a dog on a silver chain guarding his bed.[14] Once the General Chapter was informed of an issue, it usually appointed a delegation consisting of abbots from neighbouring houses to investigate the matter and report back. Transgressions of individual abbots were not the only matter which the order's authorities wanted to know about. They were often faced with conflicts between Cistercian houses. In such cases, the General Chapter, always at pains to restore peaceful and brotherly relationships within the Order, usually delegated abbots of neighbouring houses to act as judges to hear allegations, inspect the documents presented by the parties and not only pass judgement but see to the enforcement of sentences and the payment of expenses and damages. Abbots of other neighbouring houses in the areas would then act as witnesses to a charter of settlement signed by all the parties.[15]

Apart from the General Chapter, the other peculiar feature of the Cistercian order was the 'filiation' system, which established a mechanism for connecting individual monasteries, designated as 'mother' and 'daughter' houses. Abbots were not only involved in the election of abbots in the daughter houses, but were obliged to make annual visitations to maintain uniformity of practice and discipline. These were vital to the maintenance of personal connections and communication channels between monasteries belonging to the Order, and the commitment of a father-abbot to the spiritual and economic prosperity of filiation was essential to the effectiveness of an inspection. Visitations also served as a means of transferring knowledge of problems further up the Order's chain of command to the General Chapter, and their framework was based on the Order's legal structure specified in the *Instituta* and reiterated in the ruling of the General Chapter of 1193.[16] Cistercian female houses were also subject to visitation by the abbot of the male house who was overseeing their spiritual needs. Sometimes, depending on the specific status of the nunnery, a visitation was carried out by the diocesan bishop (see chapter 4).

As with many other Cistercian procedures, standardised written documentation was developed. In 1202 the General Chapter ruled that the written reports should contain exactly the same information as had been given by the abbot conducting the inspection to the community under inspection in a chapter meeting. The cantor of the monastery kept this document until the next visitation.[17] From the thirteenth century onwards the order developed a number of formulae books explaining and regulating all aspects of the visitation, types of questions to be asked, issues to investigate and models of visitation reports.[18]

Such material is particularly useful for our understanding of the internal working of the monastic communities and the problems which visitors might have encountered. There seemed to be a fear of 'conspiracies' against abbots and of fragmentation of the community into opposing cliques, whilst instances of possible favouritism were also investigated. The welfare of the community was to take priority over the wants of individuals; monks who were particularly rebellious, arrogant and unwilling to change were to be expelled to prevent them from 'infecting' the rest of the community. In some extreme cases an entire community could be dissolved. When in 1285, for example, reports of 'scandals' in Sulejów Abbey in southern Poland reached the General Chapter, four abbots from neighbouring monasteries were appointed as investigators and the decision they reached was radical: the community of Sulejów was divided into two groups and moved to abbeys at Byszew and Szpetal. The father superior of Sulejów Abbey, Abbot Hugh of Morimond, endorsed this decision and the original community was replaced by a group of monks from neighbouring Wąchock Abbey.[19]

To safeguard the corporate image of the Order, the actions of individual monks were also subject to scrutiny, especially if they involved the world beyond the monastery. Indeed, the risk that such actions, and gossip that reached the ears of outsiders, might bring the entire order into disrepute was taken very seriously. During Abbot Denis of Beaulieu's visitation of Dore Abbey (Herefordshire) in 1261, he reminded the community that no monk was allowed to sell his cowl to any secular person without the permission of the abbot as it may endanger the reputation of the whole Order – presumably by the actions of an impostor equipped with such a cowl – which all testified to both the corporate nature of the order, and its contacts with the outside world.[20] If many of the issues under investigation, such as the speed at which psalms were sung, or the depth of bows performed by monks before the altar, seem petty to the modern eye, they were closely linked with the issue of proper observance, which was central to the life of the Order.[21] Nor was this issue concerning the authorities of the Order merely at the level of individual houses. By the thirteenth century, the General Chapter was organising visitations that covered whole kingdoms or regions in which all abbeys were inspected – Spain in 1221, Southern Italy in 1226 and Ireland between 1227 and 1229.[22] These visitations were not only concerned with occasional failings in proper observance, but with a widespread departure from Cistercian standards, the adoption of local practices, and other acts of insubordination that were seen as a threat to the unity of the Order. Tension between centralisation, uniformity and regionalism was inevitable in an organisation spanning such vast areas and was to become a significant issue in the later middle ages.

The filiation system was hierarchical, the hierarchy between abbeys being organised according to 'generations' from each proto-monastery in Burgundy (Cîteaux, La Ferté, Pontigny, Clairvaux and Morimond) to its direct daughter houses, then to their daughters and so on. Within each group of monasteries the date of foundation determined the abbatial precedence and lists and tables showing the 'genealogy' of the Cistercian houses were kept in many monasteries, with a special list maintained by the cantor at Cîteaux with the day and year of foundation. Although the accuracy of this list was much contested by the abbots who wanted to improve their own ranking, the widespread production of lists and genealogical trees, often included in cartularies, by Cistercian abbeys in the later middle ages was eloquent testimony to the vitality of the idea of belonging to the international network.[23]

Foundations: How Did the Monasteries Come into Being?

A Cistercian monastery could come into being in a number of ways. Most commonly, a group of monks would be sent from a mother house to establish a daughter house in a new location; but it was also possible to incorporate an existing monastery into the Cistercian Order. The incorporation model was very prevalent in the twelfth century, particularly in the Cistercian heartland in France, but also, in some cases, on the European frontiers. The majority of the 43 Cistercian houses in southern France examined by Constance Berman, including Pontigny, Begard, Les Écharlis, Sylvanès and Reigny, had already been in existence as independent communities or hermitages before they joined the Cistercian Order;[24] and many of the oldest Danish Cistercian houses founded between 1144 and the end of the twelfth century had been Benedictine foundations, which were turned into Cistercian communities:[25] the Benedictine Sorø Abbey in Zealand (Denmark) had been founded in the late 1140s by three sons of one Skjalm Hvide, an important man in the region, but by 1161 the poorly endowed community had been turned into a Cistercian monastery by the next generation of the Hvide family, who provided a much more generous grant.[26] There were also cases of re-settling Cistercian communities on sites previously occupied by other monastic communities. Heisterbach Abbey was founded in 1189 by the archbishop of Cologne as a daughter house of Himmerod Abbey on the site previously occupied by the Augustinian canons, which itself grew out of a hermit cell.[27] Not only independent, reform-minded communities adopted Cistercian *ordo*, but also whole groups of monasteries, such as the congregations of Savigny and Obazine in 1147; and although the Sempringham (or Gilbertines) Order's application for a similar incorporation in the late 1140s was rejected,[28] the accession of Savignac houses – 40 abbeys and priories in England, Ireland, Wales, Flanders and France – was a significant enlargement of the Cistercian family.[29]

Established communities which joined the Order, although themselves a result of the reform movement, retained various practices that differed from those of the Cistercians, and while Obazine was obliged upon its incorporation to make its liturgical books follow the version used by the white monks, neither Obazine nor Savigny was obliged to abandon its peculiar economic practices.[30] Traditionally, historians have seen in this the emergence of practices that deviated 'from the Cistercian norm' and the 'purity of Cistercian practice'. In fact, however, it merely shows that for the Cistercian movement, as for many other religious orders, identity and unity rested on shared monastic observance, liturgy and spirituality, and not on shared economic practices or possession of identical types of property.

The process by which a new Cistercian monastery came into being was a complex and lengthy one, usually taking several years and involving a large number of people from within and outside the Cistercian Order. The usual form of the foundation process can be deduced from the statutes and consisted (with occasional variations) of several steps:

1. The prospective founder would apply to the General Chapter with a request for permission to establish a new house.
2. The General Chapter would appoint a commission, usually including two or three abbots familiar with the locality, to visit the prospective site of the new foundation and assess the suitability of the initial grant of land, its legal status and the distance between the proposed abbey and existing Cistercian houses in the area.
3. The report of the commission was considered at the next meeting of the General Chapter, and, if it was positive, the actual foundation was initiated.
4. A group of monks from the mother house would arrive at the new location.
5. The new community, with the concurrence of the founder, built a temporary church and accommodation for the monks.
6. The founder would issue the foundation charter describing the initial grant of land.

7. The community would organise the consecration ceremony of the monastic church, which was performed by the diocesan bishop.[31]

As we can see from this schedule, the founder was an indispensable element in the process, whether laymen and women – kings, queens, princes and nobles – or high ranking prelates. If, as indicated in chapter 1, bishops had been important in the early phases of Cistercian movement, they were also crucial later as founders outside the Burgundian core: Bishop William Giffard of Winchester founded the first Cistercian abbey in England in 1128.[32] Bishops were also crucial in introducing Cistercian houses to more peripheral areas such as the Polish kingdom. As the foundation of Cistercian houses required a smaller material investment than Benedictine houses, the social spectrum of their founders was wider; but as even the founding of a Cistercian abbey entailed a considerable sacrifice by the founder (in terms of permanent alienation of land and revenues), the foundation of a regular canon house or nunnery was a still a more attractive option for wealthy knights than a Cistercian abbey.[33]

The establishment of a new Cistercian house, therefore, was not simply a matter of sending a group of monks from the mother house, but required prior consultation between the prospective founder and the abbot of the mother house. Prior to the arrival of the monks and lay brothers, a set of temporary wooden buildings – the oratory, a refectory, a dormitory, a guest house and a gate-keeper's hut – would have to be erected. With this rudimentary set of buildings, specified in the *Summa Cartae Caritatis* as a prerequisite to sending out a new colony, the new community would at least be able to function.[34] For how long the temporary structures would have to serve differed in every case, but they could last several decades, especially if the endowment was small and further grants slow in coming.

Hence, the foundation was not a one-off event, but a process, lasting several years, and culminating only in the foundation ceremony. The building of more permanent structures in stone or brick – depending on the region – required the employment of a large number of hired hands and master masons working with the assistance of lay brothers. The image that later became a part of the reform rhetoric in the later middle ages (see chapter 8) of monks labouring on the construction of their own house is largely a late medieval myth of 'good old times' when monks were truly self-sufficient.[35] There is, however, evidence that some monks participated in building projects, usually in skilled and supervisory roles. The plans for the construction of Walkenried Abbey (*c.* 1207), were drawn up by two monks, Jordan and Berthold, who also supervised 21 lay brothers working as masons, bricklayers and carpenters;[36] and many others who joined the Cistercian Order in the twelfth century had significant lay careers behind them and skills useful in the 'project management' of building sites. In the Cistercian community of Byland a certain Henry Bugge, one of a group of knights who had been in the service of the community's patron Roger de Mowbray, acted as a warden (*custos*) of the abbey between 1139 and 1143, overseeing the finances of building operations and supervising the masons.[37] Monastic precincts tended to be permanent building sites, with new structures being erected and older buildings frequently remodelled, with the result that communities that functioned for several centuries went through several phases of construction work (see chapter 5).

The initial grant was immensely important for the viability of a new community: even if it could always be supplemented by later donations, it was the generosity of the original founder that was crucial for future success. Other valuable assets, such as forest, pasture and fishing rights, and grants of tithes and parish churches were often attached to the land, which in addition enjoyed freedom from feudal obligations, as the Cistercians were usually exempted from various secular taxes. For example, Valmagne Abbey (Languedoc) received a number of grants of tithes from its benefactors in the mid-twelfth century, while Paradyż Abbey (Greater Poland), founded in 1230 by the *comes* Bronisz on his family's land, received from the bishop of Poznań the tithes of the local parish church.[38] On the whole in East-Central Europe donors, both lay and ecclesiastical, were typically giving the Cistercian monasteries the types of properties and income that all other religious institutions were used to receive. Such donations occurred in western Europe too,[39] albeit less frequently; but the 'non-standard' elements of the endowments were not evidence of corruption or diminishing standards, but a rational response to the varying social and economic conditions under which Cistercian monasteries came into being.

The motivations which the founders gave in their charters of foundations were overwhelmingly devotional. Lay nobility often manifested their deep piety by founding a monastery, and the foundation charter of the oldest Cistercian abbey in the Polish kingdom, Jędrzejów (*c.* 1147), expressly stated that that the founder – *comes* Zbylut – was giving through this act a 'true testimony of his eager devotion'.[40] Cistercian charters across Europe were replete with similar references to the salvation of founders' souls, and those of their wives, husbands, parents, children, dead ancestors and the future generations of their families and demonstrate clearly that these foundations were not the sole act of an individual, but involved the whole kin group – living, dead and not yet born – who in return for the alienation of its land could expect to benefit from the power of the monks' prayers. There were three important elements of the benefit which founders and their descendants – the patrons – could expect from the monastic communities which they supported materially: burial, commemoration and intercessory prayers.[41]

There were, perhaps, less explicit motives at work too: if the status of the founder signified piety and commitment to the Christian ideal, it was also highly prestigious, and eloquent testimony to his wealth and social status. Many founders trusted that the material help they gave to the monasteries would be reciprocated by the spiritual help of the monks. It was not a cynical transaction. King Valdemar I of Denmark, for example, in a charter assigning a forest of Villingehoven to the monks of Esrum Abbey, declared his conviction that the prayers of monks would not only help his salvation, but also strengthen his rule.[42] The example set by royalty as generous protectors of the church also motivated members of the elite to become Cistercian founders. For most of the twelfth century there was a veritable 'fashion' for the Cistercian Order – witness, for example, the large number of Cistercian foundations by Scottish King David I – Melrose, Newbattle and Kinloss – although he also patronised several other reformed orders, such as Augustinians and Tironensians. Straightforward political motivation also played a role: in England, the leading barons of English King Henry I, who was a strong supporter of the Cistercians, were also founders of new houses of the Order, among them Walter Espec who founded Rievaulx Abbey on the land he received from the king in Yorkshire. In fact, the founders of the first four English Cistercian houses were all prominent members of the royal court. Soon, support for Cistercian communities became something of a 'family tradition': one of the leading barons in mid-twelfth-century Yorkshire, Roger de Mowbray, was a generous benefactor and patron of Cistercian houses as well as Augustinian priories. He was clearly influenced in his choice by his mother Gundreda de Gourney; and his own influence as a lord was shown by the fact that his tenants also in turn became benefactors of 'his' monasteries.[43]

Paradoxically, royal weakness and political instability could also be of benefit to the Cistercians: the biggest wave of foundations in England occurred during the 'anarchy' of King Stephen's reign. Some of these foundations were expiatory gestures for violence committed during the civil wars, whilst other benefactors might have preferred to give land to a monastery rather than lose it to an enemy.[44] The largest Cistercian house in Pomerania – Kołbacz Abbey – received a number of grants and confirmations in 1230 and 1240 from the rulers of neighbouring duchies, which were all set to expand their territories northwards, and saw in such grants a possible legal tool on which future claims could be built – as obviously confirmations of monastic estates implied that any territory granted was under the grantor's control.[45] Sometimes the political and cultural alliances of the founders were projected on to the monastic houses: the Cistercian houses of Neath, Margam, Tintern and Grace Dieu founded in southern Wales by the Anglo-Norman nobility in the twelfth century were from the start regarded by the native population as closely associated with the incomers, whereas Cistercian houses located in the territories remaining in the hands of the native rulers in the thirteenth century were closely connected to the Welsh elites. In a letter to Pope Gregory X from March 1275, Prince Llywelyn ap Gruffudd was described by the Cistercian abbots of his principality as 'a vigorous and special protector of our order'.[46]

It would seem that the Cistercian houses on the frontiers of twelfth-century Europe were founded from a mixture of political, cultural and devotional reasons rather than from any simple desire to settle the 'wilderness' (see chapter 6). Certainly Dargun Abbey (1172) on the eastern fringes of Brandenburgian control and subject to Danish, Saxon and Pomeranian influences came into being partly as a result of a variety of political pressures and not only the desire to colonise empty lands. Admittedly, subsequent changes in the structure of existing villages and the emergence of new settlements were the result of Dargun expanding and consolidating its estates, but that is not to say that these economic developments were the chief aim of the founder, for whom religious motives would have been just as rational as economic ones.[47]

It was not uncommon for a monastic site to be abandoned, sometimes more than once, in favour of a more suitable location. These migrations occurred for a variety of reasons: a chosen location might prove to be particularly unproductive and unable to support the community; or it might suffer from bad air, excessive humidity or lack of water. However, the struggle to create a habitable place against all the odds was a popular topos in the foundation narratives (see chapter 7), which should perhaps not always be taken too literally as a faithful depiction of real conditions.

Similarly, the myth of the Cistercians setting up their monasteries in deserted places far away from human habitation was perhaps for the most part a useful rhetorical device to present the founding of a community in a heroic light and to provide an ideal for maintaining ascetic standards – although for breakaway groups, such as Fountains in Yorkshire, it could also provide a legitimate justification for leaving their original 'decadent' houses to become Cistercian communities.[48] There was in fact no 'ideal' location for a Cistercian abbey, although certain characteristics appeared more frequently than others: for example, they were often located in the valleys, which provided 'ready-made' boundaries – witness such names as Schöntal, Clairvaux, Bellevaux, Droiteval, Valmagne, Chiaravalle, Orval, Rosenthal, Vale Royal or Vallbone.[49] But this was by no means a universal feature of Cistercian settlements, many of which were established on flat land or on hills.

The Organisation of Cistercian Monasteries

Close emotional bonds and inclusive ties of friendship between the monks on the one hand and an emphasis on the importance of the community on the other were central to the Cistercian interpretation of monastic life. These were frequent themes in the writings of white monks throughout the middle ages and beyond. The importance of the close personal bonds between the monks and between the abbot and the monks, often described as a strong emotion or 'love', were stressed by all the key twelfth-century Cistercian thinkers: Bernard of Clairvaux, William of St Thierry, Ailred of Rievaulx, Hugh of St Victor, Guerric of Igny, Isaac of Stella, Adam of Perseigne and Stephen of Sawley. William of St Thierry described Cistercian monasteries as 'schools of charity';[50] and Ailred of Rievaulx explained, in his *Speculum Caritatis*, that the supremacy of *caritas* as *imitatio Christi* guaranteed harmony and equality between the monks and was the way in which the tradition of the Apostles and Desert Fathers was recreated by the Cistercians.[51]

Friendship, according to Ailred of Rievaulx, provided a fruitful setting for the virtues of compassion and humility: 'charity raises our soul up to that for which it was created; but self-centeredness degrades it to what it was sinking towards of its own accord'.[52] The close community was supposed to foster humility through obedience to others and appreciation of their virtues, while compassion for the failings and sufferings of others in the community would help the monks to perfect their own virtues. Positive examples were also more likely to influence the brothers in such a close-knit community. The close emotional ties within the community were primarily between monks, of equal status, but also between junior and senior brothers and between the abbot and his monks. It was not a question of hierarchical instruction, but rather of learning from each other – in contrast to the Benedictine tradition, where instruction from and obedience to the abbot or some other superior was the key. Their emphasis on both the community and the importance of the individuals within (and their spiritual journeys) were vital factors in the Cistercian success in enlisting new members in the twelfth century. The role of friendship in the secular culture of the time, notably the companionship of knights – one of the central themes of the Arthurian legends – as incorporated into Cistercian culture, was particularly appealing to those whom Bernard of Clairvaux was especially keen to recruit – the knights.[53]

Although casual interactions between monks and non-essential conversations were forbidden and silence was indispensable for prayer and individual meditation, the community was nevertheless based on the interdependence of its members. Essential communication between the monks could always be conducted in sign language. Not that the Cistercians were the first monks to have recourse to this device, as silence and a ban on all unnecessary talking had been part of the monastic tradition since its very beginning. The first attempt to codify monastic sign language had been undertaken as early as 816 by Abbot Benedict of Aniane and Emperor Louis the Pious; and in the first half of the tenth century Cluny developed a fixed system of signs. The Cistercians developed their own sign language, for communicating short, practical messages, and all novices had to memorise it. The signs are described in a number of late medieval manuscripts and ranged from everyday terms (salt, bread, water, horse), to actions (seeing, hearing, walking), people (abbot, king, pope, woman, guest) and abstract terms (anger, humility, sadness). Meaning was usually denoted by visually representing a key feature or characteristic: the sign for lay brother was a hand-gesture symbolising beard, as a beard was a key visual characteristic of a *conversus*. Even the use of sign language was strictly circumscribed, however, and Cistercian regulations prohibited its excessive use – for example, for the purpose of holding a conversation.[54]

Although in theory all choir monks were equal, there was in practice a hierarchy based on the length of their tenure in the community. Similarly, within each monastery monks were obliged to perform functions necessary for the smooth running of the community, according to the organisational structure described in the table below. In practice, however this too might vary to reflect local conditions and needs and size of the community, just as the number of officials varied greatly over time and between different monasteries.

Table 1 The organisational structure of a Cistercian monastery

ABBOT (abbas, pater monasterii)
PRIOR (prior)
SUBPRIOR (subprior)
Officials (*obedientarii*):

novice master	cellarer (*cellerarius*)		librarian (*armarius*)
	bursarius		master of scriptorium
sacristan (*vestarius*)		the guest-master	refectorian
porter (*portarius*)		infirmarian	cantor (*precentor*)

CHOIR MONKS
LAY BROTHERS
Masters of the granges
FAMILIARES
Servants, paid workers, and other employees

Source: Terryl Kinder, *Cistercian Europe: Architecture of Contemplation* (Kalamazoo, MI: Cistercian Publications, 2002), pp. 75–78.

The abbot, the father of the community, was elected by the whole community under the supervision of the father superior (from the mother house) or other senior Cistercian abbot appointed by the General Chapter. First, the abbot-elect made an oath in the chapter house, after which he was invested with the symbol of his office by the father superior, and received 'obedience' from his community. Finally, he was consecrated by the diocesan bishop. In Benedictine and Cistercian houses, the symbol of abbatial office was traditionally a crozier and a ring worn on the middle finger of the right hand. The crozier, symbolising a pastoral staff, embodied the leadership and pastoral authority of the abbot and featured frequently on abbatial tombs, whilst the ring was the sign of the spiritual marriage between the abbot, his community and the church.[55]

Although the monastic leadership was in the abbot's hands, the practical aspects of running the monastery were delegated to different offices, which by the mid-twelfth century had developed into a complex system serving all monastic houses, whether Benedictine, Cistercian or Augustinian. The fairly fluid structure sketched in the Rule of Benedict of rotating offices of cellarer, guest-master, a brother responsible for the sick members of the community and a brother in charge of property was not appropriate for the large, complex structures of monasteries in the high middle ages. Not only did new offices develop, but also the existing ones acquired assistants and became more managerial, whilst their holders were often exempt from certain parts of the daily liturgical observance so that they could perform their duties.[56] Monastic budgets were divided into compartments supporting different monastic offices responsible for certain aspects of the life of the communities, while the growing detachment of the abbot's office from the community was manifested by a separate residence and separate budget. During the increasingly frequent abbatial absences the prior was left in charge of the monastery, with sub-priors acting as his assistants in matters of monastic observance.

As for the running of the practical aspects of monastic organisation, the cellarer was responsible for the material well-being of the community as he managed the economy of the monastery, including supervision of the hired labour and the 'home grange' (located nearest to the abbey). In larger monasteries, one or more sub-cellarers assisted him. According to the Rule of Benedict, the ideal cellarer was 'prudent, of mature character, temperate, not a great eater, not proud, not headstrong, not rough-spoken, not lazy, not wasteful but a God-fearing man who may be like a father to the whole community'.[57] The office was not only the most practically oriented of the monastic offices, but also a highly responsible one. In some Cistercian communities in the later middle ages a separate office of procurator (who represented abbots in legal and business matters) developed from that of the cellarer, whilst yet another position, that of the bursar, was devoted to supervising of cash incomes (such as rents) of an abbey.[58] Other offices, too, had relatively large remit. The cantor, for example was a chant and choir master, acted as a librarian in the *armarium* and was also often responsible for record keeping, for example recording visitations. In some monasteries with extensive book-holdings there was also a separate office of *armarius*, whose sole task was caring for the library – as at Stična Abbey (Carniola) as early as the 1150s.[59]

The care for the physical well-being of each monk was part of the collective obligation of the monastic institution. Each monastic house had its own infirmary, so the monks who were too ill or too weak to take part in the normal routine of the daily liturgy were sent there to recover in order be able to return to their spiritual obligations. If a monk was deemed to be too ill to carry out his normal routine, he was sent to the infirmary with his bedding and eating utensils. Although ill monks were officially *extra chorum* ('outside choir', i.e. did not follow normal *horarium*), the infirmaries were a type of 'mini-monastery' where the patients were to observe the offices as far as possible. In the large abbeys the infirmary complex had its own cloister.[60] Infirmaries were also permanent homes to old monks who were too infirm to follow the monastic routine. The patients in the infirmary were cared for by the infirmarian, who was not academically trained in medicine – Cistercians were not allowed to study it at university – but was equipped with practical knowledge.[61] As restrictions on speaking were less severe in the infirmary than in the rest of the monastery, the infirmarian was able to communicate with his patients. No one was allowed to enter the infirmary without his permission and he was answerable only to the abbot.[62]

Illness affected monks and dealing with it was often an object of reflection in spiritual texts. Sicknesses were sent by God and they were both a punishment and a purification of sins. Illness was not necessarily something entirely negative, since excessive preoccupation with one's own health and malingering was much condemned by monastic writers, including Bernard of Clairvaux.[63] Death was not the end of a monk's life, but a beginning of the true life for which the monastic discipline was only a preparation. In reality, for some monks, the rigours of monastic life brought health problems. Bernard of Clairvaux suffered from poor health as a result of his excessive ascetic practices, which was noted by his contemporaries. Abbot Ailred of Rievaulx was chronically ill with osteoarthritis and kidney stones in later life, and some adjustments to the monastic accommodation were made for his comfort. Because of his illness Ailred received the permission of the General Chapter to leave the common dormitory and separate sleeping quarters were built for him near the infirmary, where two monks cared him for. However, he tried to maintain, as far as possible, his abbatial duties.[64] In the eyes of their fellow monks, Bernard's and Ailred's patient suffering under painful afflictions was one of the manifestations of their holiness and a process of purification in preparation for heaven.

The key element of Cistercian *cura corporis* was blood-letting, which was considered a beneficial, preventative measure. It was connected to the theory of humours, the most widespread medieval medical theory, in which health was dependent on the balance of four humours (blood, phlegm, yellow bile and black bile). Alongside diet, blood-letting was considered crucial for keeping the right balance of humours and cleansing the body of impurities. It was practised by monastic communities from the ninth century until the sixteenth.[65] Four times a year (in February, April, September and near the feast of St John the Baptist) all the monks of the Cistercian communities were bled. This practice was considered highly beneficial, but was recognised as a risky procedure because of the possibility of haemorrhage and infection. A significant amount of blood was taken from each individual, possibly as much as four pints. The statute of 1180 specified that bleeding should be performed by a competent practitioner (*minuator*) at a time least disruptive to the community, hence not during the harvest and high feasts of Nativity, Easter or Pentecost.[66] It was organised in the warming room for the monks and, at the abbot's discretion, for the lay brothers. Monks and lay brothers recovering from bleeding rested in the infirmary for a few days and were given better and larger portions of food, including fine white bread and meat and more comfortable bedding. The restrictions on silence were lifted too, so it was an occasion for greater sociability among the monks.[67]

The role of master of novices was a particularly responsible one. The novitiate, lasting a year, was a period of acculturation to the monastic life and learning of its routines and rituals prior to permanent admission into the monastic community at the solemn ceremony of profession. Cistercians did not accept children brought by their parents as oblates and required entrants to be over the age of 15, increased to 18 by the General Chapter in 1175. As only literate applicants – i.e. these able to read Latin – were accepted, they required no basic training but went straight into theological and spiritual instruction. During the preparatory period the novices studied under the direction of the novice master, focusing on the Rule of Benedict. They followed the same daily routine as the monks and had the same diet, but were not full members of the community. This was manifested in various ways: novices wore monastic habits without the cowl, were not tonsured, and ate and slept separately from the monks and always walked behind the monks in the processions.[68] Although the novitiate was a probation period, a novice who left a monastery was regarded as an apostate; a very popular collection of stories by Caesarius of Heisterbach, written for a Cistercian audience, told of the dangers that novices brought upon themselves by returning to the lay world.[69]

Because the master of novices was responsible for their spiritual formation, he had to have a good theological grounding, but also be able to show by his own example what a monk should be like. According to a letter from Adam, master of novices at the abbey of Perseigne (d. c. 1221), to a novice master at Mortemer Abbey, the novice master should above all talk frequently with his charges about spiritual matters and the observance of the Rule. He should also probe their sincerity for monastic vocation and prevent his charges becoming despondent and melancholic. During the probation period novices were expected to detach themselves from their worldly families in the process of becoming monks; but although Ailred of Rievaulx 'explicitly condemned relationships between clerics and monks, which were only based on familial bonds',[70] for all the members of the monastic community the renunciation of the world and family ties were compensated by the closeness of the community and affectivity of the abbatial authority. In short, the master of the novices was responsible for their salvation, just as the abbot was responsible for the salvation of the monks.[71]

The role of the abbot combined several crucial aspects of leadership, both spiritual and material. Within the monastic community the abbot was the principal preacher, delivering sermons during the chapter meetings and at the feast days of the liturgical calendar. Bernard of Clairvaux described the abbot's role as that of a nurturing and loving mother; and since the Cistercians placed great importance on the individual and on free choice in entering the monastery, many entrants gave a great deal of thought to their spiritual life, and expected guidance from the abbots.[72] Of course, spiritual leadership was only one aspect of the abbatial role. The quality that monastic communities valued in their leaders was the combination of spiritual, moral and practical skills. This is reflected in numerous 'Lives of the abbots' (*Gesta Abbati*), which told the story of venerated leaders of Cistercian houses. Abbot Charles of Villers (elected in 1197) was recorded as having exactly this mixture of qualities: If his spiritual qualities made him a popular confessor to both monks and lay people, he was personally strict in his monastic observance, and his reputation soon attracted benefactors; whilst he was ascetic himself, he spent generously on the abbey, replacing temporary cloistral wooden buildings with stone structures and continuing to build the monastic church.[73]

In terms of an abbey's public image the office of abbot was, of course, of prime importance and involved its holder deeply in the affairs of the wider world. Abbots were often away from their houses on business delegated by the Order, or sometimes by ecclesiastical or royal authority, and these 'external' aspects of the abbot's role increased in the later middle ages (see chapter 8). The business of the abbey often required the abbot to host and entertain guests, and until the development of abbatial residences within the monastic precinct, the infirmary buildings were often used for feasts with important guests. The General Chapter was often unhappy about this, however, and in 1205, for example, punished the abbots of Pointigny and Rigny for hosting and accommodating the Queen of France and a local bishop in their infirmaries.[74] Clearly, abbots were not figureheads – indeed, the post they held was so demanding that retirements and even resignations were not unheard of.[75] Abbot Hugh de Chapstow of Gracedieu Abbey resigned from his office during the visitation of his house in July 1351, explaining that he was tired of endless conflicts with disagreeable lay neighbours. Usually, a retiring abbot would be awarded an annual pension for the rest of his life, a private chamber in his monastery and the right to have private servants and a generous supply of food.[76] Even so it is clear that in some cases abbots remained in office despite their incapacity: a visitation of Buckfastleigh Abbey (Devon) in 1422 by Abbot William of Hailes Abbey revealed that Abbot William Beagle was old and frail and unable to fulfil his duties. Worse, he was plundering the abbey's finances in order to obtain expensive and useless privileges from Rome. The visitor found a solution that helped all the parties involved to 'save face': the abbot escaped deposition and was granted an annual pension and provision to live in appropriate style; but the actual leadership and financial powers were transferred to the prior, Abbot William was prevented from causing further harm to the abbey.[77] Sometimes retired abbots spent many productive years engaged in intellectual pursuits. Thomas de Burton was the bursar of Meaux Abbey for a significant length of time and was elected the abbot of his community in 1396. It was a disputed election and Thomas resigned in 1399 and busied himself until his death in 1437 with composing a detailed chronicle of Meaux based on his own knowledge of the monastery, its archives and interviews with the oldest members of the community.[78]

The daily routine of the monastic community was organised around work and liturgical duties, the monks performing the canonical hours that formed the core of Cistercian *Opus Dei* seven times a day, with psalms, hymns and readings (see Table 2). They were not a group of individuals, but a community; for in the monastic world there was little room for individual activities. All Cistercian monks and nuns knew all 150 psalms by heart and chanted them every week. On weekdays the liturgy was supplemented by the Office of the Dead, and on two of the great feasts and during the Lent by a daily mass. Those monks who were ordained as priests could also perform mass privately.[79]

It was a harsh regime with a limited amount of sleep, sparse food and long prayers in a cold church. Although there was variation in the timetable for summer and winter, there was no official adjustment for the very different lengths of the daylight in southern and northern Europe. To curb divergent local traditions, seen as a breach of the common observance, the General Chapter established in 1429 a uniform rule for 2 am wake-up on weekdays and 1 am on Sundays and feast days, regardless of the season and geographical location.

Table 2 Schedule of the Cistercian day

Activity	Summer	Winter
Rising	1:45 am	1:20 am
Vigils (night office)	2:00–3:00 am	1:30–2:30 am
	Break	*Lectio divina* (religious reading)
Lauds (at first light), canonical hour	3:10 am	7:15 am
Prime (at sunrise), canonical hour	4:00 am	8:00 am
Chapter (meeting of the community)	4:15 am	9:00 am
Manual labour	4:40–7:15 am 11:35–12:50	9:55–11:10 am
Terce, canonical hour	7:45 am	9:20 am
Mass (whole convent)	8:00–8:50 am	8:20–9:10 am
Reading	8:50–10:40 am	None
Sext (midday prayers), canonical hour	10:40 am	11:20
Midday meal	10:50 am	1:35 pm
Rest	11:30–1:45 pm	None
None, canonical hour	2:00 pm	1:20 pm
Manual labour	2:30–5:30 pm	*Lectio divina* (religious reading)
Vespers, canonical hour	6:00–6:45 pm	2:50–3:30 pm
Evening meal	6:45 pm	None
Collation (monks gather in the gallery to listen to reading)	7:30 pm	3:45 pm
Compline, canonical hour	7:50 pm	3:55 pm
Sleep	8:00 pm	16:05 pm

Source: Terryl N. Kinder, *Cistercian Europe: Architecture of Contemplation* (Kalamazoo, MI: Cistercian Publications, 2002), p. 56.

The chapter meeting held every morning played a special role in the communal life of the monastery. All monks except novices were expected to attend. The meetings, held in the chapter house, were devoted to the internal matters of the community, assigning tasks, giving announcements, correcting mistakes and punishing offenders; and to readings from the martyrology for a given day and extracts from the Rule of Benedict with the abbot's commentaries. The chapter closed with the commemoration of dead members of the community and the recitation of the *De Profundis*. On Sundays there were also readings from the statutes of the General Chapter and other Cistercian regulations, and on the first Sunday of Lent novices were admitted into the monastery during the chapter. The centrality of the chapter houses in the life of the monastic community was heightened by the fact that they were the traditional resting places of deceased abbots, whose tomb slabs covered the floor.[80]

All key daily functions were performed together: not only liturgical services, but meals in the refectory and rest in the common dormitories. As a result, punishments for the transgressing monks often involved public humiliation, such as eating on the floor of the refectory, symbolising temporary exclusion from the community. Meals were eaten in silence but accompanied by reading from the Scripture by one of the monks. The Rule of Benedict prescribed vegetarian food, but fish and eggs were allowed outside the periods of fasting. Bread was the staple of Cistercian diet. Traditionally, Cistercian food was very bland, as spices were considered a corrupting luxury. Meat was became commonly eaten from the fourteenth century (see chapter 8), but its preparation and consumption was restricted to designated spaces.

The unity of the community was underlined by the habits worn by all the monks: a white tunic and scapular, a cincture, which was a rope worn around the waist over the tunic, and a deep hood (cowl), which when placed over the head completely covered the face. The colour and cut of the Cistercian habit had a symbolic meaning often discussed by monastic writers: according to Otto of Freising the six panels of the tunic symbolised the wings of the seraphim, the wider sleeves embodied an upward movement towards God.[81] Cistercian monks, like their Benedictine predecessors, kept tonsure, that is a narrow crown of hair just above the ears while the rest of the head was shaven. The cutting of the tonsure was one of the symbolic elements of the profession rites when a novice became a full member of the community. Unlike lay brothers, the monks did not wear beards.

Apart from the monks a number of other people lived in the monasteries. Lay brothers (*conversi*) were a distinctly separate group who were clearly of lower status than monks and had no voice in major decisions, such as the election of the abbot.[82] Like many Cistercian innovations, they were not an entirely new development: there had been lay associates in the workforce of the Benedictine abbey of Hirschau and other eleventh-century reform establishments (Vallombrosans, Congregation of Fonte Avellana, Camaldoli, Order of Grandmont, Carthusians, Premonstratensians); but Cistercians came to make more use of them than their predecessors or contemporaries and their induction into Cistercian houses was a far simpler affair than the training of the novices.[83] Surviving texts addressed to the *conversi* speak loftily of the 'spiritual rewards for manual labour' and 'shared brotherhood with the monks', but in fact the liturgical obligations of the *conversi* were much reduced in favour of physical work in the monastic home farm and the granges.[84] Lay brothers got up after the night office of the monks and said their prayers where they worked instead of returning to the church. Only on Sundays and on just over 20 feast days a year did their timetable correspond to the schedule of the monks. They were illiterate – they were not even allowed to own books – and the only prayers which *conversi* were obliged to learn by heart were *Paternoster*, the *Credo in Deum* and *Miserere mei, Deus*.[85] The lay brothers lived and prayed separately from the choir monks – the western section of the nave behind that allocated to the latter. The separate refectory, dormitory and latrine of the *conversi* were on the western side of the precinct. Indeed, the majority of lay brothers were actually not allocated to the abbey itself, but to a grange, where they lived and worked, and entered the abbey only on particularly important feast days. Not surprisingly, they tended to be recruited from the peasantry, and in 1188 a regulation of the General Chapter formally laid down that a nobleman could not become a lay brother, only a monk.[86] Despite all these restrictions, the sources provide eloquent testimony to the great variety of roles fulfilled by lay brothers. Not all of them were illiterate and there are even references to *conversi* who were clearly educated and worldly men: Alain of Lille (d. 1203), an important theologian, became a lay brother at Cîteaux in 1192;[87] and apart from these employed in skilled and managerial roles (see chapter 6), such men might on occasion be involved in complex political missions to the papal curia on behalf of the General Chapter, or in negotiations with secular powers.[88]

There is, as yet, no agreement between historians as to how far the numbers of lay brothers cited in the twelfth century were a reflection of the great popularity of this semi-monastic status and how far this was a phenomenon peculiar to western Europe only. Certainly, the sharp decline in the number of lay brothers in the later thirteenth century and their almost complete disappearance after the Black Death has also been attributed to wider social and economic reasons. Constance Berman has argued recently that in the early history of the Cistercians (up to the 1160s or 1170s) lay brothers and sisters were much closer in status to the monks and nuns, being recruited from among knights and free peasants; and that their social status in the monastic community was not transformed into the second-rate status assigned to lay brothers recruited from unfree peasantry.[89] Not that the few scattered references to the great number of lay brothers can give any comprehensive picture of the proportion of choir monks and lay brothers in the early period either. According to a hagiography of Abbot Ailred of Rievaulx, that abbacy had 140 monks and 500 *conversi* during his time in office (1147–1167), but how typical this proportion was is impossible to say. Evidence from the next century, however, certainly suggests a relative decline in the number of *conversi*: in 1249 Meaux Abbey recorded only 60 monks and 90 *conversi*; while by 1280 the ratio of monks to lay brothers in several German houses of the Morimond line (Kamp, Walkenried, Volkenroda, Amelungsborn, Michaelstein and Neuenkamp) had shrunk to between 1:1 and 1:2, which gives some indication of a numerical decline in *conversi*.[90]

Of course, the decrease in the number of lay brothers did not mean that the need for a workforce had disappeared. There were various hired servants on the monastic precinct supplementing the lay brothers, or even replacing them when their numbers dwindled and they were taken up with managerial roles. In 1237 the General Chapter allowed houses which had fewer than eight lay brothers to hire servants for kitchen work.[91] By 1457 Marienstatt Abbey, a community of only 27 monks and 4 *conversi*, was employing no fewer than 81 persons on its four granges – all of these figures are pertinent to the wider issue of the economic role of the lay brothers (see chapter 6).[92]

A further distinct group within the monasteries were the *familiares*, who were engaged in manual work alongside the lay brothers, but whose status was not formalised. Even so, their entry into the community was marked by some ritual solemnity: in return for food, drink, clothing and accommodation, the *familiares* had to renounce private property and make an oath of obedience to the abbot. Although their presence in the monastic houses is scarcely documented, they existed in significant numbers, and with the drop in numbers of lay brothers in many parts of Europe their importance increased – despite the fact that the General Chapter formally abolished *familiares* in 1293.[93] Several historians have suggested that the term *familiares* included not only workers, but also individuals who retired to the Cistercian houses, having purchased a kind of 'retirement plan' from the monastery entitling them to food and board in old age, as well as others who did not live within the precinct, but were entitled to a share of spiritual privileges. *Familiares* defined in this way were not identical to the benefactors and appeared to come from a lower social stratum than the donors; but Cistercian necrologies show *familiares* to have been a large body of people – men, women and whole kinship groups – associated with the monastery. Such people did not have a productive economic role within the monastery, but rather formed a religious corporation connected with the Cistercian house, a part of its 'family' linked by the spiritual bonds of prayer and commemoration.[94]

There are many other examples of different types of lay people living within the monastic precinct, such as corriodians, or long-term guests, and the precise relationship between them and the abbey was connected to the local context. In areas of instability and violence, Cistercian abbeys frequently employed 'security' troops, armed employees to guard the abbey and particularly the granges; and it was also common for travelling abbots to be accompanied by armed guards on long journeys, especially if they were transporting money or other valuables.[95] On the other side of the legal divide, however, as Cistercian abbeys also had the status of sanctuary, they could attract those on the run from the law. The Order's regulations left to the abbots' discretion what to do with such fugitives.[96]

In short, Cistercian precincts were busy places in which many different individuals and groups of people performed various roles: practical and economic activity was essential for sustaining the spiritual functions of the house. Cistercian monastic communities were established on the rule of *stabilitas*, like those of the Benedictines, but in contrast to the latter, the white monks enjoyed, thanks largely to their filiation networks, a much wider institutional perspective and far greater mobility within the Cistercian filiation.

Cistercian Networks and Career Structure in the Order

The effectiveness of the filiation system was based on the presumption of frequent communication between houses within the 'chain', and obedience of the daughter house towards the mother. One of the most obvious tools of maintaining connection and cohesion within the filiation was through carefully managed appointments to the offices of abbot, prior, cellarer and master of novices.

Internal promotion was largely determined by the existing career structure, but the entry of prominent figures – often a real asset to abbeys – into the Cistercian Order could sometimes lead to fast advancement, as their connections, experiences and intellectual capital set them apart from 'ordinary' monks. This phenomenon was particularly noticeable in the twelfth and thirteenth centuries. Ailred, future abbot of Rievaulx, before becoming a monk, had been a key member of King David I of

Scotland's court. When he joined the Cistercian house his career accelerated very fast, from novice master, to the abbot of Revesby and finally abbot of Rievaulx.[97] Prominent theologians from the secular church were sometimes attracted to Cistercian spirituality and joined communities of white monks. Alain of Lille (d. 1203), a prominent academic in Montpellier, author of works on theology, grammar and a dictionary, and an active participant in preaching campaigns against heresy, entered Cîteaux in his later years. His *Distinctiones dictionum theologicalium* was an important theological aid for preachers and copies of it produced in the scriptorium at Cîteaux bear witness to the wider ecclesiastical concerns of the monks.[98]

The quality of information about appointments of abbots varies widely, but in certain areas, such as England, we are able to trace Cistercian careers in some details. Stephen of Sawley, for example, was a native of Yorkshire who became a monk of Fountains, where in 1215 he was appointed to the office of cellarer. From there he went on to become abbot of Sawley (a daughter house of Fountains) in 1223 and abbot of Newminster a decade later, returning in 1247 to become the abbot of Fountains itself. In the course of his illustrious career Abbot Stephen also wrote four didactic-devotional treaties, including *Speculum novitii* ('Mirror of a novice'). In the Cistercian world the management of 'human resources' was usually orchestrated from the leading monastery within the filiation and region. Rievaulx Abbey played such a role in the twelfth and thirteenth centuries in northern England, as did its daughter house, Melrose Abbey in Scotland: Abbot Silvan of Dundrennan (a daughter of Rievaulx) resigned in 1167 to take up the abbacy at Rievaulx, holding it until he resigned in 1188 to move to the neighbouring Byland Abbey, where he died and was buried; while Ernald, abbot of Melrose for ten years from 1179, resigned to succeed Silvan in the abbacy of Rievaulx, which he held for a further ten years until 1199.[99] In the next century William de Courcy was the head of three monasteries in the course of his career – originally abbot of Holm Cultram (a daughter house of Melrose), he was elected in 1215 to Melrose itself, and a year later to Rievaulx, where he remained until his death. Leonius, who started his career as a monk of Melrose, was then promoted to the abbacy of Dundrennan in 1239 and elected as abbot of Rievaulx in 1240.[100]

The career pattern that culminated in the appointment of a Cistercian abbot commonly involved a period of service in a number of offices, demanding the qualities, abilities and skills desirable in an abbot, especially managing resources and spiritual and practical leadership. Thus the offices of cellarer, prior and master of novices were frequently stepping stones to the leadership of the abbey. As the cellarer's role in managing the economy of the monastery required a combination of practical management skills and personal qualities that were also required in the leadership of the entire monastic community, it is not surprising that successful cellarers were often elected as abbots. On the other hand, a successful master of the novices, equipped with a number of skills desirable in a leader of a large community, could also be a good candidate for the office of abbot. The path to promotion via successive offices with the filiation helped to strengthen the ties between mother and daughter house and also between 'sister' monasteries; and, like the visitation, helped to maintain uniformity and transfer information and ideas within the filiations, which often encompassed different regions and even whole kingdoms.

Monks promoted by the mother house to the abbacy of a daughter monastery were not always welcomed by the new community, nor did they, in turn, always prove up to the task. In 1235 Prior Hugh of Melrose was elected as the abbot of its granddaughter Deer Abbey (from Kinloss) in Aberdeenshire, but resigned and returned to his old community after a year, as he could not cope with the harsh climate or possibly the scale of leadership duties. In 1267 the sacristan of Melrose, Adam of Smailholm, resigned after five years as abbot of Deer. According to the chronicle's 'official' account of these events (written some 20 years later) he preferred the 'sweetness of Melrose' to the 'hovel' of Deer, but this was written much later, after Easter 1286. The 'unofficial' account, written in the lower margin of the chronicle in or soon after 1267 and later erased, tells us that Abbot Adam has resigned because the monks of Deer had opposed him 'as one'.[101]

Despite the often peregrinatory character of career structures, the idea of *stabilitas*, permanent membership of a particular monastic community, remained very important for the functioning of monastic houses, and unauthorised movements between monasteries were discouraged or even punished. The strength of the bond with the original community of origin can be seen in the cases of abbots who, after retirement from the office, returned to their home communities to die. Sometimes ordinary monks were able to keep a connection with their old home through casual contact and visits: when Thomas, a monk in Val-Dieu Abbey, went to visit the former mother house of Heisterbach and happened to die there on 1 June 1483, he was recorded in the necrology of this house as a guest (*hospes*).[102]

For some Cistercian abbots the headship of a monastery was not the pinnacle of their careers. Some Cistercian monks and abbots became bishops (see chapter 1) and in the later middle ages the reform movements within the Order required particular abbots to become reformers and inspectors operating above the level of individual houses (see chapter 8).

The filial connections often stretched across the borders of regions and kingdoms as Cistercian abbeys appeared in almost all parts of medieval Europe. The organisation system not only helped to spread new foundations, but also keep this vast network connected.

Spread of Foundations and Geographical Expansion of the Order

As Cistercian abbeys with filial connections crossing the frontiers of regions and kingdoms sprang up through most of medieval Europe, their organisational system not only maintained existing interconnections within this vast network but furthered the spread of new foundations (see map overleaf). The geographical expansion of the Cistercian family beyond the Burgundian heartland was a fast, but also a complex, process. Cistercian monasticism soon won the avid support of both laity and reform-minded churchmen, and the first Cistercian house in the German lands was funded in 1123 in Kamp (Rhineland). Six years later the first English house was established in Waverley, Surrey, and was followed by others in both southern and northern Europe. The first Spanish abbey in Fitero was established in 1123, and Italian Chiaravalle Milanese in 1135. In 1131 the first monastery was founded on the territory of modern-day Switzerland in Bonmont (diocese of Geneva), and Les Dunes Abbey (1138) in the present territory of Belgium and in 1133 in Heiligenkreuz in Austria and Melrose in Scotland in 1136. The next decade saw the first Cistercian monastery founded in Ireland at Mellifont (1142), in Castile in Moreruela in 1143 and in 1140 the first Portuguese house in Tarouca was established and a whole wave of foundations in East-Central Europe and northern Europe: Hungary (Cikádor), Bohemia (Sedlec, 1142–1145) and Poland (Jędrzejów, 1140–1149), Denmark (Herrisvad, 1144), Sweden (Alvastra and Nydala, 1142) and Norway (Lyse, 1146). Historians have traced the origins of this expansion to the five oldest Cistercian houses in Burgundy – Cîteaux, La Ferté, Pontigny, Clairvaux and Morimond – the first original mother houses, which seem to have divided Europe in their areas of influence. Cîteaux's and Clairvaux's daughter houses were located in western Europe, the British Isles and northern Europe; Morimond's in central and eastern Europe. Pontigny and La Ferté were less active in these distant areas and their daughter houses were located primarily in France and Italy. The chronology of the establishment of new foundations seemed to reflect their location: whilst in in western Europe 49 per cent of Cistercian houses were established in the first half of the twelfth century, activity continued apace in East-Central Europe, where 31 per cent of new foundations were established during the first half of the thirteenth century.[103]

THE CISTERCIAN ORDER IN MEDIEVAL EUROPE 1090–1500

Figure 2.1 The Medieval Cistercian Abbeys
Source: Terryl N. Kinder, *Cistercian Europe: Architecture of Contemplation* (Kalamazoo, MI: Cistercian Publications, 2002)

THE FIRST MULTINATIONAL?

Although the Cistercian model was undoubtedly very popular among the prospective founders across Europe, and although, within a region, the oldest foundation usually acted as the local mother house for expanding the filiation network further, for much of the twelfth century the Cistercian organisational structure was still fluid; nor do we know what proportion of 'new' houses were in reality pre-existing monastic communities 'adopted' into the Order.[104] By the last decade of the twelfth century, however, the General Chapter was asserting its supreme authority in the matter of establishing new houses, and statutes of the 1190s related to penalties imposed on abbots who established daughter houses without the General Chapter's permission.[105]

The rapid increase in Cistercian foundations continued in the twelfth century, and although it slowed down in the second half of the twelfth century in western Europe new foundations still continued to appear in the thirteenth century. Very few Cistercian monasteries were founded after 1350, however, and in the fifteenth century only 14 in the whole of the Empire, France and the Law Countries (or 2.3 per cent of the total).[106]

These numerous Cistercian houses would never have been possible without the support of lay people and powerful church figures – bishops and archbishops. These links with the founders and patrons through which the white monks gained new friends and supporters were crucial for the geographical expansion of the Order. At the time the Cistercians reached the Baltic and Scandinavia, church structures were still in the process of formation. This not only provided ample material for conflicts between archbishops seeking to extend their powers to the new and distant dioceses, but offered Bernard of Clairvaux an opportunity to pursue his great object of spreading the Cistercian family: for 'any person who helped Bernard with this purpose deserved to qualify as his friend, whether or not Bernard knew this person well or not',[107] Archbishop Eskil of Lund, for example, who was engaged in resisting the encroachments of Archbishop Hartvig of Hamburg-Bremen, decided, in order to strengthen the Danish church practically and spiritually, to found a new Cistercian house in Esrum (Northern Zealand). Through this action Eskil gained a friend and a powerful supporter in Bernard of Clairvaux, whilst the Cistercian Order gained a number of new foundations: Esrum went on to become a mother house of several other monasteries further north and east: Vitskøl, Sorø, Ryd, Kołbacz, Dargun and Doberan. Eskil and Bernard became friends first through correspondence, and then when the Scandinavian prelate came to Clairvaux to meet the charismatic Cistercian leader in 1152 or early 1153.

Eskil was not the only churchman from the frontiers of Europe to develop a mutually beneficial relationship with Bernard of Clairvaux. Archbishop

Malachy of Armagh's introduction of the first Cistercian house to Ireland (Mellifont, 1142) was the beginning of the dense network of white monks' monasteries in Ireland, where Cistercian houses were the core institution of church reform and brought the Hibernian church in line with the continental diocesan and monastic model.[108] Although Mellifont was a direct foundation from Clairvaux, its subsequent daughter houses were members of the Order by incorporation, being pre-existing communities, which adopted Cistercian customs. Even so, the Cistercian success was in no small part due to the support that the reformed communities received from the Irish kings.[109]

The location of the Cistercian houses was determined by the wishes of the founder, the availability of land, pre-existing settlements and natural conditions. They were often located in quite civilised surroundings near residences of the founders and patrons, and the frequent, almost routine, reference to the 'uncultivated' and wild nature of the areas where the white monks established their houses should not be taken too literally. The *Exordium Cistercii*, for example, the major source of Cistercian imagery, describes vividly the site of the new monastery as a 'place of horror, a vast wilderness', and this became a common formula in foundation narrative across the Order, rather as a symbol of humility, regardless of whether it had any resemblance to the actual landscape in any given location.

Like the term 'uncultivated', the concept of 'seclusion' so prominent in the early Cistercian writings was not so easily translated into practice. In reality, practical considerations of a sustainable location were likely to be decisive factors in the long-term survival of a monastic houses. Cistercian houses in Norway, for example, were situated close to the large centres of population and of episcopal power: Lyse (1146), a daughter house of Fountains, Hovedøya (1147), founded from Kirkstead, and Tautra (1207), established as a daughter of Lyse.[110]

One frequent choice for a location was an abandoned site, perhaps an earlier stronghold no longer needed by the founder, but still offering a viable base for a community. This was particularly the case in East-Central Europe where secure locations were of prime importance. Łekno Abbey was founded on a site of a former stronghold, Marienwalde Abbey on a hill securely surrounded by a lake and marshland. Proximity to a river and water supplies was another important consideration – witness the profusion of names such as Fountains, Clairefontaine, Font-Vive, Fontfroide, Fontevivo, Sept-Fons, Königsbronn and Acquafredda. In France, several of the oldest Cistercian houses in France were founded near water-courses dividing the lands of competing lords; and monasteries such as Pontigny (1114), founded on the border between two regions – Champagne and

Burgundy – and three counties and bishoprics, acquired something of the status of independent buffer zone.[111]

In the course of the twelfth and thirteenth centuries the white monks reached the very frontiers of expanding Christian Europe. The first Cistercian house beyond those frontiers was established in 1157 in Belmont (south-west of Tripoli) followed by Salvatio in 1161, both from Morimond. The former seemed to have survived only until 1174, but Salvatio survived until the early thirteenth century. In 1209 a Cistercian monk from La Ferté, Peter of Ivrea, became the Patriarch of Antioch and made vigorous attempts to expand the Cistercian networks – albeit with somewhat mixed results. For example, he persuaded an independent Benedictine foundation in Jubin to join the Cistercians, but the community was plagued by internal strife and disputes with the patriarchs of Antioch over tithe payment until, following in the path of other retreating Latin orders, the house at Jubin moved to Beaulieu in Cyprus after the fall of Antioch.[112]

The emergence of Cistercian monasteries in Greece, conquered by the Crusaders in 1204, was a part of a papal campaign to strengthen the Latin Church in the Orthodox world. In 1205 Innocent III appealed to French prelates to send capable Cistercian and Cluniac monks to Greece. Although it was not spelled out in the papal letter, it seems that just as in the Baltic, Cistercians were to act in some degree as missionaries in Greece. For the most part, they established their monasteries in orthodox abbeys that had been abandoned or confiscated by the Crusaders, most prominent of them being Daphni Abbey. The whole experiment was largely a failure thanks not so much to any internal deficiencies as to changes in the political situation: when the influence of the Franks declined in the 1260s to be replaced by the Venetian Republic, the Cistercian houses lost their supporters and backers; and with the Greek resurgence of 1276 almost all these Cistercian communities collapsed.[113]

In the Iberian peninsula the Cistercian Order played a part in the *Reconquista* in two significant ways: by establishing monastic houses in newly conquered areas and by inspiring and fostering military religious orders. The military Calatrava Order was founded in 1158, taking the Rule of Benedict and following Cistercian customs. It owed its origins to the defence of the town of Calatrava by Abbot Raymond of the Cistercian house of Santa Maria de Fitro in Navarre, who assembled a large army to defend the city. The lay knights who followed Abbot Raymond adopted the habit of Cîteaux and formed themselves into a military order under his direction. The Order was formally recognised by a papal bull in 1164.[114] In other areas of Europe, too, Cistercian houses played a variety of roles in accordance with the local conditions. Whereas in western Europe they were part of a long and rich monastic tradition, in East-Central Europe – Bohemia, Poland and Hungary Christianised in the late tenth century – they formed the second wave of monastic foundations, whilst in Scandinavia Cistercians were frequently among the first monastic institutions. In the pagan regions inhabited by Slavonic tribes between Germany and the Polish lands Cistercian foundations were established immediately in the wake of conquest and Christianisation in the twelfth century, and constituted the first ecclesiastical structures – for example, the Cistercian abbey of Doberan near Rostock in Mecklenburg was founded in 1171 by Duke Pribislaw of Mecklenburg and Rügen as a manifestation of his conversion.[115]

Once established, the Cistercian communities were much occupied with the internal missions. The *Book of Miracles* by Herbert of Clairvaux contains a number of stories based on information obtained from Abbot Henry of Vitskøl and the monks of Esrum. For example, one story tells that in the 'Sclavonia' region, which had recently been Christianised, Cistercian monks went every day to the villages to baptise, under the papal licence, the inhabitants who gathered for that purpose in great numbers. The abbey from which they came is unnamed by Herbert, but it has been identified as Dargun Abbey in Mecklenburg. The same monks discovered an old battlefield nearby (identified by historians as that of the battle of Verchen in 1164), where skulls of fallen Christian warriors bore a miraculous sign of the cross on their foreheads to distinguish them from the bones of pagans. What is interesting in this account is the fact that the monks of Dargun reported that local people were not at all familiar with the sign of cross, i.e. they were still largely pagan and the Cistercians were involved in missionary activities.[116]

In Sweden links between the royal power and the Cistercians were close. The first monasteries were established during the reign of King Sverker I, but the rival Erik dynasty was also in a symbiotic power relationship with the Cistercian Order. The lay power's desire for religious legitimisation was manifest in the use of two Cistercian monasteries as necropolises by the rival dynasties – Alvastra by the Sverker and Varnhem Abbey by the Erik dynasty. The formation of the written form of government was also furthered by Cistercians who worked in the proto-chancery of King Knut Eriksson in the late twelfth century. As elsewhere along the northern frontier of Europe, Cistercians were involved in establishing the structures of the secular church too: Stefan, the first archbishop of Uppsala, was a monk of Alvestra; and the prominent role of the abbots of this monastery in Sweden – holding high appointments and advising the king – lasted into the 1270s, when the priors of the Dominican house at Sigtuna superseded them.[117]

Adaptation to Regional Differences

Accommodation to different local conditions took place at both the practical/material and the cultural levels, and the impact of the local climate, food culture and access to imported goods all influenced the customs prevailing in Cistercian monasteries. Whilst the Rule of Benedict provided for the monks consuming a moderate amount of wine, for example, local availability and custom dictated that in most areas of northern Europe this was replaced by beer.[118] Problems of supply might cause discomfort or even subvert proper monastic observance, and inadequate knowledge of the local environment was often behind failures of Cistercian foundations on the very frontiers of Europe: the monastery of Munkeby founded between 1150 and 1180 some 80 km from Trondheim, and not far from the Article Circle, had to struggle to survive until 1207, when the monks moved to the more hospitable Tautra Abbey.[119]

A further pointer to the accommodating nature of the Cistercian model was the introduction of the cults of local or national saints to the general Cistercian calendar and liturgy. Successful approaches to the General Chapter in the thirteenth and fourteenth centuries included an appeal in 1221 from the abbot of Ourscamp Abbey (Picardy) for the addition of the feast of St Eligius to the Cistercian calendar and another from the abbot of Egris (Hungary) in 1222 to add the feast of St Stephen. In 1263 Kamp Abbey secured the addition of the martyr Victor of Xanten, a member of the Theban Legion.[120] Cistercians were also involved – and this was of particular importance in recently Christianised areas – in establishing completely new local cults: when, according to Herbert's *Book of Miracles*, the body of a certain Margaret from Roskilde, murdered by her barbarian husband in 1176, was moved by her relatives to Søro Abbey, it soon started to perform miracles. A cult grew around it, supported by the Cistercians.[121]

The problems of adapting to local conditions on the cultural level were particularly acute in areas where there was a wide divergence between established monastic traditions and 'standard' Benedictine customs. The introduction of Cistercian monasticism in Ireland and Scotland was part of the greater reform of the local churches, which brought them into the mainstream of the post-Gregorian church. As in Scotland, where the Scottish kings sponsored the reform, in Ireland it was supported by various native rulers, but also, by the late twelfth century, closely connected with the growing area of Anglo-Norman conquest and their political and cultural influence. The expansion of Cistercian monasticism in Ireland occurred largely through the incorporation of the existing communities. In some cases these communities continued 'native' traditions such as the practices of combining the office of the bishop with that of the abbot, separate hermitages for the monks instead of a communal dormitory, extensive use of the vernacular and even non-standard habits.[122] Indeed, by the early thirteenth century the Cistercian model had, according to the Order's authorities, become altogether too 'diluted'; and the General Chapter was particularly alarmed in 1216 and 1217 by the violent opposition of Mellifont and its daughter houses to a visitation.[123] The conflict between the ideas of the General Chapter and the particularism of the Irish Cistercians reached its apogee during the visitation of Irish monasteries in 1227/28 by the reforming Abbot Stephen of Lexington, who discovered the so-called 'Mellifont conspiracy'. In Abbot Stephen's view Irish monks represented barbarity and ignorance and he could not value their traditions. His response was rather heavy-handed, and included deposing Irish abbots and replacing them with Anglo-Norman monks to ensure uniformity of observance. The fear that the separatist tendencies of the Irish houses might lead to some kind of a schism in the Order moved the General Chapter to cancel the filiation of Mellifont and hand over its daughters to the French-speaking mother houses; and as a further precautionary measure against Irish separatism, the monks in Ireland who could not speak French were barred from entering Cistercian houses.[124] Clearly the much vaunted adaptability of the Cistercians had its limitations, especially when it came to matters of observance.

Nevertheless, such flexibility as the Order managed to display in relation to local conditions was particularly attractive to the 'native' rulers on the frontiers of medieval Europe. For such semi-independent rulers as Fergus, lord of Galloway (d. 1161), a semi-independent native ruler in the south-west of Scotland, who was the founder of Dundrennan Abbey, and such native Welsh princes as Lord Rhys (founder of Valle Crucis in 1201), becoming the founders and patrons of Cistercian houses was an opportunity to participate in the fashionable form of piety. It was also a signal to their powerful neighbours that they were in cultural and religious terms full members of the 'family' of European elites.[125]

Cistercians, Heretics, Non-Christians and Crusaders

The involvement of the Cistercian Order in the central issues of medieval church and society in the twelfth century and early thirteenth century exemplifies its commitment to the reform of the church, and to fighting its enemies in alliance with the papacy – witness its participation in the battle against heresy, in crusades, its efforts to implement papal policies of pastoral care, and, to a lesser degree, its relationship with Judaism. As preachers, missionaries and persecutors of heresy, Cistercians were precursors of the mendicant orders of the 1220s.[126] Pope Innocent III certainly had a very high opinion of the quality of Cistercian monks, indeed, of the whole Order as the 'frontier guards of the faith' preaching against heresy and organising crusades.[127] In political terms, he also saw in the Order a useful ally in containing the power of the Empire – hence the donations he lavished on Cistercian monasteries located on key routes towards Rome: Casamari, Fossanova, Marmosolio, S Martino, Falleri.[128]

Innocent III had an unflinching faith in Cistercian loyalty and ability, and frequently appointed Cistercians – for example Abbot Arnaud Amaury of Cîteaux – as legates; and it was Cistercians who implemented his plans at the turn of the century to fight heresy in southern France: abbots Gui of Cîteaux and Berthold of Morimond and numerous monks investigated suspected cases of heresy in Languedoc and the Midi and conducted extensive preaching campaigns and disputations with the heretical leaders in order to bring them back to orthodoxy.[129] The event that put an end to the largely non-violent methods of the Cistercians was the assassination of the papal legate and Cistercian monk Peter of Castelnau in 1208, following which the pope launched a crusade against the heretics. Here again, the Cistercians were very active in preaching to recruit crusaders, and as the project of eradicating heretics ran into difficulties, their message became increasingly violent. Indeed, it was with pride that Caesarius of Heisterbach in his Cistercian tales recorded the instruction given to crusaders about to take the heretic stronghold of Béziers by Abbot Arnaud Amaury, the papal envoy with the army: 'kill them all, God will recognize his own'.[130]

If less bloodily, Cistercians also supported papal policy through prayers. Faced with the failure of the Christians to hold the Holy Land in the second half of the thirteenth century, the General Chapter demanded special prayers from all abbeys across the Order: in 1268 it ordered every community to perform a mass each Wednesday in support of the Holy Land; and in 1270, at the request of King Louis IX and his queen, a special monthly procession after the chapter meeting was instituted for all Cistercian communities in addition to special prayers and psalm chanting in aid of the crusade's success. The General Chapter decreed further liturgical performances to help the recovery of the Holy Land in 1272, 1273 and 1274.[131]

The adoption by the church of an aggressive stance against heresy, and the increasing demonisation of heretics and other outsiders was accompanied by a sharpening of the church's attitude towards Jews.[132] Like every other aspect of his character and writings, the attitude of Bernard of Clairvaux towards the Jewish people has been much debated by historians. Norman Cantor argues that Bernard had no interested in converting the

Jews and was motivated simply by racial hatred; for him, the Jews had 'no place in European civilization committed to Latin Christianity'.[133] Christopher Holdsworth points out that Abbot Peter Venerable, whom many historians find more 'pleasant' than his Cistercian counterpart, was far more vituperative in his views on Jews and Muslims.[134] Peter Donzelbacher suggests that in Bernard's world-view Jews did have a role to fulfil in relation to the story of salvation, but that there is no indication of a tolerant attitude either.[135] In fact, during the Second Crusade Bernard issued a letter in 1146 condemning the violence perpetrated against Jews by the crusaders in the Rhineland, not because it was wrong to kill 'enemies of Christ', but because there was hope that Jews might yet be converted.[136] Jean Leclercq argues that Bernard's main objection to the pogroms was not that they were violent, but that they resulted from the actions of unauthorised preachers.[137] Yet although other significant Cistercian figures of the twelfth century – Guerric of Igny (d. 1157) and Ailred of Rievaulx (d. 1167) – also devoted some sermons to the issue of the Jewish rejection of Christ, there is very little evidence of the participation of Cistercian monks in campaigns to convert the Jews.[138]

The active engagement of Cistercians in preaching, missions and defence of the church against its 'enemies' was played out not only in the core French areas of the Order's development, but was felt in the north-eastern part of the continent, from the second half of the twelfth century, on the southern coast of the Baltic from Mecklenburg and Pomerania, to Livonia and in Prussia in the 1220s and 1230s. The first identifiable Cistercian monk involved in the missionary activities in these northern regions was Berno from Amelungsborn Abbey, who was appointed as missionary bishop to pagan Obodrites in 1155. According to the contemporary chronicler Helmold of Bosau, Berno, following in the tradition of early medieval bishops, took part in the military conquest of the pagan island of Rügen by King Valdemar of Denmark in 1168. He worked in close co-operation with Duke Henry the Lion of Saxony, who gave him the newly created bishopric, from where he was instrumental in founding Doberan Abbey in 1171 as a daughter house of Amelungsborn.[139]

In the later twelfth century the south-eastern Baltic was the last remaining 'pocket' of paganism in Christian Europe and, with the fervour and limited effectiveness of the crusades in the Holy Land, combined with the possibility of conquest and enrichment for the northern European knights, this area became an arena for a number of campaigns. The first missionary bishop of Estonia was a Cistercian monk, Fulco, from La Celle Abbey, who was appointed in 1162, although it is not clear that he ever got to the Baltic coast. However, the Cistercians also played a major part in the later stages of Christian conquest, in the 1180s and

1190s: Meinhard, an Augustinian canon from Segeberg, both before and during his activities as a missionary bishop in Livonia (1188), had Cistercian monks in his entourage, including Dietrich of Treiden, who baptised the Livonian chieftain Kaupo. After Meinhard's death in 1196, Dietrich, now abbot of Dünamünde, continued to work very closely with Bishop Albert of Riga (d. 1229), and in 1202 founded a military order, the Livonian Sword Brothers (*Fratres milicie Christ*). In 1211 he was ordained bishop of the missionary diocese of Estonia.[140] The second bishop of Livonia, Bertold (1196–1198), had also been a Cistercian monk, and then abbot, in Loccum Abbey. He not only participated in military expeditions himself, but was instrumental in bringing crusaders to the region, primarily from northern Germany. This marked a move by the Cistercians from pursuing a peaceful mission to engaging in violent crusades in the Baltic; and it was during the course of one such expedition that the bishop, sword in hand, was killed in a battle with pagans.[141] Berthold's successor, Bishop Albert of Buxhövden (a formerly canon in Bremen), was more peacefully inclined, and employing Cistercians as missionaries.[142]

By the second decade of the thirteenth century, however, the Cistercians had growing competition in the Baltic. The Order of Teutonic Knights, originally set up in the late twelfth century in the Holy Land, was transferred, after a brief spell in Hungary in 1226, to Prussia on the Baltic coast, with a mission to convert pagans there and protect the neighbouring Christian states. Before long, the Knights had created an entity, albeit in theory directly subordinate to the papacy, that was in reality a virtual state, subjugating the local population, striving to create large landed estates for the Order, and increasingly threatening its Christian neighbours. Since 1206 missionary work in Prussia had been conducted, with the explicit approval of Pope Innocent III, by a group of Cistercians from Łekno Abbey under the leadership of monk Christian from Kołbacz Abbey. The peaceful mission had, however, brought only limited results, while neighbouring Polish princes were keen for territorial expansion under the guise of a crusade, which was authorised by the pope in 1217.[143] The upshot of this, however, was to wipe out even the limited success of the Cistercian mission. Retaliatory attacks by the Prussians into Mazovia led Prince Conrad of Mazovia to invite the Teutonic Knights to take over the crusade.[144] As a result, Cistercians who wanted to undertake further missionary work now found themselves prevented from setting up a monastery in Prussia and opposition from the Knights brought Christian's plans to set up an 'episcopal' state in Prussia to nothing.[145] Eventually the Cistercian efforts in Prussia were completely overshadowed by the mendicants, who although not rivals had very a different relationship to the dominant political power in the region: because the mendicants were not interested in accumulating land, the Teutonic Knights did not perceive them as competition for land resources and became their political allies and supporters. Hence the houses of Dominican friars in the Baltic coastal towns were able to organise a number of successful preaching campaigns.[146]

The Cistercians were more successful in the territory of modern-day Estonia, where, following the Danish crusades, from 1219 onwards, Cistercian abbeys made territorial gains too. According to a royal census in 1241, three Cistercian houses owned 15 per cent of land in Danish Estonia. However, they were all located outside the regions – Dünamünde in the diocese of Riga, Falkenau in the diocese of Dorpat and Roma in Gotland. Moreover, the Sword Brothers, although originally connected to the white monks, feared their competition in Livonia and prevented the foundation of further Cistercian houses.

Altogether, the engagement of the Cistercian monks in the campaigns against heretics, preaching and missionary work show that the contemplative character of the Order was not in conflict with its wider mission; and the adaptability of the Cistercian model to very different conditions was certainly one of its strengths, given that the Order's most intensive involvement in preaching and Christianisation occurred at the very peripheries of the Latin world.

Conclusions

The central governing body of the Cistercian Order – the General Chapter – enforced a certain degree of uniformity and provided a forum for the exchange of ideas between abbots that helped to make the collection of hundreds of monastic houses into a family of communities. However, the General Chapter would have achieved very little if the Cistercian monasteries had not been connected to each other by the filiation system. This gave Cistercian abbeys a highly organised form of control and communication across the vast network. Because the shared 'corporate identity' of spirituality, liturgy and monastic observance was very strong, there was room for regional adjustment and accommodation to local socio-economic conditions, without losing the core practices, standards and spirituality that constituted Cistercian *ordo*.

One important manifestation of the highly structured nature of the Cistercian Order's organisation was the pattern of establishing new monasteries, which allowed the General Chapter to retain control of the process and monitor it through an established procedure. The mother house was obliged to provide a 'starter kit' of people, liturgical books and basic provisions such as buildings for every new community, which then followed a designated path.

The idea of the community, the horizontal bonds between the monks and the vertical ones linking them to the abbot, were the building blocks of Cistercian existence. The monks lived, worked, ate, slept and prayed together. The monasteries were run by different officials, responsible for various aspects of community functions, but overall leadership was in the hands of the abbot. Whilst all monks were equal, lay brothers, whose main role was physical labour and limited liturgical functions, were a separate group of lower status. Like many Cistercian innovations common to the wider reform movement of the twelfth century, the *conversi* were a development that went further than the experiments of other reform movements in this area.

The spread of the Cistercian houses to the very frontiers of Christendom, their engagement in the missions to pagans and combating of heresy, and the support of the order for the crusades were closely linked to the practical and ideological alliance of the Cistercian movement and the papacy. In the twelfth century the influential leaders of the white monks were members of a powerful ecclesiastical network; and with the appointment of a significant number of Cistercian monks and bishops, and even a pope (Eugenius III), the members of the Order continued to support a particular idea of the church and model of prelates. The white monks did not reject the world but strove to engage with it on its own terms, often, as will be seen, with great success.

Notes

1. Robert Bartlett, *The Making of Medieval Europe: Conquest, Colonization and Cultural Change 950–1350* (London: Penguin, 1994), pp. 139–140, 153–155, 227–229, 256–260.
2. David Bell, 'From Molesme to Cîteaux: The Earliest "Cistercian Spirituality"', *Cistercian Studies Quarterly* 34 (1999), p. 479.
3. Louis Lekai, 'Ideals and Reality in Early Cistercian Life and Legislation', in *The New Monastery. Texts and Studies on the Earliest Cistercians*, ed. E. Rosanne Elder (Kalamazoo, MI: Cistercian Studies, 1998), p. 227, p. 7; new edition of the oldest fragmentary series between 1157 and 1161 in *Twelfth-Century Statutes from the Cistercian General Chapter: Latin text with English notes and commentary*, ed. Chrysogonus Waddell (Brecht: Cîteaux, Commentarii Cistercienses, 2002), pp. 65–75.
4. Bell, 'From Molesme to Cîteaux', p. 479.
5. Brian Patrick McGuire, 'Norm and Practice in Early Cistercian Life', in *Norm und Praxis in Alltag des Mittelalters und der frühen Neuzeit*, ed. Gerhard Jaritz (Vienna: Österreichische Akedemie der Wissenschaften, 1997), p. 111.

6. *Twelfth-Century Statutes*, pp. 37–38.
7. *Twelfth-Century Statutes*, pp. 38–39.
8. *Twelfth-Century Statutes*, p. 39.
9. *Twelfth-Century Statutes*, 1197: 50.
10. *Twelfth-Century Statutes*, 1197: 19.
11. Elke Goez, *Pragmatische Schriftlichkeit und Archivpflege der Zisterzienser. Ordenszentralismus und regionale Vielfalt, namentlich in Franken und Altbayern (1098–1525)* (Münster: Lit Verlag, 2003), pp. 139–140.
12. Peter King, *The Finances of the Cistercian Order in the Fourteenth Century* (Kalamazoo, MI: Cistercian Publications, 1985), pp. 8–9, 33–37, 74, 80–81, 173, 194–196.
13. Jean-Baptiste Van Damme, 'Les pouvoirs de l'abbé de Cîteaux aux XIIe et XIIIe siècle', *Analecta Sacri Ordinis Cisterciensis* 24 (1968), p. 85.
14. Janet Burton, 'Homines sanctitatis eximiae, religionis consummatae: The Cistercians in England and Wales', *Archaeologia Cambrensis* 154 (2005), p. 38; *Statuta capitulorum generalium ordinis Cisterciensis ab anno 1116 ad annum 1786*, ed. Joseph Canivez, 8 vols (Louvain: Bureaux de la Revue, 1933–1941), 1215: 48.
15. Jane Sayers, 'English Cistercian Cases and their Delegation in the First Half of the Thirteenth Century', *Analecta Sacri Ordinis Cisterciensis* 20 (1964), pp. 86–89.
16. *Twelfth-Century Statutes*, 1193: 1; Jörg Oberste, *Visitation und Ordensorganisation. Formen sozialer Normierung, Kontrolle und Kommunikation bei Cisterzienser, Prämonstratensern und Cluniazensern (12. – frühes 14. Jahrhundert)*, Vita regularis 2 (Münster: Lit Verlag, 1995), p. 117.
17. Jörg Oberste, *Die Dokumente der Klösterlichen Visitationen*, Typologie des Sources du Moyen Âge Occidental 80 (Turnhout: Brepols, 1999), p. 34.
18. Jörg Oberste, 'Normierung und Pragmatik des Schriftgebrauchs im Cisterciensischen Visitationsverfahren bis zum beginnenden 14. Jahrhundert', *Historisches Jahrbuch* 114 (1994), pp. 327–334.
19. Józef Dobosz, 'Kryzys w opactwie cysterskim w Sulejowie w drugiej połowie XIII wieku', *Docendo Discimus. Studia historyczne ofiarowane Profesorowi Zbigniewowi Wielgoszowi w siedemdziesiątą rocznicę urodzin*, ed. Krzysztof Kaczmarek, J. Nikodem (Poznań: Instytut Historii UAM, 2000), pp. 133–146; *Statuta*, vol. 3, 1284: 11, p. 232; *Kodeks Dyplomatyczny Wielkopolski*, vol. 3 (Poznań: Poznańskie Towarzystwo Przyjaciół Nauk, 1879), no. 2034; *Kodeks Dyplomatyczny Wielkopolski*, vol. 1 (Poznań: Poznańskie Towarzystwo Przyjaciół Nauk, 1877), nos. 328, 558.
20. Christopher Harper-Bill, 'Cistercian Visitation in the Late Middle Ages: The Case of Hailes Abbey', *Bulletin of the Institute of Historical Research* 53 (1980), pp. 107, 109–110.
21. Harper-Bill, 'Cistercian Visitation', pp. 105, 107–108.
22. Oberste, *Die Dokumente der Klösterlichen Visitationen*, p. 35.
23. King, *The Finances*, pp. 14–15; Francis R. Swietek, 'Et Inter Abbates de Majoribus unus: the Abbot of Savigny in the Cistercian Constitution, 1147–1243', in *Truth as Gift: Studies in Medieval Cistercian History in Honor of John R. Sommerfeldt*, ed. Marsha Dutton (Kalamazoo, MI: Cistercian

Publications, 2004), p. 98; René Locatelli, 'Les Cisterciens dans L'Espace Français: filiations et Réseaux', in *Unanimité et Diversité cisterciennes: filiations, réseaux, relectures du XIIe au XVIIe siècle: actes du quatrième colloque international du CERCOR, Dijon, 23–25 septembre 1998*, ed. Nicole Bouter (Saint-Etienne: Publications de l'Université de Saint-Etienne, 2000), p. 58.

24. Constance Berman, *Medieval Agriculture, the Southern French Countryside and the Early Cistercians* (Philadelphia, PA: The American Philosophical Society, 1986), pp. 135–136.
25. Michael H. Gelting, 'The Kingdom of Denmark', in *Christianisation and the Rise of Christian Monarchy: Scandinavia, Central Europe and Rus' c. 900–1200*, ed. Nora Berend (Cambridge: Cambridge University Press, 2007), p. 98.
26. Kim Esmark, 'Religious Patronage and Family Consciousness: Sorø Abbey and the "Hvide Family", c. 1150–1250', in *Religious and Laity in Western Europe 1000–1400: Interaction, Negotiation, and Power*, ed. Emilia Jamroziak and Janet Burton (Turnhout: Brepols, 2006), pp. 97–98.
27. Swen Holger Brunsch, *Das Zisterzienserkloster Heisterbach von seiner Gründung bis zum Anfang des 16. Jahrhunderts* (Siegburg: F. Schmitt, 1998), pp. 28–43.
28. Constance Hoffman Berman, *The Cistercian Evolution: The Invention of a Religious Order in Twelfth-Century Europe* (Philadelphia, PA: University of Pennsylvania Press, 2000), pp. 142–148, argues that the merger between Savigny and the Cistercians occurred at least a decade earlier.
29. Jacqueline Buhot, 'L'abbaye normande de Savigny, chef d'ordre et fille de Cîteaux', *Le moyen âge* 46 (1936), pp. 249–264; Bennet D. Hill, *English Cistercian Monasteries and Their Patrons in the Twelfth Century* (Urbana, IL: University of Illinois Press, 1968), pp. 80–115; Francis R. Swietek, 'The Role of Bernard of Clairvaux in the Union of Savigny with Cîteaux: A Reconsideration', in *Bernardus Magister: Papers Presented at the Nonacentenary Celebration of the Birth of Saint Bernard of Clairvaux, Kalamazoo, Michigan, sponsored by the Institute of Cistercian Studies, Western Michigan University, 10–13 May 1990*, ed. John R. Sommerfeldt (Kalamazoo, MI: Cistercian Publications, 1992), p. 289.
30. *The Primitive Cistercian Breviary with Variants from the 'Bernardine' Cistercian Breviary*, ed. Chrysogonus Waddell, Spicilegium Friburgense 44 (Fribourg: Academic Press, 2007), pp. 30–31.
31. Józefa Zawadzka, 'Proces fundowania opactw cysterskich w XII i XIII wieku', *Roczniki Humanistyczne* 7 (1960), pp. 127, 142–145.
32. Janet Burton, 'The Foundation of the British Cistercian Houses', in *Cistercian Art and Architecture in the British Isles*, ed. Christopher Norton and David Park (Cambridge: Cambridge University Press, 1986), p. 25.
33. Janet Burton, *The Monastic Order in Yorkshire 1069–1215* (Cambridge: Cambridge University Press, 1999), p. 192.
34. *Narrative and Legislative Texts from Early Cîteaux: Latin text in dual edition with English translation and notes*, ed. Chrysogonus Waddell (Brecht: Cîteaux, Commentarii Cistercienses, 1999), p. 187.

35. Matthias Untermann, '"Ratio fecit diversum" Aspekte zisterziensischer Architektur', in *Von Cîteaux nach Bebenhausen: Welt und Wirken der Zisterziener*, ed. Barbara Scholkmann and Sönke Lorenz (Tübingen: Attempto, 2000), p. 62.
36. Peter J. Fergusson, 'The Builders of Cistercian Monasteries in Twelfth Century England', in *Studies in Cistercian Art and Architecture*, ed. Meredith P. Lillich, vol. 2 (Kalamazoo, MI: Cistercian Publications, 1984), pp. 15–21.
37. *The Foundation History of the Abbeys of Byland and Jervaulx*, ed. Janet Burton, Borthwick Texts and Studies 35 (York: Borthwick Publications, 2006), p. 11; Fergusson, 'The Builders of Cistercian Monasteries', p. 11.
38. Berman, *The Cistercian Evolution*, pp. 207–209; *Kodeks Dyplomatyczny Wielkopolski*, vol. 1, nos. 126, 128, 225, 252.
39. Kateřina Charvátová, 'Mindful of Reality, Faithful to Traditions. Development of Bohemian Possessions of the Cistercian Order from the 12th to the 13th Centuries', in *L'espace cistercien*, ed. Léon Pressouyre (Paris: Comité des travaux historiques et scientifiques, 1994), p. 179.
40. 'huius mei deuoti studii factiue testamentum', in *Repertorium polskich dokumentów doby piastowskiej*, ed. Zofia Kozłowska-Budkowa (Kraków: PAU, 1937), no. 55.
41. Wolfgang Ribbe, 'Politische Voraussetzungen und Motive der Ansiedlung von Zisterziensern in England und Deutschland', in *Zisterzienser: Norm, Kultur, Reform 900 Jahre Zisterzienser*, ed. Ulrich Knefelkamp (Berlin: Springer, 2001), pp. 30–36.
42. 'quia in orationibus salus nostra protegitur. Et regni nostri stabilitas firmatur'. Thomas Hill, '*Es für mich sehr nützlich ist, mir die Armen Christi zu Freunden zu Machen*. Voraussetzungen und Motive der Anlage von Zisterzienserklöster in Dänemark', in *Zisterzienser: Norm, Kultur, Reform – 900 Jahre Zisterzienser*, p. 80.
43. Janet Burton, '*Fundator Noster*: Roger de Mowbray as Founder and Patron of Monasteries', in *Religious and Laity in Western Europe 1000–1400*, pp. 33–34.
44. Christopher Holdsworth, 'The Church', in *The Anarchy of King Stephen's Reign*, ed. E. King (Oxford: Clarendon Press, 1994), pp. 222–228; Burton, 'The Foundation of the British Cistercian Houses', p. 35.
45. Dariusz Wybranowski, 'Jeszcze raz o konflikcie Barnima I z joannitami ze Stargardu i Korytowa z lat 1268–1271. Próba identyfikacji wasali książęcych z dokumentów Alberta Wielkiego', *Przegląd Zachodniopomorski* 45 (2001), p. 16, n. 50.
46. Karen Stöber, *Late Medieval Monasteries and their Patrons: England and Wales c. 1300–1540* (Woodbridge: Boydell Press, 2007), p. 16; Huw Pryce, 'Patrons and Patronage among the Cistercians in Wales', *Archaeologia Cambrensis* 154 (2005), p. 81; *Councils and Ecclesiastical Documents relating to Great Britain and Ireland*, ed. A.W. Haddan and W. Stubbs (Oxford: Clarendon Press, 1869), vol. 1, no. 499.
47. Heike Reimann, 'A Cistercian Foundation within the Territory of a Slavonic Tribe: The Abbey of Dargun in Mecklenburg', *Cîteaux: Commentarii Cistercienses* 51 (2000), pp. 5–15.

48. Patrick Brian McGuire, *The Difficult Saint: Bernard of Clairvaux and his Tradition* (Kalamazoo, MI: Cistercian Publications, 1991), p. 292.
49. Terryl Kinder, *Cistercian Europe: Architecture of Contemplation* (Kalamazoo, MI: Cistercian Publications, 2002), p. 85.
50. Mirko Breitenstein, 'Is there a Cistercian Love? Some Considerations on the Virtue of Charity', in *Aspects of Charity: Concern for One's Neighbour in Medieval Vita Religiosa*, ed. Gert Melville (Berlin: Lit Verlag, 2011), p. 65; William of St Thierry, 'De natura et dignitatis amoris', ed. P. Verdeyen, in *Guillelmi a Sancto Theodorico opera Omnia*, vol. 3 (Turnhout: Brepols, 2003), p. 198.
51. Lars-Arne Dannenberg, 'The Juristic Implementation of a Core Monastic Principle', in *Aspects of Charity: Concerns for One's Neighbour in Medieval Vita Religiosa*, ed. Gert Melville (Berlin: Lit, 2011), pp. 14–15; Aelred of Rievaulx, *The Mirror of Charity*, trans. Elizabeth Connor, intro. and notes Charles Dumont (Kalamazoo, MI: Cistercian Publications, 1990), p. 194.
52. Aelred of Rievaulx, *Mirror of Charity*, p. 101.
53. Caroline Walker Bynum, *Jesus as Mother: Studies in the Spirituality of the High Middle Ages* (Berkeley, CA: University of California Press, 1982), pp. 62–66, 80–81; Martha Newman, *The Boundaries of Charity: Cistercian Culture and Ecclesiastical Reform 1098–1180* (Stanford, CA: Stanford University Press, 1996), p. 46; Jean-Baptiste Van Damme, *The Three Founders of Cîteaux: Robert of Molesme, Alberic, and Stephen Harding*, trans. Nicholas Grove and Christian Carr (Kalamazoo, MI: Cistercian Publications, 1998), p. 22.
54. Scott G. Bruce, 'The Origins of Cistercian Sign Language', *Cîteaux: Commentarii Cistercienses* 52 (2001), pp. 176–200, 205; Robert A. Barakat, *The Cistercian Sign Language: A Study in Non-verbal Communication* (Kalamazoo, MI: Cistercian Publications, 1975), pp. 16, 25; Bruno Griesser, 'Ungedruckte Texte zur Zeichensprache in den Klöstern', *Analecta Sacri Ordinis Cisterciensis* 3 (1947), pp. 111–137 (example cited on p. 120).
55. M. Stawski, 'Benedykcja opata cysterskiego w średniowieczu', in *Pelplin, 725 rocznica powstania opactwa cysterskiego. Kulturotwórcza rola cystersów na Kociewiu* (Pelplin-Tczew: Bernardinum, 2002), pp. 361–384.
56. Julie Kerr, *Monastic Hospitality: The Benedictines in England, c. 1070– c. 1250*, Studies in the History of Medieval Religion 32 (Woodbridge: Boydell Press, 2007).
57. James France, 'The Cellarer's Domain – Evidence from Denmark', in *Studies in Cistercian Art and Architecture*, vol. 5, ed. Meredith Parsons Lillich (Kalamazoo, MI: Cistercian Publications, 1998), pp. 2–4.
58. Patrick Brian McGuire, *The Cistercians in Denmark: Their Attitudes, Roles, and Functions in Medieval Society* (Kalamazoo, MI: Cistercian Publications, 1982), p. 215.
59. 'Maroldus tunc temporis armario' was a witness to a charter. Nataša Golob, *Twelfth-Century Cistercian Manuscripts: The Sitticum Collection* (London and Ljubljana: Slovenska knjiga in conjunction with Harvey Miller, 1996), pp. 25, 197.
60. Kinder, *Cistercian Europe*, pp. 362–364.

61. David Bell, 'The English Cistercians and their Practice of Medicine', *Cîteaux: Commentarii Cistercienses* 40 (1989), p. 150.
62. Kinder, *Cistercian Europe*, p. 361.
63. Darrel W. Amundsen, 'Medicine and Faith in Early Christianity', *Bulletin of the History of Medicine* 56 (1982), p. 342; C.H. Talbot, *Medicine in Medieval England* (London: Oldbourne, 1967), p. 180.
64. Peter Fergusson, 'Aelred's Abbatial Residence at Rievaulx Abbey', in *Studies in Cistercian Art and Architecture*, pp. 48, 51.
65. M.K.K. Yearl, 'Medieval Monastic Customeries on *Miniti* and *Infirmi*', in *The Medieval Hospital and Medical Practice*, ed. Barbara S. Bowers (Aldershot: Ashgate Publishing, 2007), pp. 176, 180.
66. *Twelfth-Century Statutes*, 1180: 11.
67. *Twelfth-Century Statutes*, 1180: 2; 1184: 5.
68. *Twelfth-Century Statutes*, 1184: 2; Mirko Breitenstein, *Das Noviziat im hohen Mittelalter. Zur Organisation des Eintrittes bei den Cluniazensern, Cisterziensern und Franziskanern*, Vita Regularis 38 (Münster: Lit Verlag, 2008), pp. 266–269.
69. Caesarius of Heisterbach, *Dialogus miraculorum*, ed. Nikolaus Nösges and Horst Schneider (Turnhout: Brepols, 2009), book 1, chapter 15; book 4, chapter 50.
70. Breitenstein, 'Is there a Cistercian Love?', p. 94.
71. Adam de Perseigne, *Lettres* I, ed. J. Bouvet, Sources Chrétiennes 66 (Paris: Editions du Cerf, 1960), p. 112; Mirko Breitenstein, 'The Novice Master in the Cistercian Order', in *Generations in the Cloister: Youth and Age in Medieval Religious Life*, ed. Sabine von Heusinger and Annete Kehnel (Vienna: Lit Verlag, 2008), pp. 153–154.
72. Bynum, *Jesus as Mother*, pp. 115, 157, 166; Chrysogonus Waddell, 'The Liturgical Dimension of Twelfth-Century Cistercian Preaching', in *Medieval Monastic Preaching*, ed. Carolyn Muessing (Leiden: Brill, 1998), p. 336.
73. Martinus Cawley, 'Four Abbots of the Golden Age of Villers', *Cistercian Studies Quarterly* 27: 4 (1992), p. 305; 'Cronica Villariensis Monasterii', ed. Georg Waitz, in *Monumenta Germaniae Historica*, vol. 25 (Hanover: Impensis Bibliopolii Hahniani, 1880).
74. Jacki Hall, 'East of the Cloister: Infirmaries, Abbot's Lodgings, and Other Chambers', in *Perspectives for an Architecture of Solitude. Essays on Cistercians, Art and Architecture in Honour of Peter Fergusson*, ed. Terryl N. Kinder (Turnhout: Brepols and Cîteaux, 2004), p. 211; *Statuta*, vol. 1, 1205: 10.
75. Hall, 'East of the Cloister', p. 206.
76. Harper-Bill, 'Cistercian Visitation', p. 106.
77. Harper-Bill, 'Cistercian Visitation', p. 106.
78. *Chronica Monasterii de Melsa*, ed. E.A. Bond, Rolls Series 43, vol. 3 (London: Longmans, Green, Reader, and Dyer, 1868).
79. Immo Eberl, *Die Zisterzienser: Geschichte eines europäischen Ordens* (Ostfildern: Jan Thorbecke, 2007), pp. 182–183; *Twelfth-Century Statutes*, pp. 33–36.
80. Jens Rüffer, 'Gedächtnis und Tradition. Der Kapitelsaal als Begräbnisort Anmerkungen zu zisterziensischen Grablegen in Yorkshire', in *Sachkultur*

und religiöse Praxis (Berlin: Lukas Verlag, 2007), pp. 61–76; Kinder, *Cistercian Europe*, pp. 245–268.

81. Otto von Freising, 'Chronica sive Historia de duabus civitatibus', in *Monumenta Germaniae Historica, Scriptores Rerum Germanicarum in usum scholarum*, ed. Adolf Hofmeister (Hanover: Impensis bibliopolii Hahniani, 1912), pp. 371–372; Gert Melville, 'Construction and Deconstruction of Religious Symbols in the Middle Ages', in *Self-Representation of Medieval Religious Communities: The British Isles in Context*, ed. Anne Müller and Karen Stöber (Münster: Lit Verlag, 2009), p. 12.
82. *Statuta*, vol. 1, 1181: 2. It is not known if the lay brothers participated in the election prior to that time.
83. James S. Donnelly, *The Decline of the Medieval Cistercian Lay Brotherhood* (New York: Fordham University Press, 1949), pp. 8–11.
84. Newman, *The Boundaries of Charity*, pp. 28–29.
85. *Cistercian Lay Brothers: Twelfth-Century Usages with Related Texts*, ed. Chrysogonus Waddell, Studia et Documenta, vol. 10 (Brecht: Cîteaux – Commentarii Cistercienses, 2000), pp. 57–62, 68.
86. *Twelfth-Century Statutes*, 1188: 10.
87. J.M. Trout, 'The Monastic Vocation of Alain of Lille', *Analecta Cisterciensia* 30 (1974), pp. 46–53.
88. Reinhard Schneider, *Von Klosterhaushalt zum Stadt- und Staatshaushalt: der Zisterziensische Beitrag* (Stuttgart: Anton Hiersemann, 1994), pp. 60–70.
89. Constance Berman, 'Distinguishing between the Humble Peasant and Lay Brother and Sister, and the Converted Knight in Medieval Southern France', in *Religious and Laity*, pp. 265–267; James Donnelly, *The Decline of the Medieval Cistercian Laybrotherhood* (New York: Fordham University Press, 1949), pp. 20–21.
90. Eberl, *Die Zisterzienser*.
91. *Statuta*, 1237: 3; Kinder, *Cistercian Europe*, p. 310.
92. Otto Volk, *Salzproduktion und Salzhandel mittelalterlicher Zisterzienserklöster* (Sigmaringen: Thorbecke, 1984), p. 30.
93. *Statuta*, vol. 3, 1292: 5; Kinder, *Cistercian Europe*, p. 308.
94. Heinrich Grüger, 'Der Nekrolog des Klosters Heinrichau (ca. 1280–1550)', *Archiv für schlesiche Kirchengeschichte* 31 (1973), pp. 57, 60; H. Meyer zu Ermgassen, 'Congregatio Eberbacensis', *Hessisches Jahrbuch für Landesgeschichte* 33 (1983), pp. 32–35; Michał Kaczmarek, 'Familiares klasztoru Kamienieckiego w świetle nekrologu', *Acta Universitatis Wratislaviensis, Historia* 77 (1989), pp. 179–187.
95. Reinhard Schneider, 'Garciones oder pueri abbatum – Zum Problem bewaffneter Dienstleute bei den Zisterziensern', in *Zisterzienser-Studien I* (Berlin: Colloquim Verlag Berlin), pp. 25–28.
96. *Cistercian Lay Brothers: Twelfth-Century Usages*, p. 78.
97. Marsha L. Dutton, 'The Conversion and Vocation of Aelred of Rievaulx: A Historical Hypothesis', in *England in the Twelfth Century: Proceedings of the 1989 Harlaxton Symposium*, ed. Daniel Williams (Woodbridge: Boydell, 1990), pp. 31–50; Douglas Roby, 'Chimera of the North: The Active Life of Ailred of Rievaulx', in *Cistercian Ideals and Reality*, ed. John

R. Somemerfeldt, Cistercian Studies Series 50 (Kalamazoo, MI: Cistercian Publications, 1978), pp. 152–169.
98. Brian Noell, 'Scholarship and Activism at Cîteaux in the Age of Innocent III', *Viator* 38 (2007), pp. 35–38.
99. *Chronicles of the Reigns of Stephen, Henry I and Richard I*, ed. R. Howlett, Rolls Series, 4 vols. (London: Longman, 1884–89), vol. 1, pp. 147–148; *The Acts of Malcolm IV King of Scots*, ed. G.W.S. Barrow (Edinburgh: Edinburgh University Press, 1960), p. 22.
100. *The Heads of Religious Houses: England and Wales*, ed. David Knowles, C.N.L. Brooke and Vera C.M. London, 3 vols. (Cambridge: Cambridge University Press, 1972–2008), vol. 1, p. 140; vol. 2, p. 302.
101. Dauvit Broun, 'Melrose Abbey and its World', in *The Chronicle of Melrose Abbey: A Stratigraphic Edition*, ed. Dauvit Broun and Julian Harrison, vol. 1 (Woodbridge: Boydell, 2007), p. 5, n. 24; *Chronicle of Melrose from the Cottonian Manuscript, Faustina B. IX in the British Museum: A Complete and Full-size Facsimile in Collotype*, ed. and intro. Alan Orr Anderson and Marjorie Ogilvie Anderson; index William Croft Dickinson (London: Percy Lund Humphries, 1936), p. 129, lxiv; *A Mediaeval Chronicle of Scotland: The Chronicle of Melrose*, trans. Joseph Stevenson (Lampeter: Llanerch, 1991), p. 103.
102. Brunsch, *Das Zisterzienserkloster Heisterbach*, p. 111.
103. Zbigniew Piłat, 'Les Reseau des Cisterciens en Europe du Centre-Est', in *Unanimité et Diversité*, p. 443.
104. Eberl, *Die Zisterzienser*, pp. 50–81.
105. *Twelfth-Century Statutes*, 1197: 22, 1197: 31, 1199: 16.
106. Piłat, 'Les Reseau des Cisterciens', p. 443.
107. Brian Patrick McGuire, 'Was Bernard a Friend?', in *Goad and Nail*, ed. E. Rozanne Elder, Studies in Medieval Cistercian History 10 (Kalamazoo, MI: Cistercian Publications, 1985), p. 208.
108. McGuire, 'Was Bernard a Friend?', pp. 208–211; Bernard of Clairvaux, 'The Life of Saint Malachy', in *The Life and Death of Saint Malachy the Irishman*, trans. Robert T. Meyer (Kalamazoo, MI: Cistercian Publications, 1978), p. 53.
109. Marie Therese Flanagan, 'Irish Royal Charters and the Cistercian Order', in *Charters and Charter Scholarship in Britain and Ireland*, ed. Marie Therese Flanagan and Judith A. Green (Basingstoke: Palgrave Macmillan, 2005), pp. 122–125.
110. James France, *The Cistercians in Scandinavia* (Kalamazoo, MI: Cistercian Publications, 1992), pp. 77–98.
111. Kinder, *Cistercian Europe*, pp. 82, 85.
112. Andrew Jotischky, *The Perfection of Solitude: Hermits and Monks in the Crusader States* (University Park, PA: Pennsylvania State University Press), pp. 58–62, 133.
113. Nicky Tsougarakis, 'On the Frontier of the Orthodox and Latin World: Religious Patronage in Medieval Frankish Greece', in *Monasteries on the Borders of Medieval Europe*, ed. Emilia Jamroziak and Karen Stöber (Turnhout: Brepols, 2013).

114. Joseph F. O'Callaghan, 'The Affiliation of the Order of Caltrava with the Order of Cîteaux', *Analecta Sacri Ordinis Cisterciensis* 15 (1959), pp. 180–187.
115. Winfried Schich, 'Zum Wirken der Zisterzienser im östlichen Mitteleuropa im 12. und 13. Jahrhundert', in *Zisterziensische Spiritualität: theologische Grundlagen, funktionale Voraussetzungen und bildhafte Ausprägungen im Mittelalter*, ed. Clemens Kasper and Klaus Schreiner (St Ottilien: EOS Verlag, 1994), pp. 269–277.
116. Stella Maria Szacherska, 'The Political Role of the Danish Monasteries in Pomerania 1171–1223', *Medieval Scandinavia* 10 (1977), pp. 143–144, n. 147.
117. Nils Blumkvist, Stefan Brink and Thomas Lindkvist, 'The Kingdom of Sweden', in *Christianizaton and Rise of Christian Monarchy. Scandinavia, Central Europe and Rus' c. 900–1200*, ed. Nora Berend (Cambridge: Cambridge University Press, 2007), pp. 197–198, 202, 205; Anna Waśko, 'Rola klasztorów i zakonników w okresie "modernizacji" Królestwa Szwecji w latach 1250–1319', in *Klasztor w społeczeństwie średniowiecznym i nowożytnym*, ed. Marek Derwich and Anna Pobóg-Lenartowicz (Opole: LARHCOR, 1996), pp. 206–207.
118. Kinder, *Cistercian Europe*, p. 285.
119. James France, 'Riddle of the Northmost Cistercian Abbey in Europe', *Cistercian Studies Quarterly* 28: 3/4 (1993), pp. 261–275.
120. *Statuta*, vol. 2, 1221: 52, vol. 2, 1222: 20; vol. 3, 1263: 21.
121. 'Margareta, pia femina, in episcopatu Rosqueliae, a barbaro marito die vexata, ac tandem crudeliter interfecta, et sacri cadaveris integritate et aliis miraculis divinitus illustratur', 'Herberti Turrium Sardiniae Archiepiscopi de Miraculis Libri Tres', *Patrologia Latina*, ed. Jacques-Paul Migne (Paris, 1855), vol. 185, col. 1378; Stella Maria Szacherska, 'Cykl duńsko-słowiański w nie publikowanym rękopisie *Księgi Cudów* Herberta', appendix in her *Rola klasztorów duńskich w ekspansji Danii na Pomorzu Zachodnim u schyłku XII wieku* (Wrocław, Warszawa and Kraków: Ossolineum, 1968), p. 83.
122. B.W. O'Dwyer, 'The Crisis in Ireland in the Early Thirteenth Century', *Analecta Sacri Ordinis Cisterciensis* 31 (1975), pp. 272–273.
123. *Statuta*, vol. 1, 1216: 32, vol. 1, 1217: 78, vol. 1, 1217: 79, vol. 1, 1217: 25.
124. B.W. O'Dwyer, 'The Crisis in Ireland in the Early Thirteenth Century', *Analecta Sacri Ordinis Cisterciensis* 32 (1976), p. 19.
125. Pryce, 'Patrons and Patronage', p. 84.
126. Noell, 'Scholarship and Activism at Cîteaux', p. 23.
127. Brenda Bolton, 'For the See of Simon Peter: The Cistercians at Innocent III's Nearest Frontier', in *Monastic Studies. The Continuity of Tradition*, ed. Judith Loades (Bangor: Headstart History, 1990), p. 147.
128. Bolton, 'For the See of Simon Peter', pp. 147–149.
129. Beverley Mayne Kienzle, *Cistercians, Heresy, and Crusade in Occitania, 1145–1229* (Woodbridge: Boydell and Brewer, 2001), pp. 144–146, 152–156.
130. Elaine Graham-Leigh, 'Justifying Deaths: the Chronicler Pierre des Vaux-de-Cernay and the Massacre of Béziers', *Medieval Studies* 63 (2001), pp. 283–303.

131. *Statuta*, vol. 3, 1268: 13, vol. 3, 1270: 75, vol. 3, 1272: 4, vol. 3, 1273: 1; Ks. Franciszek Wolnik, 'Wpływ władców i wydarzeń politycznych na kształtowanie się liturgii cystersów w średniowieczu', in *Klasztor w społeczeństwie średniowiecznym*, pp. 390–391.
132. R.I. Moore, *The Formation of a Persecuting Society: Power and Deviance in Western Europe, 950–1250* (Oxford: Blackwell, 1990), pp. 42–45.
133. Norman Cantor, 'Ideological and Cultural Foundations of European Identity in the Middle Ages', in *The Birth of Identities: Denmark and Europe in the Middle Ages*, ed. Brian Patrick McGuire (Copenhagen: C.A. Ritzel Publishers, 1996), p. 17.
134. Christopher Holdsworth, 'Bernard of Clairavulx and European Spirituality', in *The Birth of Identities*, p. 62.
135. Peter Donzelbacher, *Bernhard von Clairvaux* (Darmstadt: Primus, 1998), pp. 291–293.
136. *The Second Crusade: Scope and Consequences*, ed. Jonathan Philips and Martin Hoch (Manchester: Manchester University Press, 2001), p. 4.
137. Jean Leclercq, 'Saint Bernard's Attitude towards War', in *Studies in Medieval Cistercian History*, vol. 2, ed. J. Sommerfeldt (Kalamazoo, MI: Cistercian Publications, 1976), p. 18.
138. Noell, 'Scholarship and Activism at Cîteaux', pp. 28–29.
139. Tore Nyberg, *Monasticism in North-Western Europe, 800–1200* (Aldershot: Ashgate, 2000), pp. 232–238; Stanisław Rosik and Przemysław Urbańczyk, 'Polabia and Pomerania between Paganism and Christianity', in *Christianisation and the Rise of Christian Monarchy*, pp. 300–308.
140. Paul Johansen, 'Dietrich von Treiden', in *Neue Deutsche Biographie*, vol. 3 (1957), p. 69, http://www.deutsche-biographie.de/pnd13726075X.html
141. Christian Krötzl, 'Die Cistercienser und die Mission "ad paganos", ca. 1150–1250', *Analecta Cisterciensia* 61 (2011), pp. 278–298.
142. Priit Raudkivi, 'Cistercians and Livonia: Problems and Perspectives', in *L'espace cistercien*, p. 350.
143. *Pommersches Urkundenbuch*, vol. 1, ed. Robert Klempin (Szczecin: In Commission bei T. von der Nahmer, 1868), no. 5.
144. László Pósán, 'The Invitation of the Teutonic Order into Kulmerland', in *The Crusades and the Military Orders: Expanding the Frontiers of Medieval Latin Christianity*, ed. Zsolt Hunyadi and József Laszlovszky (Budapest: CEU Medievalia, 2001), pp. 430–435.
145. Krystyna Zielińska-Mlekowska, 'Św Chrystian – misyjny biskup Prus', *Nasza Przeszłość* 83 (1994), p. 46.
146. Maja Gąsowska, 'Klasztor cystersek w Rewalu i jego znaczenie dla duńskiego władztwa w Estonii w XIII i XIV w', in *Klasztor w społeczeństwie średniowiecznym*, pp. 212–213; Dariusz Aleksander Dekański, 'Cystersi i dominikanie w Prusach – działanie misyjne zakonów w latach trzydziestych XIII wieku. Rywalizacja czy współpraca?', in *Cystersi w społeczeństwie Europy Środkowej. Materiały z konferencji naukowej odbytej w klasztorze oo. Cystersów w Krakowie Mogile z okazji 900 rocznicy powstania Zakonu Ojców Cystersów. Poznań-Kraków-Mogiła 5–10 października 1998*, ed. Andrzej Marek Wyrwa and Józef Dobosz (Poznań: Wydawnictwo Poznańskie, 2000), pp. 227–249.

chapter 3

CISTERCIAN COMMUNITIES AND THE LAY WORLD

This chapter focuses on the twelfth and thirteenth centuries, before the Cistercian Order had to face the great challenges arising from the development of more rigid political borders, deep socio-economic changes resulting from the Black Death, and the Great Schism. Already, however, Cistercian communities were very much involved with the world around them. If patrons, benefactors and neighbours formed supportive networks, the monks in turn prayed for, commemorated and conducted business with them. Disputes sometimes arose over boundary and property rights, for the neighbours of the Cistercian houses included not only monastic communities belonging to different orders, but also institutions of the secular church – parishes, cathedrals, bishops and the lands they held. Moreover, in many regions wealthy urban strata had also entered into religious and economic relationships with the Cistercian monasteries by the late middle ages. The poor and pilgrims who received monastic charity, albeit condemned to anonymity in the sources, were another notable social group with which Cistercians interacted.

To understand the relationship between the Cistercian Order and the wider world, we need to go back to the ideas underlying the white monks' writings. The prescription of hospitality so central to the Rule of Benedict was one very much embraced by the Cistercians; just as the concept of community and love of one's neighbour was one of the central themes of twelfth-century Cistercian writing.[1] Not that this necessarily meant that Cistercians were always actively serving their fellow men in a practical way: in the writings of Bernard and Ailred, the only concrete examples cited are 'praying for' and 'weeping over'; and, after all, the monks were primarily intercessors for the fate of souls in the next world.[2] Even so, at the core of the monastic–lay relationship was the reciprocity and material support given to the monasteries in return for prayers. By giving donations to the monasteries lay people acknowledged the ideals and vocation which they themselves could not attain, but through their material gifts they could directly benefit from the monks' prayers and good works.³

Although Cistercian monks were cloistered and their contacts with the outside world were heavily restricted, they were always sensitive to the possible implications of such contacts for the corporate image of the Order. In 1186, for example, the General Chapter discussed the exemption of monks from fasting on Fridays during the summer (because they were working in the fields in oppressive heat). The church did not grant such exemptions to the laity, and the assembled abbots were afraid that if the latter observed the fast, while the monks were seen not to do so, this might sit ill with the Order's reputation for asceticism. Public appearances – for example on journeys to meetings of the General Chapter – were also liable to influence the outside world's view of Cistercian monks: in 1181 the General Chapter adjured abbots stopping over in Dijon to refrain from walking around holding hands (as a manifestation of brotherly love) or making themselves conspicuous in any other way.⁴ When two Portuguese abbots and some lay brothers en route to the General Chapter in 1217 stopped in the Benedictine monastery of Marmoutier at Tours and complained very loudly about the poor quality of food offered there, they found themselves denounced to the General Chapter, which condemned the abbots to fast for a day on bread and water at Marmoutier, and the lay brothers to walk 50 miles to the abbey and be whipped in the chapter house there – sentences which were clearly intended to serve both as a deterrent and as a manifestation of Cistercian standards of behaviour.⁵

As the white monks were steeped in deep-rooted monastic traditions, they felt no desire to dismiss altogether either the old-established Carolingian and Ottonian traditions of the 'private' church, or the expectations of lay founders. In practice, the extent of the rights of patrons over Cistercian houses was not static but evolving over time; and the power balance between patrons, benefactors and 'their' monasteries reflected local traditions and preconceptions and had a significant impact on Cistercian monasteries. In the frontier regions of central Europe – Brandenburg, Meißen, Lausitz for example – Cistercian houses tended to follow the 'Hauskloster' model, in which monasteries symbolised the consolidation of the power of their founders and served as a necropolis and a centre of family commemoration.⁶ In other regions – England for example – the abbeys were rather less manifestly dependent on their lay patrons.

Because the intercessory and commemorative activities were so central to the Cistercian mission – indeed, in the eyes of the laity, its most important distinguishing feature – this chapter will examine, first, donations and the relationship between donor and recipient that arose from them; then the ways of commemorating founders and benefactors, culminating in the most lasting form – burials within the Cistercian precinct. The chapter will go on to address the multifaceted issue of hospitality, and the conflicts with patrons that afflicted many Cistercian communities. Finally, it will examine the advantages and difficulties that characterised relations between abbeys and the secular authorities, especially territorial rulers.

Donations and Donors

The relationship between Cistercian monks and their benefactors was based on the concept of reciprocity common to all religious–lay interactions in the middle ages: in return for material donations, usually land, the monks prayed for the salvation of their benefactors. This was the fundamental purpose of the grants and the chief motive of the laity in supporting monastic houses. Sometimes the grant from a lay person would be accompanied by a countergift from monks to the donor – usually a small amount of money, an object (such as a knife, a pair of gloves, or a cloak) or some more valuable item such as a horse or cow – to symbolise not only the goodwill of the monks, but the transfer of property and the promise of prayers and to emphasise the lasting nature of the relationship resulting from the donation. Sometimes these countergifts were given to close relatives of the donors, especially children and spouses, to prevent them objecting to the donation and to confirm their assent to the alienation of the family inheritance.[7] Donations accompanied by countergifts were not in any sense clandestine 'sales' or 'exchanges' – terms used in the charters for other transactions quite different from donations were clearly described in the charters as sales or exchanges. We can find examples of countergifts all over Europe: in Burgundy a grant of pasture to Reigny Abbey in the late twelfth century was accompanied by a number of countergifts to relatives of the donor: a cow for his wife, a brooch for his oldest son, a cape for his second son and two solidi for each of his daughters;[8] and in the charters of grants to Cistercian houses in twelfth- and thirteenth-century Yorkshire we find relatively frequent references to countergifts which the donors felt obliged to accept out of 'necessity' or even 'pressing necessity', so a fairly substantial countergift enabled them to become benefactors even if their resources were relatively limited. Besides, in so far as a countergift provided partial compensation for material losses resulting from donations, perhaps they helped to prevent future disputes.[9]

Certainly, the solemn ceremonies that accompanied a donation were intended to underline its security and permanence. It was common practice across Europe for the donor, his family, kin group, witnesses, local people, abbot and representatives of the monastic community to process along the boundaries of the donated land, often marking it in some way, for example by crosses cut on the trees, which might later be replaced by more permanent stone markers. In the hope of preventing future conflicts, all those involved accepted the boundary line which was enshrined in the memory of the locality as correct. In parts of East-Central Europe in the twelfth century charters became increasingly important and valued as legal proof of rights to a property, and monastic houses including the Cistercians started using them earlier than the laity. They were sealed by both recipient and the donors, if they had their own seal. Sometimes in a further solemn act of the donation ceremony donors had to place the charter of grant on the high altar of the abbey as a promise that its terms would not be broken. This was one of the very few occasions when a layman was allowed into the most sacred spaces of the Cistercian church, normally out of bounds to any outsiders, while the act itself paid tribute to both the awesomeness of the occasion and the fear of ecclesiastical punishment if the grant was revoked.

Occasionally, benefactors would declare their preference for a particlar Cistercian abbey more than any other religious institution. The proprietary language used in the charters included a patron referring to 'my monks'. Earl Conan of Brittany, assuming the role of a patron, effectively funded Jervaulx Abbey (Yorkshire) after 1154, and in the charter recording this act he refers to 'my monks who are there to serve God and pray for me'.[10] A charter of Cecilie, daughter of Peder Ebbesen, specified that her donation to Esrum Abbey was being given to 'the place which I hold in affection before others' (*quem locum pre ceteris affectuosius diligo*).[11] Reference to abbots as 'friends' of the patrons were a further indication of close personal ties. Abbot Dietmar of Kołbacz (1296–1308) was often described in documents as an intimate and special friend (*familiarissimus ac specialissimus*) of the duke of Pomerania. Some of the ducal charters stated specifically that the abbot held a position of close friendship and goodwill at the ducal court (*locum familiaritatis et dilectionis obtinet*).[12]

Patrons, Benefactors and their Rights

In theory, lay patrons of Cistercian monasteries were debarred from exercising what had become customary in Benedictine houses – appointing the abbot, meddling in financial matters and claiming very extensive hospitality rights. Nevertheless, Cistercian houses still needed their patrons to support and defend them, and by the late middle ages the extent of patrons' privileges in relation to houses of different orders was becoming increasingly ill-defined anyway. This can be seen clearly in the case of

England, where by the fourteenth century patrons of houses belonging to all monastic orders enjoyed both spiritual and material benefits – the care of the soul as well as custody of land during the abbatial vacancies, involvement in elections and rights to hospitality. In return, the patron was supposed to show continuing support of the monastery through donations and protection of the community; but by the late middle ages the scale of patron's privileges varied greatly from house to house, whilst variety had become the hallmark of practices between and within the different orders.[13]

The growing assertiveness of lay patrons was felt increasingly in the matter of appointments to monastic offices, though it should be said that they were not acting alone so much as in collusion with members of the community, and with the laity, often their kin. For example, in the late 1390s the monks of Meaux Abbey disputed the appointment of Thomas de Burton as bursar, an office of considerable financial importance, as it provided access to the monastic funds and assets. The abbot claimed that Burton had been imposed on Meaux by the patron, the duke of Gloucester, with the collusion of the father superior, the abbot of Fountains.[14] By the fourteenth and fifteenth centuries, however, not only had many of the original patrons' families died out but many aristocratic families held the patronage over a number of religious institutions. As a result, it was becoming more common for a Cistercian abbey to have a perfunctory, almost non-existent, relationship with the patron, in contrast to the intensive interactions, positive and negative, characteristic of the twelfth and thirteenth centuries.

A circle of benefactors and neighbours whom it could count on as 'friends' was of great important in the life of any Cistercian community, especially if it represented a tradition of continuous support for the monastery over several generations. It included benefactors old and new, neighbours and donors, who, even if they ceased to be active benefactors themselves, continued to witness charters issued by and for the abbey. Not that there was ever an unchanging consistency in the attitudes of any family or kin groups, either within a single generation or over time: as Bouchard put it, 'the laymen, especially with the change in the generations, had a continually shifting view of what their relationship could or should be'.[15] In the thirteenth century donations of land declined, a result partly of the shortage of land for donations, partly of the completion of the process of the creation of Cistercian monastic estates that reduced the need for new grants. Henceforth, support for Cistercian houses more often took the form of witnessing charters, smaller piecemeal donations, exchanges of property, and grants of objects, such as liturgical vessels, vestments and books.

Commemorations of Patrons and Benefactors

The prayers of the monks were, of course, central to the relationship between the monastic communities and the laity. Commemoration of the benefactors included both those departed and those who were still alive, as the intercessory power of the prayers influenced not only the posthumous fate of the soul, but also its fortunes on earth. Some benefactors were very firm about their commemoratory expectations: in his charter for Loos Abbey in Lille (1176) Philip, count of Flanders (1157/68–1191), laid down that the monks 'will hold my commemoration both in death and in life'.[16] Such arrangements were not only indicators of high social prestige – being a patron and benefactor testified to the possession of extensive material means that made such acts possible – but were held to be of vital spiritual importance as recognised expressions of piety, always highly valued in medieval society: concerns about the posthumous fate of the soul was alleviated by the promise of perpetual prayers. The Cistercians adopted a number of established forms of liturgical commemoration, one of the oldest being inscribing the names of individuals in special books, which were placed on the altar during the mass. Such volumes (sometimes rolls) were believed to help in the salvation of souls. Historians have a variety of names for them – *libri vitae*, *libri mortuorum*, obituary or mortuary rolls, or necrologies – and they vary in their design, but all can be called 'commemorative records'.[17]

Prayers for the dead were not only an obligation on the living, but a key element in the whole reciprocity circle, creating lasting ties between monasteries and successive generations of the families of benefactors. The long-established Benedictine tradition of commemoration, which the Cistercian order inherited, had already been taken further – perhaps too far – by Cluniac houses, with their daily liturgies for the benefit of an ever-growing number of individuals, and daily distribution of large quantities of food to the poor, in the name of their dead benefactors and friends. All this imposed not only a great economic burden on Cluny but also unmanageable organisational burdens, and Abbot Peter the Venerable of Cluny tried to reform this system without much success.[18]

The Cistercians adopted a far more radical approach, drastically reducing the principle of individual commemoration in favour of annual cumulative prayers for whole groups of people: on 11 January the white monks prayed for all the benefactors of the orders and on 20 November for the members of other monasteries in a prayer confraternity with the Cistercians – Cluny, Carthusians, Augustinian Canons and Premonstratensians, the Benedictine Abbey of Monte Cassino and several houses in Burgundy.[19] The individual *familiares* – supporters and benefactors of the order – were prayed for on

17 September (15 September after 1187). Every day, except on certain holy days (Good Friday, Holy Saturday, Christmas, Easter and Pentecost), Cistercians celebrated a special mass for all the deceased members and *familiares* of the Order. Later, an additional mass was added, in honour of the Virgin Mary, for all the benefactors of the Order. Despite that, strong demands persisted for individual commemorations. After 1183 many individual houses petitioned the central Cistercian government to enter prayer community with them (sometimes in vain); and by 1200 the General Chapter had granted this privilege to some 50 individuals – royalty and high nobility, including King Louis VII of France (1120–1180), King Richard I of England (1157–1199), and Matthew of Ajello, chancellor of the king of Sicily (d. 1193). Individual abbeys compiled their own lists of benefactors, but excluded individual commemoration of the monks' relatives, who felt aggrieved about this.[20] Indeed, in the thirteenth century the persisting belief in the effectiveness of Cistercian prayers of intercession gave rise to a whole flurry of appeals to the General Chapter from various European monarchs concerned for their own and their families' salvation: Philip III of France (1270–1285), Charles I of Sicily (1266–1282), Alfons X of Castile (1252–1284), James I of Aragon (1213–1276) and Edward I of England (1272–1307), as well as the dukes of Burgundy, Brittany, Flanders and their wives and relatives.[21] The upshot was that the ban, or even limitation, on individual commemorations proved impossible to sustain, as the laity continued to see them the best guarantee of social prestige in this world and salvation in the next. At the same time, the very exclusivity of entry into the prayer community of Cistercian houses that made it so attractive to the laity gave the monastic communities a handy tool for 'rewarding' individuals who were particularly useful to them.[22]

Indeed, by the thirteenth century the noting down of names of departed friends and supporters of the abbey and their commemoration had become, and was to remain, an established feature of Cistercian practice. According to the writer of an early fifteenth-century copy of the necrology of Pelplin Abbey (Pomerania), the fraternity system regulated by the Cistercian order and agreed by the Pelplin chapter conferred on all these whose names were recorded in the book a share in all liturgical and charitable works of the abbey – masses, psalms, vigils, bodily mortifications, individual prayers and alms. Moreover, their membership, and the benefits that flowed from it, were to last 'until the end of the world'.[23]

Outside the fraternity system, many monasteries made 'individual agreements' with the lay people, setting up permanent mechanisms for liturgical commemorations. These devices were usually attached to a donation to be enacted after death: King Valdemar IV Atterdag of Denmark (d. 1375) bequeathed 50 silver marks for daily masses for his soul and a yearly pittance for all the monks in his remembrance, consisting of a three-course meal and a barrel of German beer at Esrum Abbey (for a general discussion of pittances see chapter 8).[24] His daughter, Queen Margaret I, augmented these arrangements for the fate of his soul by further donations and also, with papal permission, transferred his body to Sorø Abbey. In 1378 Margaret gave Abbot Troels of Naestved Abbey a golden reliquary in return for daily masses for her parents. On the anniversary of their deaths, all the ordained monks and secular priests from neighbouring parishes were obliged to celebrate the mass.[25] For the well-being of her own soul, and those of her parents and grandparents and her own son Olaf II, Queen Margaret donated valuable land to Esrum Abbey in 1400. Her mother was buried in the monastic church of the same abbey, and the bequest specified, in return, daily masses in the monks' choir above her mother's resting place, followed by the hymn *Salve Regina*. A candle was to burn there every day and, after consuming a yearly pittance, the monks were obliged to sing another Marian hymn, *O florens Rosa*.[26]

The importance of founders and patrons was clear from the presence of their images within the monastic precinct – visual manifestations of the bond between the abbey and its benefactors, friends and supporters. Such images could also serve to cement new bonds with families or individuals who had 'arrived on the scene', leading them to become important figures in a Cistercian house, sometimes even replacing the original patronal family. One of the most spectacular examples comes from a series of wall paintings in the chapel of St James in Ląd Abbey. The chapel had been founded by Count Wierzbięta, whom King Kazimir the Great had put in charge of Greater Poland between 1352 and 1369. His family and wider kin had no prior connection with the abbey, but as Wierzbięta came into regular contact with this Cistercian house in his official capacity, a personal bond developed between them. Wierzbięta's coat of arms and those of his political allies were incorporated in the frieze of the wall painting. The central scene shows the kneeling donor with his wife and daughter presenting a model of the chapel to St James, with the abbot of Ląd Abbey and a group of monks standing behind the saintly recipient. The rest of the chapel is decorated with biblical scenes, universal and local saints, and the figures of St Benedict and Bernard of Clairvaux, the whole seamlessly encompasses both religious and political messages.[27] In the altarpiece depicting the birth of Christ on the high altar of Vyšši Bród Abbey, benefactor Peter von Rosenberg, treasurer of the kingdom of Bohemia (d. 1349), identifiable from his coat of arms, is depicted kneeling and holding a model of the monastic church; and in the fifteenth-century *Nota fundatores monasterii Altiuadensis* Peter is described as *specialis promotor ac fundator*, especially generous to the upkeep of the fabric of the church and the monastic hospital.[28] Such decorative programmes made abundantly clear who was the donor and what was the object of donation: if founders held models of churches, benefactors were shown holding other objects which they had donated. These visual representations were both reminders of the donations and integral parts of the commemoration. Moreover, as representations of founders and donors holding models of churches and abbeys were part of a long tradition going back to the sixth century, their appearance in Cistercian houses is yet another example of continuity of much older customs connected with lay–monastic interactions.[29]

Perhaps not surprisingly the form and content of these representations was an important vehicle for preserving communal memory: when Abbot Berthold von Rosswag commissioned a number of wall paintings for Maulbronn Abbey church in the mid-fifteenth century, one of them depicted the founder, Walter von Lomersheim, resplendent in his heraldic coat of arms and wearing fashionable, late medieval armour. Although dead for three centuries, Walter remained an important element of Maulbronn's identity.[30] Not only were individual founders visually commemorated, but whole kinship groups. When a new fountain house (*lavatorium*) was built in 1295 at Heiligenkreuz Abbey, it contained a set of windows with a representation of the whole family tree of the Babenbergs from whom the abbey's founder, Margrave Leopold III (d. 1136) descended. The abbey, together with Klosterneuburg Priory (an Augustinian house), was also the family mausoleum. That the founder of Heiligenkreuz was depicted with a model of the monastic church was conventional enough, but what is interesting is that the Babenbergs' commemoration was installed after the male line had died out. The renewed interest in visual representation of the founders dates from the time when the Habsburgs had become rulers of the area, taking Heiligenkreuz under their protection and confirming all the grants and privileges of their predecessors. Although some have seen the support given to the abbey by the new rulers as intended to strengthen their claim to the Babenberg inheritance, the fact that the founder's image and the family tree were located in an area accessible only to the monastic community would point to a concern for the duty of commemoration and prayers rather than about political advantage.[31]

Although representations of patrons and benefactors in person were the most striking way to commemorate their connection to the monastic houses, the display of heraldic shields was another popular method of publicising the ties between Cistercian monasteries and the laity – and not just with individuals but with whole kin groups too. In Maulbronn

Abbey, a frieze with heraldic shields was painted over the arcades of the four east bays of the nave at the end of the thirteenth or the beginning of the fourteenth century. Over 20 of them have been identified as belonging to particular families who had been longstanding benefactors of Maulbronn and several of whom were also buried in the abbey.[32]

At the other end of the scale, even small objects could serve as links between the benefactors and the abbey and reminders of perpetual commemoration. In 1230 the provost of the collegiate church of St Peter's in Leuven donated four books to Villers Abbey, explaining that he was doing this 'in alms for the salvation of my soul, that my name is written down at the beginning of each book so that henceforth my commemoration will be held in blessing by these monks'.[33]

Lay Burials

Lay burials were one of the principal manifestations of the commemorative and intercessory function of the monastic houses. Although Cistercian monasteries were very restrictive in allowing access to the living laity, burials of lay men and women within the monastic precinct were fairly commonplace. Here again, as so often in their relations with the wider social world, Cistercians inherited a well-established tradition, according to which burials in holy ground, near the relics of saints, were held to afford 'benefit' from their proximity to the regularly performed masses and other liturgical activities of the monks; and the intercessory power and social prestige attached to them made Benedictine and Cluniac houses real 'magnets' for lay burials, in which commemoration featured very prominently. By the time the Cistercians emerged the notion was widely accepted that patrons had an entitlement to be buried in 'their' monasteries; but the General Chapter, while aware of these expectations, did not automatic permit such burials. Indeed, a Cistercian statute of 1180 restricted secular burials in the monastic churches to kings, queens and bishops – a prescription frequently reiterated until 1316, when prelates were added to this exclusive group.[34]

The importance of burials as tools for creating and sustaining relationships with the outside world had been appreciated from very early times, as several statutes bore witness. From *c.* 1147 an abbey's servants who died within the precinct were allowed to be buried in the monastic cemetery alongside a limited number of 'friends', most likely particularly important benefactors and supporters, *familiares* and their wives. In 1179, in response to growing pressure, the General Chapter allowed burials of founders and anybody else who could not be refused without 'causing a scandal'. Of course, 'scandal' was to be avoided as detrimental to the fortunes of monastic communities, and the regulation of the General Chapter gave monasteries a free hand in deciding on the burials of founders and other powerful individuals who might have a sense of entitlement. A detailed codification of 1202 listed the people who could be buried in Cistercian houses – founders, their descendants (patrons), and guests, two *familiares* with their wives, servants and travellers, and in 1217 a further clarification noted that lay burials had become a widespread phenomenon, stating simply that burials of lay people in the Cistercian cemeteries were subject to a licence from the parish priest of the 'applicant' in question.[35]

In fact, even when the early restrictions were operative they did not appear to have been implemented with much vigour, and lay burials were widely accepted, particularly on the peripheries of the Cistercian order. Already by the 1180s Melrose Abbey in Scotland, for example, was accepting many interments of both men and women, many of them in the Chapter House, a practice continued in the next century – all of which reflected the pragmatic approach of many Cistercian leaders ready to give the cultivation of good relations with powerful supporters precedence over uniformity of practice regarding burials.

The position of the General Chapter itself changed in the course of the thirteenth century. Explicit blanket prohibitions ceased, and attention focused on the specific locations of the burials and on banning interments in the most sacred parts of the monastic precincts – chapter houses and churches. Although we have a number of General Chapter rulings from the late twelfth century, punishing abbots for allowing lay burials in the chapter houses or the monastic churches, there was no consistency even here. The cases in question related only to houses in France and Germany, while elsewhere lay burials were rife. Indeed, the process proved unstoppable, and by 1300 the opening of Cistercian churches to a much wider spectrum of lay people was creating a demand for more burial space, leading to the construction of special chapels located to the east end of the nave (see chapter 5).[36]

It was very much in line with older tradition that a number of Cistercian houses – like many Benedictine houses – were founded specifically as family necropolises: Doberan Abbey, founded by the dukes of Mecklenburg in 1171, continued to serve as their necropolis for hundreds of years, until its dissolution in the Reformation. Sorø Abbey, founded by the Hvide family in the early 1160s, was described in the Sorø Donation Book of *c.* 1210 as founded 'in honour of God and as a family sepulchre', whilst Bishop Peder of Roskilde noted that Sorø Abbey, 'as is well-known, was founded by our ancestors as a burial for our family'.[37] Nunneries were even more prominent than male houses in this particular role. A number of Cistercian female houses in Champagne were active in commemoration of local nobility, especially knights who made bequests before embarking on the journey to the crusades in the Holy Land and were eventually buried in Cistercian nunneries. Very typical of such relationships was Erard of Jaucourt, whose father Peter founded a Cistercian nunnery, Val-des-Vignes, near the family castle in southern Champagne in 1232. Before going on crusade with King Louis IX in 1270 Erard prepared a will containing a bequest to the nuns and deposited the document with them. After his death on the crusade his body was transported back to France and he was buried, alongside his father, at Val-des-Vignes nunnery.[38]

The Cistercian nunnery in Trzebnica was founded in 1202 by Duke Henry the Bearded of Silesia and his wife Hedwig in 1202 as their burial place. The founders were particularly generous both in the endowment and their subsequent grants, and the monastic church provided an impressive setting for the ducal mausoleum and the liturgical commemorations. After the death of Duke Henry in 1238, the widowed Hedwig retired to the abbey. The second abbess was the daughter of the founder – Gertrude – who initiated the foundation of the daughter houses in Owińska and Obłok using her family connection. In 1268 Gertrude succeeded in carrying through the canonisation of her mother Hedwig, after which, as a thriving pilgrimage centre, Trzebnica Abbey acquired a desirable holy status for the commemoration of the dead dukes.[39] Other members of royal or ducal families favoured Cistercian monasteries for their burials, including a number of the Wittelsbachs (buried in Fürstenfeld Abbey), Hohenstaufens (in Schönau Abbey), kings of Spain and Bohemia, Queen Gertrude of Hungary and the counts of Savoy, who made Hautecombe Abbey near lake Geneva a family necropolis.[40]

By the late thirteenth century burial at Cistercian houses was not confined to the very highest echelons of society, but was on offer, all over Europe, to lesser nobility or even wealthy peasants. Thirteenth-century requests for burials in Fountains Abbey reveal a whole cross-section of Yorkshire society, including a substantial number of peasants and several cases of burials from the same family over three generations.[41] These burials often took form of 'countergift': references to lay burials appear in the charters of grants, confirmations or in quitclaims of disputed properties, the grants, or the confirmations, being given 'with the body', i.e. the donor expected burials and commemoration as a countergift from the monastic community.[42]

Such burials usually took place in the monastic cemetery outside the walls of the church. Clearly, Cistercian monasteries stuck to their hierarchy of accessibility for the dead as well as for the living. The chapter house, the cloister walks and the monastic church were the most important locations – they were all liturgical spaces (see chapter 5) – and other features might enhance their significance and spiritual power. The presence of shrines was highly valued. Only when the shrine of Abbot William of Rievaulx was moved in 1250 to the entrance of the chapter house did the neighbouring space in the cloister gallery become attractive for burials.[43]

As the chapter house was so central to the life of the Cistercian community (see chapters 2 and 5), it was perhaps appropriate that the abbots should be buried there, their presence at the very heart of the community continuing, so to speak, after their deaths.[44] Lay people who were buried in the chapter houses were also held to be enjoying eternal benefit from the intercessory power of the activities that went on there. We do not know how many of the Cistercian chapter houses allowed lay burials, as written documentation was never consistent, nor have archaeological excavations been comprehensive. One of the houses which is well documented in this respect is Melrose Abbey. The thirteenth-century monastic chronicle and a separate early fourteenth-century burial list subsequently bound in the volume list 11 lay burials in the chapter house. These burials date from 1185 to 1247, but it is very likely that the others took place before and after these dates. The people interred there came from political elites closely associated with the Scottish royal court – chamberlains, royal constables, justiciars – which is not surprising since Melrose was founded by King David I, and they include one woman, Christina Corbet, the wife of William, son of the earl of Dunbar, whose family were long-standing benefactors of the abbey.[45]

The monastic church (see chapter 5) was normally out of bounds to the laity, who were only allowed to enter it on rare ceremonial occasions. The liturgical significance of the monastic church was graduated from west to east. The earliest of the lay burials in Cistercian churches started to appear first in the west porch (or *paradiscus*, also known as narthex or Galilee porch), which was the most 'secular', being the furthest away from the high altar. The choir of the lay brothers, and especially the area in front of the cross-altar, became popular locations for the aristocratic burials around 1300.[46]

The area around the high altar was the most sacred of all and patronal tombs appeared there mostly in the thirteenth and fourteenth centuries. In Lilienfeld Abbey (Lower Austria) Duke Leopold VI of Babenberg (d. 1230) and his daughter Margareta (d. 1267) were buried between the pillars of the ambulatory, giving them particularly close proximity to the high altar.[47] In Doberan Abbey an even more eminent location, in the ambulatory chapel, was given to one of its prominent benefactress, Queen Margaret of Denmark (d. 1282), who is represented in a monumental tomb sculpture *c.* 1300 realistically depicting details of her fine clothes, jewellery and royal crown.[48]

The fashion among the aristocracy and royalty for 'divided burials' (or parts of bodies) was also taken up by the Cistercian abbeys,[49] perhaps the most notable example being the heart burial of King Robert I of Scotland in Melrose Abbey, which carried important religious and symbolic connotations.[50] In Würzburg, after the death in 1287 of Bishop Bertold von Sterneberg, whose heart was buried by the high altar of Ebrach Abbey, it became customary for his successors too, as official 'protectors and defenders' of the abbey, to have their embalmed hearts displayed on the high altar 'for all to see'.[51]

Not all Cistercian abbeys were equally enthusiastic about lay burials. Rievaulx Abbey, the mother house of Melrose, was distinctly slow in allowing lay burials in the monastic church and only in the fourteenth century did the tombs of the patrons appear in the east end of the building. By the early sixteenth century, however, lay burials attracting a wide social spectrum had become a well-established practice at Rievaulx too. A will of John Clairvaux in 1510 specified a request for a burial in the choir of the Rievaulx Abbey church, supported by the establishment of a chantry; and in 1515 a will of Sir Ralph Scrope, from a leading Yorkshire gentry family, also requested burial in the abbey church, accompanied by a bequest for prayers.[52] Similarly in Denmark, when Gyde, widow of Esbern Karlsen, bequeathed 20 marks and an attractive piece of land to Sorø Abbey in 1292, she requested a burial in the monastery, adding that after the funeral the velvet pall covering the coffin should be used to make a chasuble for monks performing masses.[53]

While a sudden change of the burial location might be indicative of conflicts between patrons and monastic houses, they might also just be a result of changing fashions. Successive members of the Courtenay family, patrons of Forde Abbey, were buried there until a conflict between them and the monks in the fourteenth century drove the Courtenays to opt for burials in the less impressive parish church of Cowick (Devon).[54] Rievaulx Abbey became the necropolis of its patrons, the Ros family, only in the fourteenth century. Previously they had been buried in Kirkham Priory (Augustinian), their favoured religious house, much smaller than Rievaulx, but willing to be ruled by its patrons in a way which the Cistercian abbey was not. The priory's gate was decorated with the family coats of arms and the church came to be dominated by the Ros family tombs, notably the splendid marble tomb of Robert III de Ros, the son of William de Ros who had quarrelled for decades with Rievaulx Abbey (see below).[55] Finally, in some Cistercian houses lay burials reflected political alliances. Whilst those in south Wales were closely linked to the incoming Anglo-Norman aristocracy, others in north Wales became burial places of the native Welsh princes, their patrons and benefactors: Valle Crucis Abbey became a necropolis for Madog ap Gruffudd (d. 1236) and his sons, Strata Florida for the Lord Rhys family, while the vernacular poem *Brut* lists some 20 Welsh noblemen and women who were buried and commemorated there.[56]

It is worth noting here that certain visual aspects of patrons' commemoration (see chapter 5), namely the forms of the tombs, reflected changing fashions. The earliest lay burials, in the twelfth and early thirteenth century, were often marked by very simple, rudimentary tombs. The earliest effigies appeared in the late thirteenth century, and those of a number of lay people in abbeys all over the British Isles – Dore, Deer, Dundrennan, Fountains, Furness, Hailes, Jervaulx, Kirkstead, Margam, Neath and Strata Florida – reveal a growing complexity and level of detail as they evolved into three-dimensional sculptures.[57] In the fourteenth and fifteenth centuries monumental brasses became fashionable for high-status burials in parish churches, monasteries and friaries throughout Europe, especially in France, Italy and the Iberian Peninsula. In England, the examples of existing 'shadows' of imposing brass tombs of several high aristocrats buried in St Mary Graces Abbey in London in the late fifteenth and early sixteenth century indicate that it was a fashionable option in the later middle ages.[58]

The close connections between Cistercian communities and the secular church were reflected in the burials of prelates. The burials of bishops in the monasteries were often an offshoot of the friendship network described in chapter 1 and an expression of particular political alliances and ties of patronage. Although it was not unusual for Cistercian monks to become bishops, especially in the first half of the twelfth century, Melrose Abbey, with six bishops appointed from among its monks between 1171 and 1241, was something of an exception. Among them was Jocelin, first prior, then abbot (1170) of Melrose, and four years later he was elected as the bishop of Glasgow with strong royal backing.[59] Jocelin maintained a close connection with his old house, appearing frequently in the witness lists of Melrose charters, and was eventually buried in the monks' choir in the north end of the abbey's church.[60] His tomb was prepared in advance, indicating that he had Melrose in mind as his last resting place for some time.[61] The second episcopal burial at Melrose was that of William, bishop of Glasgow (d. 1258), who was buried near the high altar. He had been royal chancellor at the time of his election to the bishopric in 1233, which, as in Jocelin's case, reflected the influence of the kings of Scotland as patrons of Melrose.[62] There were also several instances across Europe of prominent bishops and archbishops who chose to be buried in Cistercian abbeys rather than their cathedrals, often for personal reasons: Bishop Friedrich II of Cologne was buried in Altenberg

Abbey (1158), a foundation of his brother; and Bishop Hermann of Münster was buried in Marienfeld Abbey (1203), of which he was himself a co-founder and where he came shortly before his death.[63]

Both lay and episcopal burials in the Cistercian houses must, of course, be considered in the wider context of *memoria*. The graves were reminders of the commemorative obligation that the monastic communities took upon themselves and it was important to remember who was buried and where; and the *Chronicle of Melrose* scrupulously recorded the deaths of benefactors and the location of their burials in the abbey, according to the year of their death. Similarly, the fifteenth-century *Liber ordinarius* of Bebenhausen enjoined on the community the obligation to perform the masses for the dead for those 'who are laying with us in the chapter house'.[64] Altogether, therefore, the burials that symbolised the eternal presence of the deceased patrons and benefactors gave rise to a host of written and other visual records; the presence of living lay persons within the Cistercian precincts, by contrast, through perhaps equally important and frequent, has left far fewer traces in the sources.

Hospitality

Among many of the 'founding myths' in *Exordium Parvum* is a story that before the abbacy of Harding the dukes of Burgundy held court in Cîteaux until the practice was abolished as a symbol of lay interference.[65] It is true that the Cistercians were protective of their own spaces and selective in the admission of outsiders; but they were also guided by the Rule of Benedict and their own regulations – especially *Ecclesiastica Officia* – which ranked hospitality high among monastic obligations. The prescription to show kindness to guests was frequently repeated by the General Chapter, and although guest numbers in Cistercian houses were probably lower than in Benedictine ones, it remained an important part of the white monks' ethos.[66] After all, monastic hospitality was an old tradition inherited from the Benedictine customs, and the Cistercians tried to model their own rituals closely on the prescriptions of the Rule of Benedict – for example rituals of prostration in front of the guests, and hand- and foot-washing as symbols of humility. Indeed, because Benedictines and Cluniacs took to practising these rituals in an abbreviated form, they incurred a good deal of criticism from the Cistercians.[67]

Guests were accommodated in the guesthouses, usually located west of the lay brothers' range (see chapter 5) – so as to minimise contact with the monastic community. Upon arrival, the guests' first contact was with the porter and during their stay they were well looked after by the guest-master. The guests were expected to pray separately from the monastic community, usually either in the gate chapel or in the Galilee porch in the most western section of the church, behind the lay brothers' section. Typically for the period, food played a major role in the hosting of guests. Feasts were an important element of medieval hospitality in both secular and ecclesiastical contexts. A separate kitchen catered for the abbot and his guests, who were offered far richer food than that given to the community, but had to adhere to the fasting principle on the prescribed days. One of the reasons for the development of impressive abbatial houses was precisely the need for an appropriate ambiance for entertaining important guests (see chapter 5). It is clear that it was common practice in Cistercian monasteries for the abbot to eat with his guests, but it continued to be a 'grey area' for the Order's authorities: Abbot Herman of Stratford, during his visitation of Hailes Abbey in 1394, reminded the community that secular persons must not eat regularly in the monastery, although he conceded that this was permissible if 'very great advantage to the community would come from this'.[68] Of course, as not all guests were equal, the type and quality of the accommodation and food varied accordingly, and by the end of the twelfth century Cistercian and Benedictine abbots were operating 'a two-tier system of hospitality', that is inviting selected guests to dine with them, whilst the common guests ate in the guest hall.[69]

The number, frequency and type of guests depended on the location of the abbey, its resources and its relationship with its benefactors. Travelling monks from other Cistercian houses were also given hospitality, not in the guest houses but in the host communities themselves, joining in their prayers and sharing their dormitories. Abbeys located on major international pilgrimage routes were particularly inundated with guests and often complained about the costs of providing food and shelter to the poor pilgrims.[70] Even so, the feeding of the poor and distribution of the alms at the gates remained an important obligation enunciated in Chapter 53 of the Rule of Benedict and enshrined in the notion that Christ 'was identified in particular with the poor and the needy'.[71] The eschatological benefits of the monks' charitable activities were automatically 'transferred' to the benefactors and members of the fraternity, although donors sometimes expressly requested Cistercian abbeys to distribute food to the poor on their behalf. When in 1318 Bishop Henry of Wrocław presented the parish church in Wierzbna to Kamieniec Abbey, he laid down that its income should be spent on feeding the poor, and even specified the amounts and the days when the food should be distributed at the gate of the abbey.[72] The combination of such donations and monasteries' own almsgiving meant that Cistercians across Europe were routinely providing food for the poor and hence interacting with the lowest social groups – just as Cistercian nuns were frequently involved in the care of lepers (see chapter 4), another marginalised social group.

At the other extreme, kings and queens were the most important group of all and the nature of medieval kingship required the royal court to travel around. Apart from references in monastic chronicles, the usual indication that a royal personage had stayed in a Cistercian house are the charters issued in such locations. Hosting a royal court might be a very costly business, but it also presented an opportunity to receive grants and privileges. For some rulers Cistercian monasteries were among their favourite residences: Plasy Abbey, the oldest of the Czech Cistercian monasteries, was located on the edge of extensive hunting forests and the kings of Bohemia used it as their hunting lodge throughout the thirteenth century.[73] When King Wenceslaus II of Bohemia (1283–1305) founded Zbraslav Abbey (Aula Regis) near Prague in 1292, he supervised the construction of the precinct and frequently stayed there. Indeed, Zbraslav monastery became his burial place and remained a necropolis of the Přemyslid dynasty well into the fourteenth century.[74] Scattered references in the sources across Europe indicate that Cistercian hospitals occasionally hosted high-status patients, for example royal children or relatives of the patron.

It was both related to the charitable function of the monastic community and a dimension of keeping good relationship with key friends, but the presence of a lay person within monastic buildings was not without its controversies. One of the earlier references to Cistercians offering treatment to outsiders comes from a collection of statutes dated to 1157–c. 1179 and emphasises that the monks and lay brothers who practised medicine were not allowed to stay overnight outside the monastery. They were also forbidden to administer medication to lay people away from the abbey. This regulation shows that the monks were indeed involved in providing medical treatment to outsiders, which was acceptable as long as it was done within the monastic precinct.[75] There is some anecdotal evidence for Cistercians providing hospital care to high-status patients such as royal children – for example in Kołbacz (Pomerania) and Beaulieu (Hampshire) – but it is unclear if this was a widespread practice or simply an 'extension' of the monastic hospitality. Some Cistercian abbeys have references to hospitals for the laity (*infirmitorium seculare*) in their surviving financial records, but these were most certainly located outside the monastic precinct or at least beyond the cloistral core. Some such institutions existed in Beaulieu, Furness, Meaux, Fountains, Newminster and Warden. Many abbeys had hospices for the poor, but all these establishments offered general care of food and shelter and it is difficult to assess how far they were medical hospitals and how much simply almshouses.[76] Such institutions appeared to be a frequent fixture across Europe, but the relationship between 'medical' hospital and hospitals as shelters for the poor is much debated. It has been argued that providing food and shelter was a medical activity in the medieval understanding, so distinguishing between these two types of hospitals is ahistorical. Although there is good evidence of Cistercian hospitals for the poor, there is much less information in the sources about offering medical treatment to the laity within the infirmary setting.

Monastic houses might serve as depositories for valuables of royal patrons during wars or other disturbances, although their ecclesiastical status was no absolute guarantee of safety. In 1215 English King John deposited gold, silver and jewels in 14 Cistercian houses for safe-keeping, whilst silver deposited by King Edward II at Rievaulx was stolen by the Scots in 1322.[77]

A rather less congenial type of visitor who could not be refused was the travelling army. Medieval logistics dictated the more or less forcible seizure of provisions for men and horses along the way, and the arrival of an army was often disastrous for Cistercian granges. Even more disruptive for the community, if a monastic house was in the front line it was not uncommonly pressed into service as military headquarters; in 1341/42 and again in 1356 King Edward III stayed at Melrose Abbey during his great campaigns against the Scots, using the monastic precinct as a base for a series of raids. The Welsh monastery of Strata Florida was devastated by the troops of King Henry IV in 1401, which not only stole all the abbey's liturgical vessels but also desecrated the church by using it for stabling horses.[78]

Finally, there was also another form of long-term guests of the monastery, known as corrodians, both men and women, who were given accommodation and food as a countergift for a donation or as a recognition of service given to the abbey. They lived either within the monastic precinct (as was the case in St Mary Graces London) or in hospices located within the monastic property, some distance away from the abbey (as in the case of several Silesian monasteries). The names of some of the corrodians identify them as donors, but former servants were recorded in the necrologies too. Three servants of Lubiąż Abbey – John, Simon and Martin described in the necrology as 'faithful' – secured corrody in their old age.[79] Occasionally, a document lists the terms attached to such retirements in a Cistercian abbey: in 1315, Tylon, rector of the parish church in Budzow, and his sister Gertrude signed an agreement with the abbot of Henryków Abbey granting them retirement in the abbey until their death, burial and liturgical commemoration in return for a yearly fee of 12 marks.[80] Retirement and death followed by burial in the monastery was not simply a way to secure shelter in old age, but also an act of piety to secure the posthumous fate of the soul.

Hospitality in all its forms was often very costly for the monastic houses. The dedication of a new chapter house and cloister in April 1312 at Pipewell Abbey (Northamptonshire) attracted a large number of guests, including Thomas earl of Lancaster and William Ros of Helmsley. Even two decades later Abbot Thomas recalled that 'only God knows how much was spent on this day'.[81] Prominent guests were always accompanied by large entourages also needing food and shelter and stabling for their horses. By the late middle ages it was becoming increasingly difficult to balance the intangible benefits from good relations with powerful figures, the abbots concerns for their self-representations, and financial pressures (see chapter 8).

Conflicts between Cistercian Houses and the Laity

Conflicts were a very common experience right across the Order. Sometimes benefactors changed their minds, regretting their hasty generosity when economic circumstances altered. More often it was the descendants of the donor who laid claim to donated land or challenged some aspect of the rights of a monastic house. The approximate nature of land measurement and boundaries also contributed to the frequency of disputes over properties.[82] Monastic communities were of course fully alive to the possibility of disputes, hence donation charters routinely contained consent from the relatives and kin group, and sometimes of the lord of the donor too, as a matter of routine (a custom known in French charters as *laudatio*, but practised across Europe).[83]

If relations between Cistercian houses and their patrons ranged from cordial co-operation to indifference and even downright hostility, they were also subject to 'renegotiation' with each succeeding generation. Sometimes the gap between the monks' and patrons' expectations would widen, especially under pressure of changing socio-economic conditions. When the first wave of Cistercian monasteries emerged in western Europe in the first half of the twelfth century there was still a considerable margin of land that lay landowners were willing to give to the religious houses, but by the early thirteenth century this had significantly diminished and large donations of land generally came to an end. The greater competition for land resources made itself felt in tension between patrons and 'their' monasteries. From the late 1220s to the early 1250s Rievaulx Abbey was engaged in a long series of disputes and court cases with its patron William de Ros, who tried to revoke a gift of valuable land donated by his ancestor Walter Espec and extended by Everard II de Ros, or at least to change the terms of the possession. The land in question consisted of common pasture and woods located between the abbey and William's residence of Helmsley castle, and William was particularly keen to claim hunting rights. The access to hunting was a significant marker of social status, which the lay nobility was particularly keen to preserve and extend. De Ros not only used violence against the property and employees of the abbey, but when the dispute came to court, refused to attend and simply denied the accusations. Eventually, the dispute ended with a compromise agreement in 1252 involving an exchange of land and a careful delineation of the interests of both parties.[84]

The most wearisome conflicts with the patrons were, as the case of Rievaulx shows, those over the core monastic land, but almost every monastery experienced some difficulties with benefactors and neighbours. Conflicts with the latter could often involve violence against the property and personnel of the abbey, ranging from the impounding of animals belonging to the abbey and blocking access to pastures, to attacking monastic employees and straightforward theft. Violence was most likely to increase if there was a general disorder, war or economic crisis, when a Cistercian monastery was seen as a relatively easy target for opportunistic attacks; and it was even more likely to occur if relations between the monastery and its neighbours were already strained or the monastery exercised a strong economic grip over impoverished neighbours. This was the case with Kołbacz Abbey, the largest and wealthiest Cistercian monastery in Pomerania. Although its core endowment had been given by the founder and augmented by grants from the dukes of Pomerania and bishops of Kamień Pomorski a significant proportion of its estates had been acquired by purchase and many of its neighbours had become economically dependent on the abbey. When the prolonged period of wars in the second half of the thirteenth and in the fourteenth century affected the region, Kołbacz Abbey became a target for attacks by impoverished neighbours, especially its granges for theft of livestock and other assets.[85]

The process of resolving conflicts over property sometimes involved lay or ecclesiastical courts, but often it was an informal process. As trial by battle or duel became increasingly infrequent in the twelfth century, mediation by an influential neighbour, bishop or abbots of other houses might be invoked; and in particularly bitter and lasting disputes Cistercians might turn to the king or other territorial ruler for arbitration. Informal methods of conflict resolution tended to leave little or no trace in the written records. Sometimes the only evidence for a conflict was a carefully crafted charter in which quitclaims were recorded. Juridical procedures, by contrast, generated written documentation, although the development and shape of the secular judiciary and legal structures varied greatly across Europe. In some places, especially East-Central Europe, the use of written evidence in courts was pioneered by the Cistercians, whilst their lay opponents lagged behind; and in societies only slowly starting to use written documents, Cistercian monasteries provided the additional service of chancery for their lay neighbours, authenticating and storing charters, for example at Cikádor and Toplica, both within the kingdom of Hungary.[86] It was not uncommon for monastic communities to seek to turn their enemies into friends where possible by settling conflicts through compromise involving compensatory payments in money or land.[87] This explains the frequent use of confraternity admissions to mark the transition from hostility to a new era of friendly relations. These represented not a cynical use of spiritual powers by the monks, but a genuine social and religious bond; in the relationships between Cistercian monks and their patrons, benefactors and the wider lay community the material and the spiritual were always very closely intertwined.

Cistercian Communities and Secular Powers

Cistercian abbots of prominent houses located in particularly sensitive areas were naturally heavily engaged outside the walls of their monasteries performing important tasks in the wider world. They acted as mediators, counsellors for secular rulers and spent considerable time travelling on diplomatic missions and at royal and ducal courts. Indeed, Cistercian abbots were to be found in close proximity to secular power all over Europe, for although their preoccupation with such duties could have been damaging to the internal workings of the monastery, it also offered opportunities for an abbey to win high-level 'friends' and generous donations. In France, for example, the Cistercians enjoyed a virtual monopoly of royal patronage in the early years of King Louis IX, who with his mother, Queen Blanche (daughter of a major Cistercian patron, Alfonso VIII of Castile), made significant grants to Cîteaux, Le Trésor, Saint-Antoine-des-Champs and other monasteries of the white monks, and were individually commemorated by the Order for their generosity and support. The strength of the relationship between the king, his mother and the Cistercians was further demonstrated by the foundation of Royaumont Abbey between 1228 and 1235, in which several descendants of Louis IX were buried. Blanche of Castile went on to establish Cistercian nunneries at Le Lys in *c.* 1241 and at Maubuisson in *c.* 1236, where she was eventually buried. Not that other orders – Carthusians, Franciscans and communities of Beguines – founded themselves excluded from royal patronage under Louis IX, but the importance of the white monks to the French royal house was reflected in the activities of Alfonso of Poitiers, who founded St Bernard College in Paris in 1253 (see chapter 8), and Charles of Anjou, who founded Realvalle Abbey

(Campagna) and Vittoria Abbey as a thanksgiving for his victories over Hohenstaufen at Benevento and Tagliacozzo.[88]

Of course the abbots of Cistercian houses that enjoyed ducal and royal patronage were the most likely to have close relationships with ruling houses. In England, Beaulieu Abbey, as a royal foundation, was in a different position from many other houses of the Order. Even King John, who was never a particular friend of the Cistercians and imposed very heavy taxation on them, cultivated a remarkably harmonious relationship with the abbot of Beaulieu: Abbot Hugh acted as royal envoy and was eventually promoted to the bishopric of Carlisle, and Abbot John was frequently summoned to the court to act as King John's adviser.[89] John's brother, King Richard I, had employed Adam, abbot of Perseigne (Normandy) and the author of spiritual texts, as his confessor throughout his reign.[90] In Bohemia, a number of Cistercian abbots enjoyed great influence as advisers to the late Přemyslid and early Luxemburg kings. Abbot Conrad of Zbraslav, a frequent adviser of King Wenceslaus II, was sent abroad on royal diplomatic missions, while Abbot Heydenreich of Sedlec was described as a close friend of this king and a major influence on his piety and spirituality. In the interregnum after the death of the last Přemyslid, it was the abbots Conrad and Heydenreich who led the campaign to recognise Princess Elisabeth (daughter of Wenceslaus II) as the heiress of the throne, and who went in a delegation with Abbot John of Plasy to negotiate her marriage to John of Luxemburg. Not surprisingly, the political influence of the Cistercians continued during the reign of King John, with abbots participating in the royal council and undertaking diplomatic missions – at any rate until 1319, when the king rejected Elisabeth.[91]

In England and Wales, from the late thirteenth century, some Cistercian abbots were summoned to attend parliament, which could entail long periods of absence from their monasteries. Although they saw themselves as being exempt from this duty (as Cistercian abbeys were free from all secular services), as prominent landholders they sat as peers in parliament. Between 1295 and 1377 the abbots of Beaulieu were summoned 43 times, those of Fountains Abbey 28 times, Rievaulx 17 times and Byland Abbey 12 times, whilst the abbots of the much smaller Warden Abbey were called 6 times.[92] Even so, in comparison with that of the bishops, who were far more involved with the court and whose attendance was particularly good, the actual attendance of the abbots in the House of Lords was very poor.[93]

One important feature of the relationship between Cistercian houses and secular authorities was the re-confirmations of the monastic landholding, usually after the accession of a new ruler, and especially after any significant change of political structure had occurred – conquest, or territorial changes or arrival of a new dynasty. Confirmations from new rulers acknowledging the property rights of religious houses might provide a measure of security against encroachments, but they also opened up possibilities for closer personal relationships. For monasteries, which in the course of several centuries were bound to experience cataclysmic political changes, an ability to adjust and establish new connections was vital.

Conclusions

The relationships between Cistercian monasteries, their patrons, benefactors and neighbours were based on the fundamental concept of the intercessory power of the monastic communities and on the exchange of material donations of money or property in return for prayers. This was a very old tradition, which the white monks inherited from their Benedictine predecessors. For the aristocracy and knights of twelfth-century Europe, within its core and peripheries, becoming a founder of a Cistercian house was not only likely to bring prestige and social status, but also secure commemoration and intercessory prayers believed to be of great effectiveness. Patrons and benefactors had their own expectations of their relationships with the monastic communities: hospitality, and particular aspects of commemoration such as burials. These assumptions usually reflected both local traditions and economic and social conditions in general. Contact and connections with the world outside the monastic walls were necessary elements of monastic life for all institutions. What differentiated Cistercians from their Benedictine predecessors was their much greater selectiveness, as manifested by restrictions regarding who could be buried in a Cistercian monastery and where, the shape of liturgical commemorations and forms of hospitality. The nature of Cistercian communities was also heavily influenced by their being part of a trans-European Cistercian network. All these characteristics helped to attract new patrons and benefactors by spreading the notion of the Cistercian community as a synonym for piety and effective intercession. But that all these activities were subject to change over the course of the twelfth and thirteenth centuries and even more so in the later middle ages, with a distinctly discernible tendency towards closer interactions with the lay world, was not a symptom of any 'lowering' of standards of the Cistercians. After all, the Cistercians never wanted to reject the vital connections to their patrons and benefactors. There was never a Cistercian 'golden age' when the communities of white monks remained cut off from the 'corrupting' influence of the world. Contrary to the assumptions of the older literature, there was never such a coherent set of ideas within the Cistercian movement that held the rejection of connections with the wider world to be synonymous with high standards. Certainly, the strictness of observance focused on the liturgy, claustration, and the individual and corporate piety of 'their' monks were highly esteemed by patrons and benefactors alike. But hospitality for the living and burials for the dead were also essential in maintaining good relations with the outside world; and the obligations to feed the poor and pray for the benefactors were equally central to the tradition on which the Cistercians built their form of monasticism. Pragmatism within the scope of observance was the approach that Cistercians adopted regarding trans-European networks, the General Chapter and the individual communities – witness both the prescriptions giving discretion to abbots in granting of privileges to patrons and benefactors and the inconsistencies in punishing abbots who had transgressed the norms in their contacts with the lay world. There was clearly no agreement among the abbots across Europe as to what constituted the norm in areas such as lay burials and hospitality within monastic spaces. Relations with the laity, from the royalty to the anonymous poor, show that an ability to adapt to local conditions and to respond flexibly while yet maintaining Cistercian observance and values were the most favoured norms of behaviour for Cistercians. It was a pragmatism that served them well: an ability to adjust to the changing world, whilst retaining core elements of their identity, enabling Cistercian houses not only survive, but to flourish all over Europe.

Notes

1. Caroline Walker Bynum, *Jesus as Mother* (Berkeley, CA: University of California Press, 1982), p. 61.
2. Bynum, *Jesus as Mother*, p. 71.
3. Illana Friedrich Silber, *Virtuosity, Charisma, and Social Order: A Comparative Sociological Study of Monasticism in Theravada Buddhism and Medieval Catholicism* (Cambridge: Cambridge University Press, 1995), pp. 37–172.
4. Brian Patrick McGuire, 'Norm and Practice in Early Cistercian Life', in *Norm und Praxis im Alltag des Mittelalters und der Frühen Neuzeit. Internationales Round-Table Gespräch Krems an der Donau, 7. Oktober 1996*, ed. Gerhard Jaritz (Vienna: Verlag der Österreichischen Akademie der Wissenschaften, 1997), p. 119; *Twelfth-Century Statutes from the Cistercian General Chapter: Latin text with English notes and commentary*, ed. Chrysogonus Waddell (Brecht: Cîteaux, Commentarii Cistercienses, 2002), 1186: 1, 1181: 5.
5. *Statuta capitulorum generalium ordinis Cisterciensis ab anno 1116 ad annum 1786*, ed. Joseph Canivez, 8 vols. (Louvain: Bureaux de la Revue, 1933–1941), vol. 1, 1217: 44; the case is discussed in Martinus Cawley, 'Four Abbots of the Golden Age of Villers', *Cistercian Studies Quarterly* 27 (1992), p. 310.

6. Winfried Schich, 'Zum Wirken der Zisterzienser im östlichen Mitteleuropa im 12 und 13. Jahrhundert', in *Zisterziensische Spiritualität: Theologische Grundlagen, funktionale Voraussetzungen und bildhafte Ausprägungen im Mittelalter*. ed. Clemens Kasper and Klaus Schreiner (St Ottilien: EOS-Verlag, 1994), p. 277.
7. Constance Brittain Bouchard, *Holy Entrepreneurs: Cistercians, Knights, and Economic Exchange in Twelfth-Century Burgundy* (Ithaca, NY: Cornell University Press, 1991), pp. 87–94.
8. Bouchard, *Holy Entrepreneurs*, p. 89.
9. Emilia Jamroziak, 'Making and Breaking the Bond: Yorkshire Cistercians and their Neighbours', in *Perspectives for an Architecture of Solitude: Essays on Cistercians, Art and Architecture in Honour of Peter Fergusson*, ed. Terryl Kinder (Turnhout: Brepols, 2004), pp. 64–65.
10. William Dugdale, *Monasticon Anglicanum*, ed. J. Caley, H. Ellis and B. Bandinel, 6 vols. (London: Bohn, 1817–1830), vol. 5, pp. 572–573, no. ix; discussed in Janet Burton, *The Monastic Order in Yorkshire 1069–1215* (Cambridge: Cambridge University Press, 1999), p. 194.
11. *Diplomatarium Danicum*, second series, ed. Franz Blatt, 12 vols. (Copenhagen: Munksgaard, 1938–1960), vol. 2: 1266–1280, ed. Franz Blatt and Gustav Hermansen (1941), no. 229; Brian Patrick McGuire, *The Cistercians in Denmark: The Attitudes, Roles, and Functions in Medieval Society* (Kalamazoo, MI: Cistercian Publications, 1982), p. 169.
12. Johannes Allendorff, 'Zur Geschichte des Ältesten Pommerschen Zisterzienserklosters Kolbatz', *Cîteaux: Commentarii Cistercienses* 22 (1971), p. 269; *Pommersches Urkundenbuch*, vol. 4, ed. Georg Winter (Stettin: Paul Niekammer, 1902), no. 2139.
13. Karen Stöber, *Late Medieval Monasteries and their Patrons: England and Wales c. 1300–1540* (Woodbridge: Boydell Press, 2007), p. 22.
14. Stöber, *Late Medieval Monasteries*, p. 96.
15. Bouchard, *Holy Enterpreneurs*, p. 175.
16. Arnoud-Jan Bijsterveld, '*In mei memoriam:* Hollow Phase or Intentional Formula?', in his *Do ut des: Gift Giving, Memoria, and Conflict Management in the Medieval Low Countries* (Hilversum: Verloren, 2007), p. 167.
17. Translation of the German term 'Memorialüberlieferungen'.
18. Joachim Wollasch, 'Gemeinschaftsbewußtsein und soziale Leistung im Mittelalter', *Frühmittelalterliche Studien* 9 (1975), pp. 268–286.
19. *Twelfth-Century Statutes*, 1192: 12, 1193: 5, 1194: 9, 1196: 61, 1198: 14, 1200: 1, 1201: 4, 1201: 50.
20. This issue was disused at the General Chapter meeting in 1180. *Twelfth-Century Statutes*, 1180: 8.
21. *Statuta* 1273: 68, 69, 70, 71, 72, 73, 74, 76, 77, 78.
22. Joachim Wollasch, 'Neue Quellen zur Geschichte der Cistercienser', *Zeitschrift für Kirchengeschichte* 84 (1973), pp. 188, 227, 230–231; *Statuta*, 1187: 9, 1180: 8; Bede K. Lacker, 'The Liturgy of Early Cîteaux', in *Studies in Medieval Cistercian History Presented to Jeremiah F. O'Sullivan Spencer* (Kalamazoo, MI: Cistercian Publications, 1971), p. 29; Piotr Orliński,

Cysterskie nekrologi na Pomorzu Gdańskim od XIII do XVII wieku (Toruń: Towarzystwo Naukowe w Toruniu, 1997), pp. 32–33.
23. 'Liber mortuorum Pelplinensis', in *Monumenta Poloniae Historica*, ed. August Bielowski, vol. 4 (Kraków: Akademia Umiejętności, 1884), p. 124. 'De communi consensus nostri capituli omnium missarum, psalmorum, vigillarum, disciplinarum id est castigacionum corporum, elemosinarum, oracionum, laborum et omnium spiritualium beneficiorum ac omnium bonorum, que fiunt in ecclesia nostra et que nunc procurata sunt et usque in finem mundi procurari poterunt, participles facimus fraternitatem in predictis omnibus secundum Cisterciensis ordinis consuetudinem largientes.'
24. *Repertorium Diplomaticum Regni Danici Mediaevalis*, ed. Kristian Erslev (Copenhagen: kommission hos G.E.C. Gad, 1896–1898), vol. 2, no. 3210; McGuire, *The Cistercians in Denmark*, p. 223.
25. *Repertorium Diplomaticum Regni Mediaevalis*, vol. 2, no. 3216; McGuire, *The Cistercians in Denmark*, pp. 223–224; the appearance of the Valdemars' tomb with an effigy is known from an antiquarian image, see Annegret Laabs, *Malerei und Plastik im Zisterzienserorden: zum Bildgebrauch zwischen sakralen Zeremoniell und Stiftermemoria, 1250–1430* (Petersberg: Michael Imhof Verlag, 2000), p. 163.
26. *Codex Esromensis*, ed. Oluf Nielsen, reprint ed. (Copenhagen: Selskabet for udgivelse af kilder til dansk historie, 1973), no. 187; McGuire, *The Cistercians in Denmark*, p. 225.
27. Beata Możejko-Chimiak, 'Związek starosty generalnego Wielkopolski Wierzbięty z klasztorem Cystersów w Lądzie (1352–1369)', *Nasza Przeszłość* 83 (1999), pp. 170–173; Alicja Karłowska-Kamzowa, 'Wielkopolska i Polska centralna', in Jerzy Domasłowski, Alicja Karłowska-Kamzowa, Marian Kornecki and Helena Małkiewiczówna, *Gotyckie malarstwo ścienne w Polsce* (Poznań: Wydawnictwo UAM, 1984), pp. 113–114.
28. Laabs, *Malerei und Plastik*, pp. 52–53; *Urkundenbuch des Cistercienserstiftes B. Mariae V. zu Hohenfurt in Böhmen*, ed. Mathias Pangerl, Fontes Rerum Austriacarum. Österreichische Geschichtsquellen, second series, vol. 23 (Vienna: H. Böhlaus, 1865), p. 385. The painting is now in the National Gallery in Prague.
29. Emanuel S. Klinkenberg, *The Donor's Model in Medieval Art to around 1300: Origin, Spread and Significance of an Architectural Image in the Realm of Tension between Tradition and Likeness* (Turnhout: Brepols, 2009), pp. 19–38.
30. Dagmar Zimdars, 'Ordenspropaganda der Zisterzienser in Bildbeispielen aus dem Kloster Maulbronn', in *Maulbronn: Zur 850jährigen Geschichte des Zisterzienserklosters*, ed. Dieter Planck (Stuttgart: Konrad-Theiss-Verlag, 1997), p. 464.
31. Klinkenberg, *The Donor's Model*, pp. 235–239.
32. Johannes Wilhelm, 'Die Wandmalereien in der Kirche und in der Klausur des Klosters Maulbronn', in *Maulbronn*, pp. 425–427.
33. Arnoud-Jan Bijsterveld, 'Eternal Life, Perpetual Glory: Memorialising Donors and Founders', in his *Do ut des*, p. 193.

34. *Twelfth-Century Statutes*, 1180: 5; codifications in 1202, 1220, 1237, 1257, 1289 and 1316.
35. Jackie Hall, 'The Legislative Background to the Burial of Laity and Other Patrons in Cistercian Abbeys', *Cîteaux: Commentarii Cistercienses* 56 (2005), pp. 364–369; Jackie Hall, Shelagh Sneddon and Nadine Sohr, 'Table of Legislation Concerning the Burial of Laity and other Patrons in Cistercian Abbeys', *Cîteaux: Commentarii Cistercienses* 56 (2005), pp. 373–418.
36. Matthias Untermann, *Forma Ordinis: die mittelalterliche Baukunst der Zisterzienser* (München and Berlin: Deutscher Kunstverlag, 2001), pp. 89–90.
37. Kim Esmark, 'Religious Patronage and Family Consciousness: Sorø Abbey and the "Hvide Family" *c.* 1150–1250', in *Religious and Laity in Western Europe 1000–1400: Interaction, Negotiation, and Power*, ed. Emilia Jamroziak and Janet Burton (Turnhout: Brepols, 2006), p. 101; *Scriptores rerum Danicarum*, 9 vols. (Leipzig: Viduæ Andreæ Hartvici Godiche, Frider. Christ. Pelt., 1772–1878), vol. 4, ed. Jacob Langebek, p. 476; *Diplomatarium Danicum*, ed. Niels Skyum-Nielsen, first series, 7 vols. (Copenhagen: Reitzel, 1957–1990), vol. 4, no. 41.
38. Anne Lester, 'A Shared Imitation: Cistercian Convents and Crusader Families in Thirteenth-Century Champagne', *Journal of Medieval History* 35 (2009), pp. 363–364.
39. Marian Kutzner, *Cysterska architektura na śląsku w latach 1200–1330* (Toruń: Wydawnictwo UMK, 1969), p. 22; Przemysław Wiszewski, 'Cysterki trzebnickie w społeczeństwie śląskim (czwarta ćwierć XIII wieku – pierwsza połowa XIV wieku)', in *Cystersi w społeczeństwie Europy środkowej: materiały z konferencji naukowej odbytej w klasztorze oo. Cystersów w Krakowie Mogile z okazji rocznicy powstania Zakonu Ojców Cystersów*, ed. Andrzej Wyrwa and Józef Dobosz (Poznań: Wydawnictwo Poznańskie, 2000), pp. 705–706.
40. Bernd Ulrich Hucker, 'Stauferzeitliche Zisterziensergründungen und Stiftergräber', in *Zisterzienser: Norm, Kultur, Reform – 900 Jahre Zisterzienser*, ed. Ulrich Knefelkamp (Berlin: Springer, 2001), pp. 290–291; Alois Schmid, 'Die Zisterzienserabtei Fürstenfeld als Herrschaftskloster', in *Kloster Fürstenfeld*, ed. Werner Schiedermair and Lothar Altmann (Lindenburg: Kunstverlag Josef Fink, 2006), p. 71.
41. Joan Wardrop, *Fountains Abbey and its Benefactors 1132–1300* (Kalamazoo, MI: Cistercian Publications, 1987), pp. 263–275.
42. Wardrop, *Fountains Abbey*, pp. 260–275.
43. Peter Fergusson and Stuart Harrison, with Glyn Coppack, *Rievaulx Abbey: Community, Architecture, Memory* (New Haven, CT: Yale University Press, 2000), p. 166.
44. Megan Cassidy-Welch, *Monastic Spaces and their Meanings: Thirteenth-Century English Cistercian Monasteries* (Turnhout: Brepols, 2001), p. 113.
45. Emilia Jamroziak, *Survival and Success on Medieval Borders: Cistercian Houses in Medieval Scotland and Pomerania* (Turnhout: Brepols, 2011), pp. 86–97; Dauvit Broun, 'Charting the Chronicle's Physical Development', in *The Chronicle of Melrose Abbey: A Stratigraphic Edition*, ed. Dauvit Broun and Julian Harrison, vol. 1 (Woodbridge: Boydell, 2007), pp. 129–134, 136–137, 153–154, 157–159, 161, 168–169.

46. Untermann, *Forma Ordinis*, p. 80.
47. Christine Sauer, *Fundatio und Memoria: Stifter und Klostergründer im Bild 1100 bis 1350* (Göttingen: Vandenhoeck und Ruprecht, 1993), pp. 156–157, n. 266.
48. Laabs, *Malerei und Plastik*, pp. 114–115.
49. Danielle Westerhof, *Death and the Noble Body in Medieval England* (Woodbridge: Boydell & Brewer, 2008), p. 86; Estella Weiss-Krejci, 'Heart Burial in Medieval and Early Post-Medieval Central Europe', in *Body Parts and Bodies Whole*, ed. Katharina Rebay-Salisbury, Marie Louise Stig Sørensen and Jessica Hughes, Studies in Funerary Archaeology 5 (Oxford: Oxbow Books, 2010), pp. 119–134.
50. Grant G. Simpson, 'The Heart of King Robert I: Pious Crusade or Marketing Gambit?', in *Church, Chronicle and Learning in Medieval and Early Renaissance Scotland: Essays Presented to Donald Watt on the Occasion of the Completion of the Publication of Bower's Scotchronicon*, ed. Barbara E. Crawford (Edinburgh: Mercat Press, 1999), pp. 175–181.
51. Walter Scherzer, *Kloster Ebrach in Dokumenten. Ausstellung anläßlich der Zusammenfassung der Ebracher Archivalien im Staatsarchiv Würzburg* (Würzburg: Archive Bayerns, 1980), pp. 9, 16. There is information about this custom in a papal mandate of Clemens VII (26 November 1523) and in a detailed description by the bishop's secretary in 1573.
52. *Testamenta Eboracensia: A Selection of Wills from the Registry at York*, ed. James Raine and John William Clay, vol. 5, Surtees Society 79 (London: Nichols, 1884), pp. 20–21, 63.
53. *Diplomatarium Danicum*, series II, vol. 4, 67; McGuire, *The Cistercians in Denmark*, pp. 170–171.
54. Stöber, *Late Medieval Monasteries*, p. 136.
55. Janet Burton, *Kirkham Priory from Foundation to Dissolution* (York: Borthwick Institute of Historical Research, University of York, 1995), p. 23.
56. Stöber, *Late Medieval Monasteries*, p. 40; Huw Pryce, 'Patrons and Patronage among the Cistercians in Wales', *Archaeologia Cambrensis* 154 (2007), p. 85.
57. Nicola Coldstream, 'Cistercian Architecture from Beaulieu to the Dissolution', in *Cistercian Art and Architecture in the British Isles*, ed. Christopher Norton and David Park (Cambridge: Cambridge University, 1986), p. 157.
58. Emilia Jamroziak, 'St Mary Graces: A Cistercian House in Late Medieval London', in *The Use and Abuse of Sacred Places in late Medieval Towns*, ed. P. Trio and M. De Smet (Leuven: Leuven University Press, 2006), p. 160.
59. A.A.M. Duncan, 'Jocelin (*d.* 1199)', in *Oxford Dictionary of National Biography*, ed. H.C.G. Matthew and Brian Harrison (Oxford: Oxford University Press, 2004).
60. *Liber de Melros*, ed. Cosmo Innes (Edinburgh: Bannatyne Club, 1837), vol. 1, no. 29, 30, 32, 69, 90, 94, 95, 97, 98, 106, 112, 122, 130, 138, 152, 169, 170.
61. *The Church Historians of England*, vol. 4, part 1: *The Chronicle of John and Richard of Hexham. The Chronicle of Holyrood. The Chronicle of Melrose. Jordan Fantosme's Chronicle. Documents Respecting Canterbury and Winchester*, ed.

and trans. John Stevenson (London: Seeleys, 1856), p. 30; John Dowden and J. Maitland Thomson, *The Bishops of Scotland: Being Notes on the Lives of all the Bishops, under each of the Sees, prior to the Reformation* (Glasgow: James Maclehose and Sons, 1912), p. 299.

62. *Fasti Ecclesiae Scoticanae Medii Ad Annum 1638*, rev. ed., ed. Donald E.R. Watt and Athol L. Murray (Edinburgh: Scottish Record Society, 2003), p. 189.

63. Hucker, 'Stauferzeitliche Zisterziensergründungen', pp. 293–294.

64. 'apud nos in capitulo legitur', Jürgen Sydow, *Die Zisterzienserabtei Bebenhausen*, Germania Sacra NF 16: Bistum Konstanz (Berlin: De Gruyter, 1984), p. 118.

65. Conrad Rudolph, 'The "Principal Founders" and the Early Artistic Legislation of Cîteaux', in *Studies in Cistercian Art and Architecture*, vol. 3, ed. Meredith Parsons Lilich (Kalamazoo, MI: Cistercian Publications, 1987), pp. 16–17.

66. *The Rule of St Benedict*, trans. Luke Dysinger (Trabuco Canyon, CA: Source Books, 1997), chapter 53, pp. 121–125; 'Instituta Generalis Capituli apud Cistercium', in *Narrative and Legislative Texts from Early Cîteaux: Latin text in dual edition with English translation and notes*, ed. Chryosogonus Waddell (Cîteaux: Commentarii cistercienses, 1999), clause I, p. 454; *Les Ecclesiastica Officia cisterciens du Xiième siècle. Texte latin selon les manuscripts édités de Trente 1711, Ljubljana 31 et Dijon 114, version française, annexe liturgique, notes, index et tables*, ed. D. Choisselet and P. Vernet (Reiningue: La Documentation Cistercienne 1989), chapters 87, 120.

67. Jörg Sonntag, *Klosterleben im Spiegel des Zeichenhaften. Symbolisches Denken und Handeln hochmittrlaterlicher Mönche zwischen Dauer und Wandel, Regel und Gewohnheit* (Münster: Lit Verlag, 2008), pp. 582–596.

68. Christopher Harper-Bill, 'Cistercian Visitation in the Late Middle Ages: The Case of Hailes Abbey', *Bulletin of the Institute of Historical Research* 53 (1980), p. 110.

69. Julie Kerr, 'The Symbolic Significance of Hospitality', in *Self-Representation of Medieval Religious Communities: The British Isles in Context*, ed. Anne Müller and Karen Stöber (Berlin: Lit Verlag, 2009), p. 130.

70. Julie Kerr, 'Cistercian Hospitality in the Later Middle Ages', in *Monasteries and Society in the British Isles in the Later Middle Ages*, ed. Janet Burton and Karen Stöber (Woodbridge: Boydell, 2008), pp. 28–29.

71. Julie Kerr, *Monastic Hospitality: The Benedictines in England, c. 1070–c. 1250* (Woodbridge: The Boydell Press, 2007), p. 26.

72. *Urkunden des Klosters Kamenz*, ed. P. Pfotenhauer, Codex diplomaticus Silesiae, vol. 10 (Wroctaw: Vereine für Geschichte und Althertum Schlesiens, 1881), no. 61, pp. 84–86; Michał Kaczmarek, 'W trosce o najsłabszych. Działalność charytatywna śląskich klasztrów cysterskich rodziny lubiąskiej', in *Historia i kultura cystersów w dawnej Polsce*, ed. Jerzy Strzelczyk (Poznań: Wydawnictwo UAM, 1987), pp. 422–423.

73. Marcin R. Pauk, 'Klasztor jako zaplecze ekonomiczne władzy królewskiej w państwie ostatnich Przemyślidów', in *Klasztor w społeczeństwie średniowiecznym i nowożytnym*, ed. Marek Derwich and Anna Pobóg-Lenartowicz (Wrocław: LAHCOR and Wydawnictwo DIG, 2005), pp. 228–229.

74. Kateřina Charvátová, 'Propter laudabilia abbatum merita: The Kings of Bohemia and the Cistercian Order', in *In Tal und Einsamkeit: 725 Jahre Kloster Fürstenfeld. Die Zisterzienser im alten Bayern. Band III: Kolloquium*, ed. Klaus Wollenberg (Fürstenfeldbruck: E. Wewel, 1990), p. 169.
75. *Twelfth-Century Statutes*, p. 46.
76. David Bell, 'The English Cistercians and their Practice of Medicine', *Cîteaux: Commentarii Cistercienses* 40 (1989), pp. 167–171.
77. L.S. Snell, *Suppression of Religious Foundations of Devon and Cornwall* (Marazion: Wardens of Cornwall, 1967), p. 42; *The Chronicle of Lanercost 1272–1346*, ed. Herbert Maxwell (Glasgow: James MacClehose and Sons, 1913), p. 240.
78. Michael Brown, *The Black Douglases: War and Lordship in Late Medieval Scotland, 1300–1455* (Edinburgh: John Donald, 1998), pp. 136, 186; *Knighton's Chronicle 1337–1396*, ed. and trans. G.H. Martin (Oxford: Clarendon Press, 1995), p. 39; *The Chronicle of Adam of Usk 1377–1421*, ed. and trans. Chris Given-Wilson (Oxford: Clarendon Press, 1997), pp. 144–145.
79. Kaczmarek, 'W trosce o najsłabszych', p. 431.
80. Paul Bretschneider, 'Die Ruhestands- und Sterbeversicherung eines Pfarrers und seiner Schwester vom Jahre 1315', *Archiv für schlesische Kirchengeschichte* 4 (1939), pp. 286–288.
81. Unpublished source cited in: Adrian H. Bell, Paul Dryburgh and Chris Brooks, '"Leger est aprendre mes fort est arendre": Wool, Debt, and the Dispersal of Pipewell Abbey (1280–1330)', *Journal of Medieval History* 32 (2006), p. 196.
82. David Bell, 'The Measurement of Cistercian Space: The Evidence from England', in *L'espace cistercien*, ed. Léon Pressouyre (Paris: Comité des travaux historiques et scientifiques, 1994), pp. 253–261.
83. Bouchard, *Holy Entrepreneurs*, pp. 135–137.
84. Emilia Jamroziak, *Rievaulx Abbey and its Social Context, 1132–1300: Memory, Locality, and Networks* (Turnhout: Brepols, 2005), pp. 123–129.
85. Jamroziak, *Survival and Success*, pp. 179–183.
86. Hrvoje Kekez, 'Cistercians and Nobility in Medieval Croatia. The Babonići Family and the Monasteries of Topusco (Toplica) and Konstanjevica (Landstrass) in the Thirteenth and Early Fourteenth Century', *Cîteaux: Commentarii Cistercienses* 61 (2010), p. 276; Marie-Madeleine de Cevins, 'Les Implantations Cisterciennes en Hongrie Médiévale', in *Unanimité et diversité cisterciennes: filiations, réseaux, relectures du XIIe au XVIIe siècle: actes du quatrième colloque international du CERCOR, Dijon, 23–25 septembre 1998*, ed. Nicole Bouter (Saint-Etienne: Publications de l'Université de Saint-Etienne, 2000), p. 477.
87. Bouchard, *Holy Entrepreneurs*, pp. 130, 148–149.
88. Elizabeth M. Hallam and Judith Everard, *Capetian France 987–1328*, 2nd ed. (Harlow: Pearson, 2001), pp. 298–304, 334.
89. Heather Shaw, 'Cistercian Abbots in the Service of British Monarchs (1135–1335)', *Cîteaux: Commentarii Cistercienses* 58 (2007), pp. 236–237.
90. Shaw, 'Cistercian Abbots in the Service', pp. 235–236.

91. Marie Bláhová, 'Cisterciáci ve službách české politiky za posledních Přemyslovců a při nástupu Lucemburků', in *Klasztor w społeczeństwie średniowiecznym i nowożytnym*, ed. Marek Derwich and Anna Pobóg-Lenartowicz (Opole and Wrocław: Larhcor, 1996), pp. 365–366; Charvátová, 'Propter laudabilia abbatum merita', pp. 174–176.
92. Aloyse Marie Reich, *The Parliamentary Abbots to 1470* (Berkeley, CA: University of California Press), pp. 353–357, 363–365.
93. Richard G. Davies, 'The Attendance of the Episcopate in English Parliaments, 1376–1461', *Proceedings of the American Philosophical Society* 129 (1985), p. 32.

chapter 4

CISTERCIAN NUNS: THE ROLE OF WOMEN IN THE ORDER

Women were a part of the Cistercian movement from the very beginning as nuns, founders, benefactors and supporters, but the dominant narrative of the history of the Cistercian movement is firmly rooted in the male branch of the order and its key male figures. The story of women has remained on the margins of Cistercian history for a long time. Alongside the heated discussions about the origins of the Cistercian Order, its chronology and the role of particular individuals, the place of women in the Cistercian family has been the subject of many debates. The gradual rediscovery of the female contribution accelerated in the late twentieth and early twenty-first centuries. It has been part of a wider examination of the religious experience of women in the middle ages and their role as active 'producers' and contributors to knowledge, ideas and sensibilities, rather than just passive 'consumers' of ideas created by men. Present-day nuns, too, have castigated the tendency to 'eliminate' women from the narrative of the history of the Order.

Historians searching for the blueprint for all manner of things in the early years of the twelfth century have cited, not surprisingly, the oldest stratum of the relationship between the male and female branches of the Order. Whilst some pointed to the roots of Cistercian misogyny in the ideas of the founding fathers, others tried to show that there was no particular negative bias against women. Although the older historiography emphasised Cistercian opposition to giving a place to women in the movement, and the determination to shun their distracting, even polluting, influence, there has recently been a tendency to present Cistercians as 'women friendly' from the start. The discussion often conflates the general issue of the monastic attitude to women with the more specific one of the institutional relationship between Cistercian nunneries and the Order. Nor has it helped matters that the sources for the history of female, as opposed to male, houses are decidedly meagre and that there has been much less research done on the female branch of the Order.

Of course, the debate has seen the texts of the founding fathers much quoted, with the negative views of Bernard of Clairvaux himself being perceived as particularly influential. As he warned his monks in his famous commentary on the Songs of Songs: 'to be always with a woman and not to have sexual relations with her is more difficult than to raise the dead'; and in letter 79 he voiced his strong opposition to double monasteries because it was a 'fearful danger' for monks and nuns to live under the same roof.[1] All this has been taken at face value as evidence of the Cistercian rejection of female monasticism. More recently, however, it has been demonstrated that the concept of 'women' involved very different categories and that the Cistercians' perspective was not uniform. True, Caroline Walker Bynum insists that while Bernard might write to individual women who were seeking his advice on spiritual matters, especially on joining a religious community, he 'feared contamination from women'; but she also concedes that Cistercian attitudes towards women in religious life were a separate matter from their original ideas about femininity in general.[2] Among the surviving 547 letters of Bernard, 23 were addressed to women, two of them to Ermengarde (d. 1147), countess of Brittany, a pious woman and generous church benefactress, who was seeking the advice of charismatic leaders as she struggled with the desire to enter religious life and 'experimented' with various forms of observant and semi-religious life. He also advised Hildegard of Bingen, probably the most eminent contemporary female religious figure, on the matter of her visions, and corresponded with Melisande, queen of Jerusalem, acting as regent for her son.[3] In fact, Bernard was well aware of the usefulness of mothers when it came to persuading their sons to join the Cistercian movement, and his recruitment campaigns on behalf of Cistercian monasteries were directed at women as well as men.[4] Indeed, aristocratic women and the wives of rulers were an important influence on their men to become founders of Cistercian monasteries. For Bernard, therefore, while 'women' were the sacred persona of the Virgin Mary, distant figures of patronesses or, when they 'seduced' men away from the monastic life, dangerous obstacles to his plans, and although he remained detached from them and formed emotional bonds only with men, he was not 'anti-women' as such.[5]

True, there was undoubtedly a lively fear of monks having contact with women because of the temptation for carnal sin. This was the reason for trying to prevent contact with female pilgrims or even ladies of high status visiting the abbey as wives or relatives of patrons and benefactors. In the 1190s, for example, the statutes of the General Chapter recorded a series of punishments imposed on abbots for 'violation of the monastic enclosure' by allowing women to enter the church or monastic buildings.[6]

Hence, contacts between Cistercian monks and nuns were far more likely to be conducted through correspondence than personal contact. Brian Patrick McGuire has shown that friendships between them, conducted at a distance, through correspondence, became frequent in the late twelfth and thirteenth centuries. In the collection of miracles written for the monastic audience by Caesarius of Heisterbach, some 50 out of 700 stories contain references to male–female friendships in a monastic context. The growth of the cult of the Virgin Mary, the greater involvement of Cistercians in issues outside the walls of the monasteries, and the growing dislike of friendships between monks within one community all contributed, according to McGuire, to the development of such connections between monks and nuns. Some surviving correspondence between Abbot Adam of Perseigne (1188–1221) and Abbess Agnes of Clairets, for example, represents 'a new confidence among Cistercians that close relationships with women can bring monks closer to God'.[7]

The earliest Cistercian nunneries came into being as a part of the same movement as the oldest male houses and, as in the male houses, there were different paths to the *ordo*. The first female adherents were wives and relatives of the men who entered Cîteaux with Bernard. Initially, they lived at Molesme, but when it proved to be too small the community moved in 1113 to Jully, forming a dependent priory of Molesme ruled by members of Bernard's family – first his sister-in-law Elizabeth and then his sister Humbeline. A second house was created between 1120 and 1125 at Tart and embraced the Cistercian identity in a different process. The first abbess was Elizabeth de Verge, a nun at Jully, who had married earlier in her life and had children, one of them becoming the Cistercian abbot of La Ferté. Her mother, also called Elizabeth, was a benefactor of Cîteaux and knew Stephen Harding. It was she who founded Tart Abbey, not simply to provide her daughter with an office, but because of her long-standing commitment to the Cistercian ideals. The new foundation was neither a dependent priory nor a 'private' enterprise of Stephen Harding, as the older literature presented it, but an independent house closely connected to the mother house at Jully. Pope Eugenius III's bull of 1147 expressly cited Tart nunnery as following the Cistercian *ordo*, and one of the measures of its success was the fact that by the end of the twelfth century Tart had established eight daughter houses.[8]

Just as many male houses were not 'new plantations', but pre-existing monastic communities which joined the Cistercians in the first half of the twelfth century, we see the same phenomenon in the cases of female communities in the first half of the twelfth century. The nature of these groups varied, and included informal groups and Benedictine communities seeking to follow a reformed path. In fact, female houses were more prone than the male ones to change of identity. That many of the features of personal and highly emotive spirituality were common to the beguine and Cistercian milieus sometimes led a group to change its status. A community of beguines, for example, had existed in Awirs from before 1195 until 1202, when for four years it adopted the Rule of Benedict. In 1205/6, the founder applied to Pope Innocent III for incorporation into the Cistercian order, which was granted in 1210, and the nuns moved to their final location in Aywières, in Brabant (diocese of Liège), in 1211.[9]

In the twelfth century only one nunnery was formally 'incorporated' by the decision of the General Chapter, in the sense of accepting the Cistercian *ordo*, and became part of the formal structure of the Order. This has been cited as evidence that otherwise communities of nuns remained external to the Order, with any association of female houses being only unofficial in the early stages of the Cistercian development – an interpretation that reflects the old assumption that Cistercian monks were intrinsically suspicious of women and wanted to keep them out of the Order, whilst nuns sought affiliation with the Cistercian movement by any means possible.[10] According to Richard W. Southern's influential study, no other contemporary monastic organisations 'shunned female contact with greater determination or . . . raised more formidable barriers against the intrusion of women' than the Cistercians.[11] Lekai's assertion that the Cistercian authorities resisted the admission of women into the Order because their demands and expectations would 'endanger the purely contemplative character of the Order' casts a long shadow over Cistercian historiography.[12] However, these claims are unconvincing. In the first place, the structure of the Order had not been finalised in the first decades of the twelfth century but continued to evolve; hence, the fact that nuns were only formally recognised by the General Chapter in the thirteenth century does not mean that they had not been part of the Cistercian movement in the twelfth century too. The view that spiritual concerns must have lain behind the absence of formal admissions of nunneries into the Order in the twelfth century is an invention of the modern historiography for which there is no contemporary evidence.[13] Second, it is a view which confuses the nature of the relationship between Cistercian monks and nuns and the relationships of Cistercian monks with lay women. The traditional view that there were no Cistercian nuns before the thirteenth century has now been decisively refuted. On the basis of legislative sources, the Swiss historian Brigitte Degler-Spengler has demonstrated that far from being victims of antagonism from the leadership, the nuns were in fact already well integrated into the Order by the thirteenth century, when they begin to appear in the documentary records. When the first female house was established during the abbacy of Stephen Harding, neither he nor any collegial body of the Cistercian movement authorised it – or could authorise it, given that the embryonic organisation of the Order contained no structure to enable them to do so.[14] Degler-Spengler's interpretation has been developed by Constance Berman, who has incorporated it into her own radical reinterpretation of early Cistercian history. Since her re-dating has pushed the institutional development of the Order into the second half of the twelfth century, the controversy over the formal admission of nunneries to it has lost much of its meaning, as no structure existed to which they could have been admitted. She also places nuns firmly within those reform groups comprehended by the amorphous early Cistercian movement, which only actually joined the developing Order in the second half of the twelfth century.[15] Indeed, there have recently been calls to integrate the histories of the male and female branches of the Order, including the suggestion that the narrative accounts should not banish nuns to a separate chapter at the end, but treat them together with the monks as forming an intrinsic part of the same entity.[16] Not that the attempt can be made here to incorporate the history of Cistercian men and women into one seamless narrative: given the present discrepancies in the amount of research on the white monks and nuns in different parts of Europe, the result would be an unbalanced story, and one which, as the evidence for men would predominate in any case, might only serve to perpetuate the marginalisation of Cistercian nuns.

Of course, the debate extended beyond the twelfth century to encompass the crucial stage in the thirteenth century, marked by the proliferation in the statutes of the General Chapter of references to female houses as they were formally incorporated into the Order. In the process of formal incorporation, a nunnery became part of a filiation, usually either Cîteaux or Clairvaux.[17] Here, the controversy centres on the decisions taken by the General Chapter in 1213, often interpreted as the official recognition of the female branch of the order, but also referring to houses incorporated before that date.[18] In 1218 further regulations specified that female houses should be located at least 5 miles from the male monasteries to prevent direct economic competition – there was great emphasis on the strict enclosure of the nuns as a key prerequisite of any incorporation. This anxiety over the proper claustration of the religious, especially women, which had a long tradition going back to Benedict of Nursia and Caesarius of Arles in the early sixth century, surfaced very strongly in the reform movement of the central middle ages.[19]

The first formal incorporation – of the Silesian nunnery in Trzebnica (founded by a powerful ducal family for a group of Benedictine nuns from Bamberg in 1202) – was recorded in the statutes in 1218. In the same year, the General Chapter reiterated the criteria for incorporation, of which strict enclosure appears to be the most important.[20] In 1220, the first of many prohibitions of further incorporations was issued, followed in 1225 by further statutes (which, in order to prevent nunneries from becoming a burden on the male houses, made self-sufficiency and possession of suitable buildings a prerequisite); in effect maing it far more difficult for female communities to be incorporated into the Order.[21] On the whole, just as a majority of Benedictine nunneries were poorer than their male counterparts, the same was true of Cistercian nunneries: their endowments tended to be smaller and donations more limited, all of which created economic problems. Finally, in 1228 the General Chapter issued a prohibition against further incorporations, which was repeated in 1239 and again in 1241 with slightly different clauses for possible grounds of exceptions.[22] None of these prohibitions seems to have any influence on the numbers of new foundations.

These prohibitions were accompanied by grumbling about the burden which the care of female houses entailed. Certainly, formal incorporation placed additional responsibility on the male houses, which some abbots perceived as a burden; while others complained about shortages of personnel to be sent as chaplains to the nunneries. Pope Innocent IV's response was a bull of 1251 allowing the Cistercians to refuse to accept any further female houses.[23] Yet despite all these regulations and prohibitions the incorporation of female foundations increased steadily in the 1230s and 1240s, reaching a peak between 1235 and 1245.[24] The obvious conflict between the theoretical regulations and the formal recognition in practice of so many nunneries reflects disputes and difficulties within the General Chapter. Some monasteries saw themselves as being unreasonably burdened, whilst others did not; and while some abbots complained about the trouble entailed by the spiritual care of the nuns, others took a very different view. There is widespread evidence of the support given to the communities of nuns by individual Cistercian abbeys.[25] It fact, it was quite common for a Cistercian abbot to have positive connections with a female house beyond the stage of foundation and/or incorporation; and sometimes this could go beyond the usual formal obligations – witness the texts written for Cistercian nunneries by Cistercian monks: Abbot John Godard of Newnham, for example, during his retirement from office in the late 1240s or early 1250s, wrote a spiritual treaty for Abbess Margaret of Tarrant, whose nunnery was under the care of Newnham.[26]

The battles over the 'legalisation' of Cistercian nunneries and the Order's perceived opposition to it have given rise to a whole theory of the ineradicable hostility of Cistercian monks towards nuns: as soon as women managed to 'break into' the structures of the Order, the monks – given the 'troublesome nature of some of the religious ladies, and their failure to attain the Cistercian ideals' – were at pains to check the 'corrupting' influence of the growing number of female houses.[27] In reality, however, as Degler-Spengler explains, the nuns had not been reluctantly admitted into the Order by unwilling abbots, but enjoyed the shelter of an already well-established network of nunneries within the Cistercian filiation under the aegis of the General Chapter. Nor were 'the gates' of the Cistercian Order slammed in the face of new female communities. The reason why fewer nunneries were accepted into the Cistercian Order after 1251 was not because of the prohibition, but because the need for new houses for women had been largely satisfied by the great wave of foundations in the first half of the thirteenth century. In Germany, for example, there had been 15 nunneries in the twelfth century, as many as 250 by 1250, and over 300 by 1300.[28] In Portugal the number of female houses was close to that of male monasteries by the end of the thirteenth century, with a ratio of 14 to 18. Indeed, the great popularity of Cistercian life for women was noted by contemporary observers, among them Jacques de Vitry (d. 1254), who compared the multiplication of nunneries to the stars in the sky.[29]

Admittedly, Cistercian houses were only one of several options open to women in the second half of the thirteenth century. The sharp increase in women embarking on some kind of religious life – whether official nunneries (for example the Poor Clares) or unofficial, like the beguines, or even heretical communities – was an aspect of wider social changes. Equally, the Cistercian ethos and identity was often embraced by individuals and groups that shared their values but did not necessarily want to become nuns: for example, Yvette of Huy (died *c*. 1228), who left her family to care for lepers on the outskirts of her home town, did so as a lay woman, but in view of her spiritual commitment, devotion, caring work and the fact that she wore a white Cistercian tunic under her own clothes, she came to be identified with the Order.[30] In the main, women who became Cistercian nuns in the thirteenth century often came from wealthy urban backgrounds or from lower nobility associated with towns, whilst aristocratic women were still more likely to enter Benedictine houses requiring a large dowry or to become founders of Cistercian houses.

Moreover, the historiographical topos of the church hierarchy's uniform distrust of female aspirations for the Cistercian religious life quite fails to take into account the substantial support offered to the nunneries by various prelates. Bishops often took up the cause of Cistercian female communities, lobbying the General Chapter for their incorporation or simply arranging for the nuns to follow the Cistercian *ordo* outside the formal structures of the Order.[31] That two of the most important Cistercian male houses in Denmark, Sorø and Esrum, established female monasteries early on – Roskilde (before 1177) and Slangerup (before 1200) respectively – has been attributed to the influence of bishops and of Archbishop Absalon.

As already emphasised, the issue of the attitude of the Order towards Cistercian nuns has frequently been confused with its attitude towards lay women. The statutes of the General Chapter and records of the visitations frequently reminded monks that women must not be allowed into the Cistercian precincts, or even in close proximity to them, or to the granges. The Chapter feared lest the presence of women give the monks and lay brothers the opportunity to engage in carnal sin; and whilst in particular cases regarding hospitality or burials concessions might be made to patronesses and female relatives of benefactors, casual or uncontrolled connection with the female world was discouraged. Female relatives of a patron might be allowed to enter a monastic church once – for an initial dedication ceremony – but their attendance at the annual masses on the anniversary of the dedication was forbidden.[32] As for the burials of patrons and benefactors in the monastery, there are no direct references to the presence of women, but their presence at anniversary masses for their souls was certainly against the regulations of the Order. Barbeau Abbey (near Fontainebleau) was founded by King Louis VII, who was buried there in 1180. Nevertheless, in 1190 and again in 1192 the abbot was punished by the General Chapter for allowing ladies from the royal court to attend the liturgical commemorations of the founder in the monastic church.[33]

The danger from contact with women figured frequently in the visitation records. When Abbot John of Gloucester of Hailes Abbey noticed, during the visitation of Dore Abbey (Hertfordshire) in 1318, that the cross in the monastic church attracted significant veneration from the laity, he specifically ordered that if any women were among the pilgrims they should not be given hospitality within the precinct, not even in the granges, but offered food at the gate, and they should not be allowed to stay overnight. In 1317 the General Chapter gave the Abbey of Heisterbach permission to admit women to the monastic church on the feast of its dedication, but only on the days when the pilgrims could receive indulgences; in other situations where permission was given, women's access to monastic spaces was carefully delineated.[34]

Certainly, the evidence is clear that lay women were not all equal in the eyes of the monastic authorities. Cistercian monks recognised the need for patronesses and benefactresses, who were therefore given honours and privileges such as commemorations and burials in the restricted spaces of chapter houses, or even monastic churches, just like their male counterparts and relatives. Even so, the physical presence of these distinguished females was restricted to carefully selected occasions such as the dedication of the monastic church, while for the rest, monks and lay brothers were as far as possible protected from any contact whatsoever with women, especially pilgrims, female servants and the poor receiving alms, because of the possibility of sexual transgression.

Cistercian Nunneries and the Order

In practice, there was a wide variety of relationships between Cistercian female communities and the Order. Indeed, as John A. Nichols admits, it is not always easy to pinpoint even the authority responsible for confirming or denying the Cistercian status of a nunnery: was it the General Chapter, other male Cistercian houses, the diocesan bishop, the pope or even the secular ruler? 'Being a Cistercian nunnery', therefore, was by no means a fixed concept, and its meaning could change over time. To fully explore the meaning of the term, we shall begin by examining the motivations for female communities wanting to become a Cistercian house.

These were many and various. First, of course, there was the desire to be a part of a flourishing spiritual movement; and, on a more mundane level, the desire to secure exemption from taxation and to avoid interference from bishops. These pragmatic motives should not be overstated, however, as exemption from taxation could also be claimed simply on grounds of poverty – and many female houses did claim it, without seeking to become part of the Cistercian Order.[35] Certainly, both Cistercian spirituality and the autonomy of Cistercian monasteries were as attractive to women as to men.[36] The spirituality of Cistercian nuns was Christ-centric, just like that of the monks; and they shared a very strong identification with Mary as the embodiment of the pure soul given over to obedience, intercession and love.[37]

Not that participating in Cistercian spirituality necessitated formal incorporation into the Order. After all, many Cistercian nunneries regarded themselves as part of the movement and followed the Cistercian way of life without going to such lengths. Helfta Abbey, for example, an important centre of female Cistercian spirituality founded in 1229, was never formally incorporated, yet one of its chroniclers, Sophie von Stolberg, writing in the later middle ages about her house and its saints, emphasised that Helfta had been a Cistercian house.[38] This kind of self-identification, which by no means automatically implied formal recognition by the Order, also found expression in the mortuary rolls of prelates, which travelled from monastery to monastery, sometimes even internationally, with requests for prayers for deceased ecclesiastics. Each stopover in a religious house was noted on the roll, and the names of numerous English nunneries described as Cistercian appear on several late medieval mortuary rolls of abbots and bishops, even though these convents were not officially recognised by the Cistercian order.[39] There are cartularies from Cistercian nunneries which describe themselves as 'Cistercian' and 'Benedictine' interchangeably, which may mean that they changed their self-identity over time, or even that they held some sort of dual identity. Sometimes more than one identity was assigned to a nunnery by an external authority: in one of the fifteenth-century English bishop's registers the same nunnery was listed as Benedictine and Cistercian in different entries.[40] Clearly, the definition of what constituted a Cistercian nunnery was far more fluid and permeable than traditional historiography has acknowledged.

From the perspective of the institutional church the formal recognition of Cistercian female communities by the government of the Order was a part of a wider thirteenth-century trend in which the flourishing 'women's movement' established relationships with male monastic authorities. Since the nunneries were dependent on the male houses for priestly and legal care, their expectations of protection from the male orders fostered the affiliation and incorporation strategy. It was, of course, always an unequal relationship – for example, abbesses were never the equals of abbots in the process of decision making within the Order. Indeed, whilst abbots were obliged to attend the General Chapter, abbesses were expressly forbidden to do so.[41]

In a few exceptional cases, the support of powerful protectors might give female houses a special status with greater autonomy and authority. At the request of King Alfonso VIII and Queen Eleanor of Castile, the General Chapter made the royal nunnery of Las Huelgas the mother house of all female Cistercian houses in Spain and gave it prerogatives normally reserved for the father-abbot. From 1187 Spanish abbesses held an annual General Chapter in Las Huelgas and conducted visitations within their filiation. Even after the congregation of Castile was formed in 1425 (see chapter 8), the abbey upheld its independence by resisting reforming visitations to Las Huelgas and its daughter foundations by the abbot of Poblet as head of the new congregation. In the 1510s and 1520s, the abbesses continued to resist reform visitations from abbots designated by the congregation. In 1523, for example, the abbess secured a letter of protection from Emperor Charles V granting her freedom from any visitation sent by the General Chapter on the grounds that Las

Huelgas was formally exempted in view of its ancient privileges.[42] This was an interesting example of Cistercian nuns making use of the lay power to retain their independence from the authority of the Order, but Las Huelgas was quite exceptional even within the very broad spectrum of Cistercian nunneries.

Just as the male houses of the order did not all come into being by foundation from a mother house, but often by incorporation or by groups breaking away from Benedictine houses, Cistercian nunneries too could come into being in a number of ways. The history of nunneries of Upper Swabia is a case in point: in 1252 Constance Abbey, a female house under the jurisdiction of the bishop and following no particular rule, adopted the Benedictine rule with the pope's permission. A year later, however, it adopted the Cistercian customs, and was freed from the bishop's authority and allowed to have its own chaplain. Soon after the abbey moved to Felbach (Canon Thurgau in Switzerland), the General Chapter delegated the abbots of the neighbouring Wettingen and Frienisberg abbeys to make inspections in 1260 and 1262. As a result Felbach Abbey was incorporated as a daughter of the Cistercian Salem Abbey.[43] In such cases the support of a prominent figure – abbot, bishop or powerful layman – was crucial – and Abbot Eberhard of Rohrdorf of Salem Abbey supported the founding and incorporations of six nunneries in Upper Swabia and the Lake Constance region between 1212 and 1240. Similarly, all five Cistercian nunneries in Hungary were incorporated into the Order in response to petitions from their influential backers.[44]

In contrast to the hundreds of female houses which were officially part of the order on the continent, those in England have often been said to constitute a 'special case'. The traditional assumption has been that only Tarrant (Dorset) and Marham (Norfolk) were formally part of the Cistercian order, and that other nunneries claiming to be Cistercian were, in fact, not. On the other hand, the standard reference work of English monastic history lists 27 Cistercian nunneries and the most recent calculations, using a broader range of sources, registered 33 female houses.[45] These statistical discrepancies have led historians to question what constituted Cistercian status. Traditionally, a reference – or the lack of one – in the statutes of General Chapter was the litmus test. Recently, however, Elizabeth Freeman has turned to other sources in search of a more adequate measure of Cistercian identity, and the cases she has analysed suggest that there were many ways of assessing the Cistercian status of female houses in England. In the 1270s King Henry III, the bishop of Canterbury and the abbot of Kirkstall recognised seven nunneries in the Canterbury province as being Cistercian, even though they were not recognised as such by the General Chapter. When, in the early sixteenth century, the reforming abbot of Fountains, Marmaduke Huby, fought to emancipate a number of nunneries from episcopal authority on the grounds of their Cistercian status, he was acting on pre-existing informal connections between male and female houses, not the official documentation of the Order.[46] Similarly, in Lower Saxony, out of 18 nunneries which appear in the sources as Cistercian only one – Lillienthal Abbey (near Bremen) – is mentioned in the statutes of the General Chapter. Yet many of these monasteries clearly followed the Cistercian *ordo*, identified themselves with the Cistercian spirit and became involved in the cult of Holy Blood (see chapter 8), which was very popular in the Cistercian male houses in northern Germany.[47] Janet Burton has shown that the Cistercian status of the nunneries in Yorkshire was not something permanent, but subject to change over time: while 12 claimed at various times to be Cistercian, some started doing so only in the late middle ages. As for reasons why they chose to follow the *ordo* even if only informally, she argues that the most obvious (i.e. financial considerations, particularly freedom from the payment of tithes) were not much in evidence in the Yorkshire cases. Rather, it was the interests of patrons and the personal connections with neighbouring male and female houses that influenced the nuns' desire to follow the Cistercian way of life.[48]

A claim to Cistercian status might involve a variety of authorities. How far was it simply a matter of the legal position as defined by the central authority of the Order? How far was it a matter of following Cistercian customs and being acknowledged as part of the Order by some local authority? Such 'unofficial' Cistercian nunneries sought confirmation of their status with varying degrees of success: in the late 1260s seven nunneries in Lincolnshire which were never incorporated into the Order managed to convince various secular and ecclesiastical authorities of their Cistercian status, and hence of their right to exemption from the tithes for a crusade called by King Henry III. A well-attested method of proving membership was to secure written confirmation from authorities within and outside the Cistercian order: St Michael's Stamford (Lincolnshire) secured, at various times, letters of confirmation from both King Henry III and his successor, the bishop of Lincoln, the archbishop of York, the abbot of Kirkstall (Cistercian) and prior of Healaugh Park (Augustinian). Yet whilst all these authorities acknowledged the Cistercian status of the nunnery, Abbot John of Cîteaux bleakly declared in 1270 that neither St Michael's Stamford nor other Lincolnshire nunneries had ever belonged to the Order.[49] Clearly, nunneries could secure recognition of their Cistercian statuses from local ecclesiastical authorities, male Cistercian houses in the region and secular rulers, whether the distant authorities of the Order accepted it or not – a phenomenon that became increasingly frequent in the later middle ages as the trans-European structures of the Cistercian organisation weakened, to be superseded by the regional and national structures exemplified by the activities of abbots such as Marmaduke Huby.

For the central powers of the Order the issue of the claustration and obedience of nuns became increasingly important during the thirteenth century, as the increasing financial pressures of ecclesiastical and secular taxation and collation was paralleled – and Anne E. Lester argues that the issues were indeed connected – by an increase in the financial demands made on the nunneries by the General Chapter. Whereas many women had entered the Cistercian communities to pursue active charity and care of the poor and sick, the male authorities wanted greater financial contributions from the female convents, especially once the Order was faced with demands from King Louis IX and King Philip III for the crusades. At the same time, the enforced total seclusion of the nunneries from the world hampered their charitable activities. As the records of the visitation by Stephen Lexington, abbot of Savigny Abbey, to several nunneries in north-western France in the 1230s demonstrate, the main concern of the male authorities was that the number of nuns should be kept at a level that would allow the monasteries to sustain themselves without needing to beg for alms. The practice of begging would require the nuns to interact with the lay people and even leave the convent. In any case, according to the abbots, the charity provided by the Cistercians should be confined to the 'suitable' needy: i.e. hospitality and charity denied to all men, and unmarried pregnant women or those with small babies, who might bring scandal upon the nuns.[50] Thus, the Order's handling of these issues of claustration and charity, especially its fear that nunneries might become impoverished and a burden on the male houses, led to restrictions on their charitable activities, the very activities that attracted many women to the Cistercian life; and it was clear that the Order's authority, not least because the abbesses were not a part of the order's governing structures, usually had the upper hand in their dealings with the female houses.

The Organisation of Cistercian Nunneries

If male Cistercian houses varied in terms of size and wealth, the disparities between female houses were even more pronounced; and if the economic self-sufficiency of female communities was always on the minds of the Order's authorities, this did not mean that all nunneries were small and poor. Although most convents housed about 20 nuns and many had fewer, larger houses could have over 100. Communities were restricted in size according to their ability to support their nuns, especially as claustration made them particularly dependent on income from rents. They were divided into fully professed choir nuns, novices and lay sisters. The status of this last group was similar to that of lay brothers: they were seated separately in the church, wore different habits and performed manual tasks such as cleaning, cooking, laundry and gardening. Although they took vows of poverty and chastity, the rules of enclosure were applied less strictly to them. In the later middle ages their practical duties were largely taken over by paid maidservants.[51]

Female communities were headed by abbesses (or, in the small houses, prioresses), whose symbol of office was the crozier, just as it was for abbots. By the later middle ages the crozier was often highly ornate, incorporating the coats of arms of the abbesses that testified to their high social status and kinship connections. Responsibility for monastic functions – economic, liturgical or reception of guests – was organised in a similar way as in the male monasteries. Unlike their male counterparts, however, Cistercians nuns ran schools for girls, teaching both basic *trivium* (grammar and logic and rhetoric) and advanced *quadrivium* (arithmetic, music, geometry and astronomy); and other duties – caring for the sick and the poor, penitentiary activities and intercessory prayers for the patrons and benefactors – figured prominently among their activities. In northern France many Cistercian nunneries were founded in association with hospices for the poor and lepers.[52] Indeed, Lester has established that over half the communities in Champagne which became Cistercian nunneries in the course of the 1230s originated in groups of women associated with hospices and leprosoria. If the 'culture of caregiving' in the female Cistercian houses was valued by the patrons and benefactors, for the nuns themselves the close association between charity and penitential piety was at the very core of their spiritual mission.[53]

Conventual prayers were no less important for nuns than for their male counterparts, but nuns also copied and illuminated manuscripts and engaged in the communal production of tapestries and embroidered liturgical vestments. The subjects depicted in these textiles frequently reflected local devotions to particular saints: a tapestry representing the legends of saints Elisabeth and Anne made in Wienhausen Abbey also shows St Alexander, the patron of the nunnery.[54] Manuscripts produced in nunneries were often of very high quality: the Rulle Abbey gradual, for example, commissioned or copied out (*c.* 1300) by the nun Gisela von Kerzenbroeck, was decorated with exquisite miniatures and golden initials. The initial letter of the liturgy for Christmas depicts the Birth of Christ, with Gisela herself with five other nuns of Rulle community beneath.[55]

Lay brothers, housed separately in the outer court near the workshops, were responsible for any necessary physical work. They followed the same custom as the lay brothers in the male houses. They also undertook administrative duties associated with the management of the estates, granges and urban properties, as well as representing the abbess in court proceedings.[56] By the fourteenth century, however, just as in the male houses, lay brothers disappeared from female houses in western Europe, their function being largely taken over by paid servants and more loosely associated *familiares*.[57]

Not surprisingly, female communities depended on male assistance and authority in several practical respects. In the first place, they needed a chaplain to celebrate mass, to preach and to hear confessions and perform all the liturgical roles restricted to priests. Second, nunneries were subordinated to the abbot of a male house (the father superior or 'father immediate') within the Cistercian organisational structure. Resident chaplains, of whom in large communities there were often more than one, lived in their own rooms outside the nuns' cloister. In formally incorporated nunneries, the nuns' confessors were appointed by the father superiors, but the choice of a chaplain was often a controversial matter. Abbesses frequently complained about the intellectual and moral qualities of the appointees, whilst the father superiors criticised the female convents for not giving the confessors adequate food and clothing: abbots of Himmerod Abbey, for example, often caused much resentment by sending elderly or even sick monk-priests to the nunneries under their control.[58] For the Cistercian houses not formally incorporated in the order, the choice of chaplain was less restricted (subject to nomination by a bishop), and such houses often had Dominican or Franciscan confessors, whose spiritual and social ethos was close to that of the Cistercian nuns.[59]

Incorporated female houses were subject to visitation from a father-abbot, whose role, as head of the male house exercising supervisory authority (usually located in the same region), resembled that of the of the abbot of a mother house in respect of its male filiations. In practice, however, lines of obedience were often poorly defined, and occasionally it was not even clear who the father superior was. As for abbesses, only those of Tart and Las Huelgas had the right to act as 'mother superiors' towards nunneries in their filiation. The purpose of visitation was the same as in the case of male houses – to check that the *ordo* was being observed and the economic conditions were sound. The visitors were particularly exercised over issues of internal discipline – of the claustration of the nuns, and the prevention of any unauthorised contacts with the world beyond the walls of the nunnery – all of which reflected the assumption that 'women needed firmer discipline on account of their natural weaknesses'.[60]

Indeed, the regulations of the Order provided for physical obstacles to prevent interaction with the outside world: in 1242, for example, the General Chapter decreed that the conversations of the Cistercian nuns with anybody from outside the community could only be conducted through a small window with dense grills, which would not only prevent any physical contact, but also completely obscure the face of the nun.[61]

The notion that it was the innate weakness of women that made it difficult for them to adhere to the monastic observance is reflected in the visitation records. There was a good deal of criticism of the nuns' aristocratic habits, which they allegedly continued to indulge inside the cloister walls, with luxurious clothing, fancy shoes and lavish food.[62] For example, a letter from Abbot William of Æbelholt (a Danish Augustinian house) to two nuns in the Cistercian house of Slangerup who were members of the royal family criticised them for being too concerned with upholding their social status and for drinking too much alcohol, which he described as the deplorable 'custom of the country'.[63] In England, meanwhile, it was common practice for Cistercian nuns not formally incorporated into the Order and simply following Cistercian custom to be subject to visitations from bishops, who like the Cistercian father superiors were primarily interested in the internal discipline of the houses.[64]

As visitation records from the late middle ages often paint a bleak picture of disorder, the appropriation of communal property and unchaste behaviour, historians have seen in them evidence of the decline of traditional female monasticism. We must not forget, however, that the purpose of visitations was to seek out and correct irregularities; hence the visitation reports, with their exclusively negative content, can only present a very one-sided view of the internal life of the nunneries. There are almost no records produced by nuns themselves about the internal workings of their communities which might help to redress the imbalance. It should also be noted that the restrictions contingent on the enclosure of a community put serious constraints on its ability to look after its own economic interests; between 1298 and 1302 the lay manager of the estates of Cañas Abbey (Castile) took advantage of a prolonged vacancy of the abbatial office to use the seal of the prioress to forge several receipts of rents. The thefts from the nunnery continued until an energetic abbess from the Haro family – the patrons – was appointed. Maria Diaz de Haro and the father superior put a stop to it by destroying the misused seal and the forged documents.[65] Such effective interventions by patrons and superiors were not, however, something that could be taken for granted by any nunnery whose economic interests happened to be in jeopardy.

After all, many Cistercian nunneries were poorer than their male counterparts and had smaller land-holdings. Detailed studies of particular regions have shown how Cistercian nunneries had adjusted their interests to those of their more powerful male counterparts. In Burgundy, the majority of the 14 nunneries were located close to male monasteries, which were overseeing them by virtue of historical or juridical filiations. Although recent research has shown many female houses to be far older than was previously assumed, their economic life was nevertheless dominated by the male abbeys.[66] Of course, as strict claustration allowed Cistercian nuns far less scope to manage their finances directly, they were particularly dependent on income from rents; their control of parish churches and tithes and their right to appoint the priest were other useful sources of revenue for female houses. But as, for practical reasons, female houses were less directly involved with granges and farming, the economy of Cistercian nunneries was often based, like that of the Benedictines, on tenanted estates.[67]

In social (and also, indirectly, in economic) terms, the prestige of a convent was not unconnected to the social standing of its inmates: the low profile of two nunneries in western Bohemia, in Pohled and Sezemice, has been attributed to their lack of royal patrons, as a result of which neither could attract entrants from the influential noble families whose connections were so important for securing donations and support.[68] On the whole, however, although Cistercian nunneries, like Benedictine houses, had tended to be aristocratic establishments in the twelfth and thirteenth centuries, in the later middle ages the Cistercian nuns were increasingly coming from wealthy urban backgrounds and the lower nobility.

Cistercians Nuns as Mystics and Spiritual Writers

One of the more thoroughly explored aspects of Cistercian female monasticism is the nuns' engagement with spirituality: although very little is known about the internal workings of the nunneries, the texts associated with Cistercian mystics have been intensively studied in recent years. Like other themes, notably Mario- and Christo-centric spirituality, they were the common property of all Cistercians (see chapter 7), and the religiosity of the latter must be considered in its wider context. The thirteenth century saw a great flourishing of female mysticism and the formation of unofficial groups such as beguines, in part a response to the decline of the role of women in the official church structures relative to the growing importance of the celibate priesthood and clerical status. Although Pope Boniface VIII's *Periculoso* bull (1298), formally reinforcing the limitations placed on them by specifying their perpetual claustration, was directed at nuns of all types, the main targets were the most influential orders:

the Cistercians and the Poor Clares.[69] In the thirteenth and fourteenth centuries female Cistercian mysticism flourished, particularly in the Low Countries and parts of Germany. Several Cistercian nun-mystics entered Benedictine houses as child oblates before turning in adulthood to much stricter Cistercian communities – transitions that were usually preceded by a series of powerful mystical visions. The increased use of the vernacular as a written language after 1200 facilitated the dissemination of texts produced by the Cistercian nuns which allowed them to communicate their visions to a wider audience both inside and outside the cloister walls, and served as important links between official and semi-official religious communities.[70]

Among the Cistercian female houses that became important spiritual centres was Helfta Abbey, founded in 1229 by Count Burchard of Mansfeld and his wife Elisabeth for a group of nuns from Halberstadt who wanted to follow the Cistercian rule. In 1234 the community moved to Rodarsdorf and in 1258 to Helfta in Saxony to a site donated by the brothers of Abbess Gertrude of Hackeborn. It was a wealthy and prosperous house attracting nuns from noble families in Thuringia and Saxony; and employing Dominican friars from Halle or Magdeburg as confessors and spiritual advisers. It produced several important texts in the late thirteenth century, including *The Flowing Light of the Godhead* by Mechtild of Magdeburg, who had written the first six volumes in the Magdeburg beguine community and added a seventh after entering Helfta. *The Flowing Light* is an apocalyptic and mystical text focusing on the Eucharistic piety and the cult of the sacred heart, and it significantly influenced the spirituality of the Helfta community in the 1280s and 1290s.[71] The community also included a sister of the Abbess Gertrude, the influential mystic Mechthild of Hackeborn (d. 1298/99), who composed a set of prayers and meditations in Latin and the account of her spiritual life, *The Herald of Divine Love*. The community pressed both mystics to describe their visions in writing and arranged for their 'approval' by Dominican and Franciscan theologians.[72] Indeed, Mechthild of Hackeborn's text became very popular among Carthusian monks in the fifteenth century. For women excluded from priestly functions and from holding any clerical authority, the mystical visions gave them direct access to the authority of Christ without explicitly challenging claims to priesthood.[73]

Gertrude of Helfta (d. 1302) pursued the typically Cistercian theme of devotion to the Virgin Mary: the role of Mary's pregnancy was central to the incarnation of the Word and was expressed in Gertrude's vision through convoluted symbols. Gertrude declared that the Virgin had asked her to recite the *Ave Maria* 45 times a day during the octave (six days) of the feast of the Annunciation; and, as the number 45 multiplied by 6 gives 270, being the number of days of Mary's pregnancy, Gertrude could 'accompany' the pregnancy mystically, offering her service and assistance as if actually present.[74]

The propagation of such mystical ideas through visual representations was widespread in Cistercian and Dominican nunneries of South Germany between 1300 and 1500. They took the form of small figures of Christ and John the Baptist in front of their mothers' bodies or even depicted inside their transparent wombs. In the latter depictions, the womb often resembled a heart – a clear allusion to the concept of spiritual pregnancy, i.e. the idea that Christ can enter the hearts of devout Christians.[75] The maternal aspects of Christo-centric spirituality often found expression in visions of the Christ-child, which were particularly common among the Cistercian and Dominican nuns in the Upper Rhineland and involved visions of the infant Christ moving, talking and playing with the nuns as a real child might do. Sometimes, the vision was of a statue of Christ or of a doll dressed as an infant Jesus coming to life as a result of nun's fervent prayers.[76]

According to Brian Patrick McGuire, the developments in mysticism and the role of spirituality in the female communities led to closer ties between Cistercian monks and nuns. From 1170 to 1220, for example, there was a significant increase in letters exchanged between male and female Cistercians, expressing friendship and reflecting their shared intensity of devotion – witness the correspondence between Abbot Adam of Perseigne and Abbess Agnes of Les Clairets Abbey (both located in Normandy) and the numerous instances of friendships between monks and women cited in the *Dialogus Miraculorum* by Caesarius of Heisterbach.[77]

It was really only mysticism and ascetic practices, moreover, that enabled cloistered nuns to join in debates on the key issues of the church, as other routes were closed to them. The Flemish nun Lutgard (b. 1246), a child oblate in a Benedictine monastery, who entered the Cistercian nunnery of Awirs (Aywières) as an adult, had had visions from the age of 15 and was believed to have healing powers. On three occasions she embarked on prolonged seven years' fasting 'on behalf of the church' – for the conversion of Albigensiens, for the redemption of sinners and in expiation of the misdeeds committed by the 'enemies of the church' (in particular Emperor Frederick II, whose death was regarded by some as proof of the effectiveness of Lutgard's fasting).[78] Indeed, Lutgard was posthumously venerated as a saint and was among a small group of Cistercian nuns who were believed to experience stigmata bleedings.

Although such women made a strong impression on their associates, both male and female, for all 'ordinary' nuns the main focus of spiritual life was the liturgy. Like their male counterparts, Cistercian nunneries needed books for the performance of the office, for the education of the novices and additionally for the girls in the monastic schools. The size of book collections in the female houses varied greatly across Europe. Large and well-endowed nunneries had significant libraries: by the early sixteenth century the Marienstern nunnery (Brandenburg) had a library of 'respectable size', including liturgical manuscripts, among them extremely high-quality antiphonaries, and graduals made in Altzella Abbey, residence of the father superior, officially responsible for the spiritual development of the nuns. Marienstern had also benefited from the intellectual and spiritual input from a number of university-educated monks of Altzella in the later middle ages.[79] The abbot superiors and chaplains were not simply preoccupied with the strictness of claustration, but saw the spiritual development of nuns as their obligation. Supplying texts for Marienstern's women was an element of it. Many books were private prayer books, which nuns had brought with them on entering the monastery or received as gifts: when Marguerite Lenfant, from a wealthy family of Douai, entered the monastery of Notre-Dame-des-Prés in Douai, her family gave her a splendid illuminated martyrology manuscript depicting nuns at prayer and at work.[80]

In the later middle ages, female houses saw a significant increase in the number of vernacular books, many of which were popular devotional texts which the laity and nuns with little or no Latin education could read; and mystical texts in the vernacular were an important spiritual link between the world of the cloister and lay religiosity. For smaller and poorer houses, gifts from the laity were an important source of books: in her will of 1448 a certain Agnes Stapilton of Carleton bequeathed a book – *Chastisyng of goddeschildern* – to Easholt Abbey in Yorkshire and an English translation of *Meditationes vitae Christi* to Sinningthwaite Priory. In the will of Robert Est of York, dated 1467, another Yorkshire nunnery, Hampole, received a glossed English Psalter which had belonged to the mystic Richard Rolle.[81]

The Cistercian model of spirituality remained influential with women well beyond its apogee in the thirteenth century, one of its most important manifestations being the emergence of the Bridgettine order. The founder, the future St Brigitta (d. 1373), was a powerful Swedish aristocratic woman, whose key inspiration came from Alvastra Abbey, a Cistercian house located very near her estate. Both she and her husband, frequent visitors to the abbey, were accompanied on a pilgrimage to Santiago de Compostela by a Cistercian monk, Svenung, who later became the abbot of Varnhem (a daughter house of Alvastra). For many decades, Brigitta cultivated a close friendship with the sub-prior of Alvastra, Peter Olafson, her life-long confessor, who translated her book of visions into

Latin and co-authored a Life, written shortly after Brigitta's death as part of the canonisation campaign. After the death of her husband, Brigitta lived for five years at Alvastra before leaving for Rome in 1349. The Cistercians, and specifically those at Alvastra, were an inspiration for Brigitta in setting up her own monastery. Her aim was to create an order for women which would include a male component, but which, unlike the Cistercian model, would not subject women to male authority. Thus, in addition to nuns, Brigettine communities contained priests, deacons and lay brothers, but the leadership remained in the hands of the abbess. The rule of the community (*Regula sancti Salvatoris*), which had its centre in Vadstena – the 'Cîteaux' of the new Order – was dictated by Brigitta to Prior Olafson, who later added a further volume of *Constitutiones* and provided help and general advice. Brigitta's book of visions (*Revelaciones*) placed great emphasis on the non-physical meaning of the Virgin's pregnancy as the mystical embodiment of Christ – very much a Cistercian theme (see chapter 7).[82] Many Brigettine houses were dedicated to the Virgin, following the Cistercian custom, just as the attention paid by the founder to the uniformity of practice also strongly echoed Cistercian concerns.[83]

Female Cistercian Communities and their Patrons and Benefactors

Cistercian nuns often enjoyed a close relationship with their patrons – which was just as well, given that the patrons were officially equipped with much greater formal and informal powers over nunneries than they enjoyed over male houses. The constraints of claustration, moreover, made nuns particularly dependent on their patrons: they needed patronal assistance in a host of legal and economic matters; and some patrons even lobbied bishops and popes to circumvent the General Chapter on behalf of 'their' nunneries.

Close relationships between the nuns and their patrons might be facilitated by the setting up of Cistercian nunneries in urban locations or close to a patron's principal residence, and by their functioning as prestigious necropolises for the founders and their descendants. All benefactors attached importance to the intercessory prayers of the nuns, and having a female relative in a monastery who could offer her own private prayers on behalf of her family was considered particularly beneficial. It was a well-established belief, long predating the emergence of the Cistercian movement, that the virginity of the nuns gave particular intercessory power to their prayers, reducing the 'burden of the founders' sins in the other world'.[84] Nor, in this particular, was there ever any doubt as to the motives and preoccupations of founders and benefactors: the Dominican friar Nicolas du Mans, preaching to the Cistercian nuns of Saint-Antoine-des-Champs outside Paris in 1293, told them: 'Surely, such donors made gifts to you not for your beautiful eyes, but in order to have part in your prayers'.[85] It has been suggested that the benefactors of Cistercian nunneries were able to exercise more control than in the case of male houses over how the grant should be used – whether for pittances, anniversary masses, chantries or other forms of commemorations – but no systematic work has been done on this, and it is more likely that the economic strength of a house and specific local conditions were more decisive factors than the gender of the monastic inmates.[86]

As in the male Cistercian houses, the fullest benefit of the intercessory power of the nuns' prayers was reserved for the patrons buried in 'their' churches. An impressive example of this was Las Huelgas Abbey, founded by Alfonso VIII of Castile and his queen Eleanor in 1187 and richly endowed as their dynastic necropolis. The iconography of their sarcophagi in the abbey's church emphasises on one hand their devotion to the Virgin Mary and their connections with the Cistercian community and on the other its intercessory power.[87] Their daughter, Blanche of Castile, queen of France (d. 1252), was a very generous founder of two Cistercian nunneries, Le Lys and Maubuisson, where she was eventually buried. The queen made careful preparations for her burial, entering Maubuisson as a nun a few days before her death; and according to a well-attested tradition that her heart was buried in Le Lys, Blanche was able to maintain her connections with and secure intercession from both of her foundations.[88] Not surprisingly, like male founders, their female counterparts wanted to emphasise closeness to 'their' nunneries. The tomb of Agnes of Wetting, the second wife of Henry the Count Palatine, who co-founded with him the nunnery of Wienhausen in 1221 (originally located in Ninhagen), was located directly under the nuns' gallery to ensure her eternal closeness to the community, and the limestone carving on the tomb, depicting Agnes holding a model of the church, further emphasised the significance of her devotional act.[89]

Like male houses located on the frontiers of Latin Europe, nunneries in areas recently converted to Christianity also benefited from patronage. The first monastic foundation on the island of Rügen, a former pagan political and religious centre, after its forced conversion by the Danes in 1168, was initiated by the recently baptised Prince Jaromir of Rügen. It was a small Benedictine nunnery established in the immediate proximity of his residence, on a hilltop (and soon to be known as Bergen: 'on the hill'). The nuns came from Roskilde Abbey in Denmark and the community was turned into a Cistercian convent in 1193. The nunnery established a number of parishes in the principality and helped with the

Christianisation of the island, its church also serving as a parish church for the settlement that grew around it. Although it is very likely that Bergen nunnery was originally intended as the necropolis for the Christian rulers of Rügen, with the conquest of the neighbouring mainland and the subsequent foundation of a male Cistercian house in Neuenkamp in 1232 by Prince Wisław I, the nunnery found itself side-lined.[90]

Like the smaller male houses, smaller nunneries attracted burials of lesser people and by the fourteenth century were graced by the prestigious tombs of middling knights, gentry and, in some cases, wealthy burgesses. The church of the small Yorkshire nunnery Swine Priory (founded by Robert de Veri before 1153) contains a number of fashionable alabaster tombs dating from the 1370s to the Reformation, with full-size effigies and heraldic shields, testifying to not only the piety but also the social standing those buried in the nunnery.[91]

The influence of the patrons was most obviously seen in the area of appointments. As early as 1205, Pope Innocent III's appointment of the abbot of Lubusz as *custos* and *provisor in spiritualibus* for the nuns of Trzebnica was attributed to the influence of Duke Henry the Bearded of Silesia;[92] and until 1515 all abbesses in Trzebnica nunnery came from the ruling ducal family or other related dynasties of the Polish kingdom.[93] Even so, having well-connected and personally wealthy abbesses, even if they had been 'imposed' by patrons, offered advantages to the communities concerned: for example, one of the oldest surviving monstrances in any Cistercian church comes from Herckenrode Abbey and was donated to the convent by the Prioress Hedwig in 1286.[94] Incidentally, this extremely valuable object was not only a manifestation of her prestige and her generosity, but also an early sign of a female community's interest in the Eucharistic cult, which was to flourish in many Cistercian houses in the later middle ages (see chapter 8).

Although women were often an important influence behind foundations established by their fathers and husbands, there were instances of powerful women, especially widows, using their own economic resources to act independently as founders. Three daughters of King Sancho I of Portugal (1185–1211), infantas Teresa, Sancha and Mafalda, were the key influence in establishing Cistercian nunneries, to which they continued to lend their strong support and protection.[95] Throughout northern France women from the high aristocracy were prominent in using land and income from their dowries or inheritances to found Cistercian nunneries, which they directly controlled – for example, the countesses of Chartres, Auxerre and Flanders and Countess Blanche of Navarre, who founded Argensolles in 1222.[96] In practice, foundation charters and monastic chronicles often obscured the role of women as founders and cited their husbands or fathers, even if it was the women who were supplying the endowments and devising and implementing them.[97] The Scottish earls of Lothian, for example, were prominent patrons of female communities, but it was the women of the family who were actually behind these foundations. Deirdre, the wife of Earl Gospatric III (d. 1166), was involved in the foundation of Coldstream Abbey (1136–1166) and was eventually buried, along with her husband, in Eccles nunnery, another Cistercian house of their foundation.[98]

To powerful widowed women Cistercian nunneries offered an opportunity to spend the remaining part of their lives in an environment that was both spiritual and in conformity with their high social standing. Queen Elizabeth Richenza, widow of King Wenceslaus II of Bohemia, founded a Cistercian nunnery at Staré Brno in 1323, retiring there in the final years of her life, and was buried in the abbey in 1335.[99] Rather more varied was the career of Béatrix (d. 1354), a daughter of King Charles of Hungary, who was married to Jean II Dauphin of Vienne. Widowed at 34, she entered the Cistercian nunnery of Val-Bressieux from whence, after ten years as a nun and apparently seeking a humbler position, she transferred as a simple nun to Les Hayes Abbey. After a few years there, however, Béatrix clearly desired more comfort and established herself in a semi-religious setting in a château of Beauvoir with a group of nuns, two chaplains and large household of servants. The final stage of her journey through the Cistercian world came in 1349 when her son founded a new nunnery for her in St-Just near the town of Romans, where she eventually died as a nun.[100] This rather peculiar story illustrates not just the variety of possible responses to Cistercian spirituality and the ascetic model, but also the influence which powerful lay women could exercise over religious groups to shape them according to their own wishes.

Many female founders demonstrated great energy in seeing their projects through. One Valborg, the wealthy widow of a Danish gentry landowner, founded Opager monastery in the 1320s, whereupon some of her neighbours immediately occupied the lands of the new nunnery, claiming that Valborg's late husband owed them a debt. In defence of her nunnery, Valborg went as high up as the papal court in Avignon to fight the case, and indeed died there – but her suit was successful: a papal bull of 1329 specified that the lands in question should be transferred to the abbot of Sorø to establish and care for a nunnery.[101] In 1220, another widow, Amice, lady of Breteuil, decided to found a Cistercian nunnery at Villiers-to-Nonnains (Île-de-France) instead of a Dominican priory as had originally been intended; she had to work for six years to extract from the Dominican prior and the bishop of Sense (in whose diocese the nunnery was located) permission to alter the original bequest.[102]

Charters and wills of the benefactors of Cistercian houses sometimes provide evidence of close personal connections between individual lay women and Cistercian nuns, often linked to family relations. The will of Gyde, widow of Esbern Karlsen, for example, left a golden ring with a crucifix to the prioress of the Cistercian nunnery in Roskilde, and two marks, a chest and a cooking pan to her own granddaughter Kristine, who was a nun in that house.[103] Several nuns of Saint-Antoine-des-Champs Abbey (Paris) enjoyed private incomes given to them by their families when they entered the abbey – which, as not all the nuns had such financial backing, led to conflict within the community, which was only resolved when Abbess Gile established in 1302 a funds for nuns who did not have private revenues. For this purpose the abbess used a gift of 10 *livres* in rents, which she received for her own personal use from her cousin Lady Marguerite of Beaumont. This was, as Berman remarks, a pragmatic solution: instead of trying to enforce vows of poverty and the ban on the private property, the abbess simply established a private income for nuns who had did not have one.[104]

Conclusions

Cistercian nunneries varied a great deal in terms of shapes and sizes of the communities, their association with the Order, their economic standing and their relations with the outside world. In their economic life, large and wealthy Cistercian nunneries, like their male counterparts, followed extensive land acquisition programmes, whilst smaller communities, which were more numerous, often struggled to function for decades below the monastic 'poverty line'. However, as so many Cistercian nunneries, especially these in northern France and Flanders, began their lives as leper houses and hospitals where poverty, charity and penitential spirituality were at the core of their mission and the major reason for women to seek entry, so it is important not to regard poverty as a simply an economic phenomenon.

Relations between Cistercian nunneries and the male half of the Order varied from formal incorporation to various degrees of informal association, including self-identification with the Cistercian movement without being legally a part of it. Historians seeking neat classifications and trying to distinguish between 'true' and 'imposter' nunneries have made too much of these distinctions, and recent work has shown that the status of 'Cistercian female community' was one that could have different meanings, according to various external authorities or the nuns' own convictions, all of them equally valid.

Of course, strict claustration was a major obstacle for the nunneries, obliging them to seek clerical assistance and that of patrons or friends in managing their estates, dealing with disputes and legal issues, and various other types of contact with the outside world. For many female founders and patronesses 'their' nunneries were an important place to express their own piety, retire to lead a contemplative life and finally be buried and commemorated, often amongst their relatives. However, the spiritual life in many Cistercian houses gave an opportunity to women searching for a meaningful role in the church. Despite the permanent unease about female authority, Cistercian communities gave many nuns the power to influence spirituality through their visions and texts. The influence of charismatic figures such as Mechtild of Magdeburg, Mechthild of Hackeborn or Lutgard was significant beyond the walls of their monasteries and even beyond the Cistercian Order. Although it was the men in the Cistercian movement who built the structures of the Order and gathered at the annual General Chapter from which the abbesses were barred, friendships and correspondence between monks and nuns were nevertheless important for the development of the monastic ethos. Many Cistercian monks who were chaplains to the nuns took their pastoral role very seriously, and visions and texts of Cistercian female mystics were infused with ideas shared by all Cistercians, regardless of their gender.

Notes

1. Bernard of Clairvaux, *Sermones in Cantica canticorum*, ed. Jean Leclerq, *Bernard Opera* (Rome: Editiones Cistercienses, 1957), vol. 2, p. 157, trans. in Caroline Walker Bynum, *Jesus as Mother* (Berkeley, CA: University of California Press, 1982), p. 145; *The Letters of St. Bernard of Clairvaux*, ed. Bruno Scott James (London: Burns Oates, 1953), letter 81, p. 119.
2. Bynum, *Jesus as Mother*, pp. 145, 168.
3. Shawn Madison Krahmer, 'Interpreting the Letters of Bernard of Clairvaux to Ermengarde, Countess of Brittany: The Twelfth-Century Context and the Language of Friendship', *Cistercian Studies Quarterly* 27 (1992), pp. 217–226, 230–231; *Letters of St. Bernard*, letters 119 and 117; *Sancti Bernardi Opera*, ed. J. Leclercq, H. Rochais (Rome: Editiones Cistercienses, 1974), vol. 7, pp. 296 and 297; Jean Leclercq, *Women and St Bernard of Clairvaux*, trans. Marie-Bernard Saïd (Kalamazoo, MI: Cistercian Publications, 1989), pp. 62–67.
4. Gillian R. Evans, *Bernard of Clairvaux* (Oxford: Oxford University Press, 2000), p. 28.
5. Brian Patrick McGuire, *The Difficult Saint: Bernard of Clairvaux and his Tradition* (Kalamazoo, MI: Cistercian Studies, 1991), pp. 31–32; for Bernard's theology of Virgin Mary see Leclercq, *Women and St Bernard*, pp. 87–104.
6. *Twelfth-Century Statutes from the Cistercian General Chapter: Latin text with English notes and commentary*, ed. Chrysgonus Waddell (Brecht: Cîteaux, Commentarii Cistercienses, 2002), 1190: 2, 29, 38, 55, 1191: 5,

21, 1192: 47, 48, 52, 1193: 11, 17, 27, 33, 41, 66, 1194: 28, 38, 55, 1195: 65, 67, 78, 79, 1196: 11, 1197: 6, 1198: 4, 1199: 43, 54, 69.
7. Brian Patrick McGuire, 'The Cistercians and Friendship: An Opening to Women', in *Hidden Springs: Cistercian Monastic Women*, 2 vols., ed. John A. Nichols and Lillian Thomas Shank (Kalamazoo, MI: Cistercian Publications, 1995), vol. 1, pp. 177, 182.
8. Eleonor Campion, 'Cîteaux Our Mother? Early Cistercian Women's History Revisited', *Cistercian Studies Quarterly* 34 (1999), pp. 485–490; Constance Berman, 'Were there Twelfth-Century Cistercian Nuns?', *Church History* 68 (1999), pp. 852–826.
9. Jean-Baptiste Lefèvre, 'Deux Cas Conjoints d'une evolution du monde Béguinal au monde Cistercien La Communauté des Awirs – Aywières (1195–1211) et Sainte Lutgarde (1194–1211)', in *Unanimité et diversité cisterciennes: filiations, réseaux, relectures du XIIe au XVIIe siècle: actes du quatrième colloque international du CERCOR, Dijon, 23–25 septembre 1998*, ed. Nicole Bouter (Saint-Etienne: Publications de l'Université de Saint-Etienne, 2000), pp. 281–293.
10. Ernst Günter Krenig, 'Mittelalterliche Frauenklöstern nach den Konstitutionem von Cîteaux', *Analecta Sacri Ordinis Cisterciensis* 10 (1954), pp. 1–105; Sally Thompson, 'The Problem of the Cistercian Nuns in the Twelfth and Early Thirteenth Century', in *Medieval Women*, ed. Derek Baker, Studies in Church History, Subsidia 1 (Oxford: Blackwell, 1978), pp. 227–252.
11. R.W. Southern, *Western Society and the Church in the Middle Ages* (Harmondsworth: Penguin, 1970), p. 314.
12. Louis Lekai, *The Cistercians: Ideals and Reality* (Kent, OH: Kent State University Press, 1977), p. 347.
13. Brigitte Degler-Spengler, 'The Incorporation of Cistercian Nuns into the Order in the Twelfth and Thirteenth Centuries', *Hidden Springs*, vol. 1, p. 119.
14. Degler-Spengler, 'The Incorporation of Cistercian Nuns', p. 88.
15. Constance Hoffman Berman, *The Cistercian Evolution: The Invention of a Religious Order in Twelfth-Century Europe* (Philadelphia, PA: University of Pennsylvania Press, 2000).
16. Elizabeth Freeman, 'Cistercian Nuns in Medieval England: Unofficial Meets Official', *Studies in Church History* 42 (2006), p. 111.
17. Gerd Ahlers, *Weibliches Zisterziensertum im Mittelalter und seine Klöster Niedersachsen* (Berlin: Lucas, 2002), pp. 90–95.
18. *Statuta capitulorum generalium ordinis Cisterciensis ab anno 1116 ad annum 1786*, ed. Joseph Canivez, 8 vols. (Louvain: Bureaux de la Revue, 1933–1941), vol. 1, 1213: 3.
19. Donald Hochstetler, 'The Meaning of Monastic Cloister for Women According to Caesarius of Arles', in *Religion, Culture, and Society in the Early Middle Ages: Studies in Honor of Richard E. Sullivan*, ed. Thomas F.X. Noble and John J. Contreni (Kalamazoo, MI: Medieval Institute Publications, 1987), pp. 27–40.
20. *Statuta* vol. 1, 1218: 84.

21. *Statuta* vol. 1, 1220: 4; 1225: 7.
22. *Statuta* vol. 2, 1228: 16; 1239: 7.
23. *Statuta* vol. 2, 1251: 4.
24. Elizabeth Freeman, '"Houses of a Peculiar Order": Cistercian Nunneries in Medieval England, with Special Attention to the Fifteenth and Sixteenth Centuries', *Cîteaux: Commentarii Cistercienses* 55 (2004), p. 248.
25. Jean de la Croix Bouton, *Les moniales cisterciennes*, 4 vols. (Grignan: Abbaye d'Aiguebelle, 1986–1989), vol. 1, pp. 37–82.
26. C.H. Talbot, 'Two Opuscula of John Godard First Abbot of Newenham', *Analecta Sacri Ordinis Cisterciensis* 10 (1954), pp. 208–267; Freeman, '"Houses of a Peculiar Order"', p. 259.
27. Thompson, 'The Problem of the Cistercian Nuns', p. 239; Campion, 'Cîteaux Our Mother', pp. 494, 497.
28. Degler-Spengler, 'The Incorporation of Cistercian Nuns', pp. 97–99, 106.
29. Jacques de Vitry, *The Historia Occidentalis: A Critical Edition*, ed. John Frederick Hinnerbusch (Fribourg: The University Press Fribourg, 1972), p. 117.
30. Anne E. Lester, 'Cares beyond the Walls: Cistercian Nuns and the Care of Lepers in Twelfth- and Thirteenth-Century Northern France', in *Religious and Laity in Western Europe 1000–1400: Interaction, Negotiation, and Power*, ed. Emilia Jamroziak and Janet Burton (Turnhout: Brepols, 2006), pp. 197–199.
31. Jo Ann McNamara, *Sisters in Arms: Catholic Nuns through Two Millennia* (Cambridge, MA.: Harvard University Press, 1996), p. 301.
32. *Twelfth-Century Statutes*, 1191: 21.
33. *Twelfth-Century Statutes*, 1190: 38, 1192: 52.
34. *Urkundenbuch der Abtei Heisterbach*, ed. Ferdinand Schmitz, Urkundenbücher der Geistlichen Stiftungen des Niederrheins 2 (Bonn: Peter Haustein, 1908), no. 238, p. 316.
35. Freeman, '"Houses of a Peculiar Order"', p. 263.
36. John A. Nichols, 'Introduction', in *Hidden Springs*, vol. 1, pp. 3–9.
37. Caroline Walker Bynum, 'Patterns of Female Piety in the Later Middle Ages', in *Crown and Veil: Female Monasticism from the Fifth to the Fifteenth Centuries*, ed. Jeffrey F. Hamburger and Susan Marti, trans. Dietlinde Hamburger (New York: Columbia University Press, 2008), pp. 179–181.
38. McNamara, *Sisters in Arms*, pp. 301–302.
39. Freeman, '"Houses of a Peculiar Order"', pp. 265–266.
40. Croix Bouton, 'Nuns of Cîteaux', in *Hidden Springs*, vol. 1, p. 16; Freeman, '"Houses of a Peculiar Order"', p. 273, n. 119.
41. Degler-Spengler, 'The Incorporation of Cistercian Nuns', p. 97; *Statuta*, vol. 2, 1237: 4.
42. Peter Feige, 'Filitation und Landeshoheit. Die Entstehung der Zisterzienser- kongregationen auf der iberischen Halbinsel', *Zisterzienser-Studien*, vol. 1, ed. Peter Feige, Wolfgang Ribbe and Reinhard Schneider (Berlin: Colloquium Verlag, 1975), pp. 46–47.
43. Maren Kuhn-Rehfus, 'Cistercian Nuns in Germany in the Thirteenth Century', in *Hidden Springs*, p. 149.

44. Werner Rösener, *Reichsabtei Salem* (Sigmaringen: Thorbecke, 1974), pp. 163–164; Bede Lacker, 'Cistercian Nuns in Medieval Hungary', in *Hidden Springs*, vol. 1, p. 159.
45. David Knowles and R. Neville Hadcock, *Medieval Religious Houses: England and Wales* (London: Longman, 1971), pp. 222–226; Freeman, ' "Houses of a Peculiar Order" ', pp. 284–285.
46. Freeman, 'Cistercian Nuns in Medieval England', pp. 114–119.
47. Nicolaus Heutger, 'Zisterzienser-Nonnen im mittelalterlichen Niedersachsen', *Cîteaux: Commentarii Cistercienses* 38 (1987), pp. 193–200.
48. Janet Burton, *The Monastic Order in Yorkshire 1069–1215* (Cambridge: Cambridge University Press, 1999), pp. 125–152.
49. Freeman, ' "Houses of a Peculiar Order" ', pp. 261–262.
50. Anne E. Lester, 'Cleaning House in 1399: Disobedience and the Demise of Cistercian Convents in Northern France at the End of the Middle Ages', in *Oboedientia: Zu Formen und Grenzen von Macht und Unterordnung im mittelalterlichen Religiosentum*, ed. Sébastien Barret and Gert Melville (Münster: Lit Verlag, 2005), pp. 425, 431–436.
51. Werner Rösener, 'Household and Prayer. Medieval Convents as Economic Entities', in *Crown and Veil*, p. 253.
52. Lester, 'Cares beyond the Walls', pp. 200, 222–223.
53. Anne E. Lester, *Creating Cistercian Nuns: the Women's Religious Movement and its Reform in Thirteenth-Century Champagne* (Ithaca, NY: Cornell University Press), pp. 39–40, 129.
54. Hedwig Röckelein, 'Founders, Donors, and Saints: Patrons of Nuns' Convents', in *Crown and Veil*, p. 220.
55. *Krone und Schleier: Kunst aus Mittelalterlichen Frauenklöstern. Ruhrlandmuseum: Die frühen Klöstern und Stifte 500–1200. Kunst- und Ausstellungshalle der Bundesrepublik Deutschland: Die Zeit der Orden 1200–1500*, ed. Jutta Frings and Jan Gerchow (Munich: Hirmer Verlag, 2005), no. 326, pp. 420–421.
56. Rösener, 'Household and Prayer', p. 254.
57. M. Kuhn-Rufus, 'Zisterzienserinnen in Deutschland', in *Die Zisterzienser: Ordensleben zwischen Ideal und Wirklichkeit*, ed. Kaspar Elm (Cologne: Rheinland-Verlag, 1980), pp. 132–134.
58. Anja Ostrowitzki, 'Der "Liber dictaminum" des Abtes von Himmerod als Zeugnis für die "cura monialium" im spätmittelalterlichen Zisterzienserorden', *Deutsches Archiv für Erforschung des Mittelalters* 55 (1999), p. 176.
59. Klaus Schreiner, 'Pastoral Care in Female Monasteries. Sacramental Services, Spiritual Edification, Ethical Discipline', in *Crown and Veil*, pp. 238–240.
60. Schreiner, 'Pastoral Care in Female Monasteries', p. 242.
61. *Statuta*, vol. 2, 1247: 17.
62. Roger de Ganck, 'Marginalia to Visitation Cards for Cistercian Nuns in Belgium', *Cîteaux: Commentarii Cistercienses* 40 (1989), pp. 232, 236; Lester, 'Cleaning House in 1399', p. 425.
63. *Diplomatarium Danicum*, series I, vol. 3(2), ed. C.A. Christensen (København: C.A. Reitzels, 1977) pp. 266–469; Patrick Brian McGuire, *The Cistercians in Denmark: their attitudes, roles and functions in medieval society* (Kalamazoo, MI: Cistercian Publications, 1982), pp. 99–100.

64. Freeman, ' "Houses of a Peculiar Order" ', pp. 267–270.
65. Ghislain Baury, 'Patronage et Gestion des Domaines Chez les Cisterciennes Castillanes. Les Fausses Quittances de Cañas (1298–1302)', *Cîteaux: Commentarii Cistercienses* 59 (2008), pp. 237–250.
66. Benoît Chauvin, 'L'integration des femmes à l'Ordre de Cîteaux au XIIe siècle, entre hauts de Meuse et rives du Léman', in *Cîteaux et les femmes*, ed. Bernadette Barrière and Marie-Élizabeth Henneau (Paris: Créaphis, 2001), pp. 193–211.
67. Rösener, 'Household and Prayer', p. 254.
68. Kateřina Charvátová, 'Les abbayes de nonnes cisterciennes dans le royaume médiéval de Bohême leurs relations avec le milieu laïc', in *Cîteaux et les femmes*, pp. 232–233.
69. Elizabeth Makowski, *Canon Law and Cloistered Women: Periculoso and its commentators, 1298–1545* (Washington, DC: Catholic University of America Press, 1997), pp. 19, 31.
70. Bynum, *Jesus as Mother*, pp. 174–180, 250–252.
71. Mechthild of Magdeburg, *The Flowing Light of the Godhead*, trans. Frank Tobin (Mahwah, NJ: Paulist, 1998); Amy Hollywood, *The Soul of the Virgin Wife: Mechthild of Magdeburg, Marguerite Porete, and Meister Eckhart* (Notre Dame, IN: University of Notre Dame Press, 1995).
72. Anna Harrison, '"Oh! What Treasure is in this Book?" Writing, Reading, and Community at the Monastery of Helfta', *Viator* 39 (2008), pp. 75–106.
73. Dennis D. Martin, 'Carthusians as Advocates of Women Visionary Reformers', in *Studies in Carthusian Monasticism in the Later Middle Ages*, ed. Julian Luxford (Turnhout: Brepols, 2008), p. 136.
74. Anne Clark, 'An Uneasy Triangle: Jesus, Mary and Gertrude of Helfta', *Maria: A Journal of Marian Studies* 1 (2000), p. 46.
75. Ira Westergård, *Approaching Sacred Pregnancy: The Cult of the Visitation and Narrative Altarpieces in the Late Fifteenth-Century Florence* (Helsinki: Suomalaisen Kirjallisuuden Seura, 2007), pp. 52–53.
76. Elisabeth Vavra, 'Bildmotiv und Frauenmystik – Funktion und Rezeption', in *Frauenmystik in Mittelalter*, ed. Peter Dinzelbacher and Dietrich R. Bauer (Ostfildern: Schwabenverlag, 1985), pp. 201–230.
77. McGuire, 'The Cistercians and Friendship', pp. 176–177, 182.
78. Amandus Bussels, 'Saint Lutgard's Mystical Spirituality', in *Hidden Springs*, pp. 211–213, 215–216, 218.
79. Marius Winzeler, 'Die Bibliothek der Zisterzienserinnenabtei St. Marienstern und ihre Beziehungen zum Kloster Altzella', in *Die Zisterzienser und ihre Bibliotheken: Buchbesitz und Schriftgebrauch des Klosters Altzella im europäischen Vergleich*, ed. Tom Graber and Martina Schattkowsky (Leipzig: Leipziger Universitätsverlag, 2008), p. 224.
80. Gaëlle Lachambre-Cordier, 'Les moniales de Notre-Dames-des-Prés de Douai à travers un martyrologe gothique. Le manuscript 838 de la Bibliothèque municipale de Valenciennes', in *Cîteaux et les femmes*, pp. 249–265.
81. David N. Bell, *What Nuns Read: Books and Libraries in Medieval English Nunneries* (Kalamazoo, MI: Cistercian Publications, 1995), pp. 138, 141, 168.
82. Westergård, *Approaching Sacred Pregnancy*, pp. 47–48.

83. James France, 'From Bernard to Bridget: Cistercian Contribution to a Unique Scandinavian Monastic Body', in *Bernardus Magister: Papers Presented at the Nonacentenary Celebration of the Birth of Saint Bernard of Clairvaux, Kalamazoo, Michigan, Sponsored by the Institute of Cistercian Studies, Western Michigan University, 10–13 May 1990*, ed. John R. Sommerfeldt (Kalamazoo, MI: Cistercian Publications, 1992), pp. 484–494.
84. Röckelein, 'Founders, Donors, and Saints', p. 212.
85. Translation from an unpublished manuscript in Constance Hoffman Berman, 'Cistercian Nuns and the Development of the Order: the Abbey at Saint-Antoine-des-Champs outside Paris', in *The Joy of Learning and the Love of God: Essays in Honor of Jean Leclercq*, ed. E. Rozanne Elder (Kalamazoo, MI: Cistercian Publications, 1995), p. 126.
86. Berman, 'Cistercian Nuns and the Development of the Order', p. 138.
87. Rose Walker, 'Images of Royal and Aristocratic Burial in Northern Spain, c. 950–c. 1250', in *Medieval Memories: Men, Women and the Past, 700–1300*, ed. Elizabeth van Houts (Harlow: Pearson, 2001), pp. 162–165.
88. Alexandra Gajewski, 'The Patronage Question under Review: Queen Blanche of Castile (1188–1252) and the Architecture of the Cistercian Abbeys at Royaumont, Maubuisson, and Le Lys', in *Reassessing the Roles of Women as 'Makers' of Medieval Art and Architecture*, ed. Therese Martin (Leiden and Boston: Brill, 2012), p. 217; Kathleen Nolan, *Queens in Stone and Silver: The Creation of a Visual Imagery of Queenship in Capetian France* (New York: Palgrave Macmillan, 2009), pp. 123–129.
89. Emanuel S. Klinkenberg, *Compressed Meanings: the Donor's Model in Medieval Art to around 1300: Origin, Spread and Significance of an Architectural Image in the Realm of Tension between Tradition and Likeness* (Turnhout: Brepols, 2009), p. 204.
90. Heike Reimann, 'Cistercian Nuns in the High Middle Ages: The Cistercians of Bergen in the Principality of Rügen (North Germany)', *Cîteaux: Commentarii Cistercienses* 55 (2004), pp. 233–238.
91. John A. Nichols, 'The Cistercian Nunnery of Swine Priory: Its Church and Choir Stalls', in *Studiosorum Speculum: Studies in Honor of Louis J. Lekai, O.Cist*, ed. Francis R. Swiietek and John R. Sommerfeldt (Kalamazoo, MI: Cistercian Publications, 1993), pp. 277–278.
92. *Schlesisches Urkundenbuch*, ed. Heinrich Appelt and Josef Joachim Menzel, vol. 1 (Cologne: Böhlau, 1971), no. 84; Franz J. Felten, 'Der Zisterzienserorden und die Frauen', in *Weltverachtung und Dynamik*, ed. Harald Schwillus and Andreas Hölscher (Berlin: Lukas Verlag, 2000), p. 75.
93. Marian Kanior, 'Pierwsze fundacje cysterek na ziemiach polskich', in *Cysterki w dziejach i kulturze ziem polskich, dawnej Rzeczpospolitej i Europy Środkowej*, ed. Andrzej Wyrwa, Antoni Kiełbasa and Józef Swastek (Poznań: Wydawnictwo Poznańskie, 2004), p. 42.
94. Archdale A. King, 'Eucharistic Reservations in Cistercian Churches', *Collectanea Ordinis Cisterciensium Reformatorum* 20 (1958), p. 247.
95. Maria Alegria Fernandes Marques, 'Les premières nonnes cisterciennes au Portugal. Le role des femmes de la familie royale', in *Cîteaux et les femmes*, pp. 213–226.

96. Lester, *Creating Cistercian Nuns*, pp. 69–70.
97. Penelope D. Johnson, *Equal in Monastic Profession: Religious Women in Medieval France* (Chicago, IL: University of Chicago Press, 1991), pp. 36–37.
98. R. Andrew McDonald, 'The Foundation and Patronage of Nunneries by Native Elites in Twelfth- and Early Thirteenth-Century Scotland', in *Women in Scotland c. 1100–c. 1750*, ed. E. Ewan and M.M. Meikle (East Linton: Tuckwell Press, 1999), pp. 5–6.
99. Kateřina Charvátová, 'Propter laudabilia abbatum merita: The Kings of Bohemia and the Cistercian Order', in *In Tal und Einsamkeit: 725 Jahre Kloster Fürstenfeld. Die Zisterzienser im alten Bayern. Band III: Kolloquium*, ed. Klaus Wollenberg (Fürstenfeldbruck: E. Wewel, 1990), p. 172.
100. *The Primitive Cistercian Breviary with Variants from the 'Bernardine' Cistercian Breviary*, ed. Chrysogonus Waddell, Spicilegium Friburgense 44 (Fribourg: Academic Press, 2007), pp. 36–37.
101. McGuire, *The Cistercians in Denmark*, p. 195.
102. Lester, *Creating Cistercian Nuns*, p. 70.
103. *Diplomatarium Danicum*, series II, vol. 4, p. 67; McGuire, *The Cistercians in Denmark*, p. 171.
104. Berman, 'Cistercian Nuns and the Development of the Order', pp. 140–141.

chapter 5

VISUAL CULTURE OF CISTERCIAN COMMUNITIES

The life of the monks and nuns took place in specific areas in the monastic precinct – the cloister and the church – places specifically designed to provide a focus for the community, emphasise the central role of the liturgy and reinforce claustration. The precinct was largely exclusive to the community, with only restricted access for outsiders. Of course, the external appearance of Cistercian monasteries between the twelfth and early sixteenth centuries changed in line with architectural and artistic fashions; and changes in attitudes to the commemoration of patrons and benefactors and the comfort and privacy of abbots and monks impacted on the shape and form of the buildings. There was no one architectural style that can be labelled as 'Cistercian', but the Cistercian way of life nevertheless shaped the architecture, decorations and objects surrounding monks and nuns into a Cistercian aesthetic.

Just as the myths of the Order's origins were reinterpreted, first by generations of medieval Cistercians and then by historians, so Cistercian architecture and visual culture has its own core 'myths', two of which have influenced popular ideas about medieval Cistercian communities: firstly, the idea that Bernard of Clairvaux designed the ideal model of a Cistercian church and, second, that certain features of Cistercian architecture, especially ornamentation, were codified by the General Chapter, and all Cistercian monasteries should be measured against these criteria.

In Bernard's polemical 'Apologia ad Guillelmum' (1125) two chapters criticised contemporary monastic architecture, especially Cluniac, for its visual excesses and richness. But the abbot of Clairvaux did not stop there, and even designed an ideal plan for monastic churches allegedly implemented in the Cistercian churches built during Bernard's lifetime. The centre of Bernard's 'plan' for churches, as defined by Karl Heinz Esser in 1953 on the basis of evidence from Himmerod Abbey, a direct foundation from Clairvaux, was a polygonal chancel of a church exuding austerity and simplicity, minimal decorations inside and outside the cloistral buildings, and especially an absence of any figurative motifs.[1]

Yet the idea that Bernard had created something resembling a blue-print remained very influential for the rest of the twentieth century and although simplicity and austerity were indeed important features of Cistercian architecture, Bernard 'would have been astounded', as Anselm Dimier observed, to hear that he was solely responsible for this.[2] In fact, just as Bernard did not create the Cistercian Order single-handed, so he was not solely responsible for Cistercian architecture.

Students of the architectural and archaeological evidence and of the manuscript sources have discovered a pretty coherent, and very early, Cistercian programme of how the interiors of monastic churches should look. Prescriptions restricting the use of particular precious and decorative materials can be found in the *Carta Caritatis Prior* and *Exordium Parvum*: silk, the most luxurious of medieval fabrics, was almost completely excluded from the altar cloths; the liturgical vestments worn by the priest were to be of one colour only; gold and precious jewels were not to be used in any ornaments, containers or utensils in the monastery, except for the chalices used in the celebration of the mass. But trying to see these simplifications as exclusively Cistercian phenomena misses a crucial point: it was not so much a case of the early Cistercians' restricting visual excesses, as one of many early eleventh-century reforming prescriptions aimed at standardising the sacred utensils. In that respect Cistercian ideas were not original, but it must be said that the white monks took them to an extreme, not only standardising the material used, but trying to eliminate precious metals from liturgical objects.[3] Another prescription tried to eliminate paintings or painted sculpture; stained glass windows, a staple of monastic decoration, were rejected as a distraction from spiritual pursuits, since 'when attention is turned to such things the advantage of good meditation or the discipline of religious gravity is often neglected'.[4] Besides, sculpture, being expensive to produce, conflicted with the reformist ideas of austerity and poverty.[5] The rejection of decoration was also linked to the Cistercian refusal of parochial duties and unwillingness to attract pilgrims, which for many Benedictine monasteries were important functions and sources of income.[6]

Historical – or rather historicist – concepts of the 'true' Cistercian life and its decline also characterised the approach of some historians to Cistercian architecture. The assumption that the General Chapter's codifications formed a coherent plan, applicable to all the Cistercian churches, was not universally accepted by art historians: on the one hand, evidence that these allegedly clearly defined rules of simplicity and poverty in architecture and decoration were being ignored as early as the second half of the twelfth century was much cited in the debate about 'ideals and reality' in the history of the Order; on the other, some scholars explain these variations as evidence of the adjustment of the Cistercian model to changing needs and expectations rather than a 'departure from original ideals' – which after all never existed as a clearly defined prescription. Most strikingly, the first Cistercian mother church to enlarge the east end with a chevet was Clairvaux. This work had already begun before Bernard's death, in order to create a focus for the future cult – a clear manifestation that even the abbot of Clairvaux was not following the 'Bernardine plan', if there ever was one.[7]

Of great importance in Cistercian architecture was the desire for silence, an essential condition for prayers, which found expression in the plainness of lines and the absence of narrative designs and colours in the architectural designs, while the simple effects of light and shadow on various monastic buildings created an ideal environment for contemplation.[8] Not that coloured glass was rejected for financial reasons, or from any 'puritanical' dislike of gothic ornamentation.[9] The fact was that the imagery of light was of great significance in Cistercian theology and spirituality – witness the sacralisation of time through the timetable of the daily Divine Office, the large number of references to the changes of light during the day, and the many Cistercian writers, notably William of St Thierry, Ailred of Rievaulx and Gilbert of Hoyland, who used metaphors of light. In the writing of Bernard of Clairvaux himself, light is separated from colour; and whilst light symbolised the truth, Christ and the divine Word, colour in his writing symbolises 'false value'. The dichotomy of light and darkness represents the demarcation between the divine and the human: whereas windows are the gates to divinity and walls stand for the confinement of the human condition. The application of these ideas to Cistercian architecture was seen in the interplay between light and darkness when colour-free windows allowed the full intensity of light to enter the nave and chancel.[10]

Most modern scholars agree that the restrictive theoretical prescriptions of the General Chapter and the *Carta Caritatis*, *Exordium Parvum* could never have served to inspire Cistercian communities all over Europe to adopt one standardised architectural model, and that, rather, the broad Cistercian formula of simplicity was in practice flexible enough to accommodate different stylistic interpretations created by monastic and lay workshops in response to a variety of local traditions and materials. There is no evidence that either the patrons or the monastic communities themselves were inclined to follow any 'plan' when it was much easier to follow the local traditions; nor is there evidence that the General Chapter objected to the variety of architecture in Cistercian churches.

In fact, as Marcel Aubert has argued, while there was a 'Cistercian spirit' in architecture there was never a Cistercian 'architectural style'.[11] As Cistercian churches, whenever and wherever they were built, tended to follow current fashions (and pre-existing communities which joined the Cistercian Order continued to use their 'pre-Cistercian' buildings), there was never any such thing as a 'typical Cistercian Church'.[12] Some architectural features (for example, the use of local decorative motifs, or of different types of stone, or bricks) simply reflected the variety of local conditions in the wide geographical area involved. But the thankless task of trying to reconcile the variety displayed in Cistercian architecture with alleged stylistic 'prescriptions' becomes entirely superfluous if we adopt Terryl Kinder's thesis that Cistercian architecture was not tied to a specific design or model, but reflected the Order's spirituality and monastic ideals.[13] The architecture served its purpose 'as long as the standards of simplicity answered the needs of the community'.[14] Simplicity remained an important value for the monastic communities, and its manifestation in the architecture took recognisable yet different forms. Although no one would claim that no monks ever helped to cut a stone or lay a brick, the notion that white monks generally laboured on the monastic building sites – that, in fact, the Cistercians built their own abbeys – is a myth that flies in the face of the evidence that professional stone-cutters and masons built the abbeys. Indeed, from the last quarter of the twelfth century, as technological advances and the complexity of the early Gothic architecture required far greater specialisation, the construction of buildings became increasingly professionalised – many professional masons' marks survived on Cistercian buildings.[15] As Cistercian houses linked in a filiation often made use of the same masons, the architecture and decoration of such houses often displayed many similarities: for example, the dominance of the brick architecture among the Cistercian monasteries of the southern Baltic coast came from their Danish mother houses. This was possible because the artistic ideas, technological knowledge and trained personnel travelled using connections of the filiation system.[16]

Cistercian Churches

The design of the Cistercian churches was closely linked to their liturgical function, and as monastic life was centred on the liturgy and communal prayer the church occupied the highest place within the precinct.[17] Plain in its design and free from distracting ornamentation it was intended to generate an atmosphere of simplicity, harmony and tranquillity.[18] It was

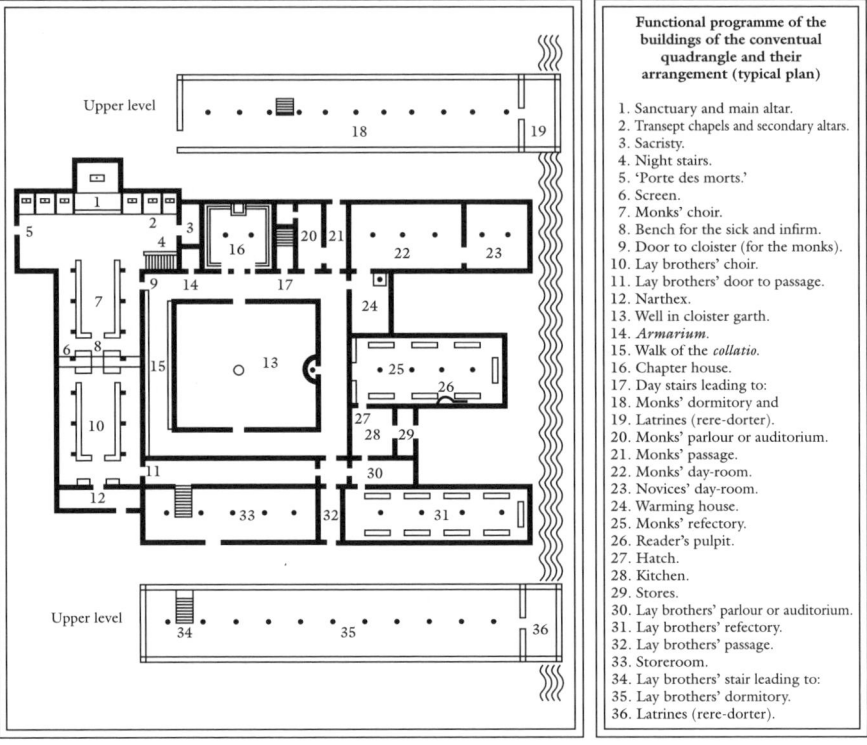

Figure 5.1 Typical ground plan of the Cistercian conventual buildings
Source: Jean-Francois Leroux-Dhuys, *Cistercian Abbeys: History and Architecture* (Cologne: Könemann, 1998), p. 52.

also the most prestigious building within the precinct and the abbots and patrons often influenced the artistic choices. Monastic churches tended to be rebuilt many times according to the changing fashions. The growth in the size of the communities also led to rebuilding and enlargement of the choir.

The most common plan of a Cistercian church was a cruciform shape, the nave and the side being traversed by transepts ending in one or more chapels at the ends, and a chevet for the altar at the east end (see Figure 5.1).[19] Unlike cathedrals and parish churches, Cistercian churches, not being open to the public, did not usually have doors at the west end. Within the hierarchy of space the east end with the high altar – presbytery or sanctuary – on a raised platform, a few steps above the level of the nave, was the most important. Here sacred vessels used in the mass were kept in a niche on the wall. There was usually a transept running across the top of the nave – not essential from a liturgical point of view – providing additional space for separate chapels. This became increasingly important from the thirteenth century, when the majority of monks were ordained priests and needed separate altars to perform the mass. A striking architectural solution to this problem is to be found at Fountains Abbey, where the Chapel of the Nine Altars had a full-height transept added across the east end of the church in imitation of nine chapels around the apse at Clairvaux.[20]

A flight of steps from the dormitory to the transept gave direct access to the church when the monks came for the first office of the day (see chapter 2). At the far end of the transept arm was the 'door of the dead', leading to the cemetery where the monks were buried, its proximity emphasising that the departed monks remained members of the community forever. As a sign of humility, the graves themselves were not marked. Some larger Cistercian abbeys established charnel houses (*ossuaria*) within the monks' cemetery where bones of the monks were gathered. A good example of such a building comes come from Doberan Abbey (Mecklenburg), built in mid-1250 as an octagonal-shaped chapel with an *ossuarium* in the cellar and the altar dedicated to St Michael, who was often represented escorting souls to heaven and hence a suitable patron for a graveyard chapel.[21]

The largest part of the church – the nave – was subdivided into three sections, or 'choirs'. The choir was the space reserved for the monks and novices (positioned behind the monks) during services and for private prayer. Each monk had his own seat (stall), arranged according to his seniority within the community. The abbot's seat was usually more prominent, especially in the later middle ages. Stalls were usually wooden and decorated with complex carvings, which like many other monastic furnishings were subject to changes according to fashion, therefore very few medieval Cistercian stalls survive. In the middle of this choir there was a portable lectern for a large copy of the antiphonary with chants. The second choir, further west, equipped with stalls and a further lectern for the Psalter, was reserved for elderly and infirm monks, but during services novices also moved there to chant from the Psalter. The third choir, a separate liturgical space, was firmly divided off from the first two by a screen and was used by the lay brothers. They entered the church by a separate entrance door in the aisle connecting it directly with the lay brothers' domain (hence avoiding all contact with the monks and novices); and although they were unable actually to witness the daily celebration of the high mass, they could hear the voice of the priest. According to the evidence from fourteenth-century Maulbronn, Heilsbronn, Vyšší Bród and Doberan, the late medieval development of the visual programme of the *chorus conversorum* was intended to transmit a penitential message (often the story of the Christ's Passion) to those gathered in the third choir.²² The area beyond the lay brothers' choir was available to hired workers, *familiares* and occasionally guests of the abbey. In the course of the fourteenth century it became possible for male lay guests to participate in the solemn mass at the back of the lay brothers' choir, which increased the importance of devotional images in this space.²³

This stratification of space, emphasising the internal hierarchy of the community, was a manifestation of the exclusivity of Cistercian churches: access to the cloistral range, even if only to the westernmost part of the church, was a special honour for an outsider for there were very few occasions during the liturgical year when the Cistercians came in contact with the lay people – for example the yearly procession around the cloister with candles on the Feast of the Purification of Mary (2 February), in which the entire community, lay brothers, *familiares* and guests took part.²⁴

The design of Cistercian houses was strongly influenced by their patrons, especially in the cases of abbeys that were founded as, or later became, mausolea for the laity (see chapter 3). Here, it was not simply a matter of the placing of tombs or of their iconography, but of creating an appropriate 'stage' for the liturgy and other commemorative practices. One of the most striking examples is Altenberg Abbey, founded by the Berg family in 1133: a new Gothic choir with nine altars and chevet, where the whole of the floor was liturgically functional, was built between 1259 and 1285; and the architectural scheme, which even incorporated elements of the royal Capetian architecture, reflected the growing power and ambitions of the Berg family.²⁵ Indeed, not only the overall shape of a church, but the form and function of particular sections of the building were influenced by the expectations of the patrons: in Zbraslav Abbey, a royal Bohemian foundation (1297) and a necropolis of several Premyslid kings, the monastic church exhibited several 'atypical' features – for example, the portal in the north transept of the Cistercian churches usually led to the monks' cemetery, but in Zbraslav the portal was an access route to the royal tomb.²⁶

Shrines and other features of the cults of saints also left their mark on the Cistercian churches. Particularly important for monastic communities (usually as part of their myth of origin) were the cults of holy abbots, who were believed to exercise a protective power over their home communities and to intercede on behalf of their brethren in the next world. The figure of the holy abbot was strengthened by the canonisation of Bernard of Clairvaux in 1174, and the visual splendour of his cult at Clairvaux Abbey became a model which spread across the Order. Cistercian abbots were normally buried in the chapter houses, and if later venerated, their remains would be transferred to more elaborate tombs or shrines. By the 1230s these shrines were frequently sited behind the high altar of the monastic church, a space traditionally associated with the cult of relics.[27] In the absence of holy abbots other important figures associated with the community played a similar protective role in some monasteries: the first major rebuilding of the monastic church in the Cistercian nunnery in Trzebnica, following the canonisation of Duchess Hedwig in 1267, saw the addition of a Gothic chapel to house her shrine.[28]

In Cistercian nunneries, designed to preserve the claustration of the nuns (see chapter 4), their choir was separated from the space allocated to lay brothers, guests and many others associated with the community, and in some cases, also the lay congregation. Their churches were divided into inner (for the nuns) and outer (for the laity); and while the community remained invisible to the laity, the outer church's artistic programme sought both to project the holiness of the nuns and to commemorate the patrons and benefactors for whose souls the nuns prayed.[29]

One common architectural device for ensuring the claustration of the nuns took the form of western galleries (or nuns') galleries (*emporia*), which also provided a good view of the elevation of the host during the mass, increasingly important in the spiritual life of thirteenth-century female communities. Many female Cistercian communities were much poorer than the male ones, and their churches were also often smaller, adapted from other buildings and less likely to be rebuilt in the latest fashionable style;[30] however, those in Cistercian nunneries whose prime function was to serve as necropolises for the founders and their families included specific features in the design to accommodate prominent tombs and special chapels.[31]

The growing involvement of the Cistercians with lay spirituality and visual commemorations in the later middle ages was often an aspect of their active search for lay benefactors to invest in the fabric of the church. During the successful reform and renewal of Cestello Abbey in Florence in the 1480s, when the entire church was remodelled in the Renaissance style, the abbey began to add chapels to the nave of the church and actively sought patrons for them among wealthy Florentines, many of whom had no prior connection to the Cistercians. In this, they were so successful that instead of the planned eight, twelve chapels were erected, of which the two most prestigious, located by the high altar, were dedicated to St Bernard and St Benedict. The design of these chapels was standardised to give a unified visual appeal to the church, but the altarpieces, stained glass and vestments and upkeep of the chapels were financed by individual patrons. The altarpieces, the majority of which focused on the special relationship between the Virgin and Christ, and among which was Sandro Botticelli's *Annunciation* (*c.* 1490), reflected a core theme of the Cistercian spirituality: but others included portraits of the donor and his or her patron saint, and the chapels were decorated with the coats of arms of the patrons. In 1498, in a rather bold gesture, the monks' choir was moved behind the high altar, making the nave accessible to the laity, who came specifically to see the new chapels. Clearly, the new programme was intended for a much wider audience than the monastic community, and Cestello is probably one of the most striking examples of engagement with benefactors through the architecture of a church.[32] Even in quite 'average' Cistercian houses, however, the fourteenth and fifteenth centuries saw a greater openness to lay burials, many of them in the choir or specially erected chapels.

Cistercian Monastic Precincts: Conventual Buildings and the Courts

While the precincts of Cistercian monasteries were primarily designed so that the community could perform its *Opus Dei* obligations, they also testify to the centrality of the community in Cistercian life. The buildings had not only to serve a practical purpose – to house large numbers of people – and to express symbolic meanings; they were also a response to changes of fashion and the changing needs of growing or shrinking monastic communities and changing obligations towards the wider world. Despite regional variations in form, materials used and decoration, the Cistercian precinct always consisted of three main parts – the conventual buildings, the inner court and the outer court – which was inherited from the Benedictine tradition, although variations were introduced to suit particular sites and the different practical needs of Cistercian communities, such as accommodation for lay brothers, which was unknown in the Benedictine houses.

In the innermost part of the precinct and central to the life of the community, the cloister (see Figure 5.1) was based directly on the Benedictine model going back to the eighth century, which itself was based on the structure of a Roman villa with its enclosed central atrium. Its name, derived from the Latin word *claustrum*, denoting an enclosed space, emphasises that the monastic space was protected from the outside world. In northern Europe the cloister was usually located to the south of the church for maximum exposure to the sun, and in southern Europe to the north, to benefit from shade. The cloister provided access to all key buildings – the church, chapter house, warming room, dormitory and refectory. Its central feature was square without a roof (cloister garth), and was surrounded on sides by covered galleries. There was always a water fountain, or at least a well, opposite the refectory, to which water was delivered by pipes running underneath and from which dirty water was taken away by other pipes. This feature, the *lavabo*, had both symbolic and practical functions, as hand-washing was necessary in the liturgical context and before meals. The designs of *lavabos* varied, but whether a cascade of water from a higher to a lower basin enclosed within a small fountain house, or a long basin or series of basins attached to a wall in the cloister gallery, all forms of *lavabo* were intended to be used by several people at a time.

The galleries in the cloister were multifunctional areas, devoted to practical and liturgical activities at different times – it was a space for manual work, washing and mending clothes, ablution, shaving and hair cutting, as well as meditation, study and reading. On certain occasions the gallery was also used for solemn processions. The four sides of the cloister also had specific functions. The east gallery was the pathway to the church used by monks several times a day. On the wall near the entrance to the church there was a wooden noticeboard covered by a thick layer of wax (*tabula*), on which notices and announcements were written, some relating to internal matters, some emanating from other Cistercian abbeys – announcing the deaths of abbots, for example. Another wooden board nearby served as a gong to summon the monks to various tasks and duties: different rhythms indicated a different message – calls to prayer, work or mealtimes, or the death of a member of the community. The east gallery was used for storing books in special cupboards, around which were benches for monks to sit for silent reading during prescribed times (see chapter 7). Because of that, the east gallery was known as the 'collation gallery' and it was devoted to spiritually oriented activities, the monks gathering here to listen to readings at the end of every monastic day. The same gallery was also used for para-liturgical purposes, such as the weekly ritual washing of feet on Saturday afternoons commemorating Christ's washing of the feet of his disciples and symbolising humility and charity, performed by the monks on a rotational basis and on Holy Thursday for poor men selected from those staying in the guest-house. The abbot, meanwhile, washed the feet of 12 members of the monastic community in another Maundy ceremony.

The refectory gallery located opposite the collation space provided a connection to the common dining room; and the west gallery, located parallel to the lay brothers' dormitory, was the part of the cloister most likely to be rebuilt and turned to different uses after the disappearance of the lay brothers (see chapter 6). In Byland Abbey the west range was converted into a granary in the fifteenth century, whilst the refectory of the lay brothers in Marienfeld Abbey was converted for storage of books and in Altzella Abbey became in 1506 an impressive library with at least 36 individual study desks for the monks. In other abbeys – Rievaulx, Fontenay, Sénanque and Santes Creus – redundant west ranges were simply demolished.[33]

The chapter house, traditionally located off the east gallery of the cloister between the sacristy and monks' day room or parlour, was probably the most important building within the monastic complex after the church. It could be square, rectangular or even polygonal. Columns supported vaulting, and the abbot's chair (sometimes in the form of a throne) was placed in the centre of the eastern wall and flanked by the seats of the prior and sub-prior. The community sat, in order of seniority, on benches along the other walls, the monks who had joined most recently sitting by the door. As an indication of its importance, the chapter house tended to be decorated, even in small and poor establishments, with marble capitals, sculpted columns and elaborate window openings into the cloister gallery. Just as the choirs of the monastic churches were rebuilt to accommodate expanding numbers of monks, chapter houses too were frequently rebuilt and extended. In the 1150s, only two decades after the foundation of Rievaulx Abbey, its third abbot, Ailred, rebuilt the chapter house, and its vast size suggests that the space accommodated not only monks, but also, unusually, lay brothers who were there to hear the abbot's preaching, most likely delivered in the vernacular, not in Latin, for the lay brothers' benefit.[34]

The chapter house was central to all communal matters. Monks assembled there for daily meetings – known as the chapter or office of the chapter – devoted to the current issues of the community and to receive spiritual instructions from the abbot. The content of the meeting was strictly confidential and not to be revealed to anybody who had not been present. Practical matters, such as announcements and the assignment of tasks to individual monks were combined with business central to the communal life – correcting mistakes and punishing monks who had transgressed. It was during the chapter that letters from popes and bishops were read to the community and on Sundays there were also readings from the statutes of the General Chapter and other Cistercian regulations. The first Sunday of Lent was the day for the admission of novices as fully professed monks, and, when necessary, the election of a new abbot following a death or resignation. The spiritual aspect of the chapter meeting involved prescribed readings from the martyrology, and extracts from the Rule of Benedict with the abbot's commentaries. Monks who had transgressed then confessed their misdemeanours and crimes to the community and, after prostrating themselves on the floor, awaited the abbot's the decision on their punishment. Lesser offences entailed humiliation, temporary exclusions from communal activities such as meals, compulsory fasting, corporal punishment or dismissal from office, while for more serious misdemeanours monks could be incarcerated in the monastic prison, excommunicated or even expelled from the monastery. To emphasise the continuity of belonging to the monastic family beyond the grave, chapter meetings always closed with the commemoration of the deceased members of the community and a recitation of *De Profundis*.

The bond between the living and departed members of the community found more material expression in abbots' tombs in the floor of the chapter house. Early tombs were not always distinguished by more than an image of a crozier – a symbol of the abbatial office – but by the later middle ages full-sized effigies with inscriptions were becoming common, reflecting the enhanced status of the abbot. If any former abbots, especially founding leaders of the community, became the subject of a cult their shrines were positioned at the centre of the community, either behind the high altar in the monastic church or in the chapter house: William, the first abbot of Rievaulx (d. 1145), was originally buried in the chapter house and his body was moved twice before 1250 in connection to his cult. An inscription on his shrine, erected at the entrance to the chapter house, proclaimed 'St William the abbot'.[35] In Melrose Abbey, a daughter house of Rievaulx, the cult of the second abbot, Waldeof (d. 1159), flourished very soon after his death. When his tomb was opened in 1171, in a solemn ceremony attended by Bishop Jocelin and four Cistercian abbots, his body was found uncorrupted (a clear sign of sanctity) and the influx of pilgrims begun.[36] The proliferation of cults in the later middle ages obliged Cistercians to seek new architectural and practical solutions to provide access while preserving the exclusivity of the monastic space (see chapter 8).

Further rooms leading off from the cloister galleries served various practical needs of the community – for example, in view of the restrictions on speaking, an 'auditorium' where conversations could be conducted. Here, the prior and other officials could conduct their business and address individual monks or groups. Access to the communal warming room (*calefactorium*), particularly welcome in the cold northern climate, was forbidden during reading time. According to the twelfth-century regulations, the warming room was, alongside the infirmary and the kitchen, one of only three locations in which heating was permitted. Heating methods changed with advancement in technology, progressing from the least efficient open hearth to fireplaces and eventually to under-floor heating (*hypocaustum*), of which examples are known in Maulbronn, Bebenhausen and Chorin abbeys. The warming room was multifunctional, being used as a scriptorium, a work-room and a room for greasing shoes, and for blood-letting. In the later middle ages, however, with the introduction of stoves to other parts of the monastery, including individual cells, the role of the warming room declined (see chapter 8).[37]

To emphasise their special status, monks and novices lived in separate quarters and had their own refectories and dormitories. Apart from the church, the monks' dormitory was often the largest building in the complex; and its centrality to the community, as laid down in the Rule of Benedict, was manifested, among other ways, in the communal arrangements for sleeping. The accommodation was on the first floor above the chapter house, with staircases ('day stairs'), connecting it to the cloister where most of the daytime activities of the monks took place, and giving direct access (through the 'night stairs') to the church, so the monks could go directly there for the Vigils prayers in the early morning. The *calefactorum* on the ground floor kept the sleeping area slightly warmer, and the dormitory had easy access to the latrines. Originally, to emphasise the unity of the community, the dormitories were large open spaces shared by all the monks and the abbot together. The monks slept in their clothes as a sign of modesty, and any display of the naked body, even only the feet, and even if accidental, was strictly forbidden. Apart from the beds there was little rudimentary furnishing for storing spare habits and other items. By the late thirteenth century, however, there was a tendency, for various complex reasons (see chapter 8), to subdivide dormitory space to provide more privacy and comfort.[38]

There were separate latrines for choir monks, novices, lay brothers, patients of the infirmary and guests in the guest-house. In abbeys with large communities, they were often extensive and impressive structures above a channel that carried away the waste. At Rievaulx Abbey the latrine building was three storeys high with openings on the top floor for about 30 wooden seats. Wooden partitions or screens were added in the fourteenth century, but privacy and modesty was achieved, according to the *Ecclesiastica Officia*, by putting the hood of the habit over the head to give anonymity to the users of the latrine. The top level of this structure was accessible from the dormitory building and two doors – one for entrance and another for exit – facilitated its use by a large number of people at the same time. At the lower level another latrine with a smaller number of seats was accessible from the day room.[39]

Eating and sleeping were communal activities in the Cistercian houses, and refectories, like dormitories and choirs, were frequently rebuilt to accommodate changing numbers of monks. In contrast to Benedictine refectories, those in Cistercian houses were often built at an angle of 90 degrees to the cloister, leaving room in the western range for other buildings. The large, undivided, rectangular refectory was well lit with windows, sometimes on two levels, on both walls, resembling the nave of a church. The tables and benches ran along the walls and the monks sat facing the centre of the room. Conversation was forbidden. The spiritual character of the communal meals was emphasised by a reading by one of the monks, elected, according to suitability, on a weekly basis. A raised pulpit, usually located at the centre of the west wall, provided good acoustics for the readings, traditionally taken from the Bible, although by the fourteenth century vernacular summaries of the Latin passages were becoming common. As the communal meals were supposed to nourish not only the body but the soul, it was appropriate that the architecture of the church and that of the refectory should display a certain stylistic kinship.[40]

Food was prepared in the kitchen by a team of monks who changed on a weekly basis, often assisted by paid servants. This was not simply a mundane task, but an element of *Opus Dei*, and as each monk took up the role of cook he said special prayers and blessings. For practical reasons, the kitchen building was located next to the refectory and dishes were passed between them through a hatch in the wall. Frequently, for reasons of convenience, the kitchen was located between the monks' refectory and that of the lay brothers and there was always a supply of clean water. It was probably the most utilitarian building in the precinct and as such was subject to frequent rebuilding to accommodate new technologies, the replacement of damaged or worn-out elements and alterations of size according to the needs of the community. The inclusion of meat in the Cistercian diet (see chapter 8) from the fourteenth century onwards led to the building of separate meat kitchens and separate dining rooms for the consumption of meat dishes.[41]

A number of other buildings, enclosures and rooms (such as offices and various workshops) were added over time as needs changed, and by the thirteenth century it was common for Cistercian houses to have prisons. These were used for the incarceration of violent monks and those who committed apostasy but had been captured and returned to their house. Imprisonment was the punishment of last resort for monks after all other methods – admonitions, exclusions from communal meals and prayers, flogging in the chapter – had failed. Prisons were usually located to the east of the cloister, near the infirmary or as a part of it. A cell in the gatehouse cellar was sometimes used for the same purpose.[42]

The infirmary, an essential part of the monastic precinct, was located in the eastern part of the precinct at a considerable distance from the conventual buildings in order to keep the sick away from the healthy. According to Hippocratic and Galenic theories, which were the basis of medieval medical ideas, the east had particularly healthy properties. By the thirteenth century the infirmary was a large building with a vaulted ceiling and large windows. In communities with a significant number of monks, the building for the sick was proportionally large too. At Eberbach

Abbey (*c.* 1200), for example, the infirmary was over 15 metres wide and 35 metres long, divided into three naves and containing eight bays in its length. By the fourteenth century the large open space of the infirmary was divided into individual cells, just as the space of the dormitory was partitioned (see chapter 8) to provide more privacy.[43] The accommodation for the sick was equipped with comforts to speed the return to health. There is, for example, evidence that infirmary halls were heated by fireplaces and had a good supply of water for hygienic reasons. Baths were also used as a therapeutic treatment. This was recommended by Hippocrates, a major ancient medical authority, well-known in monastic circles, as well as advocated for the sick in the Rule of Benedict. It was believed that recovery was not only the result of medical treatment, but also due to the power of liturgy. In the large halls of the Cistercian infirmaries there was always a chapel in the east end, so the ill could hear, if not see the mass. Seeing the elevation of the host was believed to help recovery, and ease the passage to paradise for the dying monks. There was no division between 'scientific' medical methods and spiritual healing.[44] The ritual of purification of the monastic building was performed weekly and involved sprinkling of holy water, especially in the church, chapter house, warming room, dormitory, latrines, refectory kitchen and storage rooms, in order to get rid of 'bad air' causing illnesses.[45]

The lay brothers were excluded from the monks' cloister and confined to the western part of the church and an area to the west of the cloister consisting of dormitory, refectory, latrines and often a separate passage to the church. While the expansion of the community was often accompanied by the extension of the refectory, the disappearance of the lay brothers led to changes in the use of the western part. Further out, the area beyond the lay brothers' domain was dedicated to utilitarian functions. While it divided the area restricted to the community from the outside world, its outer court connected the monastery and its estates, especially the home granges located in the immediate vicinity. Arrangements varied, but the outer court usually housed industrial buildings such as the tannery, brewery, smithy and mills, and service buildings such as stables, usually grouped together into yards or courts. The gatehouses were the key points controlling contacts with the outside world. The main gatehouse of the inner court was usually a two-storey structure with accommodation for the porter and two vaulted entrances for pedestrians and vehicles. It sometimes had its own chapel, for the use those who were not allowed to enter the precinct, especially women. The gatehouse was also a distribution point for charity to the poor, under the porter's supervision. Indeed, in times of famine, food hand-outs from Cistercian houses were often very substantial.[46]

The abbot's residence too, as an important point of interaction with the outside world, especially with high-profile guests, was located outside the inner monastic space. According to the Rule of Benedict, the abbots were supposed to share their dormitory with the rest of the community. Although initially Cistercians tried to adhere to this principle, this was highly impractical and soon abandoned in favour of separate abbatial accommodation. The chronology of this shift differed from abbey to abbey, but the earliest examples of separate accommodation dates from the second half of the twelfth century. In its simplest form, the abbot's private chamber was located near the dormitory and only later became a separate building. Frequently, old infirmaries were converted into abbatial residences as they were conveniently located, but sometimes new buildings were erected. The variety of technical and stylistic details found in abbots' residences was far greater than that of the other core buildings of the precincts and many abbeys modernised them several times, to make them more fashionable, with larger windows, fireplaces and modern fittings. A good example of development of living arrangements has been reconstructed for Villers Abbey (Brabant): until the end of the thirteenth century the abbot's accommodation was a room above the sacristy, when a separate building was erected in the south-west of the cloister as the abbot's residence; by 1459 this building, now considered too small and old-fashioned, underwent a remodelling; in 1487 the lay brothers' infirmary was converted into an imposing abbatial residence, and further decorated with a renaissance portico in the sixteenth century.[47]

The transition of the abbots' accommodation, from a communal arrangement through progressively more elaborate residences, reflects the change in the relationship between the abbot and the community of monks, with the former increasingly became the 'public face' of the monastery engaged in a great variety of issues involving the outside world. Large open spaces on the outer parameter of the outer court might contain meadows and fishponds with walls or other natural barriers such as rivers surrounding the whole area. In politically unstable conditions precinct walls could, of course, also serve defensive purposes, and partially surviving examples of such walls can be found in Cîteaux, Clairvaux, Pontigny, Vauluisant (all in France), Poblet in Spain, Maulbronn in Germany, Rievaulx in England and Melrose in Scotland.[48] These arrangements were based on the prescription of the Rule of Benedict, which stipulated that all necessary practical resources such as water, mills, workshops and gardens should be located within the monastic enclosure, so that securing the daily necessities of life would not oblige monks to expose themselves to the temptations and spiritual dangers of the outside world. Indeed, in some monasteries the main gatehouse was virtually a fortified structure, that at Maulbronn, for example, being equipped with a drawbridge.[49]

A reliable supply of water was necessary in all Cistercian abbeys. Kitchens needed to be supplied with water for drinking and cooking; the *lavabo* in the cloister supplied water for cleaning and washing before the meals, for liturgical practices such as the weekly foot washing (*mandatum*), and for the holy water used in various ceremonies. The delivery of clean water required a complicated system of pipes, tanks, valves and filters to take it from a spring located above the site, using natural pressure or mechanical means such as a water wheel; and the myriad different technical solutions adopted testify to the difficulties contingent on managing the supply of water in varying local conditions and times of drought or floods. Similarly, the construction of Cistercian latrines in such a way as to ensure that the human waste and rubbish was carried away by the 'the main drain' underneath the precinct often required significant re-engineering of the existing water courses to separate clean from dirty water and to supply several locations in the precinct through pipes or channels.[50]

Visual Culture of Cistercian Monasteries

The appearance of Cistercian monasteries today, those in ruins and those which have survived in Catholic parts of Europe as standing buildings, usually in a Baroque style, can give very little sense of the role decoration – painting, sculpture, glass and various furnishings – played in the medieval context as a focus for the spirituality, communal and individual devotion and liturgical activities of the community, and the commemoration of the patrons and benefactors. Just as the styles of buildings changed in line with fashion, so the devotional art, images, liturgical utensils, shrines and ornaments in the church were also transformed (and sold, stolen and destroyed), with the result that very few still retain their original form. Yet while, as in architecture, silence, light and simplicity were aesthetic choices underlining many of the decorative schemes, changing forms of spirituality, often focused on images, significantly influenced the appearance of Cistercian artefacts. This was not a matter of 'corrupting' some original spirit, but of responding to changes in religious sensibilities and new spiritual expectations.

The oldest images mentioned in Cistercian sources are the crucifixes, often painted and bearing a figure of Christ, that were placed on the high altar, on the east wall of the chapter house and above the abbot's seat in the refectory. They were also carried in the processions.[51] From the thirteenth century onwards monumental crucifixes, usually painted, flat or three-dimensional, became particularly popular in the north German and Scandinavian abbeys, and were usually placed above the partition separating the monks' choir from that of the lay brothers.[52] As the tradition continued into the fifteenth century, they became increasingly naturalistic in their portrayal of Christ's suffering on the cross. Meanwhile, the representations of Christ in the Pietà that were common in Cistercian monasteries by the fifteenth century reflected devotional trends common to both monastic and lay settings. A specifically Cistercian depiction of Christ on the cross embracing Bernard of Clairvaux had its roots in a miracle story from Herbert of Clairvaux's *Liber Miraculorum* and Conrad of Eberbarch's *Exordium Magnum*, according to which a monk of Mores Abbey observed Bernard at prayer in the church there when suddenly the figure of Christ came down from the cross to embraced the future saint.[53] In fact, this became the basis for a very popular iconographical model, the so-called *Amplexus Bernardi*, which spread very widely through such media as woodcuts, manuscript illuminations, stained glass, sculpture, wall paintings and panel painting. It was also frequently depicted in altarpieces and dramatic free-standing sculptures – most strikingly in a relatively early version from the 1340s, which depicts Bernard as actually present at Golgotha and receiving the unconscious body of Christ into his arms.[54] If this acknowledged the holiness of St Bernard, who was able to experience such closeness to Christ, it also emphasised the importance of empathy with his suffering, a significant theme of late medieval religiosity.

The visual manifestation of the Christo-centric spirituality of the Cistercians converged in the themes of late medieval lay spirituality in the form of the so-called Eucharistic Mill or Host Mill, an allegorical representation of the mystery of transubstantiation. Its symbolism is based on Biblical passages: Luke 17,35: 'Two women shall be grinding grain together; The one shall be taken, and the other will be left' – and the same passage in Matthew 24,41, which refers to the second coming of Christ. It invokes *Ecclesia et Synagoga*: whilst corn symbolises Christ, God is the miller, and the corn and ploughed field are Marian symbols. The earliest Eucharistic Mills are found in twelfth-century French sculpture, but in late medieval Cistercian churches they were represented on full-scale retables: the centrepiece depicts a hand-turned mill into which angels or symbols of the four evangelists throw corn in the form of banners with Biblical quotes, whilst the mill is turned by the Apostles, also accompanied by banners with quotes. A little figure of the incarnated Christ-child is coming out of the mill to be captured in a Eucharistic cup held by the Church Fathers. The oldest examples of altarpieces depicting the Eucharistic Mill come from Pomerania: Doberan Abbey from the first quarter of the fifteenth century and the Cistercian nunnery of Holy Cross in Rostock – perhaps not surprising as the region was a very active centre of the Holy Blood cult (see chapter 8).[55]

Extensive collections of relics and their elaborate displays became typical for many late medieval Cistercian houses. From 1182 Altenberg Abbey held a most impressive treasury of relics centred around St Ursula and the 11,000 virgins. A relics list of 1528 shows that its size and variety could rival many cathedrals of medieval Europe, with 250 pieces of more than 100 saints. Meanwhile, the cult of St Ursula had spread via the filiation of Altenberg to its daughter houses Mariental (Lower Saxony), Haina (Hessen), Zinna (Brandenburg) and Ląd (Greater Poland) and became an important element of filiation identity.[56]

The dedication of every Cistercian abbey included the name of Mary, the mother of Christ, and the images of her played an increasingly important role in Cistercian spirituality from the beginning of the thirteenth century. Representations of the Virgin took different stylistic forms according to changing fashions: Gothic three-dimensional figures of Mary holding the baby Christ appeared not only inside the Cistercian churches but also in the tympana, stone reliefs and on the carving of the stalls where the monks. The northern Europe fashion for large altarpieces reached many Cistercian abbeys in the thirteenth century and by the fifteenth century these complex structures became very extensive, incorporating painted scenes, sculptures, crucifixes and relic containers. Many of these monumental structures – for example, the high altar in Doberan Abbey (*c.* 1300) – had Mary as their central figure.[57] Devotion to the Virgin also featured in late medieval depictions of St Bernard, one of the most spectacular of which – the miracle of lactation, or *lactacio*, emphasising the humanity of Christ and the mystery of the Incarnation – shows St Bernard (identifiable by his Cistercian habit, abbatial staff and saint's halo) kneeling in front of the Virgin Mary holding the infant Christ, whilst a fine stream of milk shoots from Mary's breast towards the saint.[58] Not that this, perhaps to the modern sensibilities rather shocking depiction, was particularly Cistercian: it refers rather to the older symbolism of milk and honey in the Old Testament, especially the Song of Songs, and was very typical of late medieval spiritual imagery with its focus on bodily substances such as blood and milk. The theme of the healing power of the Virgin's milk also featured in many of the collections of Marian miracles, familiar to Cistercian communities.[59] The imagery of nursing was typical not just for the Cistercians, but also wider lay community, especially female spirituality; and there was also a clear link between milk as nourishment and the blood of Christ in the Eucharist feeding the souls of the believers.[60]

Finally, the most widespread and popular of the images showing the connection between the Cistercians and the Virgin Mary was that of monks and nuns sheltering under her cloak. It originated in the ever-popular collection of *Dialogus miraculorum* by Caesarius of Heisterbach, which tells of a particularly pious Cistercian monk who had a vision of encountering the Virgin Mary in the afterlife. Since among the multitude of figures in heaven he could not see any of his fellow Cistercians, he asked Mary:

> Oh! Most Holy Lady, why is it that I see no one here of the Cistercian Order? Why are your servants, who serve you so devotedly, shut out from sharing in so great happiness?' Whereupon, the queen of heaven, seeing him so greatly troubled, replied: 'Those of the Cistercian Order are so dear to me and so beloved that I cherish them in my bosom'. And opening her cloak, with which she seemed to be clothed, and which was of marvellous amplitude, she showed him an innumerable multitude of monks, lay brothers and nuns.[61]

This image – known as *Mater Misericordiae* (The Mother of Mercy) became very popular across the Cistercian Order, through cheap and easily accessible woodcuts, in a monumental form on altarpieces and in wall paintings, and in miniature versions on conventual seals. Indeed, it personified the 'special relationship' between the Cistercian order and the Virgin Mary in the later middle ages; and the power of the iconographical model was such that it was also adopted by other religious orders, becoming after the Black Death one of the most popular votive images. The centrality of this image to the Cistercian identity is exemplified very well by a woodcut in the printed volume of Cistercian privileges published in Dijon in 1491 under the auspices of Abbot Jean de Cirey; the privileges contained in the volume were of course important, but they would be nothing without the special heavenly protectoress.[62]

Cistercian communities, like their Benedictine predecessors, produced illuminated manuscripts primarily for devotional use. In general, however, the prohibition against ornamentation in buildings was also believed to extend to manuscripts, and Cistercian regulations issued between 1145 and 1151 specified that initials 'should be of one color and not decorated with painting'.[63] Certainly, important works from the 1140s adhered to this prescription: fragments of the Bible of Cîteaux and four complete volumes of the Bible of Clairvaux are all in monochrome. Their simplicity and austerity gives the manuscripts a special beauty; and the best example of this type is a manuscript from Cîteaux created in the 1180s as a master copy for liturgical volumes and core regulations (*Ecclesiastica Officia* and *Usus conversorum*) for other houses belonging to the Order, which seems to have been devised as a model, not only for the content of the text but for its visual presentation. Meanwhile, the regulations of the General Chapter repeated, in rather vague terms, prohibitions against ornamented initials in the manuscripts and added clauses against decorative covers in 1202 and in 1220.[64]

Before the prohibitions of the 1140s and from the early thirteenth century onwards, however, Cistercian manuscript illumination followed the mainstream Benedictine tradition of elaborate and colourful ornamentation. Just as in regard to Cistercian architecture, there was no prescribed artistic form for manuscripts and great diversity of design prevailed among the productions of twelfth-century Cistercian scriptoria.[65] One of the oldest known Cistercian manuscripts – the Bible of Stephen Harding (Dijon, Bibl. Mun., MSS 12–15) created in Cîteaux in four volumes – contains very high-quality miniatures and impressive illuminated initials with real and imaginary animals. A contemporary manuscript of *Moralia in Job* (Dijon, Bibl. Mun., MS 170), also a product of Cîteaux during the abbacy of Harding, is particularly famous for its highly decorative initials with depictions of the Cistercian monks engaged in various types of manual labour. In the later middle ages, however, scriptoria ceased to function as large centres of manuscript production and most books for the monastic libraries were bought from different sources, and were no longer 'Cistercian' in their visual character.[66]

The artistic programmes of Cistercian liturgical books reflected not only the transmission of styles but also the theological and spiritual ideas behind them. Just as the masons' workshops were used by the different Cistercian houses within the filiation networks and regions, so new artistic models and the spiritual concepts that they represented spread through the borrowing and copying of manuscripts. The earliest representation of Mary as *Mater Misericordiae* – sheltering Cistercian monks and *conversi* in the folds of her cloak – in Silesia can be found in the Gradual volume from Lubiąż (1320–1330), which was the source of numerous representations of this kind in other Cistercian and non-Cistercian contexts in that region; while an Antiphonary (*c.* 1280–1290) in the same monastery contains the earliest representation in Silesia of Christ as *Vir Dolorum*.[67] Clearly, Cistercian manuscript production was influential in spreading devotional ideas of the white monks within and outside the Order.

A significant number of devotional objects came into Cistercian monasteries as gifts from the laity. It was common practice to donate liturgical vessels that reflected the benefactor's wealth and social standing: an elaborate silver paten donated by Duke Mieszko the Elder of Greater Poland for Ląd Abbey between 1193 and 1202 depicted Abbot Simon and the abbey's patron St Nicholas as recipients alongside a representation of the donor.[68] Liturgical vessels were central to the performance and the power of the Mass; hence the donor, through his act of generosity and the image itself, was forever to benefit eschatologically from his gift. Sometimes donations of liturgical vessels were accompanied by explicit requests for commemoration: when in 1356 the son of Peter and Katherina von Rosenberg, very prominent benefactors of Višši Bród Abbey, donated a golden chalice decorated with gems and pearls, a monstrance depicting St Benedict and a golden reliquary with hair of Mary Magdalene, he did so on the first anniversary of his mother's death and expressly for her commemoration. Since that was also the day when the anniversary Mass for Katherina's soul would have been performed at the abbey, the object might no doubt have been used then and at the subsequent occasions for the benefit of her soul in the afterlife.[69]

Bonds with the outside world could also be strengthened by iconographical schemes to exploit real or imaginary connections with past founders and patrons to achieve particular aims in the present. In the first half of the fourteenth century two reliefs were added to the cemetery portal in Ebrach Abbey (Bavaria), in what was a clear attempt to 're-write' monastic history: as Ebrach Abbey was angling for the support of Emperor Louis IV (d. 1347) against the powerful bishops of Würzburg, the tombs of Queen Gertrude (d. 1146) and her son Duke Frederic were cited as evidence that the abbey was founded by Hohenstaufen King Conrad III (d. 1152), whilst the role of the real founders, the much more lowly ministeriales Erbo and Riwin, was minimised. Hence the portal shows King Conrad and his wife as the founders, with the real founders relegated to supporting roles, thereby emphasising Conrad's role as a direct link to the policy of close co-operation between the abbot and Emperor Louis IV and the Ebrach campaign to become 'imperial abbey' (*Reichskloster*).[70]

Conclusions

Cistercian visual culture, architecture, liturgical and devotional objects were the material framework of the monastic observance. The chief objective in designing the layout of the precinct was to uphold the Rule of Benedict, the principle of communal life and all the liturgical functions of the community. We can never fully understand the history of any Cistercian community without looking at its material remains. The changing fortunes of every monastery, and its relationship with the patrons, benefactors and the wider world are written in the architecture and shape of the buildings.

As Terryl Kinder has shown, the regulations of the General Chapter cannot be used to reveal a model Cistercian architectural style, or some master theory behind the construction of Cistercian abbeys: hence there were no clear 'rule-breakers' among Cistercian churches because there was never a defined and prescriptive Cistercian style. The characteristics commonly associated with the churches of the white monks were simply typical of the style popular in Burgundy in the late eleventh and early twelfth centuries. Apart from the local idiosyncrasies and the availability of building materials, contemplative spirituality was by far the greatest influence behind the artistic choices in Cistercian architecture. Simplicity and a relative lack of ornamentation were not governed by economic choices, but a concern for an environment that was particularly conducive to prayer. However, in practice, the shape of the buildings and many of the furnishings were heavily influenced both by the desire of patrons and benefactors for commemoration and the Cistercian attachment to emotive spirituality, with its focus on Christ's suffering and protective role of Mary.

The monastic precinct was a microcosm safely separating its inhabitants from the outside world by walls and gates, so the contemplative observance could be maintained. The white monks were following an old Benedictine tradition in adopting a cloister scheme with buildings radiating out from galleries, a design that embodied the central principle of Cistercian life in which eating, sleeping and praying took place in the shared spaces. An important innovation was the addition of buildings specifically designed for the lay brothers, who, although a part of the monastic community, remained in a separate and inferior position to the professed monks. Nor was the shape of monastic buildings ever static: there was never a stage when the monastery's buildings had been completed once and for all. Structures continued to evolve as the size and composition of the community changed, the relationship between the abbot and the rest of the monks became more distant and the lay brothers ceased to exist.

In its outer forms, Cistercian architecture of the fourteenth and fifteenth centuries increasingly followed mainstream fashionable styles and there was usually little to differentiate it stylistically from contemporary non-Cistercian religious and monastic buildings of the time. Rich late medieval decoration has often been invoked to show how far the white monks had abandoned the simplicity of the twelfth century; and art historians have often pointed a moralising figure at the 'failure on the part of the order to maintain its distinctive visual tradition'.[71] If we look deeper, however, we see that the meanings behind the iconographical schemes and altarpieces were deeply Cistercian – emotive and focused on the Virgin Mary and her relationship with Christ. The frequent representations of St Bernard of Clairvaux also testify to the strength of the tradition of the founding fathers and are direct reminders of their spiritual teachings embodied in visual form.

Notes

1. Bernard of Clairvaux, 'Apologia ad Guillelmum Abbatem', in *Sancti Bernardi Opera*, ed. Jean Leclercq and Henri Rochais (Rome: Editiones Cistercienses, 1959); Karl Heinz Esser, 'Les fouilles à Himmerod et le plan Bernardin', in *Mélanges Saint Bernard, XXIV Congrès de l'Association Bourguignonne des Sociétés Savantes* (Dijon, 1953), pp. 311–315; for a full analysis of this theory see Alexandra Gajewski, 'Another Look at Cistercian Artchitecture. Part One: The Idea of a Cistercian Architecture as a Mirror of its Times', *Cistercium Mater Nostra* 4 (2010), pp. 9–20.
2. Elisabeth Melczer and Eileen Soldwedel, 'Monastic Goals in the Aesthetics of Saint Bernard', in *Studies in Cistercian Art and Architecture*, vol. 1, ed. Meredith Parsons Lillich (Kalamazoo, MI: Cistercian Publications, 1982), pp. 31–44; Anselme Dimier, *Stones Laid Before the Lord: A History of Monastic Architecture*, trans. Gilchrist Lavigne (Kalamazoo, MI: Cistercian Publications, 1999), p. 137.
3. Conrad Rudolph, 'The "Principal Founders" and the Early Artistic Legislation of Cîteaux', in *Studies in Cistercian Art and Architecture*, vol. 3, ed. Meredith Parsons Lillich (Kalamazoo, MI: Cistercian Publications, 1987), pp. 3–6; *Twelfth-Century Statutes from the Cistercian General Chapter: Latin text with English notes and commentary*, ed. Chrysogonus Waddell (Brecht: Cîteaux: Commentarii Cistercienses, 2002), 'Instituta Generalis', chapter XXV, p. 516.
4. *Twelfth-Century Statutes*, 'The Instituta', p. 541, trans. in Rudolph, 'The "Principal Founders"', p. 6, 22.
5. Melczer and Soldwedel, 'Monastic Goals in the Aethetics of Saint Bernard', p. 35.
6. Rudolph, 'The "Principal Founders"', pp. 7–17.
7. Alexandra Gajewski, 'The Architecture of the Choir at Clairvaux Abbey: Saint Bernard and the Cistercian Principle of Conspicuous Poverty', in *Perspectives for an Architecture of Solitude. Essays on Cistercians, Art and Architecture in Honour of Peter Fergusson*, ed. Terryl N. Kinder (Turnhout: Brepols and Cîteaux, 2004), pp. 72–73; Peter Fergusson, 'Programmatic Factors in the East Extension of Clairvaux', *Arte Medievale*, 2nd series, 8 (1994), pp. 87–101.
8. Terryl Kinder, *Cistercian Europe: Architecture of Contemplation* (Kalamazoo, MI: Cistercian Publications, 2002), pp. 374–375, 385–386.
9. Meredith Parsons Lillich, 'Recent Scholarship concerning Cistercian Windows', in *Studiosorum Speculum: Studies in Honour of Louis J. Lekai*, ed. Francis R. Swietek and John R. Sommerfeldt (Kalamazoo, MI: Cistercian Publications, 1993) p. 233.
10. Emero Stiegman, 'The Light Imagery of Saint Bernard's Spirituality and Its Evidence in Cistercian Architecture', in *The Joy of Learning and the Love of God: Studies in Honour of Jean Leclercq*, ed. E. Rozanne Elder (Kalamazoo, MI: Cistercian Publications, 1995), pp. 334–370.
11. Marcel Aubert, 'Existe-t-il une architecture cistercienne?', *Cahiers de Civilisation Médiévale* 1 (1958), pp. 153–158; Marian Kutzner, 'Cysterska architektura na Śląsku w latach 1200–1330', *Nasza Przeszłość* 83 (1994), pp. 321–324.
12. Kinder, *Cistercian Europe*, pp. 162–165.

13. Kinder, *Cistercian Europe*, pp. 13–26, 374–388.
14. Gajewski, 'The Architecture of the Choir at Clairvaux', p. 74.
15. I want to thank Prof. Terryl Kinder for clarifying this issue for me. Peter J. Fergusson, 'Builders of Cistercian Monasteries in Twelfth Century England', in *Studies in Cistercian Art and Architecture*, ed. Meredith P. Lillich, vol. 2 (Kalamazoo, MI: Cistercian Publications, 1984), p. 25.
16. Ernst Badstübner, 'Klöster der Zisterzienser in Nordeuropa und die Backsteinbaukunst on der südlichen Ostseeküste', in *Weltverachtung und Dynamik*, ed. Harald Schwillus and Andreas Hölscher, Studien zur Geschichte, Kunst und Kultur der Zisterzienser 10 (Berlin: Lukas Verlag, 2000), pp. 144–145.
17. Kinder, *Cistercian Europe*, p. 85.
18. Kinder, *Cistercian Europe*, pp. 143, 161.
19. Kinder, *Cistercian Europe*, p. 168.
20. Nicola Coldstream, 'Cistercian Architecture from Beaulieu to the Dissolution', in *Cistercian Art and Architecture in the British Isles*, ed. Christopher Norton and David Park (Cambridge: Cambridge University Press, 1986), pp. 146–147.
21. Hermann Josef Roth, 'Das Beinhaus von Doberan und Parallelen zu anderen Zisterzienserklöstern', *Cistercienser Chronik* 117 (2010), pp. 331–332.
22. Annegret Laabs, *Malerei und Plastik im Zisterzienserorden. Zum Bildgebrauch zwischen sakralem Zeremoniell und Stiftermemoria 1250–1430* (Petersberg: Michael Imhof Verlag, 2000), pp. 64–69.
23. Laabs, *Malerei und Plastik*, p. 62.
24. Kinder, *Cistercian Europe*, pp. 167–175; Laabs, *Malerei und Plastik*, p. 62.
25. Michael T. Davis, 'The Choir of the Abbey of Altenberg: Cistercian Simplicity and Aristocratic Iconography', in *Studies in Cistercian Art and Architecture*, vol. 2, ed. Meredith Parsons Lillich (Kalamazoo, MI: Cistercian Publications, 1984), pp. 130–160.
26. Hubert Ječný and Michal Tryml, 'Zur Rekonstruktion der Klosterkirche in Zbraslav (Königsaal)', in *Historia i kultura cystersów w dawnej Polsce i ich europejskie związki*, ed. Jerzy Strzelczyk (Poznań: Wydawnictwo Naukowe Uniwersytetu im. Adama Mickiewcza, 1987), pp. 146–147.
27. Peter Fergusson and Stuart Harrison, with Glyn Coppack, *Rievaulx Abbey: Community, Architecture, Memory* (New Haven, CT: Yale University Press, 2000), pp. 166–169.
28. Jerzy Rozpędowski, 'Opactwo pań cysterek w Trzebnicy', in *Historia i kultura cystersów w dawnej Polsce i ich europejskie związki*, p. 265.
29. Jeffrey F. Hamburger, Petra Marx and Susan Marti, 'The Time of the Orders, 1200–1500', in *Crown and Veil: Female Monasticism from the Fifth to the Fifteenth Centuries*, ed. Jeffrey F. Hamburger and Susan Marti (New York: Columbia University Press, 2008), p. 53.
30. Kinder, *Cistercian Europe*, pp. 166–167.
31. Claudia Mohn, *Mittelalterliche Klosteranlagen der Zisterzienserinnen. Architektur der Frauenklöster im Mitteldeutschen Raum* (Petersberg: Michael Imhof Verlag, 2006), pp. 35–36, 39.
32. Ira Westergård, *Approaching Sacred Pregnancy: the Cult of the Visitation and Narrative Altarpieces in Late Fifteenth-Century Florence* (Helsinki:

Suomalaisen Kirjallisuuden Seura, 2007), pp. 127–133, 157; Alison Luchs, 'Alive and Well in Florence: Thriving Cistercians in Renaissance Italy', *Cîteaux: Commentarii Cistercienses* 30 (1979), pp. 116–122.

33. Tom Graber and Martina Schattkowsky, 'Einführung', in *Die Zisterzienser und ihre Bibliotheken. Buchbesitz und Schriftgebrauch des Klosters Altzella in europäischen Vergleich*, ed. Tom Graber and Martina Schattkowsky (Leipzig: Leipziger Universitätsverlag, 2008), pp. 12–13; Elke Goez, 'Zur Bedeutung der Schriftlichkeit im Zisterzienserorden', in *Die Zisterzienser und ihre Bibliotheken*, p. 43; Kinder, *Cistercian Europe*, pp. 131–138, 329–330.
34. Kinder, *Cistercian Europe*, pp. 245–247, 265–268; Fergusson and Harrison, *Rievaulx Abbey*, pp. 57–68, 94–99.
35. 'S[an]c[tu]s Willmus abbas', Fergusson and Harrison, *Rievaulx Abbey*, pp. 99, 166–167.
36. *The Chronicles of John and Richard of Hexham. The Chronicle of Holyrood. The Chronicle of Melrose*, ed. Joseph Stevenson (London: Seelys, 1866), vol. 4(1), pp. 133–134.
37. Kinder, *Cistercian Europe*, pp. 277–280.
38. Virginia Jansen, 'Architecture and Community in Medieval Monastic Dormitories', in *Studies in Cistercian Art and Architecture*, vol. 5, ed. Meredith Parsons Lillich (Kalamazoo, MI: Cistercian Publications, 1998), pp. 61–65, 70–71.
39. Fergusson and Harrison, *Rievaulx Abbey*, pp. 108–109.
40. Kinder, *Cistercian Europe*, pp. 282–287.
41. Kinder, *Cistercian Europe*, pp. 280–283.
42. Megan Cassidy-Welch, 'Incarceration and Liberation: Prisons in the Monastery', *Viator* 32 (2001), pp. 24, 40.
43. Kinder, *Cistercian Europe*, pp. 361–364.
44. David N. Bell, 'The Siting and Size of Cistercian Infirmaries in England and Wales', in *Studies in Cistercian Art*, vol. 5, pp. 212–215, 218–221, 226–228.
45. Anselme Dimier, 'Encore les emplacements malsains', in *Mélanges Anselme Dimier*, ed. Benoit Chauvin, 1:2 (Arbois: Benoît Chauvin, 1982–1987), pp. 545–546.
46. Kinder, *Cistercian Europe*, pp. 368–370; Jacki Hall, 'English Cistercian Gatehouse Chapels', *Cîteaux: Commentarii Cistercienses* 52 (2001), pp. 61–91.
47. Kinder, *Cistercian Europe*, pp. 355–359.
48. Glyn Coppack, 'The Outer Courts of Fountains and Rievaulx Abbeys: The Interface between Estates and Monastery', in *L'espace cistercien*, ed. Léon Pressouyre (Paris: Comité des travaux historiques et scientifiques, 1994), pp. 415–425; James France, 'The Cellarer's Domain – Evidence from Denmark', in *Studies in Cistercian Art and Architecture*, vol. 5, ed. Meredith Parsons Lillich (Kalamazoo, MI: Cistercian Publications, 1998), p. 13.
49. *The Rule of St Benedict*, trans. Luke Dysinger (Trabuco Canyon, CA: Source Books, 1997), ch. 66, p. 159; France, 'The Cellarer's Domain', p. 2; Dietrich Lutz, 'Die Maulbronner Klosterbefestigung', in *Maulbronn. Zur 850jährigen Geschichte des Zisterzienserklosters*, ed. Dieter Planck (Stuttgart: K. Theiss, 1997), pp. 360–361.

50. Kinder, *Cistercian Europe*, pp. 86–87.
51. David Park, 'Cistercian Wall Painting and Panel Painting', in *Cistercian Art and Architecture*, p. 197.
52. Laabs, *Malerei und Plastik*, pp. 71–74.
53. Anthony N.S. Lane, *Bernard of Clairvaux: Theologian of the Cross* (Collegeville, MN: Liturgical Press, 2013), pp. 230–231.
54. Franz Posset, '*Amplexus Bernardi* the Dissemination of a Cistercian Motif in the Later Middle Ages', *Cîteaux: Commentarii Cistercienses* 54 (2003), pp. 251–254, images on pp. 279–399.
55. Pia Esther Wipfler, *'Corpus Christi' in Liturgie und Kunst der Zisterzienser im Mittelalter* (Münster: Lit Verlag, 2003), pp. 189–234.
56. Petra Janke, *'Dat Werde Leve Hiltom'. Zur Verehrung der Heiligen und ihrer Reliquien am Altenberger Dom*, Studien zur Geschichte, Kunst und Kultur der Zisterzienser 29 (Berlin: Lukas Verlag, 2009), pp. 41–47, 105–132, 290–295.
57. Laabs, *Malerei und Plastik*, p. 21.
58. See examples from Bukow Abbey, Esrum Abbey. *Die Zisterzienser, Katalog*, p. 545. The vision of St Bernard, south Germany, end of the fifteenth century.
59. James France, *Medieval Images of Saint Bernard of Clairvaux* (Kalamazoo, MI: Cistercian Publications, 2007), pp. 205–207, 236–237.
60. Caroline Walker Bynum, *Holy Feast and Holy Fast: The Religious Significance of Food to Medieval Women* (Berkeley, CA: University of California Press, 1987), pp. 270–271.
61. Caesarius of Heisterbach, *Dialogus miraculorum*, ed. Nikolaus Nösges and Horst Schneider (Turnhout: Brepols, 2009), 4.36, 1:456.
62. James France, 'Cistercians Under Our Lady's Mantle', *Cistercian Studies Quarterly* 37 (2002), pp. 401–411.
63. Kinder, *Cistercian Europe*, p. 341.
64. *The Twelfth-Century Statutes*, 'The Instituta', p. 540.
65. Nataša Golob, *Twelfth-Century Cistercian Manuscripts: The Sitticum Collection* (London and Ljubljana: Slovenska knjiga in conjunction with Harvey Miller, 1996), p. 18.
66. Kinder, *Cistercian Europe*, pp. 338–343.
67. Alicja Karłowska-Kamzowa, 'Znaczenie iluminatorstwa cysterskiego dla rozwoju gotyckiej dekoracji rękopisów na ziemiach polskich, Śląsk, Pomorze, Wielkopolska', in *Historia i kultura cystersów w dawnej Polsce*, pp. 368–370.
68. Piotr Skubiszewski, 'La patène de Kalisz: Contribution à l'étude du symbolisme typologique dans l'iconographie', *Cahiers de Civilisation Medieval* 5 (1962), pp. 183–191.
69. *Urkundenbuch des Cistercienserstiftes B. Mariae V. zu Hohenfurt in Böhmen*, ed. Mathias Pangerl (Vienna: an dem Kaiserlichen Hof- und Staatsdruckerei, 1865), p. 386.
70. Christine Sauer, *Fundatio und memoria. Stifter und Klostergründer im Bild 1100 bis 1350* (Göttingen: Vandenhoeck and Ruprecht, 1993), pp. 130–132.
71. Lillich, 'Recent Scholarship concerning Cistercian Windows', p. 242.

chapter 6

ECONOMY: NOT JUST SHEEP AND GRAIN

The fact that all over Europe some Cistercian monasteries came into being as new foundations and others by incorporating pre-existing monastic communities meant that their economic structures were diverse and did not conform to any mythical Cistercian 'model'. White monks were not so much pioneers and innovators as adept at exploiting the opportunities that different localities offered. Certainly, they had an advantage of scale over many other landholders; and unlike lay property, Cistercians, and all other ecclesiastical institutions, were not subject to inheritance and partition. Strategic land acquisitions, the extension of landholdings by grants, exchange, sale and purchase were the result of planning over long periods of time and enabled the Cistercians to create well-connected, coherent estates, and improve their crop production in terms of both quality and quantity. This was neither evidence of any Cistercian master plan nor the accidental result of taking marginal empty land into cultivation, but a consequence of actively participating in a rural economy of which Cistercian houses were an integral part.

The interpretations of the 'Cistercian economic model' are closely linked to the wider debates on the origins of the Order discussed in the first chapter. According to these traditional explanations, the link between poverty and simplicity was a key element of the original monastic programme and the economic practices of the early Cistercians were based on self-sufficiency and independence from the 'feudal' world; and the economic success of the Cistercian monasteries evident by the second half of the twelfth century was 'an accidental by-product' of self-sufficiency. In consequence, this accumulation of wealth was a major reason for the 'crisis and decline' of the Cistercian Order.[1] As with many other aspects of Cistercian history, however, a literal reading of the early texts has led historians to classify any practices that diverged from the prescribed 'ideal' as deviations and symptoms of decline. In particular, the norms recommended by the *Exordium Cistercii* for upholding the purity of monastic observance – making a living from the land cultivated by the community's own labour and the rejection of ownership of parish churches, tithes, serfs or mills – were regarded as absolutely fundamental to Cistercian monasticism.[2]

Economic historians took a very different interpretational approach in the 1970s. They perceived the Cistercian Order's economic practices as being based on a deliberately designed model of monastic economy, which was applied by every house. These historians were not concerned with the religious aspects of Cistercian life, but focused exclusively on the economic function of the monasteries; and their fundamental assumption was that standardisation was a key element in the white monks' economic success. The normative regulations of the Order were seen as a driving force behind an aggressive trend towards relentless growth and expansion – Cistercians were to some extent the forerunners of capitalism.[3] Certainly, application of modern micro-economic theories can be helpful in analysis of individual houses as units of production to understand their role in the local and regional economy, and the reasons behind the changes in the profile of production, consolidation, sale and landholdings. However, the whole interpretation becomes very problematic if we try to apply it to the entire Cistercian network. In fact, the two diametrically opposed interpretations – 'victims of accidental wealth' and 'proto-capitalists' – both rest on the same misinterpretation of the early Cistercian documents as evidence for the existence of a monastic economic master-plan.[4]

Indeed, neither interpretation has stood the test of time and the proliferation of detailed studies of Cistercian houses has revealed a great variety of economic practices, which cannot be fitted into any single 'Cistercian economic model'; nor can they be dismissed as deviation from the Order's prescription. Gifts from lay benefactors came in a great variety of forms and refusing a donation was not in the interest of the monastic houses, even if the gifts were of 'forbidden' types – parish churches, mills or tithes. The fixation on the economic underpinnings of the Cistercian houses as the criterion for judging the 'quality' of the Cistercian way of life is very limiting. As Constance Bouchard points out, 'the spiritual integrity of their way of life did not and could not rest solely on the question of whether or not they owned certain kinds of property'.[5] That would most certainly have been regarded as irrelevant by medieval monks, for whom correctness of observance, in its minutest details, was the true benchmark.

Recent discussions about the Cistercians have argued that the practical differences that distinguished Cistercian from traditional Benedictine economic structures had their roots in Cistercian thinking about the role of work. However, images of physical labour by monks in the early Cistercian manuscripts and references to the monks on the fields in the texts are not glorification of work for its own sake. Physical work had its uses as penance, but was never as important as spiritual exercises. For all their engagement with manual labour, Cistercians were essentially a contemplative order in which communal and individual prayers were always of prime importance.[6]

While the monastic economy was important for the physical well-being of the community, it never actually defined monastic identity. The lands held by the abbeys, food production, crafts and all that encompassed the monastic economy were simply means of ensuring that the community was physically able to perform the Divine Office, pray for the patrons and benefactors and seek the salvation of their own souls. Contrary to the old myth, Cistercian houses never operated on totally 'new' land cultivated only by the work of monks and lay brothers. True, foundation grants often included various types of marginal and under-used land; and the monks often took on abandoned sites, disused castles and early medieval forts. They also took on land previously developed by their benefactors, however, and the reorganisation of land that had already been under cultivation was the hallmark of Cistercian activities to a much greater degree than taking virgin land into cultivation and other pioneering activities, which for a long time was believed to be the 'Cistercian speciality'.

The central feature of the Cistercian economic structure was the grange, a type of self-contained farm. The size and form of granges varied greatly, from upland pasture with simple sheep enclosures to large farms with a 'mini-monastery' encircled by walls and a gatehouse, with their own chapel, refectory, accommodation for the lay brothers and a guest house, numerous farm buildings, mills and workshops. Statistical surveys of the south German Cistercian houses have shown that the average manor of a lay lord reached only one-quarter or one-fifth of the size of a Cistercian grange in the same region. As for numbers, in German-speaking areas the average number of granges for small and medium-sized monasteries was 10 to 15 at the height of economic self-sufficiency in the thirteenth century, whilst large abbeys had 16 to 20 granges. Cistercian monasteries which were founded relatively late were disadvantaged in the process of land accumulation and tended to have fewer granges.[7]

The grange located closest to the monastery was known as the 'home grange' and its purpose was to provide food for the community; large monasteries sometimes had more than one home grange. It also served as a storage facility: many home granges had particularly large granaries or barns of almost monumental proportions. Of course, the creation of an extensive grange system required a long-term strategy, effort and money, but as an effective way of organising rural production and improving net and gross yields, it was the most significant contribution of the Cistercian Order to high medieval agriculture and landscape development.[8]

Within each grange the *conversi* (lay brothers) constituted the workforce, but by the late thirteenth century their numbers were in decline (see above p. 65) and there was also a changing number of paid workers, especially at the busy time of harvest. They were all supervised by a grange master (either a monk or a lay brother) answerable in turn to the cellarer, who was responsible for running the economic affairs of his monastery: supervising the workforce, overseeing payments in money and kind, planning of planting and harvesting, land management, and the marketing and selling of produce. In many large abbeys a new office of bursar developed in the fourteenth century, to manage the financial aspects of the economy, whilst the cellarer remained responsible for the commodity aspect of the material wellbeing of the community.

Another myth about the Cistercians concerns the spread of technological innovations. In fact, the evidence that the Cistercians played a pioneering role in introducing new and better breeds of farm animals, especially sheep and cattle, fruit trees and vegetables and new farming techniques, is very fragmentary; but there is no doubt that technological knowledge travelled through the monastic networks. It has been archaeologically attested that new varieties of fruit trees – cherries, peaches, a certain variety of apple – were introduced by the Cistercian monasteries in southern Poland, possibly from seedlings brought by the abbots travelling to the General Chapter.[9] Similarly water-mills were not invented, but adopted by the Cistercians.[10] Moreover, the old assumption that these farming improvements accounted for the popularity of new Cistercian foundations with founders and patrons is quite incorrect. Cistercian foundations on the frontiers of Europe in particular were often credited with a 'technological and civilising mission', the generosity of their founders being attributed primarily to economic reasons: by planting communities of white monks, they were consciously investing in the economic development of the region. Kołbacz Abbey, founded in 1173 in Western Pomerania, used to be credited with bringing technological advances to this 'backward region'. The heavy and fertile soils in the area of the future Kołbacz Abbey and along the Baltic coast were inaccessible to agriculture because the light wooden plough used by the Slavonic population was not suitable. A heavier steel-capped plough was introduced to Western Pomerania, most likely by the Cistercians, and as a result more land was taken into cultivation at the end of the twelfth and beginning of the thirteenth century.[11] However, Kołbacz and several other Cistercian houses in this region were not established to spread this technical innovation, but for devotional reasons and because of the cultural capital which they represented to the founders on the frontiers of Christian Europe.

Historians have long since abandoned the idea that the agricultural techniques of the Cistercians were superior to their contemporaries and the high output of the Cistercian estates is now associated with better management structures and the sizes of their domains.[12] As Constance Berman has persuasively argued, the distinctiveness of the Cistercian economy lay not in the taking up of uncultivated land, but in the systematic building of large granges.[13] However, the process always entailed the acquisition of seigniorial rights in order to control the population living on the land and to eliminate external interferences. The acquisition of tenanted land was a frequent practice of Cistercian monasteries from the start and dependent peasants had always constituted an intrinsic part of the grange economy.[14]

There was a close connection between granges and peasant communities in north-western Spain: many of the granges of Moreruela Abbey (founded in 1131–1143) originated in villages granted to the monastery together with their inhabitants, the dependent peasants providing labour for the monastic land and being directly employed in other economic activities such as mining.[15] Cistercian houses in Bohemia operated a grange system too, often including manorial elements: while lay brothers had a largely managerial role (often specialising in livestock or a particular aspect of agriculture such as vineyards), they also supervised mixed types of labour, including serfs. Many granges produced for the market as well as for internal monastic consumption, and storage facilities within the granges held not only the produce of the farms, but taxes paid in kind by the serfs.[16]

There is other evidence too that Cistercian economic activities were not pioneering in the way that has traditionally been assumed. Certainly the lands on the sparsely populated frontier between Silesia and the Duchy of Greater Poland were subjected to colonisation according to the *ius Tutonicum*, which encouraged settlement; but the white monks were far from being the only landowners involved in attracting settlers. Indeed, the statistical data shows that the Cistercian monasteries were less to the forefront in setting up new villages than previously been believed: although some 28 per cent of land under colonisation was held by the secular church and another 30 per cent by the laity, only 11 per cednt was colonised by the Cistercians.[17] In Bohemia, among the Cistercian abbeys, only Zlatá Koruna Abbey was involved in the large-scale colonisation of its estates.[18] On the other hand, if the role of the Cistercians in colonisation east of the Elba River has often been exaggerated, their contribution to settlements in western Europe has been under-estimated. In Gascony between 1250 and 1320 Cistercians established around 40 bastides – fortified towns – some of them, especially those distant from the abbey, developed around granges. For the inhabitants, bastides gave protection and functioned as market centres, but for the Cistercians they were primarily another method of management of the estates.[19]

The variety of economic practices across the Order also resulted in a variety of formal and informal ties with different groups of people who worked for, or held property of, the abbey. These included *familiares*, *mercenarios* or tenants (often heavily indebted) of the Iberian Cistercian houses and, in the cases of Polish, Hungarian or Bohemian monasteries, serfs were routinely owned. Although there has never been a comprehensive study of Cistercian lay brothers in East-Central Europe, it has generally been assumed that their numbers were always smaller than in western European houses and that they tended to occupy specialised or managerial roles and never formed the main workforce at any stage, and that the bulk of the manual work was done by the hired workers (*mercenarii*) or the unfree peasantry.[20] Such an assertion has been repeated frequently in the literature, but there are no sources from the twelfth and thirteenth centuries that could confirm or contradict it.[21]

That there was no single Cistercian model of land exploitation was even acknowledged by the General Chapter, whose normative regulations in the early thirteenth century allowed monastic houses to lease out land to lay tenants if there was no suitable workforce and/or property was located too far away.[22] This fitted in with wider economic changes in western Europe that were pushing landowners, including the Cistercians, towards greater reliance on tenants – both a cause and a symptom of the decline of the role of the lay brothers in the Order. This last manifested itself in a growing dissatisfaction of the lay brothers with their status within the monastic community, and the *Statuta* speaks of a series of 'rebellions' (sometimes violence) against abbots. Between 1190 and 1308 there were 103 incidents of revolts, 27 of them involving both monks and *conversi*, and almost all of them in western Europe (mainly in France, Italy and England). Apart from wider economic grievances, and the reorganisation of the methods of land cultivation leading to leasing the land and less reliance on the monastic workforce from the 1180s, a series of prohibitions on the drinking of alcohol by the *conversi* was causing a lot of resentment: some revolts seemed to have a disciplinary dimension connected with attempts to limit the lay brothers' consumption of beer. From the point of view of the authorities, however, if the lay brothers were ceasing to be essential element of the monastic community, and if the numbers of recruits were falling anyway, they were increasingly coming to be seen as troublesome individuals.[23]

Recently, a radically new interpretation of the lay brothers' revolts has been put forward. From the second half of the twelfth century, lay brothers were coming to play prestigious roles within monastic structures as representatives of abbots in legal matters, negotiators with merchants, and as managers and supervisors of various enterprises. It was their demands for better living conditions, food and clothing appropriate to their enhanced status, and the Order's refusal to meet them, that lay behind some of the rebellions. In the thirteenth century, dissatisfaction was further intensified by the trend towards leasing monastic land. The decision to reduce the amount of directly exploited land was a pragmatic one, as leasing it out became more profitable; but it had devastating consequences for many lay brothers, now threatened with obsolescence, and prompted a number of rebellions like that in Ter Duine Abbey in Flanders in 1308, when the lay brothers denounced the policy of leasing that was depriving them of their livelihood and even their reason for existence.[24]

Rural Economy of the Cistercian Monasteries

The development of Cistercian landholdings was largely determined by grants from patrons and benefactors, but it was also common for Cistercian houses to buy or exchange land. To function effectively the grange system needed compact, well-connected fields, and in order to transform a patchwork of grants into a viable estate, land might have to be bought from smaller landowners unwilling or unable to become donors. The proportion of the exchanges to purchases varied greatly between Cistercian abbeys in different parts of medieval Europe and was linked to the local socio-economic conditions and pre-existing patterns of landholding; but the process itself of creating large, well-defined granges through exchange and purchase has often been characterised as typically Cistercian. Certainly, there was never any prohibition of such transactions in the Cistercian regulations, although many historians have assumed in the past that the buying and selling of land must have been against the spirit, if not the letter, of the Cistercian regulations. Indeed, purchases of land were common practice in the Cistercian movement from the start; and while grants in free alms accounted for one-third of the estates of Orsance grange of Cîteaux Abbey, built in the mid-twelfth century, two-thirds were acquired by purchases.[25]

Virtually every Cistercian house went through periods of consolidating its estates by selling off or exchanging those that were too small or too distant to be profitably farmed. If not sold, such land was also frequently leased out. With variations according to regional and local conditions, these developments – whether on a grand scale or merely an accumulation of small adjustments – were certainly clear in the thirteenth century and accelerated fast in the fourteenth: in September 1391, for example, Heisterbach Abbey (Rhineland) exchanged half of two granges for land located in the immediate vicinity of the abbey and in 1392 sold property located 275 kilometres away in Dordrecht.[26] An extensive process of consolidation at Løgum Abbey resulted in 170 of its 193 landholdings being located within a radius of 15 kilometres from the abbey. The steady diminution of the proportion of land directly exploited by abbeys reflected the declining importance of the granges in the Cistercian economy: the proportion of granges within the total of Søro's landholdings, which had been as high as 71 per cent in 1186, had fallen to 47 per cent in 1198 and only 29 per cent in 1248.[27]

In the rural economy arable fields were only one of many resources. Monasteries located in upland and arid regions received significant amounts of pastures, for example in central Spain, northern England and Scotland, which gave many of the houses a chance to develop a successful pastoral economy. Although sheep and wool became almost synonymous with the economic success of Cistercian houses, white monks also specialised in other types of animal husbandry: in Denmark, for example, many Cistercians houses specialised in horse breeding, a very significant element of the local economy.[28] Forest pastures were an attractive resource, coming with rights – depending on the local legal context – to pasture pigs and take timber and firewood, and perhaps even much-coveted hunting rights. Water itself was yet another profitable natural resource. Depending on the location, a frequent type of donation to a Cistercian monastery was fishing rights on the lakes, rivers and seas. Water was useful because it could power mills. Sometimes monastic houses received an actual mill as part of their endowment, as in the case of Bordesley Abbey (1138) and Louth Park (1139), and sometimes a share of the income from a particular mill, Waverley Abbey receiving one mark a year from the income of a mill at Midhurst. When a donor gave land with a watercourse, it might well include permission to set up mills, and might be combined with monopoly rights in particular areas. It was a favourite tactic of Cistercian houses to establish a virtual monopoly by acquiring all the mills in an area. By steadily following a conscious plan, Fürstenfeld Abbey (Bavaria) brought nearly all the mills on the Amper River into its control between 1301 and 1328; and as it already had exclusive fishing rights on the river, it was able to enjoy the two most profitable assets that water could provide.[29] Not that mills were used only for grinding corn: the monastic economy also profited from fulling-mills, paper-mills and bark-mills for the tanneries and mills to power ironworks. Other grants associated with mills might be earmarked for specific purposes: Ollerton mill was granted to Rufford Abbey in the late twelfth century in order to provide fabric for the church, whilst Woodhall mill was given to Kirkstead Abbey to pay for the light (candles) at masses in the church.[30]

Since Cistercian estates were not only large, but also often scattered over large areas, good communication 'corridors' between granges were essential for efficient land exploitation, which necessitated investing in the upkeep of roads and the building of bridges. Indeed, some donations – a substantial number of those made to Warden Abbey between 1180 and 1250, for example – were specifically linked to enhancing the communication between monastic properties.[31] Many patrons and overlords swelled the profits of Cistercian trade by granting tax exemption for the passage of Cistercian goods through their lands and freedom from toll and custom payments on the markets. The consolidation of large blocks of land was not the only reason why Cistercian houses founded in the first half of the twelfth century were beginning to restructure their landholdings by the second half of the thirteenth century. Various usage rights were also being steadily accumulated: rights to pasture, forests for timber, firewood, berries and honey collection, pastures for pigs, water courses, and a miscellany of 'small' rights such as the right to collect stones in areas where building material was scarce.[32] In fact, in England and Scotland it was often the issue of exclusive access to, and rights to exploit, different aspects of land use, rather than the actual ownership of land that caused the conflicts between Cistercian houses and their neighbours. Hunting and pasture rights were among the most contested assets; and one of the most spectacular conflicts, between Melrose Abbey and Patrick Earl of Dunbar, over 2,000 hectares of arable land and hill pasture in north Roxburghshire, lasted from 1198 to 1207. Hunting and pasture rights had been claimed by various neighbours of the property – the former by the de Morevilles and the Dunbars, and the latter by Dryburgh Abbey, the de Morevilles and the Dunbars – while King David I granted Melrose Abbey the right of pasture, pannage and tree-cutting (in the south-eastern part) as part of its initial endowment.[33] Between 1170 and 1198 Melrose Abbey had managed to resolve the claims of all the parties in question apart from the earl of Dunbar, which took another nine years and involved a number of ecclesiastical and secular authorities before the case was resolved by the royal court in 1207.[34]

As the primary aim of the monastic economy was to provide essential resources for the community, its dependants and guests, food production was a priority. Hence the importance of fish, the key protein source in any non-meat diet, and still important when, in the later middle ages, Cistercian monks were eating meat fairly frequently (see chapter 8). Not that the Cistercians were pioneers of new technologies so much as skilled in adapting to different ecological conditions, whether in inland waters, rivers or the sea. They used such existing wild fisheries as could be found locally, accepted fish in dues and rent payments, imported fish from a distance and, above all, established their own fisheries. The simplest form of harvesting fish was by using dams and weirs of mills to catch migratory fish – such as the salmon of the river Mulde at Altzell Abbey in Saxony – which were then often stored in holding tanks. Starting in the late twelfth century, far more advanced fisheries became widespread in Cistercian houses by the later middle ages. These often entailed far greater modification to aquatic habitats, for example by damming a valley, as at Henryków Abbey in Silesia or Byland Abbey in Yorkshire, or diverting streams to fill man-made ponds, as at Chaalis Abbey in Valois. Channels and sluice gates were in regular use for emptying the ponds to harvest the fish. These artificial fisheries could cover large areas – some 60 hectares in the case of Byland Abbey's fishponds in the early fourteenth century.[35] Norwegian monasteries were involved in the production of dried cod, while Danish Cistercian houses sold salted herrings to the Hanseatic merchants.[36] Just like pastures or forests, water was a contested natural resource. Hiddensee Abbey competed with the burgesses of Stralsund over sea resources – especially herring fisheries and saltpans. The latter was particularly profitable, producing half the total income of Hiddensee Abbey by 1500.[37]

Cash crops were particularly important for the Cistercian economy in areas where arable farming was not profitable or even possible, for example northern England, Scotland and parts of Iberia. Pastoralism, focusing on sheep and wool production, especially in upland areas, required a smaller workforce than arable farming and made good use of lands that would otherwise have remained largely unproductive. All stages of wool production were done in-house, including the final steps of washing, dressing and packaging prior to selling. Thirteenth-century records of agreements between Italian merchants and English Cistercian monasteries show clearly that monastic wool was highly valued on the international market. Buyers specified that the preparation should be done in-house to ensure quality and wool sold by an abbey that had purchased it from other smaller producers (known as *collecta*) was clearly distinguished from that produced in-house.[38]

The agricultural activities of the Cistercians, whether directed towards satisfying the needs of the communities or producing a surplus for sale on the open market, were closely linked to artisan production of all kinds: bakeries, breweries, wine production, weaving and cloth production, tanneries, shoemaking, smithies, the manufacturing of parchment and paper (made from cloth rugs from the fifteenth century onwards) and many others. Even proto-industrial activities were in evidence, especially mining – of silver, iron, coal and salt. Iron ore was either extracted via shafts or simply collected from the ground and then smelted in a charcoal furnace.

Salt was a very valuable commodity. Not all abbeys were large-scale producers, but all needed salt for the monastic kitchen, where large quantities were essential for the preservation of meat, fish, cheese and butter. Since it was expensive, its use in the kitchen was controlled by the cellarer and it was distributed in the refectory on request.[39] Any surplus could be sold, and salt was eminently marketable. Several monasteries also had privileges to mine salt. In 1260 Wąchock Abbey in southern Poland secured a privilege to mine salt both on the surface and below the ground.[40] Monasteries which had access to the sea, especially the North Sea and the Baltic, often established saltpans to extract it through evaporation or from salt springs through wells. In areas rich in minerals, several monastic houses and other corporate and lay landholders may have had extraction privileges. High concentrations of salt occurred, for example, in Lüneburg on the Elba River downstream from Hamburg, where seven Cistercian monasteries operated their saltpans. Indeed, they, together with other religious institutions and prelates from Mecklenburg, and the cathedrals of Lübeck and Hamburg owned no fewer than 19.5 saltpans. The consequent proliferation of ecclesiastical owners enjoying toll privileges led to a prolonged conflict with the city of Lüneburg, which wanted the ecclesiastical corporations to contribute to the city coffers, while the monasteries and prelates stubbornly refused to do so – a typical clash of economic interests being exacerbated by the perceived privileged position of Cistercian communities in terms of taxation and of other freedoms which they had received from the secular rulers.

In some cases salt, like other foodstuffs or goods which were not produced by the monasteries themselves, had to be paid for in cash, and the Cistercians were involved in the economy not only as producers but also consumers and players on the medieval financial market. Changes in the medieval economy from the thirteenth century, leading to a much greater role of money and credit, were linked to the wider processes of the growth of towns, and the intensification of trade, which are sometimes described as the 'commercialisation' of the medieval economy. Social and economic change became increasingly interlinked with commercialisation, leading to increased productivity and the acquisition of wealth becoming increasingly dependent on money and trade.[41]

All these changes had an impact on the way in which the white monks ran their economic affairs. At first glance it amounted to a shift from the 'ideal' model of self-sufficiency and manual labour performed by the monks and lay brothers towards leasing out the land and reliance on rent. However, this was never a universal phenomenon, and just as a great variety of economic practices had existed from the very beginning of the Cistercian movement, so the transition to a market-based economy varied in terms of both forms and chronology all over Europe. In the second half of the fourteenth century, especially after the Black Death, the Cistercian land economy was everywhere very different from what it had been in the twelfth century; but whereas in western Europe Cistercian houses leased out most of their granges to the laity and collected cash rents, in eastern Europe there was a shift towards the demesne farm and a workforce of serfs.

Cistercian Monasteries, Trade and Money Markets

It was trade that provided monastic communities with one of its very few means of access to the liquid capital it needed for building projects, devotional images, liturgical and other materials for the monastic church, luxurious foodstuffs and other items needed for purposes of hospitality and enhancing the status of the abbot. Credit was not only difficult to obtain but expensive – hence the problem of endemic debt that according to the General Chapter was besetting many French Cistercian houses as early as the twelfth century. Indeed, in 1182 the General Chapter decreed that abbeys which already owed 50 marks for land purchases must not buy any more land or begin new projects until the debt had been cleared; and it returned to the problem again in more detail in 1188, specifying punishments for abbots who transgressed.[42] Financial problems of this kind emerged in other parts of Europe in the thirteenth century, but the scale and many details were strongly regional and specific to individual houses. Whilst some abbeys were active and successful themselves on the money market, lending money to their patrons, benefactors and neighbours, others were heavily in debt. Inevitably, French abbeys were more exposed to the supervision of the General Chapter, hence their problems are better documented.

Of course, lending and borrowing money usually carried the danger of involvement in usury, which by the late twelfth century was a major concern of the church. The Councils of Lyon in 1274 and Vienne in 1312 codified ecclesiastical punishments for usury, including the denial of death-bed absolution and Christian burial and the threat of excommunication for secular powers that permitted the practice. The main objection against it was that lending money with interest was a lack of charity, and a way of gaining 'something for nothing', as the lender was making a profit without any labour. The main theological argument against usury was formulated by Thomas Aquinas, who wrote that charging interest was akin to stealing time, which belongs to God, so charging it on the amount of a loan was equal to stealing.[43] However, in medieval legal thinking there was a concept of 'just price', so mortgaging of land was supposed to be done in such a way that if the property ended up in the hands of the creditor the amount of borrowed money was close to the market value of the land. Even so, as all monastic communities needed access to finance especially for expensive building projects, complex financial tools were devised to avoid open use of credit, with the result that the regulations of the General Chapter forbidding both borrowing and the giving of credit were largely ignored in practice.[44]

English Cistercian monasteries, for example, used forward contracts to sell their wool as a way of raising large amounts of cash. These were sophisticated financial instruments used primarily by thirteenth-century Italian merchants, who were the almost exclusive trading partners of the Cistercians in England and Wales and served as middlemen for the rapidly expanding cloth industry in Flanders. These contracts were in all but name loan agreements in which future wool production was used as security; and they were concluded between 2 and 20 years in advance. The system had several advantages for Cistercian abbeys. First, the amount of money that a monastery was going to receive was known in advance and fixed, which made financial planning less risky. Second, the payments from the merchants were made in large lump sums, ideal for financing the extensive building projects in which many monasteries were engaged. On the other hand, this system of buying wool ensured the merchants a significant discount, as much as 20 per cent in relation to the price level if the monks sold their crop on a yearly basis; and monasteries particularly desperate for cash were more likely to concede an even higher discount.[45]

The system ran to the advantage of all concerned until the outbreak of the devastating sheep disease known as 'murrain', which decimated wool production between 1272 and 1317. This affected all producers, but had particularly dramatic consequences for the ability of the Cistercians to sustain the level of credit they had assumed.[46] On several occasions the monastic houses of northern England that had based their economy on wool production became insolvent: Rievaulx Abbey in 1276, 1288 and 1292, Kirkstall in 1276 and 1281, Fountains in 1274 and 1291, Flaxley in 1277, 1281 and 1283. This did not mean that the monastery in question disappeared, but an administrator appointed by the crown took over while the monks were sent to neighbouring Cistercian houses to keep running costs to a minimum. The administrator's role was to pay off the debtors and bring monastic finance into solvency again. It seems that the 'safety-net' of calling for royal help in the case of dire financial trouble encouraged high-risk strategies. On the other hand, English kings, who frequently turned to the Cistercian monasteries for taxes and ad hoc payments, had an interest in preserving these useful sources of money for the future whilst appearing to be protectors of the church. As for the monasteries, although advance sales and chronic indebtedness became, in the late thirteenth century, almost a way of life for many English Cistercian houses, and although it was certainly disruptive for a community when it had to be dispersed, advance sales remained the only practical way for a house to acquire cash in an economy in which merchants were disproportionally rich in contrast to permanently impecunious agricultural producers.[47]

The Cistercians' involvement in trade and the market economy meant that many houses possessed liquid capital, and were not only borrowing money, but also acting as creditors across Europe. The credit instruments used were varied, from rent contracts and rent purchase to pawning. The social profile of their customers varied according to region, and ranged from middling knights and tenants of monastic lands to cathedral chapters, higher clergy, nobility and even rulers. By the fifteenth century the debtors of Cistercian monasteries tended to be more urban-based, whilst impoverished knights were the least likely to be able to pay off the debts and became even more economically dependent on their monastic neighbours.[48] The earliest examples of Cistercian houses acting as creditors, by taking property in pawn from middling knightly families, occurred in the mid-twelfth century. In return for a piece of land, Cistercians would give a lump sum, lower than the actual sale price. The land could be redeemed after an agreed period, usually within six years; if not, it stayed in the hands of the monastery. Such transactions became frequent among the Burgundian houses and usually involved knights going on crusades. In southern France, the mortgaging of land to Cistercians became a common way to raise cash not just for crusade expeditions or ransoms but also for more mundane purposes not specified in the charters; and for Berdoues Abbey it became a device for putting landholdings together.[49]

In the money market the role of the Cistercians varied according to the regional conditions: in Wales, where the commercialisation of the economy remained very low until the early decades of the thirteenth century, Cistercian abbeys were one of the very few sources of silver coins and Cistercians benefited from being able to purchase the lands of native rulers and landholders who needed liquid capital for purchases and consumption.[50]

Credit given to those lower down the social scale who were not landowners, such as tenants on monastic estates, was often provided on the security of goods and for a relatively short period. In 1320 Fürstenfeld Abbey lent its tenant Chunrat von Hattenhofen three pounds of Munich pfenning, on the security of goods in his farm, repayable on St George's day (23 April). It was agreed that if he defaulted, the monastery was to take the goods away.[51] Another form of dealing in credit practised by English Cistercians in the late twelfth and early thirteenth centuries was to buy properties from landowners heavily indebted to Jewish creditors, with the Cistercian house redeeming the debt and retaining the land. The practice has been documented for Rievaulx, Thame, Flaxley, Meaux and Fountains, and could prove particularly useful when the amount of land that could be obtained by free alms diminished drastically.[52]

On the whole, the credit activities of the Cistercian abbeys, far from being predatory, were often manifestations of lasting relationships between the monasteries and their patrons and benefactors, who could turn to 'their' monks for a loan in times of need. Their perceived or real economic success, however, also made them a target for the monetary demands of the state; and apart from their voluntary involvement in lending there were also instances when the Cistercians were creditors under duress. In England the crown, from at least the reign of Richard I, was mindful of the wealth possessed by the Order: the money raised for King Richard's ransom from captivity by Emperor Henry VI, negotiated in 1193, included a year's worth of wool from the Cistercian monasteries in the kingdom. The opportunity to extract money from the Cistercian houses was taken up very enthusiastically by King John, who in order to raise money for military campaigns imposed special taxation on the entire church, regardless of the Cistercian exemption. Eventually he managed to extract between 25,000 and 39,000 marks from Cistercian monasteries in England, much of it by force. His son, Henry III, was less violent, but he too was very effective at extracting money – in return for repeated confirmations of Cistercian exemptions and privileges. The financial imposition on the English houses reached their height with King Edward I's demands for money for campaigns in Wales and Gascony in the 1270s and 1280s, when a large part of the taxation imposed on the English clergy, four times between 1279 and 1290, came from Cistercian houses.[53]

Similarly, French kings regularly extracted money from the Cistercian Order. In 1284 King Philip IV imposed a levy on the Cistercian houses in his kingdom for a campaign in Flanders and a crusade in Aragon; and in 1296 and 1297 Cistercians in France contributed 60,000 livre *tournois* for the French king's war against the English in Gascony. Because Cistercian houses in France did not have a cash surplus of such magnitude, they were forced to borrow money at a high interest rate and fell deeply into debt.[54] By the later middle ages the continuance of this trend was causing serious financial problems for the French monasteries (see chapter 8).

Cistercian Monasteries and Urban Settlements

Although Cistercian houses were predominantly situated in the countryside and their economic basis was land, they were linked to urban economic networks in a variety of ways. Almost all Cistercian monasteries and nunneries owned properties in towns, usually warehouses for storage of goods and houses to accommodate travelling monks and lay brothers, which provided a connection between the rural economy and the expanding market economy.[55] Since Cistercian monasteries were not established in the wilderness and were frequently in close proximity to important transport routes, many had access to local, national and international trading centres where they could sell their produce and buy specialised or imported goods. Regions marked by particular concentrations of monastic urban properties included the Rhineland, the Moselle valley, Champagnes (Troyes, Lagny, Provins, Bar-sur-Aube) and the territories of the Hanseatic league (Lübeck, Wismar, Rostock, Szczezin, Gdańsk and Riga).

The urban properties of Cistercian houses were usually referred to as *curia* or *domus* in the sources, to emphasise that they consisted essentially of a building or buildings as opposed to open land. In the papal privilege for Ebrach Abbey (Upper Franconia) there is a clear distinction between the grange, denoting a rural estate, and the *curia*, denoting urban property.[56] Some abbeys, if the size and concentration of their urban properties was very high, established 'town granges', consisting of several buildings and a chapel, under a *magister* like the rural granges. One of the oldest identified examples of a 'town grange' was the late twelfth-century property belonging to Himmerod Abbey in Trier, a major centre of trade in the Moselle region and an important link in the chain of wine production and marketing.[57]

Cistercian properties in urban centres facilitated access to specialised and important items unobtainable in the countryside. The accounts from the court belonging to Fürstenfeld Abbey in Augsburg from the mid-sixteenth century list purchases of olive oil, imported foodstuffs and wine, gold items made by highly skilled artisans, silver tablewear, liturgical objects and medical instruments.[58] The urban properties of Salem Abbey were used for marketing monastic produce – crops, livestock, wine and salt – and bear witness to the abbey's importance in the economic relations between the towns around Lake Constance and the countryside.

It was not unusual for Cistercian houses to hold properties in a number of urban centres: Himmerod Abbey, for example, had a presence in nine towns, of which the town courts in Cologne, Trier and Koblenz were the most important for the marketing of monastic products. In Cologne in particular, the chief wine-trading centre in the Rhineland, Himmerod's property contained extensive storage facilities and was used as a transit station for large shipments of wine.[59] Monasteries in the Rhineland, northern France and upper Bavaria often owned properties in key medieval trading cities such as Cologne, Troyes, Regensburg and Augsburg. In the thirteenth century Eberbach Abbey was already selling its own salt production through its city court in Cologne; and the fact that the abbey held privileges exempting it from customs payments on salt brought into the city made the trade even more profitable for Eberbach.[60]

Monastic outposts in important trading centres were often quite extensive, and a concentration of Cistercian buildings covering one or more blocks became a distinct feature of many medieval cities. A group of properties belonging to Doberan Abbey in Rostock was so large that in the late middle ages it came to be called 'Little Doberan'. Meanwhile, the special 'exterritorial' character of the Cistercian properties in relation to the rest of the urban space was manifested by the right of many town granges to grant asylum to fugitives.[61]

The pattern of the emergence and expansion of Cistercian urban holdings indicates that this was often part of a much wider process of urban growth. The development of the urban holdings of Eldena Abbey (founded in 1199) in the city of Greifswald began in 1278 with one house, which was augmented in 1290 by the purchase, jointly with another religious institution, the Hospital of the Holy Spirit, of further property on the border between the old and new towns. The fourteenth century saw further expansion, with the acquisition of two houses belonging to the city authorities in exchange for two other properties between the city walls and St Mary's Church. These eventually developed into the large court of Eldena Abbey within the city. Certainly, the fact that the abbey found the town court in Greifwald particularly useful as the growing city bought up much of its produce, especially salt, timber, ash and cane, illustrates the importance of the urban outposts of Cistercian houses for local trade between the rural producer and urban consumer.[62]

Beyond this, however, urban properties were important links in the chain of transport by water and road and a staging post between different monastic properties. The property of Zinna Abbey, for example, situated near the Spree in Berlin (first noted in 1543, but in fact much older) was used as a transit point for limestone. For Cistercian monasteries in Yorkshire and Lincolnshire, engaged in large-scale wool production, urban properties in York and Boston (then a North Sea harbour) were crucial for the trade with Flemish and Italian merchants. Moreover, York had a good transport connection in the river Ouse, which was navigable for sea-going vessels.[63] Since it was the access to storage and lodging facilities that was crucial for all abbeys involved in trade, some were prepared to rely on friendly connections with other Cistercian houses to secure the use of such outposts without actually owning any urban property themselves. Such an agreement existed between Melrose Abbey and its daughter Holm Cultram Abbey in Cumbria, by which a house in Carlisle was made available for Melrose monks and *conversi* to use during the annual fair there.[64]

Some Cistercian nunneries were located in the urban centres. This was sometimes the doing of their patrons, but there were also important economic considerations in play. In Champagne, many nunneries located just outside busy fair towns and along international trade routes, accumulated lands in the suburbs and rents from urban properties. In the thirteenth century Cistercian nuns came to rely heavily on urban markets to buy and sell property and to collect rents. Wealthy city dwellers became their benefactors, some joining communities as nuns and *conversi* as well as taking leaseholds on many of their lands. Besides, being located in immediate proximity to the urban world was important for the exercise of the social mission of the nuns as carers for the poor and sick; thus their presence became 'integral to the shape of the social and religious landscape of Champagne'.[65]

By contrast, male Cistercian houses in towns and cities were very rare, and the choice of a location was almost always linked to some peculiar circumstances. Some were very late foundations; for others the location reflected the wishes of the founder or perhaps some opportunity offered by a particular urban location. Often it was a combination of such factors: King Edward III founded St Mary Graces Abbey in London in 1350 as a daughter house of an older royal foundation in Beaulieu (Hampshire). The monastery was located just outside the city walls of London, on the site of a Black Death cemetery in East Smithfield, near the Tower. It was close to the royal residences along the Thames river in Baynard's Castle, Kennington, Rotherhithe and Sheen. Although the abbey received only a limited number of bequests from the citizens of London, it was particularly favoured by aristocrats associated with the royal court and became an important location for prestigious burials from that group. This was linked to the royal patronage of the house, which helped to create links between the Cistercian house and the royal court.[66] Similarly, a Cistercian monastery in Zagreb was founded in the early fourteenth century as a daughter house of a royal foundation in Toplica (Slavonia). Zagreb monastery, located on the outskirts of the city on a river island, was both secluded and well-connected, and very soon became the centre of a settlement, with workshops, mills and a population of tradesmen, abbey serfs and servants.[67]

The Cistercian incursion into urban communities was not simply a commercial phenomenon, but one that gave rise to a new 'benefactor base' of wealthy burgesses, on a different footing from the Order's land-based benefactors, and one that often reflected long-standing trade connections. Hiddensee Abbey (founded in 1296), which had extensive saltpans in Lüneburg, developed lasting business connections with a number of citizens of Stralsund. A document of 1514 acknowledges that the abbot and convent of Hiddensee owed 1750 marks to one Kersten Parow, a businessman and member of the influential Merchant Taylor's Company in Stralsund. Part of this debt was converted into a donation in his and his parents' memory and the remainder was to be paid off from the income of saltpans in Lübeck. This was only one part of much wider business deals that the abbey had with this family over two generations – between Karsten and his widowed mother and the abbey – concerning a loan in 1509 relating to some earlier joint ventures between his father Jacob and the abbey some time before.[68] Just as donations, exchanges and sales of land by rural benefactors were often blurred, so the economic and devotional motivations for the new urban donors of Cistercian houses were intertwined. Nor was it only the male houses that benefited from opportunities to acquire new benefactors among the urban elites. Already in the first half of the thirteenth century the nunnery of Saint-Antoine-des-Champs outside Paris had an increasing number of donations from the citizens of Paris, many of them in connection with the admission of burgesses' daughters into the monastic community.[69]

The close connections between urban elites and Cistercian monasteries left visual reminders – tombs and other forms of commemoration. In contrast to the mendicants, inundated with lay burials, Cistercian abbeys had the aura of selective institutions. Doberan Abbey, the 'home monastery' of Mecklenburg's ruling family, also contains the tomb of one Peter Wise (d. 1338), a burgess from Lübeck. Perhaps the fact that his two brothers were monks at Doberan explains the conspicuousness of Peter's involvement with the abbey, through donations and the establishment of chantries; and that his first tombstone was subsequently used as an altar table was not a sign of disrespect, but a reminder that Peter was still present and benefiting from the liturgy performed over his image. His second tombstone bears his coat of arms and a eulogy to him in Latin and the vernacular. Peter was not the only wealthy citizen of Lübeck to be buried in Doberan. A hundred years after his death, the members of the city council of Lübeck and their families, looking to benefit spiritually from all the good works performed by the monks, became, as a group, members of the Doberan confraternity.[70]

Conclusions

Certainly, Cistercian abbeys benefited from the general economic and geographical expansion of Europe in the twelfth century; but their success in acquiring land on which to build their economic basis was a result of the spiritual and social appeal to lay elites, particularly the growing number of aspiring knights. The growth in the wealth of many Cistercian monasteries was not an accidental by-product of their development, nor was it an obstacle to their spiritual functions. After all, funds were essential for building projects within the cloister and the church where the liturgical functions were performed, and a poor and economically failing monastery was far less likely to attract new donations and fulfil its intercessory obligations.

The economic foundations of Cistercian houses were overwhelmingly rural and many monasteries succeeded in creating extensive landholdings built over several generations through donations, exchanges, purchases and sales. The self-contained granges, the hallmark of the white monks' economy, existed only so long as the supply of lay brothers to run them guaranteed their viability. The process of commercialisation of the medieval economy from the thirteenth century onwards, the growth of trade and the importance of money made leasing out land far more profitable for many landowners in western Europe, and granges started to disappear. They had never been part of the Cistercian identity in the same way as monastic observance was; hence the end of direct exploitation of land was not a sign of Cistercian decline, but simply part of a process by which rural monasticism was adjusting itself to the new socio-economic conditions.

The local specialisation, taking advantage of pre-existing conditions (for example pastoralism, salt production, and mining) that often characterised Cistercian houses, was another aspect of the regionalisation of the Order, which can also be seen in its architecture and its relationships with the lay world. Its relationships with urban communities, large cities and smaller regional centres covered a number of different, but interconnected issues. The nature of a monastery's connection with urban centres was directly related to its location. The ownership of urban properties was not an ideological issue, but purely a pragmatic concern; hence monasteries located near important trading centres usually established facilities for the storage and marketing of monastic produce. Products varied according to regions, but usually involved bulk raw materials such as timber, wool, corn or salt. Urban outposts were also convenient points for buying imported or specialised goods needed in the monasteries, but urban–monastic relations were not exclusively commercial. As Sven Wichert points out, it is limiting to see the relationship between a monastery and a city as simply that of producer and consumer. Whilst urban communities were significant both as trading partners and benefactors, monasteries were after all primarily places of prayer and 'the professional struggle for the soul'.[71]

Notes

1. Louis Lekai, *The Cistercians: Ideals and Reality* (Kent, OH: Kent State University Press, 1977), pp. 282–333; David Knowles, *The Monastic Order in England: A History of Its Development from the Times of St Dunstan to the Fourth Lateran Council, 940–1216* (Cambridge: Cambridge University Press, 1963), p. 68; James E. Madden, 'Business Monks, Banker Monks, Bankrupt Monks: The English Cistercians in the Thirteenth Century', *Catholic History Review* 49 (1963), pp. 341–364.
2. Constance Bouchard, *Holy Entrepreneurs: Cistercians, Knights, and Economic Exchange in Twelfth-Century Burgundy* (Ithaca, NY: Cornell University Press, 1991), pp. 95–96.
3. Richard Roehl, 'Plan and Reality in a Medieval Monastic Economy: The Cistercians', *Studies in Medieval and Renaissance History* 9 (1972), pp. 83–113; Bernhard Nagel, *Die Eigenarbeit der Zisterzienser. Von der religiösen Askese zur wirtschaftlichen Effizienz* (Marburg: Metropolis-Verlag, 2006), pp. 83–95.
4. Constance Berman, 'The Development of Cistercian Economic Practice during the Lifetime of Bernard of Clairvaux: The Historical Perspective on Innocent II's 1132 Privilege', in *Bernardus Magister: Papers presented at the Nonacentenary Celebration of the Birth of Saint Bernard of Clairvaux, Kalamazoo, Michigan, sponsored by the Institute of Cistercian Studies, Western Michigan University, 10–13 May 1990*, ed. John R. Sommerfeldt (Kalamazoo, MI: Cistercian Publications, 1992), p. 305.
5. Bouchard, *Holy Entrepreneurs*, p. 97.
6. Bede K. Lackner, 'Early Citeaux and the Care of Souls', in *Noble Piety and Reformed Monasticism*, ed. E.R. Elder (Kalamazoo, MI: Cistercian Publications, 1981), p. 57.
7. Werner Rösener, 'Religion und Ökonomie. Zur Wirtschaftstätigkeit der Zisterzienser', in *Von Cîteaux nach Bebenhausen: Welt und Wirken der Zisterzienser* (Tübingen: Attempto, 2000), pp. 115–116; Charles Higounet, 'Essai sur les granges cisterciennes', in *L'Économie Cistercienne: géographie, mutations, du Moyen Âge aux temps modernes: troisiemes Journees internationales d'histoire, 16–18 septembre 1981*, ed. Charles Hugounet (Auch: Comité départemental du tourisme du Gers, 1983), p. 165.
8. Constance H. Berman, 'The Economic Practices of Cistercian Women's Communities: A Preliminary Look', in *Studiosorum Speculum: Studies in Honor of Louis J. Lekai*, ed. Francis R. Swietek and John R. Sommerfeldt (Kalamazoo, MI: Cistercian Publications, 1993), p. 16.
9. Józef Dobosz and Andrzej M. Wyrwa, 'Działalność gospodarcza cystersów na ziemiach polskich – zarys problemu', in *Monasticon Cisterciense Poloniae*, ed. Andrzej M. Wyrwa, Jerzy Strzelczyk and Krzysztof Kaczmarek, vol. 1 (Poznań: Wydawnictwo Poznańskie, 1999), p. 210.

10. Constance H. Berman, *Medieval Agriculture, the Southern French Countryside, and the Early Cistercians* (Philadelphia, PA: American Philosophical Society, 1986), pp. 87–91.
11. Jan M. Piskorski, *Pomorze Plemienne: Historia – Archaeologia – Językoznawstwo* (Poznań: PTPN, 2002), p. 219.
12. Lawrence J. McCrank, 'The Economic Administration of a Monastic Domain by the Cistercians of Poblet, 1150–1276', in *Studies in Medieval Cistercian History*, vol. 2, ed. John R. Sommerfeldt (Kalamazoo, MI: Cistercian Publications, 1976), p. 141; David H. Williams, *The Cistercians in the Early Middle Ages: Written to Commemorate the Nine Hundredth Anniversary of Foundation of the Order at Cîteaux in 1098* (Leominster: Gracewing, 1998), p. 276.
13. Constance Berman, *Medieval Agriculture, the Southern French Countryside, and the Early Cistercians* (Philadelphia, PA: American Philosophical Society, 1986).
14. Isabel Alfonso, 'Cistercians and Feudalism', *Past and Present* 133 (1991), pp. 24–27.
15. Alfonso, 'Cistercians and Feudalism', pp. 27–28.
16. Kateřina Charvátova, 'Manorial Farms of Cistercian Abbeys of Mediaeval Bohemia', in *Historia i kultura cystersów w dawnej Polsce i ich europejskie związki*, ed. Jerzy Strzelczyk (Poznań: Wydawnictwo Naukowe UAM, 1987), pp. 127–135).
17. Dobosz and Wyrwa, 'Działalność gospodarcza cystersów', p. 206.
18. Kateřina Charvátova, 'Mindful of Reality, Faithful to Traditions: Development of Bohemian Possessions of the Cistercian Order from the 12th to the 13th Centuries', in *L'espace cistercien*, ed. Léon Pressouyre (Paris: Comité des travaux historiques et scientifiques, 1994), p. 181.
19. Constance Berman, 'From Cistercian Granges to Cistercian Bastides. Using the Order's Records to Date Landscape Transformation', in *L'espace cistercien*, pp. 204–205.
20. Teresa Dunin-Wąsowicz, 'W sprawie roli konwersów w polskich klasztorach cysterskich (XII–XIII w.)', in *Wieki Średnie. Medium Aevum: prace ofiarowane Tadeuszowi Manteufflowi w 60 rocznicę urodzin* (Warsaw: PWN, 1962), pp. 126–128; Winfried Schich, 'Zum Wirken der Zisterzienser im östlichen Mitteleuropa im 12. und 13. Jahrhundert', in *Zisterziensische Spiritualität. Theologische Grundlagen, funktionale Voraussetzungen und bildhafte Ausprägungen im Mittelalter*, ed. Clemens Kasper and Klaus Schreiner (St Ottilien: EOS Verlag, 1994), p. 282.
21. Piotr Oliński, 'Konwersi pelplińscy w świetle klasztornego nekrologu (z badań nad liczebnością konwersów w klasztorach cysterskich w Polsce)', in *Cystersi w społeczeństwie Europy Środkowej. Materiały z konferencji naukowej odbytej w klasztorze oo. Cystersów w Krakowie Mogile z okazji 900 rocznicy powstania Zakonu Ojców Cystersów. Poznań-Kraków-Mogiła 5–10 października 1998*, ed. Andrzej Marek Wyrwa and Józef Dobosz (Poznań: Wydawnictwo Poznańskie, 2000), p. 738.
22. *Statuta capitulorum generalium ordinis Cisterciensis ab anno 1116 ad annum 1786*, ed. Joseph Canivez, 8 vols. (Louvain: Bureaux de la Revue, 1933–1941), vol. 1, 1208: 5, 1220: 5.

23. James S. Donnelly, *The Decline of the Medieval Cistercian Lay Brotherhood* (New York: Fordham University Press, 1949), pp. 38–60; Martha Newman, *The Boundaries of Charity: Cistercian Culture and Ecclesiastical Reform 1098–1180* (Stanford, CA: Stanford University Press, 1996), pp. 101–106; Megan Cassidy-Welch, *Monastic Spaces and their Meanings: Thirteenth-Century English Cistercian Monasteries* (Turnhout: Brepols, 2001), pp. 167–193.
24. Brian Noell, 'Expectation and Unrest among Cistercian Lay Brothers in the Twelfth and Thirteenth Centuries', *Journal of Medieval History* 32 (2006), pp. 270–274.
25. Constance Bouchard, 'Twelfth Century Burgundy: The Great Unknown?', in *Studiosorum Speculum: Studies in Honor of Louis J. Lekai*, ed. Francis R. Swietek and John R. Sommerfeldt (Kalamazoo, MI: Cistercian Publications, 1993), pp. 40–41.
26. Swen Holger Brunsch, *Die Zisterzienserkloster Heisterbach von seiner Gründung bis zum Anfang des 16. Jahrhunderts* (Siegburg: Verlag Franz Schmitt, 1998), p. 80.
27. James France, *The Cistercians in Scandinavia* (Kalamazoo, MI: Cistercian Publications, 1992), p. 273.
28. France, *The Cistercians in Scandinavia*, p. 278.
29. Klaus Wollenberg, *Die Entwicklung der Eigenwirtschaft des Zisterzienserklosters Fürstenfeld zwischen 1263 und 1632 unter besonderer Berücksichtigung des Auftretens moderner Aspekte* (Frankfurt am Main: Peter Lang, 1984), p. 269.
30. C. James Bond, 'Cistercian Mills in England and Wales: A Preliminary Survey', in *L'espace cistercien*, pp. 368–373.
31. *Cartulary of Wardon*, ed. G.H. Fowler, *Publications of the Bedfordshire Historical Records Society* 13 (1931), pp. 75–76.
32. Bouchard, *Holy Entrepreneurs*, p. 106.
33. *Liber de Melros*, ed. Cosmo Innes (Edinburgh, Bannatyne Club, 1837), vol. 1, no. 1.
34. Thomas Mackay Cooper, 'Melrose Abbey *versus* the Earl of Dunbar', *Juridical Review* 54 (1943), pp. 2–3, 6–8; Paul C. Ferguson, *Medieval Papal Representatives in Scotland: Legates, Nuncios, and Judges-Delegate, 1125–1286* (Edinburgh: Star Society, 1997), pp. 217–218; *Liber de Melros*, vol. 1, no. 101–103.
35. Richard Hoffmann, 'Mediaeval Cistercian Fisheries Natural and Artificial', in *L'espace cistercien*, pp. 401–414.
36. France, *The Cistercians in Scandinavia*, pp. 281–284.
37. Andreas Niemeck, 'Kloster und Stadt. Die Personell-sozialen Beziehungen zwischen den Zisterzienserklöstern Neuenkamp und Hiddensee und der Stadt Stralsund', in *Klöster und monastische Kultur in Hansestädten: Beiträge des 4. wissenschaftlichen Kolloquiums Stralsund 12. bis 15. Dezember 2001*, ed. Claudia Kimminus-Schneider and Manfred Schneider (Rahden: Verlag Marie Leidorf, 2003), pp. 142–143.
38. T.H. Lloyd, *The Movement of Wool Prices in Medieval England*, Economic History Review Supplements 6 (1973), p. 10.
39. Otto Volk, *Salzproduktion und Salzhandel mittelalterlicher Zisterzienserklöster* (Sigmaringen: Jan Thorbecke, 1984), pp. 28–29, 119–141.

40. Paweł Kołodziejski, 'Górniczo-hutnicza działalność cystersów wąchockich (1179–1819)', in *Ingenio et Humilitate. Studia z dziejów zakonu cystersów i Kościoła na ziemiach polskich*, ed. A.M. Wyrwa (Katowice: Biblioteka Śląska 2007), p. 118.
41. Richard H. Britnell, 'Commercialisation and Economic Development in England 1000–1300', in *A Commercialising Economy: England 1086 to c.1300*, ed. Richard H. Britnell and Bruce M.S. Campbell (Manchester: Manchester University Press, 1995), pp. 7–8.
42. Brian Noell, 'Cistercian Monks in the Market. Legal Study, Economic Statutes, and Institutional Evolution in the Twelfth Century', in *Cîteaux: Commentarii Cistercienses* 59 (2008), pp. 187–188; *Twelfth-century Statutes from the Cistercian General Chapter: Latin text with English notes and commentary*, ed. Chrysogonus Waddell (Brecht: Cîteaux, Commentarii Cistercienses, 2002), 1182: 9; 1188: 14.
43. Mark Koyama, 'Evading the "Taint of Usury": The Usury Prohibition as a Barrier to Entry', *Explorations in Economic History* (2010), http://papers.ssrn.com/sol3/papers.cfm?abstract_id=1829062
44. *Twelfth-Century Statutes*, 1180: 12, 1184: 7.
45. Adrian H. Bell, Chris Brooks and Paul Dryburgh, 'Interest Rates and Efficiency in Medieval Wool Forward Contracts', *Journal of Banking and Finance* 31 (2007), pp. 365–366.
46. Ian Kershaw, 'The Great European Famine and Agrarian Crisis in England, 1315–1322', *Past and Present* 59 (1973), p. 27.
47. Emilia Jamroziak, 'Rievaulx Abbey as a Wool Producer in the Late Thirteenth Century: Cistercians, Sheep and Big Debts', *Northern History* 40 (2003), pp. 216–217.
48. Grzegorz Żabiński, 'Mogiła – A Case Study of Credit Activity of a Cistercian Monastery in the Medieval Diocese of Cracow', *Annual of Medieval Studies at the CEU* 9 (2003), pp. 93–126.
49. Constance Bouchard, 'Twelfth-century Burgundy: The Great Unknown', in *Studiosorum Speculum*, p. 43; Constance Hoffman Berman, 'Land Acquisition and the Use of the Mortgage Contract by the Cistercians of Berdoues', *Speculum* 57 (1982), pp. 263–264.
50. Huw Pryce, 'Patrons and Patronage among the Cistercians in Wales', *Archaeologia Cambrensis* 154 (2005), p. 89.
51. Wollenberg, *Die Entwicklung der Eigenwirtschaft*, p. 329.
52. Coburn V. Graves, 'The Economic Activities of the Cistercians in Medieval England (1128–1307)', *Analecta Sacri Ordinis Cisterciensis* 13 (1957), pp. 43–44.
53. H.S. Deighton, 'Clerical Taxation by Consent, 1279–1301', *English Historical Review* 68 (1953), pp. 161–162; Graves, 'The Economic Activities of the Cistercians', pp. 37–41.
54. William Chester Jordan, *Unceasing Strife, Unending Fear: Jacques de Thérines and the Freedom of the Church in the Age of the Last Capetians* (Princeton, NJ: Princeton University Press, 2005), p. 78.
55. Berman, *Medieval Agriculture*, pp. 123–124; Wollenberg, *Die Entwicklung der Eigenwirtschaft*, p. 295.

56. Reinhard Schneider, 'Stadthöfe der Zisterzienser: zu Ihrer Funktion und Bedeutung', *Zisterzienser Studien*, vol. 4 (Berlin: Colloquium Verlag, 1979), p. 18.
57. Werner Rösener, 'Religion und Ökonomie. Zur Wirtschaftstätigkeit der Zisterzienser, in *Von Cîteaux nach Bebenhausen*, p. 117.
58. Wollenberg, *Die Entwicklung der Eigenwirtschaft*, p. 322.
59. Rösener, 'Religion und Ökonomie', pp. 117–118.
60. Wolfgang Bender, *Zisterzienser und Städte: Studien zu den Beziehungen zwischen den Zisterzienserklöstern und den großen urbanen Zentren des mittleren Moselraumes (12. – 14. Jahrhundert)* (Trier: Verlag Trierer Historiche Forschungen, 1992), pp. 37–45; privilege of 1266 for Eberbach also exempts other agricultural produce. Otto Volk, *Salzproduktion und Salzhandel mittelalterlicher Zisterzienserklöster* (Sigmaringen: Thorbecke, 1984), pp. 30–31.
61. Sven Wichert, 'Zisterzienserklöster und Hansestädte', in *Klöster und monastische Kultur in Hansastädten: Beiträge des 4. wissenschaftlichen Kolloquiums Stralsund, 12. bis 15. Dezember 2001*, ed. Claudia Kimminus-Schneider and Manfred Schneider (Rahden and Westfalen: Leidorf, 2003), p. 154.
62. Doris Bulach, 'Die Stadthöfe der Zisterzienserklöster Eldena, Neukamp und Hiddensee in Stralsund, Greifswald, Goldberg und Plau: ihre Funktionen und Bedeutung', in *Klöster und monastische Kultur*, pp. 122–123.
63. Winfried Schich, 'Grangien und Stadthöfe der Zisterzienserklöster östlich der mittler Elbe bis zum 14. Jahrhundert', in *Zisterziensische Wirtschaft und Kulturlandschaft*, ed. Winfried Schich (Berlin: Lukas Verlag, 1998), pp. 95–97.
64. The document specifying the arrangement is preserved in Holm Cultram cartulary, calendared in the edition of Holm Cultram sources and printed in the *Liber de Melrose* (from the Holm Cultram cartulary). BL, Harley MS 3891, f. 79; *The Register and Records of Holm Cultram*, ed. Francis Grainger (Kendal: T. Wilson, 1929), no. 40d; *Liber de Melrose*, vol. 2, Appendix 12.
65. Anne E. Lester, *Creating Cistercian Nuns: The Women's Religious Movement and its Reform in Thirteenth-Century Champagne* (Ithaca, NY: Cornell University Press, 2011), pp. 199–200.
66. Emilia Jamroziak, 'St Mary Graces: A Cistercian House in Late Medieval London', in *The Use and Abuse of Sacred Places in late Medieval Towns*, ed. P. Trio and M. De Smet, Mediaevalia Lovaniensia, Series 1, Studia, vol. 38 (Leuven: Leuven University Press, 2005), pp. 153–164.
67. Ksenja Brigljević, 'The Cistercian Monastery and the Medieval Urban Development of Zagreb', in *Annual of Medieval Studies at the CEU 1993–94*, ed. Marianne Sághy (Budapest: CEU Press, 1994), pp. 100–107.
68. Niemeck, 'Kloster und Stadt', p. 143.
69. Constance Berman, 'Cistercian Nuns and the Development of the Order: The Abbey at Saint-Antoine-des-Champs outside Paris', in *The Joy of Learning and the Love of God: Essays in Honor of Jean Leclercq*, ed. E. Rozanne Elder (Kalamazoo, MI: Cistercian Publications, 1995), p. 132.
70. Wichert, 'Zisterzienserklöster und Hansestädte', p. 150, image on p. 152.
71. Wichert, 'Zisterzienserklöster und Hansestädte', pp. 149–150.

chapter 7

INTELLECTUAL HORIZONS: WRITING, PREACHING AND CISTERCIAN SPIRITUALITY

However impressive the manifold economic activities of Cistercian monasteries might have been, they were never more than a means to an end, a tool for ensuring that the monks would be able to lead a contemplative life and maintain proper observance of the rules of the Order. Far more important than working to create wealth were prayers, contemplation, preaching and listening to the sermons, and also reading, writing and copying manuscripts. Contrary to popular assumption, Cistercian monks were not anti-intellectual and were involved in a broad range of activities which can be described as knowledge creation, application and consumption. Much of that work – for example keeping annalistic records, copying liturgical books and preaching – was a continuation of old monastic traditions, but the Cistercians made their own distinctive contribution to Christo-centric and Marian spirituality and also, in the later middle ages, to relatively new developments such as university education. Even if white monks were hardly in the forefront of new intellectual advances, they were skilled in making effective use of the work of others for purposes close to their heart, such as preaching and formation of the novices.

To understand the complexity of the Cistercian intellectual horizon it would be well to consider the tools they used – the libraries, scriptoria, record keeping and archives – as well as their achievements in the fields of history writing, sermons and preaching, hagiography, theology and its connection to the spirituality of the white monks.

For Cistercian monks, knowledge was not a neutral concept and some of its potential uses worried Bernard of Clairvaux. In a series of sermons he defined knowledge as good or bad according to its application and emphasised that it must not be used to fulfil empty curiosity, to feed vanity by impressing others or to gain honours; nor must it be used for profit.[1] Books were powerful things and in the early years the prescription of the General Chapter stated that no member of the Order of whatever rank – abbot, monk or novice – might produce books without the permission of the Chapter.[2] What concerned the authorities was not so much works produced solely for internal consumption, such as chronicles and hagiographic texts, but sermons and theological works which tended to be distributed outside the Cistercian communities too.[3] This relative paucity of Cistercian literary production had led many historians to conclude that the white monks were anti-intellectual, but it is a misinterpretation to see Bernard of Clairvaux as having blank objections to knowledge or the use of reason.[4] Although, as Elizabeth Freeman has pointed out, the prescription affected only unauthorised book production, not intellectual work as such, it nevertheless paid tribute to the power of the written word, which needed to be vetted by the Order's authority lest it cause damage.[5] True, the great intellectual developments of the thirteenth century did not pass the Cistercians by, but the white monks remained selective in their relationship with the universities and other innovations of the age, insisting that whatever they did should first benefit Cistercian observance and enrich communal life.

Who was involved in intellectual work in the Cistercian abbeys, in particular in spread of knowledge, and the writing and dissemination of ideas? Particularly in early Cistercian history, we encounter a number of monks and abbots who were prominent intellectuals, connected to networks of theologians and Cistercian leaders, united in the pursuit of reform and communicating across Europe in vigorous exchanges of letters. Another model, frequent from the thirteenth century onwards, was of intensive intellectual activity during retirement, following a high-flying career in the monastic structures. William of Montague, for example, after being prior of Clairvaux, abbot of La Ferté and finally, in 1227, the abbot of Cîteaux itself, withdrew in 1239 to live as a monk in Clairvaux. During his 'retirement', however, he was fully engaged in scholarly work producing two collections of *florilegia* consisting of almost 6,000 extracts from the core books of Cistercian libraries, especially of St Augustine and other Church Fathers, all carefully arranged and indexed as a useful aid to writing sermons.[6] The vigorous growth of scholasticism in the thirteenth century was very much associated with the organisation and codification of accumulated knowledge and sources of authority, in the form of indexes, catalogues and lists, which revolutionised the work of scholars. The oldest of such devices – collections of extracts for use in composing sermons, and as aids to scriptural exegesis – were the invention of the Cistercians (who needed them as preachers and for mentoring novices) in the last decade of the twelfth century.[7]

Libraries, Books and Reading

Among the most important tools of intellectual work and spiritual development in the community were the libraries – although apart from the libraries each monastery had to have a separate collection of liturgical books: the Statute of the Cistercian Order required every monastery to own the Missal, the Bible, the Epistolary, the Collectarium, the Gradual, the Antiphonary, the Rule of Benedict, the Hymnary, the Psalter, the Lectionary and the Calendar, all of which were essential for the performing of liturgical duties and training of the novices.[8] The core of the monastic libraries themselves, since the Cistercian order did not run external schools, consisted of theological works for the instruction of novices.

The creation of the monastic library was a prolonged process and book collections developed over a long periods of time. Key items were usually donated by the mother house or, if funds permitted, bought from neighbouring monastic houses whether Cistercian or not. The 'initial book package' given by the mother house to its daughter contained the essential liturgical books as well as a collection of miracles to be read to the monks as an edifying text and 'the blueprint of Cistercian identity'. Although the Cistercians strove for complete uniformity in their liturgical texts, this, needless to say, was never fully achieved.[9]

Cistercian libraries varied greatly in terms of size. Twelfth-century catalogues of Cistercian libraries of Châalis (Picardy), Hautefontaine (Champagne) and Vaux-de-Cerney (Île-de-France), Morimondo (Lombardy) and Staffarda (Piedmont), Baumgartenberg (Upper Austria) and Heiligenkreuz (Lower Austria) and Marienfeld (Rhineland) indicate book collections of between 50 and 150 volumes. By the mid-fourteenth century Himmerod Abbey (Moselle region) had 2,000 volumes, Lehnin (Brandenburg) half that number and Zwettl Abbey (Lower Austria) 500 items in its library.[10] Many smaller houses, however, had libraries consisting of a mere handful of items.[11]

As very few Cistercian collections survived intact, evidence of the precise chronology of book acquisition is scarce. The library of Neuberger Abbey in Styria, a daughter house of Heiligenkreuz and founded relatively late, in 1327, possessed 5 twelfth-, 14 thirteenth- and 84 fourteenth-century manuscripts, that is, contemporary to the foundation. In the next century, Neuberger Abbey acquired a further 136 manuscripts, 19 of which pre-dated the foundation and all came from the mother house and were primarily additional liturgical and theological books necessary for the functioning of the community.[12] The traffic of books between Cistercian houses after the initial foundation stage was an important indicator of the value of filiation links and connections to other religious institutions.

The (now dispersed) library of Eberbach Abbey in the Rhineland, a direct foundation from Clairvaux, and one of the wealthiest monasteries in the region, contained liturgical works donated by the mother house, Carolingian manuscripts of Church Fathers from Benedictine house of Lorsch, richly decorated codices brought from Paris by monks of Eberbach who had studied there, and a large corpus of theological works copied in the Eberbach scriptorium.

Many manuscripts, especially chronicles, were transcribed in-house from borrowed copies and occasionally such loans are documented: on two occasions the abbot of Dundrennan asked to borrow the manuscript chronicle from Melrose Abbey, as he wanted his community to make its own chronicle using as a starting point the text of its sister monastery – both were daughter houses of Rievaulx; and the manuscript returned to Melrose abbey *c.* 1290 has marginal notes indicating which sections the Dundrennan editor had copied.[13] The transporting of books between abbeys was clearly a routine matter, but occasionally, if a loan was not returned on time, the matter was brought to the attention of the General Chapter: in 1199 Valasse Abbey (Normandy) complained that a volume borrowed by Stratford Langthorne Abbey (Essex) was overdue, whereupon the General Chapter declared that the book must be returned by the coming Easter and the abbot of Savigny, as the abbot-superior of Stratford Langthorne Abbey, was to ensure that the daughter house returned the loan.[14] Other owners had recourse to writing warnings like that inscribed on the first folio of Gregory the Great's *Moralia in Job* (*c.* 1180), the property of Stična Abbey (Lower Carniola): 'This text is written in honour of Saint Mary. Who will take it away shall burn in the eternal fires. Sticna'.[15] For Cistercian abbeys all over Europe journeys to the General Chapter were an opportunity to source books from highly esteemed French scriptoria: Ruda Abbey (Silesia) purchased several volumes from Morimond Abbey in the thirteenth century, and Henryków Abbey, also in Silesia, purchased a manuscript copied in the scriptorium of Pforta Abbey (Saxony) in 1441, which was eventually passed on to its daughter Mogiła Abbey (Greater Poland). The relatively well-preserved collection from Pelplin Abbey (Pomerania) contains a number of high-quality illuminated manuscripts, which appear to be direct imports from France, possibly from Parisian scriptoria. The oldest of these are Peter Lombard's Commentary on the letters of St Paul (mid-thirteenth century) and a codex of medical texts including Avicenna's *Canon de medicina* (*c.* 1300). In the same library is another manuscript – A thirteenth-century *Vita Sanctorum* decorated with 'typically Cistercian' simple initials – which appears to have taken a distinctly circuitous route to its destination and which carries annotations to the effect that it was part of a monastic library at Doberan (Mecklenburg) before arriving at Pelplin Abbey. The inscription 'Liber Sancte Marie in Doberan' is followed by 'Abbas Conradus libri fecit eum' and then 'Liber S[an]c[t]e Marie in Pelplin'. In the early fourteenth century, by which time the manuscript was at Pelplin, further texts were added to the codex, including Bernard of Clairvaux's sermons.[16] It is unclear how this volume made the journey of over 400 kilometres between the two abbeys: was it linked to their distant filiation connection, or was it a purchase or even a loan that never got returned?

The inclusion of some types of texts in the monastic collection was restricted; some works, such as the *Corpus canonum* and the *Decreta Graciani*, were selected by the General Chapter in 1188 to be kept separately from the books accessible to the whole community, as the study of law might pose a danger to the monks. Only abbots were allowed to consult them. By the fifteenth century, however, Cistercian attitudes towards the study of law had changed, the practical needs of both the Order and individual houses having eroded earlier assumptions. Access to legal works was now the norm, and copies of legal volumes were being frequently loaned by one monastic house to another. Indeed, in 1496 the abbot of Sénanque Abbey opened a college at Avignon dedicated to the study of law by Cistercian monks.[17]

If the Cistercians initially tended to hold aloof from innovative forms of organised learning, new intellectual methods, the growth of new subject areas, and the rise of cathedral schools and then universities in the twelfth century had a great effect on monastic libraries. Indeed, by the end of the century learned works were proliferating in Cistercian abbeys: two Rievaulx Abbey library catalogues (*c.* 1190 and *c.* 1200), for example, listed Peter Lombard's *Sentences*, commentaries on Artistotle's *Categories*, a glossed copy of the Bible, two medical treaties and several legal volumes, including Justinian's *Codex* and Gratian's *Decretum*.[18] Other Cistercian libraries accumulated works on the *trivium* subjects (grammar, logic and rhetoric) and natural sciences. Although the classical texts in the curricula of the twelfth-century schools were not of much interest to the Cistercians, they had no prohibition against studying them.[19] The growing number of works on ancient history in Cistercian libraries were useful for Biblical exegesis;[20] and the presence of medical works testifies to an interest in medical knowledge, but it is difficult to assess how much of it was applied in practice: although Cistercian theologians, such as William of St Thierry and William of Conches, were among the first to mention Arabic medical works in their writings, they did not intend them to be used in the actual practice of medicine.[21] David Bell's catalogue of medical manuscripts from English Cistercian houses reveals a mixture of highly academic treatises and 'more practical' formulas for treatments and ointment preparations.[22]

For the most part, Cistercian libraries tended to be conservative in their scope and predominantly theological until 1400, the white monks tending, like other contemplative orders, to look to the past rather than the present.[23] Even so, some library holdings were modified in response to new fashions, new connections and new interests of the abbots. The contents of the library of Meaux Abbey (Yorkshire) are in a catalogue written *c*. 1410, but the foundations of the collection were laid by the fourth abbot, Alexander (1197–1210), whose memory as a man of learning has been preserved in the historical tradition of the community. Very few of the later abbots of Meaux seem to have been interested in intellectual matters, yet the catalogue of 1410 reveals a collection of works on theology (80 per cent of the total), grammar, logic, philosophy, law, classics, science, medicine and history that is impressive for what was, after all, a fairly typical conservative monastic library catering for the education of monks and novices. Not that Meaux was unique; the 'study library' at Altzella Abbey created in 1506 had a profile very similar to that of Meaux – 774 books out of a 960-strong collection were theological and philosophical works.[24]

Before the era of printing, of course, when libraries contained only manuscripts, many of the particularly valuable items or those accessible in the 'reference library' were chained to prevent theft. Repeated injunctions from the General Chapter to maintain inventories of books and other precious objects had a similar purpose.[25] When Archbishop Corbridge made a visitation to Keldholme nunnery (Yorkshire), he gave orders that 'no nun or other person belonging to the house was to take away books, ornaments or other things belonging to the church, without the express consent of the prioress and the convent'.[26] After all, the library was a material and spiritual asset of the community and its good upkeep was just as important as maintaining the fabric of the church. Contrary to popular belief, there was no single fixed location in the monastery for storing books, and the library catalogues indicate that they were kept in various locations according to the type of text and the needs of the community.[27] The most precious books were kept with other high-value objects, whilst liturgical texts were kept in the sacristy and copies of sermons, lectionaries and hagiographical texts in the choir. A so-called *armarium* in the cloister gallery near the chapter house was the most traditional location for books, which were stored in built-in cupboards in an arched niche or niches with wooden shelves and lockable doors. Examples of book cupboards survived in the eastern gallery in Hailes (Gloucestershire), Boquen (Britanny) and l'Escaladieu (southern France) abbeys. The key to the *armarium* was entrusted to the cantor, who was usually in charge of the books, although some monasteries had a separate *armarius* for this task. Further collections of books were available to monks in the dormitory and the infirmary.[28] On occasion, accommodation arrangements might have to be modified as collections expanded, or their contents might be adjusted in response to the preoccupations of their users: preaching, for example, demanded special library resources. During the abbacy of Arnaud Amaury Cîteaux acquired a large number of polemical works and preaching manuals, which were essential for the abbot's campaigns against heretics.[29]

Manuscripts donated to monastic communities by educated clerics who became Cistercian monks, and by well-disposed prelates, testify to both the continuing interest in academic theology, and the importance of the social networks that linked Cistercian monasteries to intellectual centres and clerical establishments. In the early 1170s, for example, a certain Master Robert donated a collection of 19 glossed Bibles – a typical teaching collection – produced in northern France, to Buildwas Abbey in Shropshire, whither he seems to have retired to continue to annotate and gloss his book collection. In the early thirteenth century, Master Martin, the archdeacon of Flavigny, donated a codex of commentary on the Psalms by Peter Lombard to Cîteaux Abbey; while a fourteenth-century necrology from Henryków Abbey notes donations of volumes of canon law from Master Henry de Lemberg and Master Tilo, and a psalter from one Master Nicholas, a goldsmith.[30]

Finally, the expansion of book collections in Cistercian monasteries reflected the educational activities of monks, sometimes pursued at universities. Sometimes volumes in the monastic libraries can be linked to identifiable monks who acquired university degrees and brought manuscripts and books back with them on returning to their communities. For example, a particular group of early printed books in Oliwa Abbey (Pomerania) can be associated with the monks Nicolas Rosenfeld and John Bornemann, who matriculated in Leipzig in 1490 and 1498 – indeed it was in the fifteenth and the early sixteenth centuries, as white monks took more interest in liberal studies and printed books facilitated the growth of the collections, that the influence of universities on Cistercian libraries reached its height.[31]

Not only the growth of university learning, but wider trends too influenced the composition of late medieval Cistercian libraries. The majority of the texts were of course in Latin, but the number of vernacular texts was beginning to grow. This was also the case in English nunneries (see chapter 4); in the late thirteenth and first half of the fourteenth century pious noblewomen in Cistercian houses in southern German were a 'target group' for translations of the works of Bernard of Clairvaux and other iconic Cistercian authors. This process accelerated in the later centuries: the library of the wealthy nunnery of Kirchheim in northern Bavaria had 122 German-language manuscripts – as opposed to only 20 in Latin (excluding liturgical books) from the fifteenth and sixteenth centuries.[32] The process of 'vernacularisation' was, however, a highly regional one, and in northern Germany Latin texts continued to dominate monastic libraries for much longer.

Not surprisingly, the rich resources of their libraries played a major role in the daily life of monastic communities. Reading of the holy texts was one of the key activities for every Cistercian monk and nun and the monastic timetable allocated set times to it. Individual *Lectio divina* took place in the eastern gallery of the cloister in winter in the afternoon, and in summer between *c.* 8:50 and 10:40 in the morning, and, if desired, during the rest-time after lunch. During Lent the morning reading time was extended. On Sundays, reading was conducted during the periods devoted on weekdays to work. In addition, texts were read aloud during communal meals in the refectory and when the monks gathered in the collation gallery in the evening (summer) or late afternoon (winter), at the end of the monastic day. The collation reading usually involved edifying texts such as *Vitae Patrum*, reminding the monks about their illustrious predecessors in the deserts of Egypt and the Holy Land.[33] 'The aim of all reading, individual or communal, silent and aloud, was to inspire prayer and meditation, and thereby achieve contemplation – mystical union with God.'[34]

Scriptoria, Record Keeping and the Archives

Contrary to popular image, Cistercian monasteries rarely had a room whose sole function was to house the scriptorium where the monks would sit at rows of desks copying and illuminating manuscripts. In fact, the scriptorium usually had no permanent location, but moved according to conditions and needs. What was required first of all was good lighting, preferably natural, and convenient access to the equipment – ink, pens, pigments, rulers, metal styli for making lines, wax tablets for making notes, as well as parchment, pumice stone to smooth it, and reading frames to hold the material the scribe was copying. These were all expensive commodities and the cellarer controlled supplies. Archaeologists have found traces of them in different parts of Cistercian cloisters, most commonly in the day room. In some abbeys, such as Clairvaux, scriptoria consisted of a series of small separate rooms located off the cloister gallery, a location that is also indicated in the prescription in the *Ecclesiastica Officia*, which states that rooms used for manuscript copying should have doors: whilst a copyist was at work, no one except the abbot was allowed to enter.

Evidence from surviving Cistercian library catalogues throws some light on the role of the scriptorium: books from the library of Buildwas Abbey shows that this monastery was producing manuscripts from the 1160s until the mid-thirteenth century.[35] In the later middle ages, however, with the growing professionalisation of the book trade, manuscript production in this and other Cistercian houses became increasingly the domain of the commercial scriptoria. Moreover, increasing production, associated with the development of the universities and the spread of literacy beyond the clerical elites, reduced the need for religious institutions, including Cistercian houses, to have a permanent scriptorium; and by the fourteenth century many abbeys were simply buying volumes on the open market.

Of course, abbeys still had to produce charters and other types of documents, but this activity was separate from copying of manuscripts.[36] The legal affairs of monastic houses were complex. The successful management of large landholdings demanded regular attention and the defence of property rights needed careful record keeping. Medieval English monastic houses such as the Cistercians were, as Michael Clanchy has observed, in the vanguard of the transition 'from oral to written word'.[37] The creation of permanent bureaucratic structures based on written documents and the use of written evidence in the legal process were European-wide, but their chronology varied according to region. For Cistercians, the keeping of careful archival records, preserving charters and other documents was crucial, not only for the defence of property rights, but for creating institutional identities. This partly explains the Cistercian practice (especially in the twelfth century) of forging charters. It was not so much a question of purveying false information as of underpinning legal claims providing evidence admissible in court regarding particular properties, privileges or tax exemptions. The forged documents frequently contained information on legal actions which had been settled orally or reconstructed from memory. The earliest charters of two Cistercian houses in southern Poland – Jędrzejów and Sulejów – were forgeries, providing (most likely recreating verbally received grants) written evidence for their properties and privileges.[38] This does not mean that the white monks were simply lying and cheating in order to enrich their monasteries, rather they believed that the objects at issue belonged by right to them.

The process of landholding accumulation and co-existence with the lay ecclesiastical world ensured that, even in relatively small institutions, monastic archives grew very fast. The Cistercian attitude to record preservation was expressed very well by Abbot Henry of Heilsbronn in 1312: the collecting and preserving of administratively important documents brought economic advantages, but it was also an act of piety.³⁹ It was important that documents should be not only secure, but also easily traceable if needed. In Cistercian monasteries the names and locations of the archives – *armarium* (literally, 'a book chest') or *scrinium* ('portable document chest') – varied and the actual term *archivum* appeared in the statutes of the Order only in 1490. It was often located in a passage between the dormitory and the church.⁴⁰ Charters were usually collected in bundles and stored according to the property to which they referred on shelves, in chests, boxes, baskets and cupboards.⁴¹ Surviving inventories suggest that monastic archivists developed a complex system of item-marks allowing for effective retrieval of documents with cross-references to other records, especially cartularies.⁴² Many abbeys with extensive documentary collections reorganised their archives several times in their history.

In order to keep precious charters safe, and for ease of consultation without having to see the originals, copies were made in the form of cartularies. In fact, the majority of the surviving documentation of monastic houses across Europe came to us in the form of cartularies, and far less frequently as original charters. Cartularies had already a long tradition emerging in the ninth century, and when Cistercian monasteries started to make them, they were a well-established form.⁴³ They were usually created for the internal purpose of organising information about an abbey's past and its possessions when the number of charters it stored reached a critical mass.⁴⁴

The amount of editing, i.e. omission of the formal parts and formulae from the charters in the copied entries, varied greatly according to the context. Usually the first cartularies were created at least 50 to 100 years after the foundation, often in parallel with the creation of foundation narratives. They were often organised geographically, by the grange or location of property, whilst the charters of particularly prominent individuals – kings, popes and bishops – had their own sections. In one of the cartularies of Holm Cultram Abbey (Cumbria), the section containing copies of the papal bulls at the end of the volume is accompanied by marginal drawings symbolising the content of each.⁴⁵ Papal bulls addressed to the whole of the Order were copied in the cartularies of many individual houses, strengthening not only the knowledge of the privileges and exemptions granted to the Cistercian order, but also emphasising the sense of belonging to the trans-European organisation. News of new privileges and actual texts travelled through the filiation system.⁴⁶ Older houses were often obliged to have several cartularies covering particular sections of their accumulated lands, granges and donations, while it became impossible, even for medium-sized houses, to keep copies of all their charters in one volume. The second of the Cîteaux cartularies containing charters up to 1260 has more than 1,000 items.[47] Sometimes editors copied material from older cartularies without going back to the original charters, although there might be – as was the case in Fountains Abbey – marginal cross-references to the original charters and other cartulary entries in different volumes.[48] In the Catholic parts of Europe Cistercian communities, while following the organisational principles developed in the middle ages, carried on making cartularies well into the eighteenth century – for instance Obra Abbey in Greater Poland and Wąchock and Sulejów abbeys in southern Poland.[49]

Cartularies also often incorporated court rulings, extracts from manorial records, memoranda and genealogies of patrons and benefactors, and served commemorative and historical functions too.[50] The fourteenth-century *Ledger Book of Vale Royal Abbey* is a good example of such a hybrid text combining a cartulary section with the foundation history and copies of Cistercian privileges. Vale Royal Abbey was founded by King Edward I in 1274, but after the initial generosity – he contributed significantly towards the cost of building the large church – royal interest diminished and the monastic community struggled to complete extensive building projects and had financial problems for most of its history.[51] The abbey also moved its location early on from Darnhall to Over (Cheshire), which was suitably depicted in the ledger book as a story of a miraculous discovery of a more appropriate site. As in many similar texts, the narrative of the history of subsequent abbots incorporates the theme of struggles with the enemies of the monastery. However, unlike many analogous volumes, the chronicle part is not followed by a cartulary, but by a collection of 'pleas and evidence' incorporating legal material (copies of pleas, fines, agreements, memoranda and charters) relating to the holding of particular properties by Vale Royal. Its final section is devoted to over 30 Cistercian privileges – bulls of exemptions and other papal grants. The ledger book is a very good example of how origin myths, anxiety over property rights, and privileges were combined in a defensive narrative, in which institutional genealogy was both a tool for asserting the legal status of lands and for providing the monastic community with a sense of Cistercian identity.

However, probably the most impressive example of the 'hybrid' commemorative–economic–legal products of a Cistercian monastery is the *Liber Fundatorum Zwetlensis* – also called *Bärenhaut* (bear skin) of Zwettl Abbey. Created in the second decade of the fourteenth century, it has been described as a founders' chronicle; but it is more than that. It is a combination of texts, genealogies and cartulary-type records with a number of illustrations, the most famous of them depicting the abbot and the patron perambulating the abbey's lands. The volume narrates the story of its founder's family intertwined with that of the monastery in three versions: as a Latin 'history in verse', an expanded Latin prose version and a vernacular (German) rhymed chronicle.[52]

Other monastic products were for internal use, related to economic activities linked to particular obligations and privileges. These included pittances lists, provided for the community by various benefactors and entitling the monks to additional portions of food on the particular days when they prayed for the donors. There were also accounts for individual granges and audits of granges, which the monasteries were obliged to conduct yearly. In order to manage their finances, monasteries often created inventories of specific incomes and assets, such as rentals. The most mundane, practical records rarely survived. They were never a part of the monastic archive; after they were no longer needed the parchment or paper on which they were written was reused; while even more ephemeral information was recorded on wax tablets, which were then wiped to accommodate new notes. Very large monastic houses also developed separate archives for particular offices, such as bursar, cellarer or prior.

In the middle ages, the lines between what we would now call practical documents, historical narrative and commemorative records were unclear. Knowledge of the history of an area and genealogy of neighbours could be vital both for the security of monastic possessions and for the corporate identity and shared history of a monastic community. Distinctions between genres are somehow artificial: chronicles might be fused with cartularies, which could in turn contain genealogical information, and volumes of copies of various charters, memoranda, agreements and narrative fragments could play several roles at once, while the spiritual and commemorative could be treated alongside legal and economic matters. Since the 'core business' of the monasteries was to intercede on behalf of others, commemorative and liturgical obligations to benefactors expanded over time and required their own documentation in the form of lists and calendars. In order to keep some control over intercessory obligations, the *Kalendarium indulgenciarum, benefactorum servitorum et pietanciarum Ebracensium* (Calendar of indulgences, benefices, services and pittances of Ebrach Abbey) brought the information together in one list.[53]

Writing History

Institutional history – the story of the communities' origins, their patrons and their development – was pursued by all medieval Cistercian communities, but survival of these texts is very fragmentary. Monastic chronicles had been a staple production for all monastic communities since the early middle ages, and as white monks were not, by any means, pioneers of this genre, they drew, like so many others engaged in history writing, on older and broader traditions. The most common method of writing history was in the form of a chronicle with yearly entries, which could be as short as one sentence or contain long narrative passages. True, for a long time, Cistercian writing tended to be marginalised in regional and national studies of medieval literature owing to their isolation from the 'great events' of their time, their 'provincial outlook' and their aversion to literary innovations.[54] But its purpose was, after all, not to inform posterity about the important historical events, but to inculcate in Cistercian monks a sense of belonging to the Order, and to teach them to learn from the past experience of their communities, and to follow the example of the holy abbots and pray for all past and present friends of the abbey.

In fact, as regards the forms and structures of their historical writing, Cistercian houses could draw on a strong and shared textual tradition. The copies of the core Cistercian narratives – the *Exordium Parvum* and the *Exordium Cistercii* – were widespread in Cistercian monasteries by the 1190s.[55] Although the former dealt with the origins of Cîteaux, while latter described the origins of the Order, they both served as models for countless narratives of the histories of the other Cistercian monasteries. Some chronicles were very explicit as to their purpose: the chronicle of Øm Abbey in Denmark (written between 1207 and 1216) sought

> to transmit to future generations how this monastery, which is called Øm, had its beginning, we wish here to make known both when and by whom it was built, with what privileges it has been ratified, how it has moved from place to place, where it is now situated, as well as the names of those abbots who have ruled it for the forty-two years until the present year when this was written.[56]

'Foundation narratives' were usually compiled within three or four generations after the foundation, often originating in some crisis or difficulty facing the community: the topos of overcoming adversity and struggles to survive was prominent in the *Exordium Parvum* and featured regularly in other Cistercian foundation narratives, including the *Historia Fundationis* of Byland and Jervaulx, the oldest text of this type in northern England.[57] Another common theme widespread in foundation narratives – e.g. those of Fountains Abbey in Yorkshire, Loccum Abbey in Lower Saxony and countless others – was the desolate, inhospitable locations in which new abbeys were established. These references go back to the biblical 'place of horror and vast solitude' (Deuteronomy 32.10); and the vocabulary was also part of an old monastic tradition used to describe the founding of Carolingian Benedictine monasteries: Fulda Abbey was allegedly 'in the wooded place of great wilderness and solitude' in the eighth century, according to a letter from St Boniface to Pope Zechariah.[58] Certainly, the topos was common among the Benedictine foundation narratives from the Merovingian period onwards: the *Vita S. Galli* presents the location of the future St Gallen Abbey in a deep mountain valley amongst wild animals.[59] In the eleventh and twelfth centuries this imagery was further promoted by the monastic reformers who used the rhetoric of going 'back to the desert', away from the corruption of the world; and it became particularly popular in Cistercian writing after it was applied to Cîteaux in *Exordium Cistercii*:[60]

> After many labours, therefore, and exceedingly great difficulties, which all who will to live in Christ must suffer, they at length attained their desire and arrived at Cîteaux – at that time a place of horror and of vast solitude. But judging that the harshness of the place was not at variance with the strict purpose they had already conceived in mind, the soldiers of Christ held the place as truly prepared for the by God.[61]

It is futile to speculate as to whether these locations really were remote, as the texts refer not to any physical reality, but to the spiritual idea of solitude. However, perhaps the rhetorical device might prove of practical value, as a way of asserting that no other landholders, lay or ecclesiastical, could have a prior claim to the land on which the monastery was founded.

Certainly, looking back into the history of the community might be one way of preserving what the monks believed to be the 'truth' of their glorious past and placing it within a narrative of overcoming difficulties and dangers; and in fact numerous texts from all over Europe testify to the adaption of local circumstances to the wider Cistercian models. The *Book of Henryków*, created in a Silesian monastery in two stages (in the 1260s and over a few decades from 1300) contains a prologue explaining why it was created; its aims – apart from preserving the story of the foundation – were to remember the founder's good deeds and to encourage the monks to pray that the founder would become a saint. The roles of various key people in the foundation of Henryków are explicitly recorded: notary Nicholas, who was the initiator of the foundation, Duke Henry, who was the founder, and his son. Part three of the book is the catalogue of the bishops of Wrocław, diocesans of Abbey, noting the days of their deaths, and asking for prayers for their souls as protectors and benefactors of the monastery. Although the *Book of Henryków* is a complex text recording legal rights to lands and possessions of the abbey and difficulties with neighbours, the genealogical and commemorative aspect was closely intertwined with the record of the holdings.

In Cistercian history-writing the genealogy of the patrons was closely intertwined with the history of the monastic houses. In the *Epytaphia ducum*

Slezie from Lubiąż Abbey the story of the monastery is intertwined with an extended genealogy of the dukes of Silesia, beginning with the life of founder Bolesław and the story of the abbey's foundation. Information about his relatives and descendants are accompanied by dates of deaths, burial locations and longer narrative sections. The format of information, according a day for each person, indicates that the volume could have been used for anniversary masses for deceased patrons and for the wider commemoration of their connection with the abbey.[62]

Sometimes the histories of Cistercian abbeys were organised in terms of the succession dates of abbots – a very old model going back to the Roman lists of consuls (*Fasti Consulares*), a form of which was later used in the lives of the popes (*Liber Pontificalis*). The *Gesta Abbatum* (histories of the abbots) format was common in Benedictine monasticism before it was used by the Cistercians. It had many functions – to tell the history of the institution through the succession to the central office, to provide model examples of perfect abbots, and to commemorate departed abbots.[63] The *Cronica domus Sarensis* of the Žd'ár Abbey in western Bohemia started with the foundation until 1300 and used the chronology of its 11 abbots and their achievements as the narrative framework, whilst intertwining the history of the monastery with that of the founders' family.[64] The focus on abbots also indicates what Cistercian communities particularly valued about their leaders: piety and spiritual qualities were of course important, but abbots who were effective in gaining lands for the abbey and rebuilding and beautifying the conventual buildings were particularly praised. In the chronicle of Croxden Abbey, Abbot Walter London, elected in 1242, who rebuilt the church and other parts of the precinct, received the highest praises from the chronicler: 'the Lord especially blessed this place, since at his arrival he enlarged the convent of Croxden in a wonderful way, and he most skilfully built very beautiful buildings there in his time'.[65]

Sometimes a Cistercian historical account – often known as *Liber Memorandum* (a book of things to be remembered) or *Liber Traditionum* (book of legal rights) – would be structured according to the geographical locations of landholdings. The *Book of Henryków Abbey* is organised in sections devoted to localities where the abbey held lands and described as 'inheritances' (*hereditates*), 'holdings' (*sortes*), 'manors' (*praedia*), villages and estates (*villae*). The book is not, however, simply a description of monastic holdings, but a complex defence, by its first author, Abbot Peter, of Henryków's legal rights based on carefully constructed arguments, and the genealogies of local people ranging from the 1160s until the time of writing a century later. Abbot Peter is very explicit about his aim of passing this knowledge on to the present and future members of the community, to equip them to defend the abbey against aggressive neighbours. Abbot Peter is not as concerned as some Cistercian writers to link local events to wider monastic or regional history; but the most important such event – the Mongolian invasion of 1241, which ravaged the abbey and led to the death of Duke Henry II the Pious at the battle of Legnica – nevertheless divides the narratives into two distinct periods: 'before the pagans' and 'after the pagans' – or the 'good old days', when everybody trusted each other under the just rule of the duke, and modern times, when written legal documents are essential to defend the status quo in an age of failing ducal power and unstable rulers.[66]

Although Cistercian historical accounts often combined elements of different genres in one text, many abbeys produced 'conventional' annalistic chronicles with yearly entries: collaborative ventures by several generations of monks. Although many of these have been denigrated as simplistic and blinkered historical records, they fulfilled various functions – as aids to correct liturgical observance by giving the date of Easter; as a source of information from missals and obituary calendars; and as reference books supplementing cartularies and inventories. Above all, they were the repositories of the historic memory of the community. In appearance they resembled monastic bureaucratic texts, with which they were closely connected. Julian Harrison has suggested that the creation of many British Cistercian chronicles was linked to the reorganisation and expansion of the monastic archives.[67]

Cistercian history writing was in some respects very specific, relating to particular regions, but the texts often exuded a strong sense of belonging to a wider Cistercian network. Filial connections were, after all, central to the Cistercian identity; hence the *Historia Fundationis* of Byland and Jervaulx were very much focused on establishing the place of the two houses within the Cistercian network (especially as Byland's relations with its mother house, a Savignac house at Furness, were very problematical).[68] The most frequent indications of the strength of filial connections were references to the events occurring in fellow Cistercian houses and General Chapter meetings. In the *Chronicle of Melrose*, the 'knowledge horizon' of the text gives further indication of what it meant for Melrose to be a part of the Cistercian family: the deaths of abbots were noted, as were appointments to abbatial offices, and the dedications of churches, not only in the daughter houses of Melrose (Newbattle, Holm Cultram, Kinloss, Coupar Angus, Balmerino), but also in those of its 'grand-daughters' founded in the second decade of the thirteenth century (Culross, Deer, Grey). Other houses which were 'sisters' of Melrose, that is also daughters of Rievaulx Abbey, both in Scotland (Dundrennan) and England (Warden, Revesby, Rufford) featured predominantly in the chronicles in relation to the monastic appointments. There are lengthy accounts of events arising from the death of an abbot and the appointment of a successor, who might already hold an office in another monastery, leading in turn to yet another appointment. Events and appointments in Scottish houses of Rievaulx filiation, such as Glenluce, a daughter house of Dundrennan, are also mentioned several times. Its connection with the mother house gave Melrose an important channel of communication with the wider Cistercian family – witness the numerous references to other Cistercian monasteries in northern England – Fountains, Byland, Sawley, Furness, Colder and Newminster.

Both the mundane and more dramatic information in the Cistercian chronicles testified to a certain sense of solidarity with the Order: King John's plundering of the Cistercian abbeys in 1210 was duly noted by the *Chronicle of Melrose*; and the attack by the army of Alexander II of Scotland on Holm Cultram in 1216, much nearer to home, was expressly disapproved of.[69] True, the chronicle tried to shift the blame away from the royal patron of Melrose Abbey on his 'barbaric' troops from Galloway, but its emotional loyalty clearly lies with fellow white monks.

Sermons and Preaching

Apart from the involvement of Cistercian monks in preaching for the crusades in the Holy Land, against the heretics in the south of France and pagans in the Baltic, the most important audiences for Cistercian preaching were always their own communities Here, the Rule of Benedict imposed special obligation on abbots, whose sermons were expected to be wide-ranging, from those delivered to monks in the daily chapter meeting, to patristic sermons read at Matins and formal sermons in the church on an impressive number of feast days. The feasts that merited sermons from the abbot were dispersed throughout the liturgical year: the first Sunday of Advent, Christmas Eve, Epiphany, Palm Sunday, Easter Ascension and Pentecost, the Birth of St John the Baptist, St Peter and St Paul, St Benedict, All Saints, the four Marian feasts (Purification, Annunciation, Assumption and the birth of Mary) and the anniversary of the dedication of the monastic church.[70] Like all Cistercian sermons produced for the monastic audiences, they tended to be inward-looking with a strong scriptural grounding and frequent use of symbols and allegory. Because they were addressed to an audience that was theologically aware and educated in the Scripture, they could afford to be extremely allusive, often using only two or three words of a passage from Scripture, the Church Fathers or the liturgy, to an extent that would have been quite incomprehensible to a lay audience.[71]

In the Benedictine and Cistercian tradition the word 'sermon' denoted both a speech delivered to a group of monks and a text intended for private reading and circulated in manuscript copies. Primarily concerned with the monks' spiritual and theological development and the proper observance of the Rule, sermons constituted an intrinsic part of the community's liturgy. Before a monastic audience they were preached in Latin, but in Cistercian monasteries on the major feasts, when lay brothers were also present, they were delivered in the vernacular. As in all medieval preaching, *exempla*, a type of short anecdotes, were used frequently to explain complex theological problems and to drive home to novices the importance of monastic observance. The most important and popular Cistercian collection of *exempla* was the *Dialogus miraculorum* of Cesarius of Heisterbach, a wide-ranging collection of intriguing, frightening, entertaining and edifying tales that testify to the importance of good story-telling for effective preaching.[72]

For reading purposes, the sermons of several authors were often collected within one manuscript or included in a volume of other theological works – although, of course, once written down, edited and revised, these sermons were no longer quite what the original monastic audience would have heard. One thirteenth-century collection from Foigny Abbey (Picardy) contains 39 sermons of 21 Cistercian authors and ranges over a variety of themes; but in other collections the sermons may focus on smaller number of exegetic themes. Filiation networks were vital for the circulation of Cistercian sermons, which were often included (sometimes in bundles) in the texts of letters sent to recipients in a filiated monastery. A number of important twelfth-century Cistercian theologians – Guerric of Igny (d. 1157), Bernard of Clairvaux and Ailred of Rievaulx (d. 1167) – left large collections of sermons.[73] Detailed studies of 400 manuscripts of Bernard of Clairvaux's sermons surviving from the twelfth and early thirteenth centuries have enabled scholars to work out how fast and how widely Cistercian sermons travelled within the Order and beyond.[74]

The concern over preaching is clear from the contents of many Cistercian libraries. Indeed, sermons, especially homilies discussing Biblical passages, often constituted as much as 80 per cent of sacred text collections of large monasteries in German-speaking lands, and copying them was one of the main functions of Cistercian scriptoria – for which they began to develop various study aids, indexing and reference systems as early as in the twelfth century.[75]

Hagiography

The proliferation of Bernard's hagiography made a substantial contribution to the development of Cistercian writing, especially among the houses of the Clairvaux line in the second half of the twelfth century. These texts contained not only accounts of the saint's miracles, but of other miraculous events witnessed and reported by monks and lay brothers from Clairvaux and houses associated with it. The oldest of them, the *Book of Miracles*, written by Herbert, a Spanish monk, between 1178 and 1180 during his stay at Clairvaux, included information supplied to him by Archbishop Eskil and other Danish ecclesiastics, among them Abbot Henry of Vitskøl (Jutland). They were the most likely source of ten stories from the Slavonic–Danish frontier, at that time the most distant outpost of the Cistercian Order. These stories, in which Cistercian monks successfully fought various 'pagan demons' (even employing one as a paid worker in Vitskøl Abbey until he was unmasked and neutralised), show that it was a region in which the veneer of Christianity was still very thin, with large sections of the population still secretly worshipping pagan gods. Stories of Cistercian missionary work and the miracles associated with it were also related by Alberic of Trois-Fontaines (d. *c.* 1252), who used a number of Cistercian *exempla* collections which no longer exist; and all these collections were used by Cesarius of Heisterbach, whose *Dialogus miraculorum* remained popular with Cistercian monks and nuns well into the fifteenth century.[76] Eventually, extensive collections of saints' lives made their way, by means of numerous copies of the manuscript *Liber de Natalitiis*, a late-twelfth-century Cistercian legendary, to monasteries in France, Italy, southern Germany and Rhineland.[77]

Certainly, the white monks' involvement with hagiography partly accounts for the 'regional flavour' of many Cistercian libraries, whose strong connections with the local area were underpinned by hagiographical works relating to the lives of locally venerated saints – often copied from volumes borrowed from older houses in the region.[78] In the late twelfth century the monks of Fountains Abbey borrowed a manuscript from the Benedictine community at Durham to make their own copy of the *Life of St Godric of Finchale*, a locally venerated hermit active in county Durham some decades before.[79] On occasion, individual Cistercian monks were commissioned to write hagiographic texts: Ailred of Rievaulx produced the *Life of St Edward of Confessor* (*c.* 1161–1163) for Abbot Laurence of Westminster and the *Life of St Ninian* (*c.* 1160) for Bishop Christian of Whithorn.[80] Jocelin of Furness was commissioned to write a life of Waltheof, second abbot of Melrose, by one of his successors, Abbot Patrick (*c.* 1206–1207).[81]

A particularly interesting aspect of Cistercian hagiographic writing was the reinterpretation of stories of long-established saints in the Cistercian spirit. In the early thirteenth century Abbot John of Forde (d. 1214) wrote the life of a hermit, Wulfric of Haselbury (d. 1154), whose cult was very popular in the locality of Forde Abbey in Somerset. It describes how the hermit, unappreciated by the Benedictine monks of Montacute, came to share a close bond with the Cistercian community. 'He [Wulfric] lauded the Order to the skies and never hesitated to direct to it those who came to consult him about reforming their lives.'[82] Abbot John's work not only brought a marginal holy figure to the attention of a wider audience and cast light on the rivalry between monastic houses in Somerset, but by linking an ascetic hermit to Cistercian ideals, it grafted a local custom on to a broader tradition and integrated the Cistercian house into the local spiritual landscape. Indeed, Cistercian involvement in the cult of saints as a facet of the interaction with the outside world was to become a striking feature of late medieval monasticism.

Theology and Spirituality

Whereas spiritual theology was absolutely fundamental to Cistercian monastic life, neither academic theology nor the vernacular theology concerned with the education of the laity was ever of comparable importance. Cistercian theological writing was primarily, if not exclusively, aimed at a monastic audience and focused on the spiritual, contemplative life. Here again, the myth of the decline and fall from an ideal affected later thinking, and the period from 1098 to the mid-thirteenth century has been depicted as the golden age of Cistercian spirituality when the pristine theory of Cistercian life was defined and truly practised. This came to an end when scholasticism penetrated Cistercian thinking and the Order ceased to produce original works.[83] Yet this scenario seems to imply that the white monks should either have cut themselves off from changes in the wider field of theology resulting from the development of the universities, or should have seized the lead in expounding the new ideas. Of course, the Cistercians did neither and the central themes of their theology throughout the middle ages was an emotional response to the divine. Cistercian spirituality was 'in essence sacramental, grounded in meeting of the worshipper with Christ on the altar'.[84]

The theological inheritance of Bernard of Clairvaux was fundamental to Cistercian spirituality. His approach, which can be described as theological anthropology focusing on the relationship between humanity and the divine, was a popular one within the wider monastic tradition, especially the reform movements of the early twelfth century, but Bernard was by far its most skilled exponent in both preaching and writing. His sermons on the Song of Songs have a central place in the corpus of his works and provide 'a methodology of spiritual development'.[85] Charity, as understood by the white monks, was the love between members of the community and, as such, was a step towards ultimate love for the divine.

This was the core idea shaping the life of Cistercian communities. In his commentary on the Song of Songs, Baldwin of Forde (d. 1190) stressed that 'the love of neighbour refers back to the love of God, because you cannot love your neighbour except according to God, in God, and because of God'.[86] One of the most important themes in Cistercian theology was the community and its connection to God. The idea of love and charity as the organising principles of monastic community was closely linked to the importance of friendship within the Cistercian communities. Ailred of Rievaulx, who produced numerous theological, spiritual and historical works, including a very important study on friendship, translated classical, pagan concepts of friendship into Christian ideas. In this text, *De spiritali amicitia* (or Spiritual Friendship), we can also see how the theological concept shaped the understanding of the working of the monastic community, especially the idea of charity and forgiveness.[87]

Along with theological debates about the Eucharist and nature of the divine presence, reflections on the nature of Christ, his humanity and suffering were important developments in twelfth-century spirituality. Cistercians were at the forefront of debates about the Eucharist: they 'look into the Eucharist for the sight of God, attempting with the eye of reason to understand the presence of Christ's body and blood in the bread and wine ... and with the eye of love to rest in union with him'.[88] This mixture of reason and emotion – the eye of reason and the eye of love – typified the approach of all the leading Cistercian theologians of the twelfth century: William of St Thierry, Ailred of Rievaulx, Baldwin of Forde and Isaac of Stella.[89] William of St Thierry, for example, described Cistercian methods of understanding the nature of Eucharist as an inseparable mixture of reason and love: 'let us strive as far as possible to see, by seeing to understand, and by understanding to love, so that by loving we may possess'.[90] For Bernard of Clairvaux, the 'affective meditation on the events of the life of Jesus' meant, in terms of monastic practice, identification with Christ by translating compassion for his suffering into pity for the suffering endured by fellow humans.[91] Henceforth, the concept of believers striving for the unity with Christ remained central to Cistercian spirituality for the rest of the middle ages. In fact, this idea became popular beyond the Cistercian world. The late medieval *Imitatio Christi* was crucial to both monastic and lay late medieval spirituality. In the fourteenth and fifteenth century, in the fashion typical of the time, Cistercian monks were reflecting on the imitation of Christ, stigmata and the mystical union. Interesting manifestations of these ideas include popular, late medieval manuscript images of a crucified Cistercian monk, which originated from three sources. The first source is the story from Caesarius' ever popular collection in which he compares strict monastic discipline with the crucifixion;

the second is Bernard of Clairvaux's *Sermo de conversion*, which compares spiritual discipline to the crucifixion; and the third, similar topos occurs in St Gregory the Great's *Moralia in Job*. This is a typically Cistercian combination of sources – the Church Father and the Cistercians' own early authorities – in this case employing the explicit imagery of crucifixion, suffering and pain so popular in late medieval religiosity.[92]

Another important element of Cistercian theological reflection and spirituality, which also had visual manifestations, was the figure of the Virgin Mary. For monks she was not only the embodiment of the perfect woman, but the bringer of the incarnation of the Word. She features very prominently as the defender of the white monks in the *Dialogus miraculorum* of Cesarius of Heisterbach, which recalls a host of Cistercian visions and apparitions of Mary and stories of her statues becoming animated and communicating with adoring monks.[93] Bernard of Clairvaux praised Mary's qualities of nurturing, caring and loving, but he also emphasised that she was unlike any earthly woman because of her unpolluted nature, and described her special nature in one of his sermons: 'at the very beginning of her pregnancy, when other women are most grievously afflicted, we find Mary ascending the mountains with all alacrity in order to minister to her cousin Elisabeth'.[94] For the Cistercians the Virgin was the symbol of spiritual, not real, motherhood and thus she was a model for a pious person receiving the body of Christ. In another of his sermons on the Annunciation, Bernard compares Mary to an aqueduct through which water runs as a metaphor for grace, hence she is a channel but not herself a source. For Bernard and his followers their closeness to Mary was a vital step in the direction of their final aim of union with Christ.[95] Hence, the Virgin was enshrined in the Cistercian liturgy through daily masses, which were preceded by the antiphon *Sub tuum praesidium*.

The theological pursuits of monks and academic theology, especially scholasticism, were divergent paths. Already in the twelfth century Bernard of Clairvaux had made clear his dislike of theological speculation, and its most dramatic manifestation was his conflict with Abelard, culminating in the charge of heresy against the latter. On the other hand, Bernard was a friend and supporter of like-minded academic scholars, including Peter Lombard, Robert of Poule and John of Salisbury, and was consulted by other prominent theologians, including Hugh of St Victor.[96] Most historians agree that although in the twelfth century Cistercians remained very sceptical about the compatibility of academic study and the monastic vocation, by the following century the Order was beginning to accept, and even make use of, the academic study of theology. Cistercian communities started to acquire works of scholastic theologians and pastoral works for their libraries, and Cistercian monks began to participate in higher education.[97]

This 'turn towards academia' fitted in with the Cistercians' commitment to participating in the next step of church reform: the Fourth Lateran council of 1215. The emphasis this body placed on the pastoral mission, the eradication of heresy, and high standards in clerical education made a great impact on the church and its relationship with the faithful.[98] Some writers on late medieval Cistercian theology have contrasted the dearth of significant authors of theological works after the end of thirteenth century with the towering thinkers of the preceding period, citing this as further evidence for the decline of the Cistercian order. But perhaps this is simplistic. Cistercian theology was always monastic rather than academic; and the purpose of Cistercian involvement in university studies was not to contribute to scholastic debates but to enrich and renew monastic communities of which university-educated Cistercians were members. It had never been the aim of Cistercian theologians even in the twelfth century to produce theological innovations, but to remain firmly rooted in the patristic tradition. Theology was to serve spirituality by bringing monks and nuns closer to the divine; and late medieval Cistercians continued in this tradition, even as the intellectual world around them changed drastically. In fact, as theology students Cistercians performed well, often better than members of the preaching orders who were more closely associated with the universities. According to the graduation lists of the Theology Faculty of the University of Paris (established by the regent masters of the Faculty) from 1373 to 1500, numbering over 1,000 individuals, and taking into account the graduates' ability, character and orthodoxy of belief, the Cistercian monks had the highest percentage of best results not only among the monks (Cluniac and Benedictines), but also significantly outnumbered the friars (Franciscans, Dominicans, Augustinian Hermits, Carmelites and Servites) in the merit ranking.[99]

Conclusions

Cistercian monks and nuns were both producers and consumers of knowledge. Theology and especially the study of the relationship between the human and the divine was central to the intellectual world of the white monks; but they never sought to be 'at the cutting edge' of theological enquiries. Cistercian spirituality was intrinsically inward-looking and the limitations of their success in academic theology were simply a consequence of the Order's attitude towards knowledge and its application. The aim of Cistercian theology was to support the contemplative nature of monastic observance. Its essence was 'its sacramentalism, its grounding in the humanity of Christ, and its willed, active intimacy with Jesus'.[100] Sermons were the key tool of spiritual development for monks and nuns and novices. Preaching and the *Lectio Divina*, listening to the Scriptures and even private reading all made their contribution to the white monks' communal experience. The most important resource for the intellectual work of the monks were the libraries, which were intended both to further the spiritual development of the monks and to help with the training of the novices. Their profiles tended to resemble those of other contemplative orders, but the works of Bernard of Clairvaux, William of St Thierry, Isaac of Stella and other important figures in the early Cistercian movement remained the building blocks of Cistercian book collections throughout its history.

The production of manuscripts and the creation or copying of new texts was intended to support the identity of the institution and community. Volumes of a seemingly practical nature, such as cartularies, were never simply tools of administration and monastic economy, but also repositories of versions of the monastic past on which members of the community built their identity for generations. Knowledge about past difficulties, conflicts with the neighbours, the names of benefactors and friends long dead, all helped in shaping the present, confronting new difficulties and sustaining the intercessory mission of the community. Cartularies of individual houses containing copies of papal bulls issued for the Cistercian Order, and monastic chronicles recording events that occurred in other abbeys, all helped to maintain the sense of belonging to a trans-regional monastic network, just as history writing, foundation narratives and chronicles were essential tools of monastic self-identification both within a particular geographical location and as part of the spiritual and organisational structures of the Order.

Notes

1. 'Sermones super Cantica Canticorum', ed. J. Leclercq, C.H. Talbot and H.M. Rochais, vol. 1–2, *Sancti Bernardi Opera* (Rome: Editiones Cistercienses, 1957).
2. *The Twelfth Century Statutes from the Cistercian General Chapter: Latin text with English notes and commentary*, ed. Chrysogonus Waddell (Brecht: Cîteaux, Commentarii Cistercienses, 2002), 'The Instituta', p. 553, 'Local Collections: Alcobaça', p. 689.
3. Helen Birkett, *The Saints' Lives of Jocelin of Furness: Hagiography, Patronage and Ecclesiastical Politics* (York: York Medieval Press, 2010), pp. 15–16.
4. David N. Bell, '*Certitudo Fidei:* Faith, Reason, and Authority in the Writings of Baldwin of Forde', in *Bernardus Magister: Papers presented at the Nonacentenary Celebration of the Birth of Saint Bernard of Clairvaux, Kalamazoo, Michigan, sponsored by the Institute of Cistercian Studies, Western Michigan University, 10–13 May 1990*, ed. John R. Sommerfeldt (Kalamazoo, MI: Cistercian Publications, 1992), p. 250.

5. Elizabeth Freeman, *Narratives of a New Order: Cistercian History Writing in England, 1150–1220* (Turnhout: Brepols, 2002), pp. 94–95.
6. Richard H. Rouse, 'Cistercian Aids to Study in the Thirteenth Century', in *Studies in Medieval Cistercian History*, ed. John R. Sommerfeldt (Kalamazoo, MI: Cistercian Publications, 1976), vol. 2, pp. 126–127.
7. Rouse, 'Cistercian Aids to Study', pp. 123–125.
8. *Twelfth-Century Statutes*, 'Capitula', p. 513; Birger Munk Olsen 'The Cistercians and Classical Culture', *Cahiers de l'institut du moyen-âge grec et latin, Université de Copenhague* 47 (1984), p. 74.
9. Thomas Falmagne, 'Le Reseau des Bibliotheques Cisterciennes', *Unanimité et Diversité cisterciennes: filiations, réseaux, relectures du XIIe au XVIIe siècle: actes du quatrième colloque international du CERCOR, Dijon, 23–25 septembre 1998*, ed. Nicole Bouter (Saint-Etienne: Publications de l'Université de Saint-Etienne, 2000), p. 196.
10. Ambrosius Schneider, 'Scriptorien und Bibliotheken der Zisterzienser', in *Die Cistercienser. Geschichte – Geist – Kunst*, ed. Ambrosius Schneider (Cologne: Wienand, 1986), p. 407.
11. David N. Bell, *What Nuns Read: Books and Libraries in Medieval English Nunneries* (Kalamazoo, MI: Cistercian Publications, 1995), p. 48.
12. Hans Zotter, 'Die Bibliothek des Zisterzienserstiftes Neuberg in der Steiermark', *Jahrbuch für Internationale Germanistik* 71 (2005), pp. 90–92.
13. Julian Harrison, 'Cistercian Chronicling in the British Isles', in *The Chronicle of Melrose Abbey: A Stratigraphic Edition*, ed. Dauvit Broun and Julian Harrison, vol. 1 (Woodbridge: Boydell, 2007), p. 25; Dauvit Broun, 'The Physical Development of the Manuscript', in *The Chronicle of Melrose Abbey*, p. 69; Dauvit Broun, 'Charting the Chronicle's Physical Development', in *The Chronicle of Melrose Abbey*, pp. 158–159.
14. *Twelfth-Century Statutes*, 1199: 17, pp. 427–428.
15. 'Librum hoc scriptum sub honore sanctae Mariae. Qui tulerit pereat et in eternum gemat. Sitik'. Nataša Golob, *Twelfth-Century Cistercian Manuscripts: the Sitticum collection* (London and Ljubljana: Slovenska knjiga & Harvey Miller, 1996), pp. 38, 177–178.
16. Kazimierz Bobowski and Elżbieta Ratajczyk, 'Biblioteka klasztoru cystersów w Henrykowie w okresie średniowiecza (na podstawie zbiorów Biblioteki Uniwersyteckiej we Wrocławiu)', in *Cystersi w społeczeństwie Europy Środkowej. Materiały z konferencji naukowej odbytej w klasztorze oo. Cystersów w Krakowie Mogile z okazji 900 rocznicy powstania Zakonu Ojców Cystersów. Poznań-Kraków-Mogiła 5–10 października 1998*, ed. Andrzej Marek Wyrwa and Józef Dobosz (Poznań: Wydawnictwo Poznańskie, 2000), p. 399; Alicja Karłowska-Kamzowa, 'Znaczenie iluminatorstwa cysterskiego dla rozwoju gotyckiej dekoracji rekopisów na ziemiach polskich, Śląsk, Pomorze, Wielkopolska', in *Historia i kultura cystersów w dawnej Polsce i ich europejskie związki*, ed. Jerzy Strzelczyk (Poznań: Wydawnictwo Naukowe Uniwersytetu im. Adama Mickiewcza, 1987), pp. 372–373.
17. David N. Bell, 'A Treasure-House for Monks? The Cistercian Chapter General and the Power of the Book from the Twelfth Century to 1787', *Cîteaux: Commentarii Cistercienses* 58 (2007), pp. 114–115; Thomas

Sullivan, 'Cistercian Theologians at the Late Medieval University of Paris', *Cîteaux: Commentarii Cistercienses* 50 (1999), p. 88.
18. David Bell, *The Libraries of the Cistercians, Gilbertines and Premonstratensians* (London: British Library in association with the British Academy, 1992), pp. 87–140.
19. Olsen, 'The Cistercians and Classical Culture', p. 63.
20. Olsen 'The Cistercians and Classical Culture', pp. 78–79.
21. Bernard McGinn, *Three Treatises on Man: A Cistercian Anthropology* (Kalamazoo, MI: Cistercian Studies, 1977), pp. 87, 93.
22. David Bell, 'The English Cistercians and their Practice of Medicine', *Cîteaux: Commentarii Cistercienses* 40 (1989), pp. 153–159.
23. David Bell, 'Printed Books in English Cistercian Monasteries', *Cîteaux: Commentarii Cistercienses* 53 (2002), pp. 141–142.
24. Elke Goez, 'Zur Bedeutung der Schriftlichkeit im Zisterzienserorden', in *Die Zisterzienser und ihre Bibliotheken. Buchbesitz und Schriftgebrauch des Klosters Altzelle im europäischen Vergleich*, ed. Tom Graber and Martina Schattkowsky (Leipzig: Leipziger Universitätsverlag, 2008), p. 43.
25. Bell, 'A Treasure-House for Monks?', pp. 116–117.
26. Bell, *What Nuns Read*, p. 46.
27. David N. Bell, 'The Books of Meaux Abbey', *Analecta Cisterciensia* 39 (1983), pp. 27–30.
28. Bobowski and Ratajczyk, 'Biblioteka klasztoru cystersów w Henrykowie', pp. 394–395; Terryl Kinder, *Cistercian Europe: Architecture of Contemplation* (Kalamazoo, MI: Cistercian Publications, 2002), pp. 133–134.
29. Brian Noell, 'Scholarship and Activism at Cîteaux in the Age of Innocent III', *Viator* 38 (2007), pp. 25–26.
30. Jennifer Sheppard, *The Buildwas Books: Book Production, Acquisition and Use at an English Cistercian Monastery, 1165–c. 1400* (Oxford: Oxford Bibliographical Society, 1997), pp. lvi–lvii; R.M. Thomson, 'Robert Amiclas: A Twelfth-Century Parisian Master and his Books', *Scriptorium* 49 (1995), p. 241; Noell, 'Scholarship and Activism at Cîteaux', p. 33; Bobowski and Ratajczyk, 'Biblioteka klasztoru cystersów w Henrykowie', pp. 397–398.
31. Dariusz A. Dekański, 'Kilka uwag o życiu intelektualnym cystersów oliwskich w średniowieczu', in *Ingenio et Humilitate. Studia z dziejów zakonu cystersów i Kościoła na ziemiach polskich*, ed. A.M. Wyrwa (Katowice: Biblioteka Śląska 2007), pp. 288–289.
32. Nigel F. Palmer, 'Deutschsprachige Literatur im Zisterzienserorden. Versuch einer Darstellung am Beispiel der ostschwäbischen Zisterzienser- und Zisterzienserinnenliteratur im Umkreis von Kloster Kaisheim im 13. und 14. Jahrhundert', *Jahrbuch für Internationale Germanistik* 71 (2005), pp. 242–244.
33. Kinder, *Cistercian Europe*, pp. 134–136.
34. Beverly Mayne Kienzle, *Cistercians, Heresy and Crusades in Occitania, 1145–1229: Preaching in the Lord's Vineyard* (York: York Medieval Press, 2001), p. 59.
35. Sheppard, *The Buildwas Books*, pp. i–lv.
36. Kinder, *Cistercian Europe*, pp. 336–343.

37. Michael T. Clanchy, *From Memory to Written Record: England 1066–1307* (Oxford: Blackwell, 1993), pp. 146–149.
38. Józef Dobosz, 'Trzynastowieczne falsyfikaty cysterskie z Sulejowa i Jędrzejowa. Motywy i okoliczności powstania', in *Klasztor w kulturze średniowecznej Polski*, ed. A. Pobóg-Lenartowicz and Marek Derwich (Opole: Wydawnictwo Św. Krzyża, 1995), pp. 225–234.
39. *Urkundenregesten des Zisterzienserklosters Heilsbronn*, ed. Günther Schuchmann and Gerhard Hirschmann (Würzburg: Schöningh, 1957), vol. 1, p. 175; Goez, 'Zur Bedeutung der Schriftlichkeit im Zisterzienserorden', p. 31.
40. *Statuta capitulorum generalium ordinis Cisterciensis ab anno 1116 ad annum 1786*, ed. Joseph Canivez, 8 vols. (Louvain: Bureaux de la Revue, 1933–1941), vol. 5, 1490: 12.
41. Elke Goez, *Pragmatische Schriftlichkeit und Archivpflege der Zisterzienser. Ordenszentralismus und regionale Vielfast, namentlich in Franken und Altbayern (1098–1525)* Vita regularis 17 (Münster: Lit Verlag, 2003), pp. 101–106.
42. Michael Spence, 'Cartularies of Fountains Abbey: Archival Systems and Practices', *Cîteaux: Commentarii Cistercienses* 61 (2010), pp. 190–193.
43. Patrick Geary, *Phantoms of Remembrance: Memory and Oblivion at the End of the First Millennium* (Princeton, NJ: Princeton University Press, 1994), pp. 81–107.
44. Constance B. Bouchard, 'Monastic Cartularies: Organizing Eternity', in *Charters, Cartularies, and Archives: The Preservation and Transmission of Documents in the Medieval West*, ed. Adam J. Kosto and Anders Winroth (Toronto: PIMS, 2001), pp. 22, 31.
45. British Library, Harley MS 3891, ff. 109–126.
46. Goez, *Pragmatische Schriftlichkeit*, pp. 212–213.
47. Goez, *Pragmatische Schriftlichkeit*, p. 219.
48. Spence, 'Cartularies of Fountains Abbey', pp. 193–198.
49. Andrzej Wyrwa, 'Obra', p. 267, Józef Dobosz and Leszek Wetesko, 'Wąchock', Józef Dobosz and Leszek Wetesko 'Sulejów', p. 323, in *Monasticon Cisterciense Poloniae*, ed. Andrzej M. Wyrwa, Jerzy Strzelczyk and Krzysztof Kaczmarek, vol. 2 (Poznań: Wydawnictwo Poznańskie, 1999).
50. Bouchard, 'Monastic Cartularies: Organizing Eternity', pp. 22, 31.
51. *The Ledger-Book of Vale Royal Abbey*, ed. John Brownbill, The Record Society for the Publication of Original Documents relating to Lancashire and Cheshire 68 (Edinburgh: Ballantyne Press for the Record Society, 1914).
52. 'Das "Stiftungen-Buch" des Cistercienser-Kloster Zwettl', in *Fontes rerum Austriacarum*, series 2 Diplomataria et Acta, vol. 3, ed. J. von Frast (Vienna: K.K. Hof- und Staatsdruckerei, 1851); Hans Patze, 'Adel und Stifterchronik. Frühformen territorialer Geschichtsschreibung im hochmittelalterlichen Reich', *Blätter für deutche Landesgeschichte* 100 (1964), pp. 72–74.
53. Goez, *Pragmatische Schriftlichkeit*, p. 263.
54. John Taylor, *English Historical Literature in the Fourteenth Century* (Oxford: Clarendon Press, 1987), pp. 8–12.
55. Freeman, *Narratives of a New Order*, pp. 24–26.

56. James France, 'Cistercian Foundation Narratives in Scandinavia in their Wider Context', *Cîteaux: Commentarii Cistercienses* 43 (1992), p. 125.
57. Janet Burton, 'Constructing a Corporate Identity: The Historia Fundationis of the Cistercian Abbeys of Byland and Jervaulx', in *Self-Representation of Medieval Religious Communities: The British Isles in Context*, ed. Anne Müller and Karen Stöber (Münster: Lit Verlag, 2009), p. 331.
58. 'locus silvaticus in heremo vastissimae solitudinis', in 'Die Brief des heiligen Bonifatius und Lullus', ed. Michael Tangel, in *Monumenta Germaniae Historica, Epistolae*, vol. 4 (Berlin: Bibliopolii Hahniani, 1916), p. 193; Sigfried Epperlein, ' "Mit fundacyjny" niemieckich klasztorów cysterskich a relacja mnicha lubiąskiego z XIV wieku', *Przegląd Historyczny* 58 (1967), pp. 590–591.
59. Dieter von der Nahmer, 'Über Ideallandschaften und Klostergründungsorte', *Studien und Mitteilungen zur Geschichte des Benediktiner-Ordens zur Geschichte des Benediktiner-Ordens und seiner zweige* 84 (1973), p. 239.
60. Freeman, *Narratives of a New Order*, pp. 158–159.
61. 'Exordium Cistercii', in *Narrative and Legislative Texts from Early Cîteaux: Latin text in dual edition with English translation and notes*, ed. Chrysogonus Waddell (Brecht: Cîteaux, Commentarii Cistercienses, 1999), p. 400.
62. 'Epitaphium ducum Silesie', ed. Georg Heinrich Pertz, in *Monumenta Germaniae Historica, Scriptores*, vol. 19, pp. 550–552; Jarosław Wenta, 'Dziejopisarstwo cystersów a "memoria" na przykładzie Henrykowa, Lubiąża i Oliwy', in *Klasztor w społeczeństwie średniowiecznym*, ed. Marek Derwich and Anna Pobóg-Lenartowicz (Opole: LARHCOR, 1996), p. 194.
63. Michel Sot, *Gesta Episcopum, Gesta Abbatum* (Turnhout: Brepols, 1981), pp. 15–19; Michel Sot, 'Local and Institutional History (300–1000)', in *Historiography in the Middle Ages*, ed. Deborah M. Deliyannis (Leiden: Brill, 2003), p. 96.
64. 'Cronica domus Sarensis', ed. Julius Dietrich, in *Monumenta Germaniae Historica, Scriptores*, vol. 30, part 1 (Hanover: Impensis Bibliopolii Hahniani, 1896), pp. 678–707; Franz Machilek, 'Stiftergedächtnis und Klosterbau in der Chronik des Heinrich von Saar', in *In Tal und Einsamkeit: 725 Jahre Kloster Fürstenfeld. Die Zisterzienser im alten Bayern. Band III: Kolloquium*, ed. Klaus Wollenberg (Fürstenfeldbruck: E. Wawel, 1990), pp. 185–208.
65. The chronicle is unpublished and survives in a manuscript, British Library MS Faustina VI. The extract from f. 74r is cited from Karen Stöber, 'Self-Representation of Medieval Religious Communities in their Writing of History', in *Self-Representation of Medieval Monastic Communities*, p. 376.
66. Piotr Górecki, 'Rhetoric, Memory, and Use of the Past: Abbot Piotr of Henryków as Historian and Advocate', *Cîteaux: Commentarii Cistercienses* 48 (1997), pp. 261–266, 274–277.
67. Julian Harrison, 'Cistercian Chronicling in the British Isles', *The Chronicle of Melrose Abbey: A Stratigraphic Edition*, pp. 18–21.
68. Burton, 'Constructing a Corporate Identity', pp. 332–335.
69. *The Church Historians of England*, ed. Joseph Stevenson, vol. 4(1), (London: Seeleys, 1856), pp. 151, 161–162.

70. Chrysogonus Waddell, 'The Liturgical Dimension of Twelfth-Century Cistercian Preaching', in *Medieval Monastic Preaching*, ed. Carolyn Muessing (Leiden: Brill, 1998), p. 337.
71. Waddell, 'The Liturgical Dimension', pp. 344–345; Beverly Kienzle, 'The Twelfth-Century Monastic Sermon', in *The Sermon*, ed. Beverly Kienzle and René Noël, Typologie des Sources du Moyen Âge Occidental 81–83 (Turnhout: Brepols, 2000), pp. 273–278.
72. Stefano Mula, 'Twelfth- and Thirteenth-Century Cistercian Exempla Collections: Role, Diffusion and Evolution', *History Compass* 8 (2010), p. 906.
73. Guerric d'Igny, *Sermons*, intro. and notes John Morson and Hilary Costello, trans. Placide Deseille (Paris: Éditions du Cerf, 1970).
74. Kienzle, 'The Twelfth-Century Monastic Sermon', pp. 285–288, 298–301.
75. Andrzej Wałkówski, 'Piśmiennictwo sakralne skryptoriów klasztorów cysterskich w Lubiążu i Herykowie do końca XIII wieku', in *Cystersi w społeczeństwie Europy Środkowej*, pp. 386–387. Calculation based on evidence from Lubiążu, Henryków, Himmerod and Altenberg.
76. There is no adequate edition of the Herbert book, it is only printed in *Patrologia Latina*. 'Herberti Turrium Sardiniae Archiepiscopi de Miraculis Libri Tres', *Patrologia Latina*, ed. Jacques-Paul Migne, vol. 185 (Paris, 1855), col. 1273–1384; Stella Maria Szacherska, 'Cykl duńsko-słowiański w nie publikowanym rękopisie Księgi Cudów Herberta', appendix in her *Rola klasztorów duńskich w ekspansjii Danii na Pomorzu Zachodnim u schyłku XII wieku* (Wrocław, Warsaw and Kraków: Ossolineum, 1968), pp. 80–84; *Monumenta Germaniae Historica, Scriptores*, vol. 23, p. 849 (story of mission). A critical edition of Alberic's text is in preparation by Stefano Mula.
77. François Dolbeau, 'Notes sur la genèse et sur la diffusion du Liber de Natalitiis', *Revue D'Histoire des Textes* 6 (1979), pp. 143–195.
78. Nigel F. Palmer, *Zisterzienser und ihre Bücher: die mittelalterliche Bibliotheksgeschichte von Kloster Eberbach im Rheingau unter besonderer Berücksichtigung der in Oxford und London aufbewahrten Handschriften* (Regensburg: Schnell und Steiner, 1998).
79. *Libellus de Vita et Miraculis S. Godrici heremitae de Finchale*, ed. Joseph Stevenson, Surtees Society, vol. 20 (London: Nichols, 1847), pp. 466–468.
80. Ailred of Rievaulx, *The Life of the Northern Saints*, trans. Jane P. Freeland, intro. Marsha Dutton (Kalamazoo, MI: Cistercian Publications, 2006); *Aelred of Rievaulx: The Historical Works*, trans. Jane P. Freeland, ed. and intro. Marsha L. Dutton (Kalamazoo, MI: Cistercian Publications, 2005); D. Roby, 'Chimaera of the North: The Active Life of Aelred of Rievaulx', in *Cistercian Ideals and Reality*, ed. J.R. Sommerfeldt (Kalamazoo, MI: Cistercian Publications, 1978), p. 159.
81. Birkett, *The Saints' Lives of Jocelin of Furness*, pp. 115–138, 201–225.
82. 'John of Forde: The Life of Wulfric of Haselbury', in *The Cistercian World: Monastic Writings of the Twelfth Century*, ed. and trans. Pauline Matarasso (London: Penguin, 1993), p. 253.
83. Louis Lekai, *The Cistercians: Ideals and Reality* (Kent, OH: Kent State University Press, 1977), pp. 227–235.

84. Marsha L. Dutton, 'Intimacy and Imitation: The Humanity of Christ in Cistercian Spirituality', in *Erudition at God's Service. Studies in Medieval Cistercian History*, ed. John Sommerfeldt (Kalamazoo, MI: Cistercian Publications, 1987), p. 34.
85. William O. Paulsell, 'Virtue in St Bernard's Sermon on The Song of Songs', in *Saint Bernard of Clairvaux. Studies Commemorating the Eighth Centenary of His Canonization*, ed. M. Basil Pennington (Kalamazoo, MI: Cistercian Publications, 1977), p. 101.
86. Cited in Martha Newman, *The Boundaries of Charity: Cistercian Culture and Ecclesiastical Reform 1098–1180* (Stanford, CA: Stanford University Press, 1996), pp. 63–64.
87. Aelred of Rievaulx, *Spiritual Friendship*, ed. and intro. Marsha Dutton, trans. Lawrence C. Braceland (Kalamazoo, MI: Cistercian Publications, 2010).
88. Marsha L. Dutton, 'Eat, Drink, and be Merry: The Eucharistic Spirituality of the Cistercian Fathers', in *Erudition at God's Service*, p. 1.
89. Emero Stiegman, 'Bernard of Clairvaux, William of St. Thierry, the Victorines', in *The Medieval Theologians*, ed. Gillian R. Evans (Oxford: Blackwell, 2001), p. 132.
90. Cited in Dutton, 'Eat, Drink, and be Merry', p. 2.
91. Caroline Walker Bynum, *Holy Feast and Holy Fast: The Religious Significance of Food to Medieval Women* (Berkeley, CA: University of California Press, 1987), p. 255.
92. Almuth Seebohm, 'The Crucified Monk', *Journal of the Warburg and Courtauld Institutes* 59 (1996), pp. 61–73.
93. Sylvie Barnay, 'Lactations et Apparitions de La Vierge: Une relecture de la vie de Saint Bernard', in *Unanimité et Diversité*, p. 164.
94. Bernard of Clairvaux, *St. Bernard's Sermons on the Blessed Virgin Mary* (Chulmleigh: Augustine Publishing Company, 1987), pp. 218–219.
95. Ira Westergård, *Approaching Sacred Pregnancy: The Cult of the Visitation and Narrative Altarpieces in Late Fifteenth-Century Florence* (Helsinki: Suomalaisen Kirjallisuuden Seura, 2007), pp. 47–48; *Sancti Bernardi Opera Omnia*, vol. 5, ed. J. Leclercq, C.H. Talbot and H.M. Rochais (Rome: Editiones Cistercienses, 1957–1977), pp. 275–299; James France, 'Cistercians under Our Lady's Mantle', *Cistercian Studies Quarterly* 37 (2002), p. 394.
96. Gillian R. Evans, *The Mind of St. Bernard of Clairvaux* (Oxford: Clarendon Press, 1983), pp. 138–147.
97. Noell, 'Scholarship and Activism at Cîteaux', pp. 21–23.
98. Noell, 'Scholarship and Activism at Cîteaux', p. 33.
99. Thomas Sullivan, 'Cistercian Theologians at the Late Medieval University of Paris', *Cîteaux: Commentarii Cistercienses* 50 (1999), pp. 86–89, table 6 on p. 99.
100. Dutton, 'Intimacy and Imitation', p. 63.

chapter 8

WAS THERE A CRISIS OF THE CISTERCIAN ORDER IN THE LATER MIDDLE AGES?

The history of the Cistercian Order after the end of the thirteenth century is even today a much neglected subject. Indeed, thanks partly to still widespread assumptions about 'monastic decay' in the later middle ages, partly to the diminished distinctiveness of the Cistercian movement as it became much like any other rurally based monastic order, few aspects of the white monks' record have aroused much interest among scholars. If, on the one hand, the very existence of Cistercian communities as independent entities was subject to erosion by the growth of the power of external authorities, notably the papacy, and, on the other, by that of the secular power, historians have pointed to the decay of the international structures of the Order generally by the end of the thirteenth century. Yet it might well be argued that the really damaging pressures on the trans-European organisation of the Cistercians came only a century later.[1]

The history of the Cistercian Order in the late middle ages is a story of change. In the first place, as new regional structures developed, linking Cistercian houses and cutting across traditionally established filiation lines, the Order became far more regionalised, with many communities focusing more on local concerns and looking for solutions to local networks and authorities rather than to the General Chapter or geographically distant mother house.[2] Second, the growth of universities and new centres of learning and intellectual power and the participation of the white monks in higher education made its impact on Cistercian communities and the expectations of the laity, especially in respect of the new forms of piety, evoking a ready response in many Cistercian communities. Third, as the social and material framework of late medieval society – especially the enhancement of living conditions, comfort and privacy – changed the appearance of Cistercian precincts, the status of Cistercian abbots came to resemble that of other late medieval prelates. Finally, the Order was exposed to pressures from external events that affected not just the church generally (like the Great Schism), but society as a whole – wars, famines and plague.

Even so, the response of late medieval Cistercians was not simply one of passive accommodation to the new, but rather one of reflective and planned adjustment. Like many other traditional rurally based Orders, the white monks recognised the need to respond to change and to the changing religious expectations of the laity if they were to revitalise their own purpose of existence. If the concept of reform as a return to an original, perfect form of worship had been familiar to the medieval church since the early middle ages, attempts at renewal mark the late medieval history of the Cistercian Order too. Yet these reforms, which always combined institutional changes with spiritual renewal, were not only a response to internal pressure within the Cistercian world, but to external pressure – for example, the papacy – without.

Reforms: Internal and External

One of the cornerstones of the idea of reform from the Carolingian period to the fifteenth century was the need to remove the distractions of material life to allow the monks to concentrate fully on the purified spiritual life.[3] Strict adherence to the monastic rule, the correct performance of the liturgy, discipline and uniformity of practice were central to the twelfth-century reform movement of which Cistercians were an integral part. Ever since the mid-tenth century, reforms developed their own rhetoric to justify change by presenting it as eradication of corruption and a return to the original perfect state. One must beware of assuming, however, that wherever something occurred that might be termed a 'reform' (perhaps simply because it was the doing of a 'reformer') and whatever had preceded it must have been 'decadence' or 'decline'. For if reformers were naturally concerned to justify their actions, their contemporaries were sometimes all too ready to regard quite minor adjustments to the changing world as momentous changes. Whereas nowadays the term 'reform' is associated with the idea of progress and the construction of something new and, by definition, better, in the medieval context 'reform' denoted a process of returning to an original, perfect, state of affairs which had, or should have, formerly existed. In practice, however, at the level of the organisation of the Order and individual abbeys, late medieval rhetoric about removing 'corruption' and going back to an original model was intertwined with the introduction of new practices; and these changes, especially if imposed from outside, were often opposed by the white monks as introducing non-Cistercian elements into the Order.

Of all these reforms, some were internally driven and implemented by Cistercian leaders, frequently, but not exclusively, abbots of Cîteaux; others were deliberately regional and involved selected communities rather than the entire Order; and the papally driven reforms, imposed by papal bulls, were part of a much wider programme of reforms affecting many monastic and mendicant orders.

Of the internally driven reforms two, each associated with an abbot of Cîteaux – Stephen Lexington in the thirteenth century and Jean de Cirey in the fifteenth century – require more detailed attention. Stephen (born *c.* 1198), an Englishman educated at Paris and Oxford, instead of pursuing clerical career opted, together with seven followers, to become a monk at Quarr Abbey on the Isle of Wight. His career progressed very fast: in 1223 he became abbot of Stanley Abbey in Wiltshire; in 1228 the General Chapter entrusted him with the visitation of the Irish houses of the Order, where he showed himself very keen to introduce uniformity and discipline. A year later he was elected abbot of Savigny. There, in an effort to raise standards, he insisted on a period of rigorous study after completion of a novitiate and wrote his reformist *Economic Ordinance for the Monastery of Savigny* on monastic management, planning, control of offices, administration and financial reporting.[4] His presence in the Cistercian delegation at the Roman synod called by Pope Gregory in 1241 testified to his standing within the Order, and the pinnacle of his career was reached when he was elected abbot of Clairvaux in 1243. This allowed him to realise the most important element of his reform programme, the establishment of a Cistercian college in Paris.

Until then, the idea of higher education had been of relatively marginal concern to the Order – while the Cistercian statute had encouraged abbots to promote studies in their houses, it had not been compulsory. Henceforth, one abbey was selected in every region as the site for a school of theology (similar to those of the mendicant orders. For Stephen Lexington, higher studies for Cistercian monks were not so much a matter of scholastic learning, as a means of promoting a common, and higher, standard of observance across the Order.[5] At any rate, on 24 January 1254 a bull of Pope Innocent IV granted St Bernard College in Paris the same status as colleges belonging to the Dominican and Franciscan orders. At the same time the pope, who was a strong supporter of the Cistercian project, gave the white monks of the college licence to preach in public and offer ordinary lectures in theology, and demanded their admission to the Faculty of Theology in Paris.[6] Innocent's support was crucial, as the wider struggle between mendicants and seculars at the University of Paris for the control of the university threatened to engulf the Cistercians too. The establishment of the college significantly raised the importance and popularity of academic study across the Order; and although Clairvaux Abbey originally ran the Cistercian college alone, when that proved to be too expensive the college was sold in 1320 to the General Chapter, which operated it on behalf of and at the expense of the whole Order.

The first of the papal reforms of the Cistercian Order was promulgated in 1265 by the bull *Parvus fons* (also known as *Clementina*) of Pope Clement IV. Typically, it used the rhetoric of a return to a mythical golden age of monasticism – hence the frequent references to the *Carta Caritatis* – but it was in reality essentially a response to the rival claims of the abbots of Clairvaux and Cîteaux to authority and executive powers and its main aim was to make the Order more effective. *Parvus fons* focused on four key areas – the organisation of the General Chapter, the organisation of the visitation system, and the procedures for electing abbots and for removing them from office. The powers of father-abbots over elections were restricted and they were forbidden to interfere in the affairs of the daughter houses when an office fell vacant; and, by the same token, an abbot could henceforth only be removed from office for serious dereliction of duties – heresy, simony, financial irregularities or the falsification of documents, and not at the whim of the father-abbot.[7]

In the fourteenth and fifteenth centuries papal interference with the religious orders was to intensify, particularly in matters of taxation and other forms of financial payment to Rome. Even so, not all papal plans for the contemplative orders became reality. In 1317/18, for example, Pope John XXII planned a wide-ranging monastic reform that called in question the exemptions enjoyed by Orders such as the Cistercians, particularly in financial matters, and sought to extract from them a large contribution to future crusades. 'The suggestion that the order might need reformation implied that there were widespread abuses within it, and that these were direct consequences of exemption.'[8]

Seeing a threat to Cistercian independence, Abbot Jacques de Thérines of Cherlieu (Burgundy) presented the pope with a dossier that argued strongly, on the basis of a mass of documentation, that the Order was in no need of reform. Indeed, as the exemption rested direct on papal authority, the shortcomings alleged in the pope's reform plans were simply inconceivable. Moreover, the Order was already bearing enormous tax burdens, especially in France; wars raging elsewhere (in Gascony, Flanders, Scotland and Wales) had brought destruction to numerous monasteries; and their charitable obligations to feed the poor had increased enormously since the Great Famine of 1315–1317. Indeed, at a time when the burden of poverty was actually forcing Cistercian communities to disperse, the abbot argued, additional contributions toward the crusades were simply out of the question. Appealing astutely to Pope John XXII's well-known devotion to the Virgin Mary, Abbot Jacques pointed out that, as the patroness of the Cistercian Order, She owned all the land belonging to the monasteries; hence any attacks on exemptions were tantamount to attacks on Her. For a time the abbot's appeal succeeded and the pope shifted his attention to others, especially the Franciscans, but within a few decades the spotlight was again on the white monks.[9]

In 1335 the most far-reaching reform devised by the papacy for the Cistercians was promulgated in the bull *Fulgens sicut stella* (also known as *Benedictina*) of Pope Benedict XII (1334–1342). The pope was himself a Cistercian monk with a doctorate in theology from the Cistercian college in Paris, but the reform of the Order was part of his wider plans for the reform of the church and monastic life generally. The *Benedictina* was followed by a bull for the reform of the Benedictine monasteries in 1336 and by another addressed to the Augustinian canons in 1339.[10] Typically, the reform spoke of returning to the 'roots' and original ideals of the Order – which was 'the notion of the earlier period of the Order as Pope Benedict understood it'.[11] It also embedded a drive for uniformity of practice across the Order. The General Chapter was placed once again at the centre of the standardisation of clothing, liturgy, rituals and correct forms of liturgical texts;[12] and in the spirit of restoring *vita communis*, practices deemed corrupt and against the original spirit, such as private cells, eating meat, and individual stipends of additional portions of food, were forbidden. In order to make sure that monks were genuinely committed, procedures for admission into the Order were strengthened; and although abbots retained the power to accept new monks, they had to consult the elders of the monastic community.[13] In a move to address the growing problem of abbatial domination, the bull specified that each house was to have a conventual seal, with an image of the Virgin, separate from the abbatial seal and representing its authority to validate documents. To prevent forgeries, the abbot's seal bore the office-holder's name and its matrix was to be destroyed after his departure from office.[14]

The weakening connections between the centre of the Cistercian Order and individual houses were clearly in need of repair and the *Benedictina* imposed high financial penalties on abbots who failed to attend the General Chapter. The bull also reorganised the central finances of the Order, replacing the laborious and unreliable system of tax collection through the filiation system with an annual collection taken and accounted for at the beginning of the General Chapter meeting.[15] In order to curb mismanagement by abbots, they were henceforth only permitted to take decisions about the alienation of monastic property or its rents and rights with the consent of the community and two neighbouring abbots and sanctioned by the General Chapter. To prevent the appropriation of communal property by abbots, the proceeds from sales of monastic land were to be held under joint control of the abbot, the bursar and one monk elected from the community.[16]

Yet despite the bull's efforts to curb excessive abbatial powers, it did not prove possible to return to the mythical *vita communis*, in which the abbot shared a living space with the community. The divide between the abbot and the community continued to deepen as abbots increasingly acquired the status of prelates.

The *Benedictina* bull also promoted higher education – teaching of grammar, logic and philosophy was henceforth to be compulsory in each monastery, and abbots were to be obliged to send bright monks to Cistercian colleges. Monasteries with 40 or more students had to send two monks to study in Paris, and smaller communities of between 30 and 40 had to send one monk to a regional Cistercian school. The oldest schools in Paris, Oxford, Toulouse and Montpellier were elevated to the position of *studium generale*. That in Paris remained open to all monks of the Order, whilst abbeys in particular regions supported other colleges, which were open to the monks from that area: the schools in Toulouse and Montpellier were open to monks from southern France and the kingdoms of Navarre and Aragon, and the college at Salamanca catered for students from Castile and Portugal.[17]

Not all Cistercians, even the reform-minded, liked the reforms introduced by the *Benedictina*. Despite papal claims that the bull was correcting corruption and restoring original observance, some authorities regarded it as a 'deformation' of the Order rather than a 'reform'; and for them its heavy emphasis on university studies, in particular, was borrowed from mendicant practice and alien to a contemplative Order.[18] Abbots saw the bull as eroding their powers over the monastic community; and its attempt to subject them to greater control by their communities by having elected delegates of the monks accompany them to General Chapter meeting was successfully opposed by the four proto-abbots (the abbots of La Ferté, Clairvaux, Morimond and Pontigny).[19] In 1493 Marmaduke Huby of Fountains (d. 1526), one of the most prominent Cistercian abbots in England and himself a tireless reformer, was outraged at Pope Innocent VIII's bull *Quanta in Dei Ecclesia* authorising the archbishop of Canterbury to conduct visitations and reform monasteries – including Cistercian houses – in his diocese. This, according to Abbot Marmaduke, could only portend 'the ruin of the Order'.[20]

The last of the reforms of the medieval Cistercian Order came from within the community itself and was instituted in February 1493 by the *Articuli Parisienses* of Abbot Jean de Cirey of Cîteaux, which were accepted by the General Chapter in 1494.[21] De Cirey came from Dijon and had been abbot of Balerne in Burgundy before taking up an office at Cîteaux in 1476. When, after the death of Duke Charles the Bold in January 1477, Burgundy came under the control of the French crown, the abbot of Cîteaux became one of the major lords of the duchy in close alliance with King Louis XI and the equal, as a member of the Burgundian parliament, of the bishops of Autun, Auxerre, Chalon and Mâcon. De Cirey, however, appeared only rarely at the royal court and remained, above all, a monastic leader, being firmly of the opinion that the problems of the Order and the decline of its trans-European networks were related to deficiencies in its institutional structure and the curse of commendatory abbots who did not care for the well-being of their monasteries or the cohesion of the Order.[22] The commendatory system (*commenda*) had been introduced by the Avignon papacy in order to get better control of, and more profit from, ecclesiastical offices. It deprived monastic communities of the right to elect their own abbots, who were instead appointed directly by the pope or even by secular rulers. Obviously, the papacy's use of the system to reward secular prelates, treating abbacies as political prizes, had a detrimental effect on the Order. Not only did it abrogate an important element of the internal career progression that made for effective monastic leadership, it also exacerbated the financial problems of monastic houses. For commendatory abbots were all too often not monks but outsiders, rarely resided in their abbeys, were indifferent to the spiritual and material welfare of the communities and simply exploited the office for financial gain.

Although de Cirey's *Articuli* did not refer directly to the evils of the commendatory system, they stressed the obligations of proper monastic observance and the centrality of the Rule. They urged that monks be discouraged from involvement in pastoral care outside monasteries and forbidden to appeal to the secular authorities against the decision of monastic superiors. As the process of collecting dues for the General Chapter was flawed, account keeping was inadequate and many monasteries were withholding contributions from the centre, the reorganisation of taxation and finances constituted a major feature of the abbot's programme. On a practical, local level he recommended the suppression of small male and female houses that were too poor and too deeply in debt to sustain viable communities that could contribute to the central coffers.[23] As regards the reorganisation of taxation, de Cirey proposed the appointment of a commissioner for every province of the Order, to supervise the collection of taxes, whilst the abbot of Cîteaux would keep the central accounts and present them to the scrutiny of the General Chapter. In fact, in de Cirey's view, sorting out the Order's financial problems was the key to freeing it to pursue the vital issues of the day – its relationship with the papacy and lay rulers and the safeguarding of its privileges. Other leading abbots of the Order, especially Abbot Pierre de Virey of Clairvaux, were both unconvinced and very unhappy about the growing power of the abbot of Cîteaux. Controversially, de Cirey's strategy was to rely on the papacy, which controlled the commendatory system at the heart of Order's problems. He secured – albeit at a high price – a number of bulls from Pope Sixtus IV (1471–1484), and from his successor, Pope Innocent VIII (1484–1492), another ally. Ultimately, however, the strategy of publicising the plight of the Cistercian Order and purchasing unenforceable bulls and confirmations of privileges proved both expensive and futile. Indeed, it brought the already impoverished Order to the verge of bankruptcy and drove the abbot of Clairvaux to declaring succession and the establishment of the Congregation of Clairvaux in 1483 (a schism that was only healed six years later when Pope Innocent VIII issued a bull reuniting the Order under Abbot de Cirey). In fact, this pope seemed to have a genuine interest in the problems of the Order and issued a number of bulls restricting the powers of the commendatory abbots and confirming the Order's exemption from the episcopal jurisdiction, before the brief spell of co-operation between Cîteaux and the papacy was cut short by Innocent's death.[24]

Although the reforms of the Cistercian Order driven by the papacy were part of a much bigger campaign targeting the whole church, contemporaries noted with frustration that this holistic approach had achieved little. Local endeavours, by contrast, were proving distinctly more successful: as one Dominican friar observed: 'a partial reform is possible in many countries and localities. We see it gaining ground day by day in monasteries and convents, through God knows amid what difficulties'.[25] Indeed, the very proliferation of these local activities testified to the vitality of Cistercian monasticism and the idea of a contemplative life generally. The fifteenth century saw the greatest expansion of the Carthusian movement, with a large number of new foundations across Europe; and the popularity of the concept of renewal among Benedictines, Augustinians, Franciscans and Dominicans eventually gave rise to the observant congregation of reformed communities dedicated to strictness of observance and precise adherence to the Rule.[26]

The filiation system was, of course, conducive to the spread of reform. The Congregation of Sibculo, centred on Cologne, was an association of reform-oriented Cistercian houses in the Low Countries and in Rhineland.[27] At Heisterbach, Abbot Christian II (d. 1448) introduced many economic and internal changes in the 1420s before proceeding to reform the Cistercian nunneries in Gnadental, Seyne in Cologne and Walberberg, paying particular attention to the enforcement of the claustration of the nuns. Meanwhile, he attended provincial chapters of the Cistercian Order, for example in January 1422 in Maastricht, where the abbots from powerful houses in the Low Countries and Rhineland met to discuss the reform of the Order and of the church at large.[28]

Local reforms and changes were usually dependent on the ideas, connections and drive of particular individuals. Although Cardinal Domenico Capranica was appointed as a commendatory abbot of Cestello Abbey in Florence in 1436, his actions were anything but those generally associated with such appointees. He recovered property that had been alienated from the monastery and increased the size of the Cistercian community by transferring Benedictine monks from another Florentine abbey to the Order. The appointment in 1441 of Timoteo di Giannino as abbot of Settino (mother house of Cestello) spread the reform further: on his orders, the Cistercian nunnery in Florence, which was in a poor financial state, was turned into the new male house of Santa Maria Maddalena di Castello on a sound economic footing. Closer ties of Cestello with the town were manifested by the introduction of the feast of St Bernard in 1444, which soon became a major event in the Florentine calendar.[29] The same regional approach to reform was seen in female Cistercian houses: if some of them were subject to male reformers, others formed their own associations, as at Marienstuhl Abbey in Saxony, which from 1464 sent a number of 'reforming teams' to other Cistercian nunneries in the region.[30]

A geographically targeted approach to reform was characteristic of programmes instituted by the General Chapter, abbots being mandated to reform houses within specifically delineated, often extensive, territories: in 1445, for example, the reform of abbeys in England, Scotland, Wales, Ireland and Denmark was assigned to the abbot of Morimond.[31] What was typical of this process was also a frequent renewal of these arrangements with different abbots in charge; and in the second half of the fifteenth century English, Welsh and Irish houses were subject to repeated bouts of reform at the behest of the General Chapter.[32]

Not infrequently, controversies over specific reformers reflected personal conflict and rivalries within and among monasteries: Abbot John Troy of Mellifont in Ireland (elected in 1486) was outraged when his rival for the leadership of the Irish province, William O'Dwyer, abbot of Holy Cross Dublin, interfered in an internal conflict at Mellifont and labelled him, in a letter to the abbot of Cîteaux, as a 'pretended *reformator*'.[33] The rhetoric of these conflicts frequently involved accusations of venality, low moral standards and *ultra vires* actions, none of which could have enhanced the reputation or authority of the abbots within their own communities.

Along with the papacy and the Order itself, the secular powers too made a contribution to the debate about 'renewal' – although from different motives. The reform of Cistercian and Benedictine houses in Iberia in the late fifteenth century, for example, was initiated by King Ferdinand and Queen Isabel, partly in order to gain more control over wealthy and powerful establishments that were linked to centres of authority outside Spain. Indeed, their reform of the administrative structures of the Cistercian houses was ultimately intended to break the connection with Cîteaux altogether. True, the reforms of Ferdinand and Isabel had many 'traditional' features – the moral and spiritual agenda of poverty, chastity and a return to the core values of Cistercian monasticism, and, in the case of nuns, a reinforcement of the rules regarding claustration. Nevertheless, the ending of the local nobility's traditional economic control over the monasteries, the strengthening of royal control over the structures of the Order, and the assault on its international ramifications were all new departures.[34]

Although these developments were to herald further changes typical of the post-medieval Cistercian Order, the traditional theme of 'renewal' continued to have repercussions to the very end of the middle ages. For the Cistercian involvement in reforms was not confined to their own Order, especially as the conciliar movement and the debates over the shape of authority and limitations of papal power within the fifteenth-century church left no area untouched. Cistercian monks held many important positions at the Council of Basel (where, apart from the formal representation of the Order, individual Cistercian monks were attached to the representatives of various nations and principalities).[35] Abbot John of Cîteaux and Abbot John of Maulbronn were appointed to the Commission of Faith; and in 1432 the latter abbot was sent with Abbot Herman of Eberbach to the Hussites in Bohemia with an invitation to join the Council. Abbot John of Cîteaux was sent to England and Scotland to summon the ecclesiastical representatives to Basel, and Abbot John of Bonneval of Rodez to the French and Spanish 'nations'. When, as the conflict between the pope and the conciliarists escalated in the summer of 1439, the Council arranged to elect a new pope (essentially an anti-pope). The group established to choose the electors included Abbot Thomas of Dundrennan, together with the Cistercian abbots of Lucelle (Alsace), Eaunes (Languedoc) and Tamié (Savoy). The strategy of the Order was to maintain good relations with both the papal and conciliarist parties with the overall aim of protecting the Order's exemptions, but this was not an easy task. In the end, the Cistercians disassociated themselves from the Council and turned back to the pope, but the damage had already been done. Several moves by Pope Eugenius IV were regarded by the Order as detrimental to its interests and integrity, especially the formation of the Spanish congregation of Cistercian abbeys and encouragement given to the Cistercians in the British Isles to hold their chapter there instead of travelling to Cîteaux.[36] The difficulties and dilemmas afflicting the Cistercians during and after the Council of Basel exemplify the wider concerns of the leadership of the Order. On one hand the white monks wanted to be active players in the wider ecclesiastical arena, to shape the church in the direction which they saw as the correct one. On the other, they were fighting for the well-being of their own organisation at a time when many different political, social, financial and personal pressures were pulling it apart. At the same time there was no internal agreement about the changes occurring within the Order.

In the case of individual monasteries, by contrast, we can see various manifestations of 'renewal' and confidence deriving from the Cistercian spiritual heritage. At Maulbronn Abbot Berthold of Rosswag (1445–1462), a keen reformer, commissioned so-called 'foundation images' for the abbey's church, depicting the abbot as a donor, the abbey's founder, and such core Cistercian themes as the adoration of the Virgin Mary and Christ, the Adoration of the magi and charity to the poor. Such compositions, by no means unique to Maulbronn, demonstrated that Cistercians were still effective intercessors for their patrons, and testified to the endurance of the Cistercian tradition even in a time of change and innovation.[37]

Universities and Cistercian Learning in the Later Middle Ages

It is difficult to overestimate the impact of university education on the Cistercian communities – on individual monks, their place in the Order, transmission of ideas and books in monastic libraries. The establishment of Cistercian colleges in the second half of the thirteenth century gave rise to, on the one hand, central structures catering for Cistercian monks and, on the other, a regional tendency for monks from different cultural and linguistic spheres to gravitate towards academic centres within their own regions.[38] First in the field was, of course, the College of St Bernard, established in Paris in 1245, followed by other Cistercian colleges in western Europe and the opening of regional schools in the larger monasteries for their own monks and those coming from smaller neighbouring houses: Valmagne Abbey (Languedoc) opened a college attached to the University of Montpellier in 1265, and Grandselve Abbey the College of St Bernard in Toulouse in 1280.[39] English abbeys founded a college in Oxford in 1281, Ebrach Abbey a college in Würzburg and

Kamp one in Cologne. The last two were short-lived affairs, but by the late thirteenth century advanced studies were enshrined in the Chapter's regulations, which decreed severe punishments for abbots who neglected the education of their monks.[40]

A second wave of opening of Cistercian colleges came in the fourteenth century with the foundation of universities in central Europe. The University of Prague was established in 1348. The College of St Bernard at Prague University was established largely though the initiative of the abbot of Zbraslav. In 1374 Emperor Charles gave the college a prominent building in the old town.[41] In 1386 a theological faculty was founded in the University of Vienna and another at the University of Heidelberg a year later, established by Reginald, a Cistercian monk from Aulne Abbey (Wallonia) who graduated from Paris.[42] Elsewhere the initiative of locally influential abbots played a decisive role too: the Cistercian college founded by Mogiła Abbey at the University of Kraków was formally recognised by the Order in 1416/17 and, like the colleges in Vienna and Heidelberg, Kraków received significant support from lay patrons. For the monks, the emergence of the Central European schools offered an alternative to costly studies in Paris, and one that was even more necessary during the Schism, when the Paris school became cut off from the rest of the Order.[43] Other universities in eastern and northeastern Germany – Leipzig, Erfurt, Rostock and Greifswald – also counted Cistercian monks among their students, with as many as 300 studying at Leipzig between 1428 and 1522.[44] By the fourteenth and fifteenth centuries, although the College of St Bernard in Paris remained open to all monks of the Order, it was reliant on monasteries around France for the great majority of its students.[45]

The recruitment areas of different Cistercian colleges were defined in terms of nationality (Oxford, Bolonia), boundaries of secular territories (Vienna, Heidelberg, Leipzig, Rostock), archdiocesan territory (Kraków) or foundation line (Metz for the monks of the Morimond line only). With each new foundation, the General Chapter specified the 'catchment area' for the new college. For example, in 1411 the Cistercian governing body decided that the newly founded St Bernard College in Leipzig (1409) would draw on monks from Thuringia, Saxony, Meißen, Hessen, Westphalia, Western Pomerania and 'neighbouring regions'.[46]

In practice, however, Cistercian monks' choices of where to study were determined increasingly by linguistic and cultural factors.[47] By the fifteenth century, for example, German-speaking monks from Pomerania preferred to study in Leipzig rather than Kraków, where Slavonic speakers predominated. The desire to study in a familiar cultural and linguistic environment that was close enough to the home community to keep the costs down was probably behind a request in 1507 by the abbots of Lehnin, Zinna, Kołbacz, Neuzelle, Paradyż, Marienwalde, Chorin, Himmelpfort and Himmelstädt to the General Chapter for the establishment of a college in Frankfurt-an-der-Oder.[48] Sometimes, choices of university reflected specific intellectual currents: when the University of Heidelberg became the centre of nominalism its Thomist Cistercian students moved en masse to Cologne or Freiburg.[49]

After the *Benedictina* bull academic study was no longer a matter of choice for Cistercians but a requirement, as the General Chapter never ceased to reiterate, ordering in 1482 that all English Cistercian house with 12 monks should send one and those with 26 should send two to study at Oxford; whilst smaller communities should pool their resources and send one monk between them. This statute was clearly disliked by many abbots as university fees were a significant expense, but the General Chapter equally clearly considered it essential, and in 1490 expressly ordered the abbots of Fountains and Stratford Langthorne to enforce the decree.[50] On the other hand there is also a number of cases of students who matriculated as laymen, but graduated as Cistercian monks: for example John Wale, who enrolled at the University of Erfurt as a layman, but graduated as a monk of Oliwa Abbey in 1407 and continued his studies in Kraków to become a *magister* in 1419.[51] Since the communities financed the studies of their monks, this may well have influenced such students to join the Order.

The impact of education on the life of Cistercian communities was manifold. Within the internal hierarchy monks with degrees had precedence over even those with longer tenure; and their perquisites included funds for books and further studies. A higher degree was also likely to speed up opportunities – holding an office, serving on reformatory missions, visitations and other inspections, or even becoming an abbot. Educated monks could have more lasting influence on their communities as owners of books, which after their deaths were taken into the monastic libraries and thus read by other members of the community. When Heisterbach's monk Peter von Jülich died in September 1497 his books, valued at 30 guilders, were added to the monastic library.[52]

The cost of higher degrees above the licentiate was formidable, and many who enrolled for a master's degree in theology never completed it. Even so, Cistercian monks, alongside Franciscans, had a far higher completion rate than secular clerics and members of other orders – 95 per cent at the University of Paris between 1422 and 1500 – no doubt partly attributed to the frequency of the appointment of Cistercian monks with a licentiate in theology to abbatial office, where they could draw on the resources of their communities to cover the expense of studying for a master degree. Unlike the mendicants, the Cistercians who graduated in theology in Paris rarely stayed on at the university to lecture, but returned to their monasteries to provide theological training to their communities.[53] There were, of course, exceptions to this general trend. Two Cistercian professors of theology at Prague University had successful academic careers: Conrad of Ebrach, author of many theological works, who started as a professor in 1375 stayed on, with the permission of the abbot of Morimond (the mother house of Ebrach), until his death in 1399. Meanwhile Jan Štěkna, who entered the Order as an MA in 1376, preached in the Bethlehem chapel in Prague from 1393 to 1397 before moving to Kraków as a professor of theology, chaplain to the Polish Queen Jadwiga, and in 1404 authored an anti-Hussite polemical work on the Eucharist.[54]

A good example of the multifarious impact of higher education on individual Cistercian monks was Arnold von Monnikendam in the Diocese of Utrecht, who probably entered the Cistercian Order whilst studying at the University of Rostock between 1427 and 1435. In 1436 he received the title of *magister* in Cologne and a doctorate in theology in 1445, after which he returned to his home community of Heisterbach where he was appointed a novice master. From there he was employed by the General Chapter on a number of missions, becoming provisor of the St Jacob College in Heidelberg from 1451 to 1456. Then he was appointed abbot of Lehnin, from where in 1467 he was promoted to the abbacy of Altenberg, a direct daughter of Morimond and one of the largest and most important Cistercian houses in Rhineland. There he set about reforming both the abbey and its daughter houses while at the same time serving the General Chapter on reforming missions and visitations, investigating conflict and abbatial usurpations in German Cistercian houses. In 1471, at the height of his career, Arnold was appointed by Pope Sixtus IV as 'Defender' of Cistercian monasteries in *totius Germaniae* and special legate to the Holy See, with a mandate covering the detrimental practices of commendatory abbots. Clearly no run-of-the-mill Cistercian monk, Arnold embodied the importance of education, leadership skills and commitment to the idea of renewal.[55] Not that the impact of higher education was always positive. By creating a privileged category of monks it could have a detrimental effect on the cohesion of communities; and it could lead some monks to abandon the Order altogether: Jacob von Jueterbord (1381–1465) from Paradyż Abbey, who as a Cistercian studied law and theology in Kraków, found the Order neither spiritual enough nor conducive to intellectual work, and later joined the stricter and more 'fashionable' Carthusian Order, which set a particularly high value on education.[56]

Probably the most neglected aspect of Cistercian intellectual activity in the late middle ages was its contribution to humanism. The central elements of this intellectual movement were the study of the biblical languages, Latin, Hebrew and Greek, philological research into original sources, and especially the preparation of editions of the Bible. These were clearly pursuits close to the Cistercian ethos, and became integral to the monastic mission. Conrad Leontorius (d. 1511), a monk in Maulbronn Abbey in the later fifteenth century, and a philosopher, poet and skilled linguist of three sacred languages, graduated from Heidelberg University and was, between 1489 and 1495, a secretary of Jean de Cirey of Cîteaux and a friend of many other monastic humanists. From 1503 Leontorius served as a caring and diligent father confessor to the Cistercian nuns at Engental near Basel. Since Basel was the very heart of Renaissance scholarship, he was able to pursue further work on ancient history and rhetoric as well as teaching, including tutoring in humanistic script. There, his most important achievement was a critical edition of the Bible using his linguistic skills and knowledge of several manuscript versions in Cistercian libraries. His multi-volume edition was printed in Basel between 1498 and 1502 and a second edition in 1503–1504, and his Biblical Concordance in 1506.[57] The name and emblem of another Cistercian monk and friend of major humanistic figures, Henricus Urbanus from Georgenthal Abbey in Thuringia, a promoter and editor of poetry on Christ Crucified by the Croatian humanist Marcus Marulus, appeared alongside those of Erasmus of Rotterdam, Johann Reuchlin, Mutianus Rufus and Martin Luther on the document marking the end of the rectorship of Critus Rubeanus at the University of Erfurt in 1521.[58]

As regards the content of late medieval Cistercian libraries, the increasing importance of academic study did not necessarily lead Cistercian monks into new intellectual areas, but rather prompted them to visit afresh what constituted the core of the Cistercian spiritual and theological tradition. Between 1350 and 1550 there was a spate of copies of manuscripts of St Bernard's works and texts attributed to him. However, this was far more than a recycling of twelfth-century ideas. For the early Florentine humanists, Bernard's writings were the antithesis of dead scholasticism and were highly valued for their spiritual power.[59] In their emphasis on the Imitation of Christ, the emotive spirituality of St Bernard and the *Devotio Moderna*, an important lay spiritual movement, had much in common: it was no coincidence that Bernard's texts had a significant influence on the movement's theology, which has even led some historians to speak of a 'Bernardine Renaissance'.[60] Nor is it a coincidence that the name 'Order of St Bernard' was often synonymous with the Cistercian Order in English ecclesiastical sources up to the Dissolution.[61]

Naturally, the invention and spread of printing after the 1440s had a major impact on the church and on religious life. An important factor in the expansion of Cistercian libraries in the fourteenth and fifteenth centuries was the reduction in the cost of book production – partly attributable, even before the advent of printing, to faster copying techniques, the use of paper instead of parchment and the development of the book trade.[62] Books that survived from English Cistercian houses suggest that the greatest increase occurred in the last decade of the fifteenth century. Many were imported from the continent; others were acquired as gifts.[63] Indeed, in many monasteries books continued to be acquired right up to the Reformation, as in Hailes Abbey, where Abbot Sagar bought three printed books for the chapter house only a year before the abbey was closed down in 1539.[64]

The shift in the role of the monastic libraries became clear in the fifteenth century. In earlier centuries, the General Chapter had stressed the need for an adequate supply of suitable books for the Divine Office, whereas in the late middle ages the emphasis was on the importance of books for educating the monks In 1454 the General Chapter issued a statute concerning the state of book collections in the English Cistercian houses:

> Since, with sorrow, it has come to the ears of the present General Chapter that some abbots of the Order in the realm of England are so negligent that they have allowed books and libraries, which are considered a treasure-house for monks, to become so old and damaged that they scarcely capable of proper repair, the present General Chapter, wishing to prevent such losses and negligence, states, ordains, and defines that to each one of the monasteries in the said realm of England where more necessary books are in need of repair there be allocated annually forty shillings in English money until such books are adequately repaired.[65]

Again, in 1495 the General Chapter authorised Abbot Marmaduke of Fountains to ask for two books from each Cistercian house in England suitable for the library of the Cistercian College of St Bernard in Oxford, founded in 1438 by Archbishop Chichele (renamed St John's College after the Dissolution). These statutes express very clearly the view prevailing in the late medieval contemplative orders that monks should be encouraged to read books and abbeys should keep them in good order. Indeed, the state of the monastic library was held to be symptomatic of the moral and spiritual state of the community.

Late medieval Cistercians, receptive to technological developments, were quick to recognise the value of printing, especially as an aid to maintaining high standards of observance. In 1487 Abbot Nicolas Wydenbosch of Baumgarten printed a number of liturgical books – missals, breviaries, diurnals and psalters – borrowing manuscript exemplars from other German Cistercian houses in order to ensure their accuracy. The General Chapter scrutinised the newly produced incunabular and was so pleased with its quality that it recommended their sale throughout the Order and even asked all the abbots and abbesses to correct their existing manuscript volumes of liturgical books according to the new printed edition.[66] Certainly, for the Cistercian authorities print was an excellent tool for ensuring the uniformity of liturgical practices, a major concern of the Order ever since the twelfth century. While recognising the many benefits that accrued to the Cistercians and their libraries from the new technology, the Order was also fully aware that it might help to spread dangerous ideas. In 1522 the General Chapter issued a warning that monks, including those in Cistercian colleges, who read, distributed or even possessed works by 'a certain person named Luther' would be excommunicated, and if student monks, they would be expelled from the school. Not that the General Chapter assuming the role of censor was without precedent by any means: already in the late twelfth century it had been warning members of the Order not to write any book without the express permission of the authorities, and by the sixteenth century this had been extended to prohibiting the printing of liturgical volumes without permission.[67]

Nevertheless, all restrictions notwithstanding, the proliferation of printed book collections was so significant that the larger Cistercian houses began to construct separate libraries to accommodate them. At Clairvaux, a new library building started by Abbot Pierre de Virey in 1495 was completed by his successor Jean Foucand in 1503. Shortly afterwards Abbot Jacques de Pontailler built a superb new library for printed books at Cîteaux; the wealthy south German monasteries of Himmerod, Kaisheim and Salem erected new library buildings at about the same time; and one of the largest libraries in Brandenburg was built at Zinna Abbey.[68] Even houses that did not build new libraries enlarged the scope of their collections. Stična Abbey acquired a large number of incunabula of humanistic authors ancient and contemporary – from Plato, Pliny, Suida and Terence to Angelo Poliziano and Niccola Perotti – in the 1480s and 1490s.[69] These fine collections were not simply the result of the lower cost of books, but a direct consequence of the spread of concepts of study and intellectual work among the Cistercian monks. Yet although the universities, humanism, printing and the influx of new books all made their contribution, they were not the only determinants shaping late medieval Cistercian monasticism: the piety and religiosity of the laity were also of vital importance.

Cistercians and Late Medieval Lay Religiosity

In the twelfth and even thirteenth centuries very few Cistercian monks, or even abbots, were ordained priests. Indeed, Conrad of Eberbach's *Exordium Magnum* contains a whole chapter on the topic, 'How dangerous it is to seek Holy Orders'.[70] Things were very different by the late middle ages, when the majority of Cistercian monks were priests, and able to celebrate mass – hence the need for additional altars in monastic churches (see chapter 5), as the priests there needed them for private masses. The multiplication of altars also helped to maintain commemoration of the benefactors and posthumous care of their souls.

Although intercessory prayers remained important, a much greater provision of spiritual services to the laity superseded the traditional patrons' rights.[71] All over Europe Cistercian houses lost their original patrons as the families died out or patronage was passed on by inheritance to others: in England, only 40 out of 61 of the Cistercian monasteries had identifiable lay patrons by 1300.[72]

At the same time an ever-increasing number of benefactors and friends were requesting intercession from the monastic communities. The proliferation of services for the dead had a major impact on the life of communities and the appearance of their churches, which had to become far more accommodating to lay burials. On a spiritual level there were important similarities between the personal nature of lay religiosity, involving images of physical contact with the holy, and the very emotive spirituality of the Cistercian monks. The twelfth-century tradition of Christo-centric spirituality was developed further in fifteenth-century Cistercian writing and visual culture: for example, the monumental altarpiece commissioned in 1496 for Esrum Abbey in Denmark depicting the Crucifixion with, in one of the side panels, St Bernard embracing the dead Jesus on the cross.[73] The very popular collection of prayers assembled by Abbot Nicolas Wydenbosch of Baumgarten in Alsace contained pseudo-Bernardine prayers with strikingly corporal images of the veneration of the body of Christ.[74] New religious movements in the fourteenth and fifteenth centuries, especially the *Devotio Moderna*, or Brothers and Sisters of the Common Life, popularised the writings of Bernard of Clairvaux, in particular the affective spirituality and the focus on the humanity of Christ; while vernacular editions, such as the translation of the *Sermons on the Canticle* into Italian (*c.* 1420) by a Camaldulensian monk, Giovanni da Sanminiato (1360–1428), from Florence, made them accessible to the laity.[75] It was not only the white monks' spirituality which appealed to the adherents of the *Devotio Moderna*, whose principles of communal life – prayer and work – echoed the Cistercian and

Carthusian ethos. Customaries developed for the Common Life communities copied many of the organisational elements of the white monks too: the structure of the day, the role of manual labour, collation meetings, humility and chastity.[76]

St Bernard himself was already, of course, a subject of vernacular prayers, often in association with the Virgin Mary; and his rise from being only a monastic patron to universal sainthood owed much to the popularity of the *Golden Legend* (*c.* 1260) by James Voragine, which was translated into various vernacular languages in the later middle ages and made its way into popular preaching.[77]

The search for meaningful spirituality led Cistercian monasteries to establish links with Carthusian houses, famous for their strict lifestyle and regarded as a spiritual elite in the fifteenth and early sixteenth centuries. The Cistercian houses of Jervaulx and Roche built connections with the Carthusians at Mount Grace and Axholm respectively;[78] and when one George Lazenby, a monk of Jervaulx, publicly refused to recognise the king as the head of the church in July 1535, he claimed inspiration from a vision of the Virgin Mary of Mount Grace. He was then imprisoned for treason and executed at York a month later.[79] Indeed, the quest for rigorous adherence even led some white monks to transfer to the Carthusian Order altogether: it was a yearning for a rule and observance much stricter than that in his Cistercian house that led Abbot Johannes Fein of Neukloster in Lower Austria to seek to resign from his office to live as an ordinary monk in a Carthusian community in 1554/55.[80]

The growing cult of saints in late medieval Cistercian houses reflected both their own devotional practices and their engagement with the laity. Some cults were indigenous to Cistercian communities while others already had a long tradition when they were taken over. Altenberg Abbey, for example, 'adopted' the important cult of St Ursula, originally based in Cologne, which thanks to the Altenberg filiation spread further eastwards to Łekno, Ląd and Obra abbeys.[81] Some cults were celebrated not in conventual churches, but in chapels (sometimes pre-dating Cistercian ownership) located elsewhere on the monastic estates – which had the major advantage of keeping lay people away from the precinct: a Cistercian nunnery in Koszalin kept its miraculous image of the Virgin Mary in a chapel a short distance from the town, which became an important pilgrimage site.[82] Fürstenfeld Abbey administered a chapel dedicated to St Leonard in Inchenhofen, a highly successful shrine with numerous instances of miracles recorded by the Cistercian monks.[83] Mariawald Abbey, south-west of Cologne, was a late foundation (1486) of Kamp Abbey and became a pilgrimage site in the sixteenth century, with a chapel containing a fifteenth-century wooden *Pietá*.[84]

By the late fifteenth century the cult of saints was not just a matter for individual communities, but for the central structures of the Order. Certainly, early abbots who were venerated as saints (for example Ailred in Rievaulx or Waltheof of Melrose) were an important symbol of their communities, but by the later middle ages the saints belonging to the Cistercian Order became 'codified' as an important spiritual symbol for all the white monks. The first printing catalogue of Cistercian saints, commissioned by Abbot Jean de Cirey of Cîteaux in 1491, consisted of 75 *sancti* and *beati* (including four nuns), arranged according to their monasteries. In the introduction, Abbot Jean explained that in creating the list he had used not only written source, but information that he acquired during his frequent visitation and reformatory travels in the localities.[85]

That Cistercian communities were responsive to the growth of lay religiosity was clear from their readiness to engage with the most 'fashionable' ideas in the fourteenth and fifteenth centuries. One particular category of cult that attracted pilgrims at that time was that associated with the 'blood cults', especially bleeding hosts (when a consecrated wafer would 'bleed' as a manifestation of the presence of Christ) prevalent in northern Germany. The cult of the host, whilst very popular among the laity, was, in many ways, rooted in the Christo-centric, affective spirituality of the Cistercians. Abbot Baldwin of Forde (d. 1190) had written two works on the Eucharist (*De sanctissimo sacramenti Eucharistiae* and *Liber de sacramento altaris*); Caesarius of Heisterbach's ever-popular collection of miracle stories contained 67 miracles involving the Eucharist; and Matthew (d. 1220), cantor of Rievaulx Abbey, had written Eucharistic hymns. In the Cistercian liturgical calendar the feasts associated with the Eucharist became ever more prominent. The feast of *Corpus Christi* which had originated in the visions of an Augustinian nun, Juliana of Liège, in 1208, was formally established by papal bull in 1264, and was flourishing by the early fourteenth century. The cult first spread throughout the diocese of Liège and then throughout the Low Countries, gaining international popularity.[86] The Cistercians were among its early devotees, with the General Chapter ordaining in 1318 that the feast of *Corpus Christi* should be marked with two conventual masses. The cult of the Eucharist required new visual arrangements: the fashion for elaborate tower-like 'sacrament houses' of metal lattice and painted wood, which allowed the viewer to see the sacrament, spread from Germany and the Low Countries at that time; and there were 'sacrament houses' in several Cistercian abbeys – Doberan (Mecklenburg), Salem (Baden), Heilsbronn (Franconia) and Altenberg (Rhineland) – by the fifteenth century. These structures, usually equipped with a permanent light, were placed not on the altar, but as the sole focus of attention in the presbytery.[87]

The miraculous hosts were a feature of the veneration attached to consecrated hosts, especially in the 'extra-liturgical' context (i.e. not as a part of mass). Doberan, Wasserleben (Saxony) and Bernstein (Neumark) abbeys were locations of bleeding host miracles. In addition, nunneries in Marienfliess, Zehdenick, Heiligengrabe (Brandenburg), and Mariengarten and Wienhausen (both in Lower Saxony) all possessed blood relics. Many Brandenburgian and Mecklenburgian Cistercian houses came to count on the income that pilgrims brought and the prestige that the possession of these relics brought. Some of these cults had a strongly anti-Semitic flavour, the supposed miraculous bleeding of the hosts being ascribed to their desecration by the Jews. In Heiligengrabe Abbey, for example, an early sixteenth-century abbess commissioned a series of panels for the new chapel that put an anti-Semitic gloss on the much older blood cult.[88]

The cults focusing on Christ, although popular, did not obliterate other types of devotion in the Cistercian houses. In southern Germany, a very popular cult of saints known as 'Fourteen Helpers-in-Need' developed from a vision of a shepherd working for the Cistercian Abbey of Langheim (Bavaria) in 1445. Several Cistercian houses in southern Germany as far as Silesia – Raitenhaslach, Waldsassen, Kamieniec, Neuzelle, Heryków and Krzeszów – established chapels and altars in honour of the saints, attracting large numbers of pilgrims.[89]

Monasteries that claimed to possess relics, blood relics or miraculous hosts could usually attract a good number of pilgrims, together with significant material gain. When Hailes Abbey in Gloucestershire acquired a Holy Blood relic, the east end of its church was rebuilt in 1270 to accommodate a prestigious shrine. The confraternity of the abbey embraced high royal officials, which testified to its popularity and status, while its pilgrims included the famous Margery Kempe (d. 1438), an Englishwoman from King's Lynn, whose itinerary even extended to north German sites.[90] If a shrine was located within the monastic space, the Cistercian authorities had to adjust the rules of admission to accommodate pilgrimage traffic, which would otherwise have breached several important regulations: in 1317, for example, the General Chapter gave Heisterbach Abbey permission to admit women to the monastic church on the feast of its dedication, when pilgrims could receive indulgences.[91] Even so, although Abbot John of Gloucester of Hailes Abbey noted approvingly during the visitation of Dore Abbey in 1318 that the cross in the monastic church was attracting significant veneration from the laity, he was adamant that if any women were among the pilgrims, while they might be offered food at the gate, they must on no account be accommodated within the precinct, not even in the granges.[92] Similarly, in 1402 Abbot Robert of Fountains, as abbot-superior of Kirkstall Abbey, permitted female pilgrims to enter the monastic church on specific days of the year, in accordance with Pope Boniface IX's indulgences, but forbade the abbot and monks, on pain of severe penalties, to allow them access to any other building in the precinct.[93]

Interestingly enough, Cistercian monks would sometimes act as pilgrims on behalf of others. The practice of pilgrimage by proxy was not unusual in the middle ages, but what is noteworthy here is the fact that the pilgrimages in question were to be undertaken by Cistercian monks. In 1287 the will of Juliane, a daughter of Tule Bosen of the powerful Skjalm family, specified not only that she wished to be buried in Sorø Abbey, but that the abbey should send pilgrims for the benefit of her soul to Jerusalem, Rome and St Nicholas' in Bari.[94] Even more strikingly, in 1411 the will of Queen Margaret I of Denmark, Sweden and Norway specified a large number of pilgrimages to be undertaken in her name within two years of her death. The abbots of Sorø and Esrum abbeys were to be paid 2,000 Lübeck marks to send their monks on 130 pilgrimages to 44 shrines in Europe and the Holy Land – the pre-eminent Christian sites such as Rome, Jerusalem, Bethlehem, Santiago de Campostela, and well-established popular shrines in Canterbury, St Denis, Cologne and Assisi, and also to Nordic sites in Vadstena, Trondheim, St Magnus Orkneys and a parish church in Hattula in central Finland which had a relic of the cross. Finally, the queen's list included 'fashionable' new pilgrimage sites, for example Wilsnack with its cult of Holy Blood, and an array of Marian churches in Denmark, Sweden and Norway. Queen Margaret died in 1412, and there is no record of whether the abbots of Sorø and Esrum carried out her intentions; but there is good evidence that monks of these houses were involved in pilgrimages both on their own and by proxy. In another pious bequest Queen Margaret bequeathed the sum of 600 Lübeck marks to the abbots of Sorø and Esrum and the prioress of a nunnery in Roskilde for various purposes including sending the poor on foreign pilgrimages. A late medieval tomb cover (*c*. 1300) from Sorø depicts a Cistercian monk, Jonas, with an inscription stating that he had been to Rome three times, to Jerusalem twice and to Santiago once – perhaps he was one of these professional pilgrims.[95] At any rate, it seems that the queen's request, and possibly others made to the Danish houses, was regarded as compatible with the principle of *stabilitas*, and that by the early fifteenth century going on pilgrimage, with the permission of the abbot, was an acceptable role for a Cistercian monk.

The Changing Character of Communal Life

The quality of life in Cistercian communities was naturally influenced by the improvement in living conditions and changes in the lifestyle of large sections of society in the later middle ages. In fact, by the end of the thirteenth century a fundamental shift was observable, away from the communal, and towards a more individual, private mode of existence.[96] In the secular world, the consumption of imported food was becoming the criteria for standards of living, and in Cistercian houses, too, this meant a richer diet, not only for the abbot, but for the whole community. Monks were not cut off from the realities of the world around them, and their perception of standard of living reflected its norms. Whereas until the second half of the thirteenth century recruits into Cistercian houses were primarily of noble origins, by the later middle ages they increasingly included townsmen or even better-off free peasantry, for whom entering a Cistercian monastery did not mean a drastic reduction in living standards: indeed, for some it may even have meant an improvement.

Better food

The 'traditional' Cistercian diet (see chapter 1), plain, meat-free and confined to two meals a day at most, gave little sustenance; already the late twelfth century had witnessed a move away from the usual meagre portions of bland vegetarian food with occasional fish, to increased allowances of white bread, wine or fish in the form of pittances. Fish dishes, in particular, were now often elaborately prepared; and landlocked abbeys welcomed imports of sea fish such as herring, plaice and stockfish. The number of days on which additional food portions were served increased steadily in the thirteenth and fourteenth centuries. In Zwettl Abbey there were 98 days a year when extra food was served to monks in the fourteenth century. In the first half of the fifteenth century the monks of Heligenkreuz Abbey, Buch Abbey in Saxony, Himmerod Abbey, Ebrach Abbey, Marienstatt Abbey and Raitenhaslach Abbey in Bavaria all enjoyed additional food portions on over 200 days a year. Benefactors gave pittances to monastic communities in return for prayers for their souls when they were consumed. These pittances might be very fancy, including specified expensive or imported ingredients and local specialities: Henry von Dosse, a benefactor of Marienwalde Abbey (Neumark), established an annual two-day pittance for the monks consisting of 'good wine, good beer, sturgeon, stockfish, eggs, good fish with appropriate pepper seasoning'.[97] Clearly monks who had partaken of such a feast could be expected to pray all the more fervently for their benefactor.

By the late fifteenth century such improvements in the monastic diet had been recognised in the regulations of the General Chapter: pittances were no longer seen as a special 'treat'. Although the eating of meat continued to be forbidden in the refectory, meat was being consumed increasingly, and special meat kitchens and special dining rooms known as 'misericords' were built to accommodate it.[98] This more nourishing diet was accompanied by more ornate and expensive plates and cutlery, silver being in common use (as among wealthy laity) by the late thirteenth century, not only at the abbot's table but in the refectory. When Andrew of Royewell, the cellarer at Pipewell Abbey (Northamptonshire), was promoted to the office of the abbot in 1298 he made a gift of 50 silver spoons with his name engraved on them for the monks to use instead of wooden ones.[99] It is easy to dismiss such behaviour as 'corruption' or departure from an 'ideal', but these monks and nuns were part of a society that was rapidly changing; and no institution can be expected to live by the standards of the twelfth century some 300 years later.

The desire for privacy and comfort
The comforts that the Cistercians enjoyed in the late middle ages were not restricted to food: accommodation, furnishings and heating all improved. First of all, there was a tendency away from open spaces towards subdivision and greater privacy. Common infirmaries, like that at Jervaulx Abbey, started to be partitioned in the early thirteenth century with wooden screens dividing beds. By 1400 these had been replaced by stone walls equipped with lockable doors. The infirmary hall at Fountains Abbey, divided into self-contained units over two floors with their own hearths and latrines, reflected a desire not only for better conditions for individual study, but perhaps for privacy for its own sake.[100]

While architectural and archaeological remains yield only fragmentary evidence of the spread of private spaces in Cistercian houses across Europe, the regulations of the General Chapter against such changes to dormitory arrangements are quite informative. The oldest of these prohibitions – 1287, 1314 and 1323 – are addressed to nuns, not monks, and stress that apart from the abbess no nun should have a private room, as it causes envy and conflict in the community. According to further admonition of 1327, such private rooms fostered egocentricity and were against the Cistercian spirit.[101] The idea that the private rooms for more might be incompatible with the spirit of the Order was first addressed in the *Benedictina* bull, which declared that only the holders of monastic offices could have separate quarters.[102] The dangers attached to private rooms were further elucidated in a General Chapter statute of 1370 directed at the whole Order: as such spaces encouraged monks to indulge in unofficial 'parties', unauthorised meals and even conspiracies against monastic officials, the General Chapter requested their demolition.[103] Such pronouncements were still being reiterated, and offenders being brought to the attention of the central authorities, until the mid-1470s; but the resistance of the monks to giving up the comforts of private space, comfortable bedding and other pleasures was equally tenacious.[104] Cistercian nuns, too, strove for greater comforts: in 1324 the abbess of Bouchet (France) even managed to secure a bull from Pope John XXII permitting her nuns to have private apartments, female companions and servants.[105]

If subdivided spaces were one innovation of late medieval domestic architecture, another was more effective heating by fireplaces; and when in the late fifteenth century the General Chapter at last gave up its struggle against private rooms, it turned its attention to 'illegal' heating. Originally dormitories were supposed to be unheated, which in the northern European climate was rather extreme. The only permitted source of warmth was a fireplace in the warming room, to which monks were allowed access only at certain times. In 1476, therefore, the General Chapter ordered the removal of portable stoves and permanent fireplaces from the communal dormitories and private rooms; but although this prohibition was repeated later in the century, it does not seem to have had much effect.[106]

The ownership of property

One issue linked to the privatisation of space in the Cistercian houses is the ownership of property by individual monks. The visitation of Dore Abbey in 1318 reiterated that monks might not own horses and that all animals should be kept in the communal stables; nor should the holders of monastic offices have greater drink allowances than the rest of the community.[107] Clearly, members of the community owned a variety of personal possessions beyond the books belonging to studying monks or graduates. A variety of sources, especially those from the fifteenth and sixteenth centuries, show monks to be giving sums of money, valuable objects and books to their relatives and friends in the secular world and in the ecclesiastical hierarchy. Equally, bequests by the laity to Cistercian monks and nuns show that despite being members of religious communities they continued to be part of their family and kinship networks. In a will of 1422, one Heinrich Vette, a burgess of Stralsund, bequeathed to his stepson Heinrich Westfal, a monk of Neuenkamp Abbey, a pension of no less than 16 marks yearly – one-third of the total inheritance.[108]

Another indication of family ties is the singling out of individual members of the community in general donations. In 1307 Cecilie, a daughter of Jon Jonsen in Northern Zealand, gave 60 marks in her will for her burial and anniversary masses and pittance at Esrum Abbey. There was nothing special about this, but that she also gave 10 marks to Abbot Jens Hvid and 4 marks to the monk Heuze Krabbe strongly suggests a personal, probably family connection between them.[109] Such behaviour is sometimes castigated as symptomatic of the 'corruption' of late medieval Cistercian communities, but the reasons for it are understandable enough.[110] In the first place, many monks had undertaken significant obligations outside their monasteries, perhaps in terms of their education, or holding an unpaid but desirable position, say as a papal chaplain, all of which required, of course, significant financial resources. Secondly, gifts of personal property had the effect of reinforcing their connections with the world outside the monastery, and in return for providing that individual commemoration which had become a standard expectation in the wealthy urban stratum from which many late medieval Cistercian monks came.

The position of abbots
The separation of the abbots from the monastic communities was becoming apparent by the thirteenth century, when they generally abandoned communal life in the dormitory to establish separate abbatial houses, which a century later became far more imposing residences: when the old infirmary at Maulbronn Abbey was converted into an abbatial residence during the time of Abbot Albrecht IV von Ötisheim (1402–1428), he saw to it that the three-storey interior, especially the large hall, was heavily decorated with wall paintings, whilst subsequent abbots left their own marks by adding their own coats of arms.[111] Not that the great expense and care put into beautifying these buildings was merely an expression of individual vanity – as one function of abbatial houses was to provide hospitality for distinguished guests they were important for gaining lay support.[112]

Although the abbot's stall in the choir had always been differentiated from those of the monks, being located on the south side of the presbytery, by the later middle ages it had become a prominent throne, sometimes equipped with a baldachin.[113] A similar process of emphasising the position of the head occurred in female houses, but a separate house for the use of the abbess on official occasions, especially those involving important guests, featured only in larger and wealthier Cistercian nunneries, where their emergence in the fifteenth century reflected the growing prestige of the office of abbess.[114]

Probably the most important visual manifestation of the status of the abbatial office was the 'pontificals' – the vestments and insignia symbolising episcopal status. 'Privilege of pontifical' was much desired by abbots, but expensive to obtain. Although the Cistercian abbots received a general privilege to use pontifical vestments in 1359, confirmed in 1483, in practice individual permission was necessary, entailing a large obligatory payment, which was, in effect, just another device for the papacy to tax Cistercian monasteries. Despite the expense, many abbots were willing to pay. These who acquired the right could display it on their abbatial seals, the iconography of which included such signs of the abbot's eminence as the pontifical ceremonial robes and a figure enclosed by an architectural frame indicating elevated status.[115] Abbot Robert Chamber of Holm Cultram Abbey, who received the right to the pontifical privilege in 1508, promptly incorporated it into his coat of arms displayed on the new western portal of the abbey church.[116] Visually, the pontificals – several pieces of heavily decorated liturgical garb worn on important liturgical and ceremonial occasions – were certainly impressive: the abbot wore a mitre on his head and carried crosier, pectoral and ring. Valuable pontifical sets were frequently recorded in the inventories of late medieval Cistercian abbeys.[117] Of these, the mitre was the most important and serves on seals and coats of arms as a 'shorthand' symbol for the pontifical privilege.[118] Although the pontifical raised the prestige not only of the abbot, there was sometimes a conflict between the personal ambition of the abbot and the good of the community: when Abbot Andrew Hoffmann of Lubusz in Silesia (1498–1534) paid 240 gulden for a papal bull to obtain the pontifical privilege, paying a further 350 gulden for a mitre and 50 for a new Benedictional, it would seem that his pleading the poverty of his house at the General Chapter in 1502, and his inability to pay for the studies of his monks, were not unconnected to his own extravagance.[119]

Alongside the symbols and signs of high spiritual office, it became a common practice by the fifteenth century for Cistercian (and Benedictine) abbots to display their own coats of arms separately from that of the abbey – an indication of their personal position, high birth and an elevated status within the community, and in some cases even a step towards the personalisation, if not the privatisation, of the abbatial office.[120] A wall painting of 1462 depicting the abbot of Žd'ár in Bohemia with both a mitre and his family coats of arm is certainly not meant to reflect any shared status with the monks.[121] On the other hand, monastic communities – and not only the Cistercians – found it advantageous to fortify their separate legal identity by adopting the coat of arms of a patron or the most prominent benefactor as the coat of arms of the community. Rievaulx

Abbey, for example, adopted the coat of arms of the Ros family, descendants of the founder.[122]

The power of abbots and the stamp of their influence on their monasteries was also reflected in their practice of founding altarpieces for their churches, presenting them in the standard pose of a benefactor with an identifying scroll bearing their names and the insignia of their abbatial office.[123] Abbots as founders of devotional images for the monastic churches were themselves commemorated both as leaders of their communities and as individuals of particular piety and standing: an early fifteenth-century fresco in the abbey church of Bebenhausen depicts Abbot Peter von Gosmaringen presenting the Virgin Mary with a large model of the bell tower that was erected during his time in office. In a woodcut in a printed psalter of 1492/93 from Zinna Abbey the central figure of Mary holding baby Christ is flanked not only by powerful secular figures (the Holy Roman Emperor Frederic III and Maximilian, King of the Romans) but by the dean of Magdeburg cathedral, Duke Adolph of Anhalt *prepositus* of the same cathedral, and significantly the abbot of Zinna with the pontifical and his coat of arms. In this way the abbot is directly connected to major contemporary figures through their shared devotion to Mary.[124] In Scotland, Abbot Thomas Crystall of Kinloss (1505–1535) was praised in the life written by monk Ferserius for donating an impressive silver monstrance to the monastic church.[125]

Yet while such gestures were undoubtedly expressions of personal piety and commitment to the monastic communities, they also testified to an abbot's separation from his monks. In earlier times, when the twelfth- and thirteenth-century abbots embarked on large-scale building projects, they did not do so in a personal capacity. Even if abbots were specifically remembered in such building projects, these were corporate ventures. The donations of valuable objects by the later medieval abbots, by contrast, were the personal gestures of wealthy individuals.

Of course, the system of commendatory abbots was notoriously abusive; and it must be said that absenteeism was not always a matter of choice: large monasteries were complex business organisations demanding travel and attention, and the proliferation of litigations could absorb a lot of abbots' time.[126] The fact remains, however, that there were enough absentee or uninterested abbots to bring a real crisis of leadership, especially of spiritual leadership, in their communities – and this was a time, in the later middle ages, when individual houses and, indeed, whole regions were experiencing serious economic and social pressures; and even the role of the papacy was often anything but conducive to the cohesion of Cistercian Order.

Difficulties and Pressures on the Order in the Late Middle Ages

The Great Schism (1378–1417) was a disaster for the trans-European network of the Cistercian Order. The French mother houses became cut off from the rest of the Order as the Roman popes Urban VI and Boniface IX forbade 'their' Cistercian monasteries to have any contact with fellow houses that were loyal to the Avignon papacy. Already in 1376 Pope Urban VI had suspended Gerard de Buxières of Cîteaux as an Avignon adherent and it became impossible for the Order to hold meetings of the General Chapter in Cîteaux until after the council of Pisa in 1409. In the meantime, the popes in Rome encouraged 'reduced' General Chapter meetings in the territories they controlled – not so much out of solicitude for the Cistercian Order as to facilitate the collection of papal taxation. As a result, the annual meetings became highly fragmented: Italian abbots assembled in Rome, abbots from the Empire in Vienna, while smaller regional chapters met in Nuremberg, Worms and Heilsbronn. That some of these gatherings were formalised as chapter meetings for different kingdoms and regions only further eroded the unity of the Order. In 1394 and 1400 English abbots met at St Mary Graces Abbey in London, a relatively recent foundation (1350) that had originally owed its rise to its location close to the centre of power and new forms of patronage associated with the royal court, but which now confirmed its standing within the Order. That the secular power was wont to obstruct the activities of the General Chapter was nothing new: as early as 1298 King Edward I of England had forbidden Cistercian abbots to travel to Cîteaux, and the prohibition was repeated several times in the next century. In France, meanwhile, the behaviour of the Roman popes pushed the French Cistercians closer to the king, to whom they looked for protection, but this also further eroded the unity of the Order.[127]

In the era of the Avignon papacy (1309–1378) and during the Schism (1378–1414), the papacy became very financially demanding. While the competing Roman and Avignon pontiffs each had a far smaller income than their unchallenged predecessors, they still had to meet the very high costs of centralised administration and of their own political ambitions: Pope Clement VI (1342–1352) needed cash to buy Avignon from Queen Joan of Naples; his successor Innocent VI (1352–1362) had to pay for wars in Italy. They therefore taxed the richest institutions within the church – the religious orders. Even popes who were considered friends of the Cistercians – like Benedict XII, himself a former Cistercian monk – made heavy financial demands on the Order. There were also requests for 'voluntary' contributions from abbeys that were considered particularly wealthy. In 1355, Pope Innocent VI, unable to access English Cistercian houses, and finding those in Italy already too poor and many within the Empire under the protection of his enemy Charles IV, launched such an appeal to the Cistercian and Benedictine abbeys in France; and it was on the French Cistercian houses, particularly 'accessible' to the papal demands, that the burden of taxation fell most heavily.[128]

Even so, it was not merely direct taxation that was draining the Order of its resources but the commendatory system, by which abbatial offices were essentially sold or given as rewards. This system often had disastrous consequences for the abbeys concerned, as commendatory abbots were all too prone to sell monastic property or use it as security for loans and to withhold funds for the maintenance of the buildings, the needs of the community and the cost of the monks' university studies.[129] At the same time, they would leave the actual running of the monastery – both practical and spiritual – to the prior, with very limited financial resources. The commendatory system impinged on some parts of Europe more than others: it was particularly rife in Italy and France, where almost all the Cistercian houses had commendatory abbots by the late sixteenth century. In Scotland on the eve of the Reformation only the abbots of Coupar Angus and Kinloss were Cistercian monks, all the other houses being in the hands of commendatory abbots. The most eminent of the Order's monasteries in Scotland – Melrose Abbey – was passed on to a succession of outsiders, all purely political appointees.[130] In England the spread of the system was obstructed by the ingrained hostility of the royal power towards any form of papal interference and Cistercian houses were generally able to appoint their own abbots. In some parts of central Europe the commendatory system was introduced only in the sixteenth century and by the secular power, kings of Poland, for example, using it to reward courtiers, relatives and royal officials.[131] The Cistercian authorities made a number of attempts to suppress, or at least curb, this damaging practice; and Abbot Jean de Cirey of Cîteaux, in particular, appointed commissioners to inspect houses headed by commendatory abbots to make inventories of the monastic property and to discover whether proper Divine Office was being held, and whether the monks were adequately provided for. Ultimately, they all failed because no pope was willing to put an end to the practice.[132]

If the central structure of the Cistercian Order was under continuous financial pressure from the papacy, the demands of the thirteenth- and fourteenth-century French kings for cash for their planned crusades, wars and other 'emergencies' were equally unrelenting. Eventually, the payments from the Cistercian houses became a regular part of the royal revenue.[133] Not that the Order remained passive in the face of pressures that were destroying its resources and undermining its unity. In the fourteenth and fifteenth centuries Cistercians lobbied the papal court in Avignon incessantly for bulls to safeguard the privileges and freedoms of the Order. It was both a very costly process and one of distinctly limited effectiveness. In 1415 the General Chapter secured (a very expensive) confirmation of privileges from Pope John XXII, who promised to appoint only Cistercians to vacant offices in the Order and to declare void all previous nominations of commendatory abbots except those that had been given to the cardinals. In 1485 Pope Nicholas V issued a similar bull against all types of commendatory abbot. In practice, however, the impact of these documents was virtually nil, as the popes purloined the fees for the bulls while continuing to reward the secular clergy with abbatial offices.[134]

Recognising at last the utility of this strategy, the Order attempted to control the damage itself by means of regulations against commendatory abbots who were draining the resources of their monasteries and eroding the leadership functions of their office. The General Chapter set limits to the income these abbots could take from their houses, and transferred the other abbatial powers to the priors, who now became, in terms of practical management and spiritual leadership, de facto abbots.[135]

Clear evidence of the developing threat to the General Chapter was the emergence of territorial structures within the Order. This phenomenon, like strife over the commendatory system, the weakening of ties with the centre and the declining effectiveness of the centre itself, was both a cause and a symptom of the problem; and while it was in one respect part of a positive drive for reform, it also furthered the fragmentation of the Order. The first such 'territorial' structure emerged as early as 1425, when the Castilian congregation was formed. Half a century later, in 1481, the abbot of the Cistercian abbey in Florence petitioned the pope to form a congregation consisting of Cestello, Settimo and Buonsollazzo in Tuscany and S. Bartolomeo near Ferrara, and secured exemption from the commendatory system. In 1484, a bull of Innocent VIII founded the Congregation of St Bernard in Tuscany, with its own General Chapter, visitations and 'career structure' for the monks within it. Finally, in 1497 Pope Alexander VI extended the Congregation of St Bernard to the rest of Italian territories.[136]

Another sign that the trans-European bonds within the Order were being replaced by territorial connections was the General Chapter's introduction of provincial visitations in 1433. The traditional system of visitation within the immediate filiation was not abolished, but in practice it became weakened and even defunct in many areas, especially across hostile political borders.[137] In order to maintain some discipline and preserve the connection between the centre and the monasteries, the General Chapter frequently replaced the father-abbot of the distant mother house who neglected visitation duties with an abbot from a locally important Cistercian house. The abbot of Fountains was criticised by the General Chapter for neglecting his duties towards his Norwegian daughter house in Lyse in 1213 and threatened with removal from the visitation role.[138]

It was not merely the central authority and the filiation structures that were coming under pressure in the fifteenth century, but individual houses too. Membership of the communities was in decline: from the 1390s it became permissible for a male member of a religious order to receive a papal dispensation to leave the order and hold a benefice as a secular priest; and to some Cistercian monks who could afford the substantial fee payable to the curia, a comfortable life as a priest seemed an attractive option. The records of the supplications and fees submitted to the Penitentiary Office of the curia illustrate the motives behind individual applications: in December 1517 a certain Olavus Magni, an ordained Cistercian monk from the diocese of Strängnäs in Sweden, was given permission to leave his abbey permanently because he:

> suffers from serious and incurable disease and wishes to move to his parents' or friends' house, so that he can be better cared for. The regent Mercurius refers the case to the archbishop of Croia (in Albania) and of Uppsala and commissions them to permit Olavus to do so and to take part in the Divine Office, to administer sacraments, preach the words of God, ask for alms and use them.[139]

Papal dispensations offered a legal way out of the monastic enclosure without resorting to apostasy; but they nevertheless tended to undermine one of the central principles of Cistercian monasticism, the *stabilitas* – the separation from the world and permanent membership of the monastic community.[140] Certainly, the authorities of the Order could only view with dismay the loss of members who, as a letter of March 1496 from the abbots of Fountains, Stratford Langthorne and St Mary Graces to the abbot of Cîteaux put it, 'wander in the world, giving great scandal to our Order'.[141]

The greatest natural disaster of the late middle ages, the Black Death, decimated many Cistercian communities. As early as 1349, in an attempt to replenish a rapidly decreasing number of monks, the General Chapter lowered the requirement for the monastic profession to anybody who was 14 years old, had completed one year of noviciate, and knew the psalms by heart.[142] In the short term, the Black Death decimated monastic communities and in the long term it helped to shift the social composition of all rural-based monastic orders, from primarily noble and knightly elements to those lower down the social scale. Of course, this was a process linked to wider socio-economic changes and the growth of wealth based on trade and commerce, but the Black Death accelerated it and one consequence was that from the second half of the fourteenth century recruitment was primarily from the upper urban stratum and prosperous peasants. The numbers of lay brothers also fell off sharply and in many regions they disappeared completely.[143]

This was the pattern all over western Europe, where paid employees replaced the *conversi*. Things were different in East-Central Europe where the urban population was smaller and where the nobles were pushing the free peasantry into serfdom – the upshot, as the sons of the nobility were not too keen to enter contemplative orders and as the socio-economic position of the peasants steadily declined, was an acute shortage of Cistercian monks. The situation was most dramatic in Hungary, where the Order suffered from increasingly poor recruitment from the fourteenth century to the sixteenth century. Indeed, there were so few Hungarian monks that Cistercian lands were in effect 'privatised' by local noble families. Several abbeys closed down altogether in the fifteenth century, moving King Matthias Corwinus to appeal to the General Chapter in 1477. The response was positive, and several German monasteries offered to send about 100 monks; but the revival of the Hungarian Cistercian houses was cut short by the Turkish invasion of 1526. In the Polish kingdom many Cistercian communities continued to recruit monks from abroad, and houses belonging to the Altenberg line in particular were staffed by German-speaking monks.[144]

In the fourteenth and fifteenth centuries wars and other disasters put a lot of strains not only on the individual Cistercian houses, but also on the international structures of the Order. It was not only the Great Schism but the disorders associated with the Hundred Years War (1337–1453) that made it impossible to hold meetings of the General Chapter in Cîteaux, which was reduced to a small coterie of abbots from the neighbouring Burgundian houses. Numerous monasteries were repeatedly looted and vandalised by passing armies, and communities were left destitute and unable to function. It was not just a matter of incidental damage from English attacks and French responses; by the second half of the fourteenth century a plague of mercenaries had emerged, specialising in deliberate plunder. In 1367 Cîteaux Abbey itself was looted and burned by a group of mercenaries and the monastic community had to move to the abbot's town-house in Dijon.[145] Cistercian nunneries were also ruined, property stolen and nuns raped, killed or dispersed and unable to even support themselves, with their buildings in ruins, their estates ravaged and rents impossible to recover.[146]

In central Europe, the Hussite wars (1420–c. 1434) were particularly destructive for many communities, not only in Bohemia and Moravia, where the heretics were strongly entrenched, but in Silesia, Saxony, Hungary and even as far as the Baltic Sea coast in Prussia where the Bohemians were at war with the Teutonic Knights. The fighting forced many monks and nuns to flee to other Cistercian houses, which were often already overcrowded and sent them to seek shelter even further away from their home communities. A study of 100 letters from the abbots of Cistercian communities in Austria from the 1420s until the second half of the fifteenth century shows that half the cases of migration by monks were linked to the destruction of their monasteries by fire, war, violence and Hussite and Turkish attacks, and that in a very large area, stretching as far as Pelplin Abbey in Pomerania to Langheim Abbey in Franconia, the devastation inflicted by Hussites was cited in no fewer than a third of the cases as a major reason for monks having to leave their houses.[147]

Even so, it should be said that although, as heretics, the Hussites had rejected all forms of monasticism, the majority of violence perpetrated against the Cistercian houses in the late middle ages seems only rarely to have had an ideological motivation: precincts were sometimes attacked, looted or even destroyed, liturgical objects and other precious items stolen and libraries burned, but it was generally the granges that were the real target. Medieval logistics required the seizing of provisions for men and horses as the armies advanced through enemy (and even their own) territories, and mercenary soldiers could be a particularly destructive force, especially if they were not paid. There are numerous examples of compulsory 'purchase' of grain and even straightforward theft from the granges of the Scottish Cistercian houses by English soldiers, and Melrose Abbey was used as a headquarters by both English and Scottish kings during the fourteenth-century Wars of Independence. Even if a belligerent force promised to protect monastic houses, this promise was rarely kept: the monastic chronicle of Pelplin Abbey noted in 1457 – during the Thirteen Years War for the control of Pomerania between the Teutonic Order state and the Polish Kingdom – that 'the abbey was looted by unknown soldiers ... they emptied the monastic mill taking a lot of corn and malt and other foodstuffs and also looted the bake-house. ... It is not known if they were soldiers of Danzig, Teutonic Knights, Poles or Czechs.'[148]

The rise of national kingdoms in the late middle ages and the spread of the vernacular languages also contributed to the erosion of the trans-European unity of the Cistercian Order. One of the major problems Stephen Lexington encountered during his reforming mission to Ireland was the Irish monks' ignorance of French – the main language of communication within the Order. Stephen's plans for higher education were aimed precisely at establishing common standards and a common language in the Order – by making fluency in French and Latin a prerequisite for admission into the Order; by holding all monastic chapters across the whole Order either in French or Latin; and by improving the monks' active knowledge of French, for example by the recitation of the Rule of Benedict in French.[149] Problems with language were, of course, most acute in areas subject to a variety of ethnic, linguistic and political influences: Wągrowiec Abbey in Greater Poland was a daughter house of Altenberg Abbey (Rhineland) and was founded (on another site in Łekno) in 1142. The community continued to have German abbots and monks in the fifteenth century and it became a contentious issue when the organisation of the Order became focused on the regional chapters. In 1487 the German community of Wągrowiec refused obedience to the abbot of Mogiła, the head of the Polish Cistercian province, and continued the recruitment of monks from Rhineland, refusing to accept Polish entrants. The issue became so politicised that successive royal decrees of 1538 and 1550 laid down that only Polish noblemen could be elected to the abbatial position in Wągrowiec and two other Cistercian houses in Greater Poland, and the conflict lasted until 1580 when the Polish monks took over control of the community.[150]

The responses of various Cistercian authorities, prominent abbots and the General Chapter to the prolonged process of fragmentation indicate that the Order was far from blind to the cultural and political divisions that were undermining its cohesion, but sought to cope with the problem by accommodating its structures to life in a fragmented world. Not that such an approach did much to slow down the process of fragmentation. On the contrary, military and political events in the Iberian peninsula in the early sixteenth century took the process of differentiation between regional chapters a stage further. Since the conclusion of the *Reconquista* in the 1490s, the descendants of Jewish and Muslims converts to Christianity had been treated with increased suspicion and intolerance and accused of secretly following their old beliefs; and the early-sixteenth-century Cistercian houses in the peninsula found themselves confronted with the controversial question of 'blood purity' (*Limpieza de sangre*) as the criterion for the admission of descendants of converted Jews and Muslims into religious orders and offices. The first royal statutes prohibiting the descendants of converts from holding ecclesiastical office were issued in the first half of the fifteenth century. In 1530 the abbot of Cîteaux forbade the abbess of Las Huelgas to admit girls of Jewish descent into the community, and in 1537 the statutes of the newly planned Cistercian Congregation of Aragon banned the admission of novices with Jewish or Muslim ancestry as far back as four generations. If such individuals were already among the monks, they were prohibited from being elected as abbots or cellarers.[151] Although the Iberian context was characterised by cultural and linguistic divisions of growing intolerance, in other parts of an increasingly fragmented Christendom too the unity of the Cistercian Order and its trans-European networks were being progressively eroded as regional chapters took precedence over the General Chapter. The Order was entering the post-medieval world.

Conclusions

The history of the Cistercian Order in the later middle ages is complex. Yet while it is all too often dismissed as an unrelieved process of decline, it was also a period of adjustment to change and renewal. The idea of reform was in fact central to the late medieval history of the white monks, much of whose rhetoric focused on returning to the 'roots' and upholding the practices and standards of the twelfth-century observance. Such a return to what was, after all, a mythical 'golden age' was, of course, not possible and even attempts to reverse the changes in the comfort and privacy of monastic buildings, especially by individual cells, heating and better food, usually failed. In the event, the most successful reforms, whether originating from the Order or the papacy, were those related to higher education. However, when it came to university education, the white monks did not strive to be at the forefront of theological debates or enter university faculties, but tried to use it for the benefit of the individual communities and the Order as a whole.

The late medieval Order was shaped by increased fragmentation, reflecting political boundaries, linguistic and cultural influences, but it still strove to maintain its trans-European filiation networks, even whilst Cîteaux and Clairvaux, given their location and the difficult political circumstances, lost effective power. True, they retained a certain influence as a point of reference, but in the circumstances neither the Cistercians in France nor the central structures there could find effective help locally and were forced to appeal to the papacy for protection. This proved a costly and unrewarding business for the already heavily indebted Order; and as papal authority weakened during the Schism it contributed to the erosion of the cohesion of the Order.[152] The final blow to Cîteaux and its structures centred on the Concordat of Bologna in 1516, when Pope Leo X gave the French king Francis I the right to nominate almost all benefices within the kingdom.[153] Although for some historians this marks the end of the medieval Cistercian Order, it was not the end of Cistercian monasticism.

Great wars had no doubt brought damage and destruction to many Cistercian communities; social and economic changes affecting landowners and burgesses and the commercialisation of the economy had marginalised many of the contemplative, rural-based religious orders. Yet while the mendicant orders played a major role in lay religiosity and in ecclesiastical politics, the Cistercians too made a number of successful attempts to reinvigorate their model of monasticism. Indeed, no one can doubt that Cistercian spirituality made a very important contribution to the late medieval religiosity beyond the monastic walls, that engagement with the cult of saints opened another point of contact between the laity and the Cistercian communities, or that intercessory prayers and burials never lost their importance. Although the lifestyle of Cistercian monks witnessed many changes between the twelfth and fourteenth centuries, from austere communal arrangements to comfortable private cells and a richer diet, and many monks were university graduates, these were not disastrous departures from the original ideal, but a natural reflection of the changes occurring in society as a whole.

Notes

1. Brian Patrick McGuire, *Cistercians in Denmark* (Kalamazoo, MI: Cistercian Studies, 1982), pp. 156–166; Bernhard Schimmelpfennig, 'The Papacy and the Reform of the Cistercian Order in the Late Middle Ages', in *Studiosorum Speculum: Studies in Honor of Louis J. Lekai O.Cist.*, ed. Francis R. Swietek and John R. Sommerfeldt (Kalamazoo, MI: Cistercian Studies, 1993), p. 337.
2. M. Kaczmarek, 'Związki modlitewne śląskich domów cysterskich z klasztorami niemieckimi w późnym średniowieczu', in *Niemcy-Polska w średniowieczu*, ed. Jerzy Strzelczyk (Poznań: Wydawnictwo Naukowe Uniwersytetu im. A. Mickiewicza, 1986), p. 41.
3. Brian Patrick McGuire, 'Spiritual Life and Material Life in the Middle Ages: A Contradiction?', in *Mensch und Objekt im Mittelalter und in der frühen Neuzeit. Leben – Alltag – Kultur*, ed. Gerhard Jaritz (Vienna: Verlag der Österreichischen Akademie der Wissenschaften 1990), p. 20.
4. Werner Rösener, 'Abbot Stephen Lexington and his Efforts for Reform of the Cistercian Order in the Thirteenth Century', in *Goad and Nail: Studies in Medieval Cistercian History*, ed. E. Rozanne Elder (Kalamazoo, MI: Cistercian Publications, 1985), p. 47.
5. Reinhard Schneider, 'Studium und Zisterzienserorden', in *Schulen und Studium im sozialen Wandel des hohen und späten Mittelalters*, ed. Johannes Fried (Sigmaringen: Thorbecke, 1986), p. 330; Daniel M. La Corte, 'Pope Innocent IV's Role in the Establishment and Early Success of the College of Saint Bernard in Paris', *Cîteaux: Commentarii Cistercienses* 46 (1995), p. 291.
6. La Corte, 'Pope Innocent IV's Role', pp. 301–302.

7. Severin Grill, 'Der erste Reformversuch im Cistercienserorden', *Cistercienser-Chronik* 36 (1924), pp. 49–54.
8. William Chester Jordan, *Unceasing Strife, Unending Fear: Jacques de Thérines and the Freedom of the Church in the Age of the Last Capetians* (Princeton, NJ: Princeton University Press, 2005), p. 75.
9. Patrick Nold, 'Pope John XXII's Annotations on the Franciscan Rule: Content and Contexts', *Franciscan Studies* 65 (2007), pp. 298–299; Jordan, *Unceasing Strife*, pp. 75–76, 79–81, 83.
10. *Magnum Bullarum Romanum: diplomatum et privilegiorum sanctorum romanorum pontificum taurinensis*, ed. Francesco Gaude, vol. 4 (Turin: Franco et Henrico Dalmazzo, 1859), pp. 203b–213b.
11. Schimmelpfennig, 'The Papacy and the Reform', p. 40.
12. Elke Goez, *Pragmatische Schriftlichkeit und Archivpflege der Zisterzienser. Ordenszentralismus und regionale Vielfalt, namentlich in Franken und Altbayern (1098–1525)* (Münster: Lit Verlag, 2003), pp. 117–118.
13. *Statuta capitulorum generalium ordinis Cisterciensis ab anno 1116 ad annum 1786*, ed. Joseph Canivez, 8 vols. (Louvain: Bureaux de la Revue, 1933–1941), vol. 3, 1335: 19; Bernhard Schimmelpfennig, 'Zisterzienserideal und Kirchenreform: Benedikt XII. (1334–42) als Reformpapst', *Zisterzienser-Studien*, vol. 3, ed. Wolfgang Ribbe (Berlin: Colloquium Verlag, 1976), pp. 29–36, tabulated content of the bull on pp. 32–33.
14. T.A. Heslop, 'Cistercian Seals in England and Wales', in *Cistercian Art and Architecture in the British Isles*, ed. Christopher Norton and David Park (Cambridge: Cambridge University Press, 1986), pp. 278, 280.
15. Peter King, *The Finances of the Cistercian Order in the Fourteenth Century* (Kalamazoo, MI: Cistercian Publications, 1985), pp. 8–10, 23, 99, 167.
16. *Statuta*, vol. 3, 1335: 4, 5; Schimmelpfennig, 'The Papacy and the Reform', pp. 341–342.
17. Louis Lekai, *The Cistercians: Ideals and Reality* (Kent, OH: Kent State University Press, 1977), p. 84; Schimmelpfennig, 'The Papacy and the Reform', p. 343.
18. Laetitia Boehm, 'Papst Benedikt XII. (1334–1342) als Förderer der Ordensstudien. Restaurator – Reformator – oder Deformator regularer Lebensformen?', in *Secundum Regulam Vivere: Festschrift für P. Norbert Backmund, O. Praem.*, ed. Gert Melville (Windberg: Poppe, 1978), pp. 281–310.
19. Schimmelpfennig, 'The Papacy and the Reform', p. 342.
20. *Letters to Cîteaux from the English Abbots to the Chapter at Cîteaux, 1442–1521*, ed. H. Talbot (London: Royal Historical Society, 1967), no. 50.
21. William J. Telesca, 'Problem of Commendatory Monasteries and the Order of Cîteaux during the Abbacy of Jean de Cirey, 1475–1501', *Cîteaux: Commentarii Cistercienses* 22 (1971), pp. 169–170.
22. Immo Eberl, *Die Zisterzienser: Geschichte eines europäischen Ordens* (Ostfildern: Jan Thorbecke, 2007), p. 326.
23. Jean-Marie Le Gall, *Les moines au temps des réformes: France (1480–1560)* (Seyssel: Champ Vallon, 2001), pp. 359, 272; Anne E. Lester, 'Cleaning the House in 1399. Disobedience and the Demise of Cistercian Convents

in Northern France at the End of the Middle Ages', in *Oboedientia. Zu Formen und Grenzen von Macht und Unterordnung im mittelalterlichen Religiosentum*, ed. Sébastien Barret and Gert Melville, Vita Regularis 27 (Münster: Lit Verlag, 2005), p. 242.
24. William J. Telesca, 'Jean de Cirey and the Question of an Abbot-General in the Order of Cîteaux in the Fifteenth Century', in *Studies in Medieval Cistercian History presented to Jeremiah F. O'Sullivan*, ed. John R. Sommerfeldt (Kalamazoo, MI: Cistercian Publications, 1971), vol. 2, pp. 190–207; William J. Telesca, 'The Cistercian Dilemma at the Close of the Middle Ages: Gallicanism or Rome', in *Studies in Medieval Cistercian History*, pp. 180–181; Telesca, 'Problem of Commendatory', pp. 171–172.
25. Johann Nider cited in Francis Oakley, *The Western Church in the Later Middle Ages* (Ithaca, NY: Cornell University Press, 1979), p. 231.
26. Oakley, *The Western Church*, pp. 231–238.
27. Lekai, *The Cistercians*, pp. 113–116; Telesca, 'The Cistercian Dilemma', p. 180.
28. Swen Holger Brunsch, *Das Zisterzienserkloster Heisterbach von seiner Gründung bis zum Anfang des 16. Jahrhunderts* (Siegburg: F. Schmitt, 1998), pp. 83–86.
29. Alison Luchs, 'Alive and Well in Florence: Thriving Cistercians in Renaissance Italy', *Cîteaux: Commentarii Cistercienses* 30 (1979), pp. 111–113.
30. Cornelia Oefelein, 'The Forgotten Library of the Sisters of Egeln: A List of the Books of the Former Cistercian Nuns' Abbey Marienstuhl in Egeln near Magdeburg', in *Truth as Gift: Studies in Medieval Cistercian History in Honor of John R. Sommerfeldt*, ed. Marsha Dutton (Kalamazoo, MI: Cistercian Publications, 2004), pp. 199–200.
31. *Statuta Capitulorum*, vol. 4, 1456: 53.
32. *Statuta Capitulorum*, vol. 4,1456: 15, 16, 115; vol. 5, 1482: 26; 1489: 43, 44.
33. Calmcille Ó Conbhuidhe, *Studies in Irish Cistercian History*, ed. Finbarr Donovan, foreword Roger Stalley (Dublin: Four Courts Press, 1998), pp. 12–47.
34. Elizabeth A. Lehfeldt, 'Gender, Order, and the Meaning of Monasticism during the Reign of Isabel and Ferdinand', *Archiv für Reformationsgeschichte* 93 (2002), pp. 145–157.
35. They came from the following abbeys: Cîteaux, Clairvaulx, Bonnevaux, Maulbronn, Cerreto, St Jean d'Aulps, la Chassagne, Preuilly, Tamié, Bonmont, Silvacane, Eberbach, Bonnecombe, Lieu-Croissant, Terdona, Acquafredda, S.M. della Columba of Piacenza, Val-St Lambert, Altenberg, Lucelle and Dundrennan.
36. William J. Telesca, 'The Order of Cîteaux during the Council of Basel, 1431–1449', *Cîteaux: Commentarii Cistercienses* 32 (1981), pp. 18–27.
37. Dagmar Zimdars, 'Ordenspropaganda der Zisterzienser in Bildbeispielen aus dem Kloster Maulbronn', in *Maulbronn. Zur 850jährigen Geschichte des Zisterzienserklosters*, ed. Dieter Planck (Stuttgart: K. Theiss, 1997), pp. 257–459, 463.

38. Reinhard Schneider, 'Zentralistische und divergierende Tendenzen in der Studienorganisationen der Zisterzienser', in *Ex Ipsis Rerum Documentis. Beiträge zur Mediävistik. Festschrift für Harald Zimmermann zum 65. Geburtstag*, ed. Klaus Herberts, Hans Henning Kortüm and Carlo Servatius (Signaringen: Thorbecke, 1991), pp. 495–508.
39. Werner Rösener, 'Abbot Stephen Lexington and his Efforts for Reform of the Cistercian Order in the Thirteenth Century', in *Goad and Nail*, pp. 47–48; Lekai, *The Cistercians*, pp. 79–81, 83–84.
40. *Statuta*, 1287: 238; Krzysztof Kaczmarek, 'Ustawodawstwo szkolne cysterskiej kapituły generalnej w XIII i XIV wieku', in *Nihil superfluum esse. Prace z dziejów średniowiecza ofiarowane Profesor Jadwidze Krzyżaniakowej* (Poznań: Instytut Historii Uniwersytetu Adama Mickiewicza, 2000), pp. 286–287.
41. Michal Svatoš, 'Obecné učení (1347/48–1419)', in *Dějiny Univerzity Karlovy 1348–1990*, ed. František Kavka and Josef Petráň (Prague: Univerzita Karlova, 1995), vol. 1, p. 56.
42. Franz Posset, *Renaissance Monks: Monastic Humanism in Six Biographical Sketches* (Leiden: Brill, 2005), p. 23.
43. Krzysztof Kaczmarek, 'Prowincja szkolna polskich cystersów w średniowieczu', *Nasza Przeszłość* 83 (1994), pp. 127, 129–131.
44. Lekai, *The Cistercians*, p. 84; Krzysztof Kaczmarek, 'Kariery zakonne cysterskich graduatów uniwersyteckich w średniowiecznej Polsce', in *Klasztor w kulturze średniowiecznej Polski*, ed. A. Pobóg-Lenartowicz and Marek Derwich (Opole: Wydawnictwo Św. Krzyża, 1995), pp. 84, 90.
45. Thomas Sullivan, 'Cistercian Theologians at the Late Medieval University of Paris', *Cîteaux: Commentarii Cistercienses* 50 (1999), p. 91, table 8 on p. 100.
46. *Statuta*, vol. 6, 1495: 31; David N. Bell, 'A Treasure-House for Monks? The Cistercian Chapter General and the Power of the Book from the Twelfth Century to 1787', *Cîteaux: Commentarii Cistercienses* 58 (2007), p. 118; Kaczmarek, 'Prowincja szkolna polskich cystersów', p. 132; *Statuta*, vol. 4, 1411, pp. 144–145.
47. Reinhard Schneider, 'Sprachprobleme in zisterziensischen Studienhäusern', in *Vita Religiosa im Mittelalter: Festschrift für Kaspar Elm zum 70. Geburtstag*, ed. Franz J. Felten and Nicholas Jaspert (Berlin: Duncker und Humblot, 1999), pp. 223–224.
48. Krzysztof Kaczmarek, 'Dlaczego cystersi z "Prus" nie chcieli studiować w Krakowie?', *Nasza Przeszłość* 96 (2001), pp. 202–206; *Statuta*, vol. 6, 1507: 15.
49. Posset, *Renaissance Monks*, p. 23.
50. *Statuta*, vol. 6, 1482: 41; *Letters to Cîteaux from the English Abbots*, no. 74; David N. Bell, 'Printed Books in English Cistercian Monasteries', *Cîteaux: Commentarii Cistercienses* 53 (2002), pp. 131–132.
51. Dariusz Aleksander Dekański, 'Kilka uwag o życiu intelektualnym cystersów oliwskich w średniowieczu', in *Ingenio et Humilitate. Studia z dziejów zakonu cystersów i Kościoła na ziemiach polskich*, ed. Andrzej Wyrwa (Katowice: Biblioteka Śląska, 2007), p. 290.

52. Brunsch, *Das Zisterzienserkloster Heisterbach*, p. 165.
53. Sullivan, 'Cistercian Theologians', pp. 90, 95.
54. Jaroslav Kadlec, 'Teologická fakulta', in *Dějiny Univerzity Karlovy 1348–1990*, ed. František Kavka and Josef Petráň (Prague: Univerzita Karlova, 1995), vol. 1, p. 146.
55. Kaczmarek, 'Kariery zakonne', pp. 89–90; Stephan Warnatsch, 'Abt Arnold von Monnikendam – eine zisterziensische Ordenskarriere', in *Spiritualität und Herrschaft*, ed. Oliver H. Schmidt, Heike Frenzel and Dieter Pötschke (Berlin: Lukas Verlag, 1998), pp. 132–162.
56. Wolfgang Ribbe, 'Zur Ordenspolitik der Askanier. Zisterzienser und Landesherrschaft im Elbe-Oder-Raum', in *Zisterzienser-Studien*, vol. 1 (Berlin: Colloquium Verlag, 1975), p. 94.
57. Posset, *Renaissance Monks*, pp. 29–39, 44–51.
58. Posset, *Renaissance Monks*, pp. 109–110, 125–131.
59. Patrick Brian McGuire, *The Difficult Saint: Bernard of Clairvaux and his Tradition* (Kalamazoo, MI: Cistercian Publications, 1991), p. 227; Charles L. Stringer, 'St Bernard and Pope Eugenius IV (1431–1447)', in *Cistercian Ideals and Reality*, ed. John R. Sommerfeldt (Kalamazoo, MI: Cistercian Publications, 1978), pp. 331–333.
60. Berndt Hamm, *Frömmigkeitstheologie am Anfang des 16. Jahrhunderts* (Stuttgart: Mohr, 1999), pp. 11–12.
61. Elizabeth Freeman, '"Houses of a Peculiar Order": Cistercian Nunneries in Medieval England, with Special Attention to the Fifteenth and Sixteenth Centuries', *Cîteaux: Commentarii Cistercienses* 55 (2004), p. 266, n. 80.
62. David N. Bell, *What Nuns Read: Books and Libraries in Medieval English Nunneries* (Kalamazoo, MI: Cistercian Publications, 1995), pp. 14–17.
63. Bell, 'Printed Books', p. 129.
64. Bell, 'Printed Books', pp. 132–133.
65. *Statuta*, vol. 5, 1454: 95, transl. in Bell, 'A Treasure-House for Monks?', p. 118.
66. Bell, 'A Treasure-House for Monks?', pp. 99–100, 113; *Statuta*, vol. 5, 1487: 14; complaints about manuscripts not being returned by Baumgarten, *Statuta*, vol. 6, 1503: 29.
67. Bell, 'A Treasure-House for Monks?', pp. 100–103; *Twelfth-Century Statutes from the Cistercian General Chapter: Latin text with English notes and commentary*, ed. Chrysogonus Waddell (Brecht: Cîteaux, Commentarii Cistercienses, 2002), 'The Instituta', p. 553; *Statuta*, vol. 6, 1522: 10; further statutes against ideas of Luther: vol. 6, 1523: 7, 1531: 54; 1557: 31, 1565/100–101.
68. Terryl Kinder, *Cistercian Europe: Architecture of Contemplation* (Kalamazoo, MI: Cistercian Publications, 2002), p. 355; Ribbe, 'Zur Ordenspolitik der Askanier', p. 93.
69. Nataša Golob, *Twelfth-Century Cistercian Manuscripts: The Sitticum Collection* (London and Ljubljana: Slovenska knjiga in conjunction with Harvey Miller, 1996), p. 24.

70. Bede K. Lackner, 'Early Cîteaux and the Care of Souls', in *Noble Piety and Reformed Monasticism*, ed. E.R. Elder (Kalamazoo, MI: Cistercian Publications, 1981), p. 57.
71. Ribbe, 'Zur Ordenspolitik der Askanier', p. 94
72. Karen Stöber, *Late Medieval Monasteries and their Patrons: England and Wales c. 1300–1540* (Woodbridge: Boydell Press, 2007), p. 40.
73. Af Sissel F. Plathe, 'Altertavlen i Esrum klosterkirke', in *Bogen om Esrum Kloster*, ed. Søren Frandsen, Jens Anker Jørgensen and Christian Gorm Torzen (Frederiksborg: Amt, 1997), pp. 156–157.
74. Patrick Brian McGuire, *The Difficult Saint: Bernard of Clairvaux and his Tradition* (Kalamazoo, MI: Cistercian Publications, 1991), pp. 238–243.
75. Charles L. Stinger, 'St Bernard and Pope Eugenius IV (1431–1447)', in *Cistercian Ideals and Reality*, ed. John R. Sommerfeldt (Kalamazoo, MI: Cistercian Publications, 1978), pp. 329–330.
76. John Van Engen, *Sisters and Brothers of the Common Life: The Devotio Moderna and the World of the Later Middle Ages* (Philadelphia, PA: University of Pennsylvania Press, 2008), pp. 142, 241.
77. Brian Patrick McGuire, 'A Saint's Afterlife. Bernard in the Golden Legend and in other Medieval Collections', in *Bernhard von Clairvaux. Rezeption und Wirkung im Mittelalter und in der Neuzeit*, ed. Kaspar Elm (Wiesbaden: Harrassowitz Verlag, 1994), pp. 179–205; Peter Ochsenbein, 'Bernhard von Clairvaux in spätmittelalterlichen Gebetbüchern', in *Bernhard von Clairvaux. Rezeption und Wirkung*, pp. 213–232.
78. Claire Cross, 'The Last Years of Roche Abbey', in *Monasteries and Society in the British Isles in the Later Middle Ages*, ed. Janet Burton and Karen Stöber (Woodbridge: Boydell, 2008), p. 231.
79. Claire Cross and Noreen Vickers, *Monks, Friars and Nuns in Sixteenth Century Yorkshire*, The Yorkshire Archaeological Society Record Series 150 (Huddersfield: Yorkshire Archaeological Society, 1995), pp. 134–135.
80. Gerhard Jaritz, ' "Transeuntes ad alium Ordinem": The Position of Cistercians and Carthusians in the Middle Ages', *Medium Aevum Quitidianum* 37 (1997), p. 39.
81. Urszula Borkowska, 'Kult liturgiczny św. Urszuli w Polsce do XVI wieku', *Roczniki Humanistyczne* 14 (1966), pp. 109–198.
82. Zofia Krzymuska-Fafius, 'Kaplica pielgrzymkowa cysterek koszalińskich na górze chełmskiej i jej wyposażenie', in *Cystersi w kulturze średniowiecznej Europy*, ed. J. Strzelczyk (Poznań: Wydawnictwo Naukowe UAM, 1992), pp. 329–335.
83. Franz Machilek, 'Die Wittelsbacher, Kloster Fürstenfeld und die Wallfahrt St. Leonhard zu Ichenhofen', in *Die Wittelsbacher im Aichacher Land. Gedenkschrift der Stadt Aichach und des Landkreises Aichach-Friedberg zur 800-Jahr-Feier des Hauses Wittelsbach*, ed. Toni Grad (Aichach: Mayer & Söhne, 1980), pp. 199–208.
84. Helen Zakin, 'Stained Glass Panels from Mariawald Abbey in the Cleveland Museum of Art', in *Perspectives for an Architecture of Solitude. Essays on Cistercians, Art and Architecture in Honour of Peter Fergusson*, ed. Terryl N. Kinder (Turnhout: Brepols and Cîteaux, 2004), pp. 261–267.

85. The list was reprinted in *Les monuments primitifs de la règle cistercienne*, ed. Philippe Guignard (Dijon: Imprimerie Darantiere, 1878); Jaap Van Moolenbroek, 'The Life and Cult of Emanuel Sescalco (d. 1298), Bishop of Cremona, but Buried in the Abbey of Aduard near Groningen', *Cîteaux: Commentarii Cistercienses* 62 (2011), p. 206.
86. Esther Wipfler, *'Corpus Christi' in Liturgie und Kunst der Zisterzienser im Mittelalter*, Vita Regularis 18 (Münster: Lit Verlag, 2003), pp. 17–18.
87. Archdale A. King, 'Eucharistic Reservations in Cistercian Churches', *Collectanea Ordinis Cisterciensium Reformatorum* 20 (1958), p. 243; Annegret Laabs, *Malerei und Plastik im Zisterzienserorden. Zum Bildgebrauch zwischen sakralem Zeremoniell und Stiftermemoria 1250–1430* (Petersberg: Michael Imhof Verlag, 2000), pp. 93–110.
88. Caroline Walker Bynum, *Wonderful Blood: Theology and Practice in Late Medieval Northern Germany and Beyond* (Philadelphia, PA: University of Pennsylvania Press, 2007), pp. 51, 55, 59, 62, 75.
89. Lekai, *The Cistercians*, p. 388.
90. Nicola Coldstream, 'Architecture from Beaulieu to the Dissolution', in *Cistercian Art and Architecture*, p. 158; Julie Kerr, 'Cistercian Hospitality in the Later Middle Ages', in *Monasteries and Society in the British Isles in the Later Middle Ages: Studies in the History of Medieval Religion*, ed. Janet Burton and Karen Stöber (Woodbridge: Boydel and Brewer, 2008), p. 31; paper of David N. Bell at the International Medieval Congress, Leeds, July 2009; *The Book of Margery Kempe*, ed. and trans. B.A. Windeatt (London: Penguin, 2004), p. 148.
91. *Urkunden der Abtei Heisterbach*, ed. Ferdinand Schmitz, Urkundenbücher der Geistlichen Stiftungen des Niederrheins 2 (Bonn, 1908), no. 238, p. 316.
92. Christopher Harper-Bill, 'Cistercian Visitation in the Late Middle Ages: the case of Hailes Abbey', *Bulletin of the Institute of Historical Research* 53 (1980), p. 105.
93. 'The Cistercians and Women: Access to Kirkstall Abbey Church', in *Monasticism in Late Medieval England, c. 1300–1535*, ed. and trans. Martin Heale (Manchester: Manchester University Press, 2009), pp. 125–126.
94. *Diplomatarium Danicum*, series II, vol. 2, no. 173; McGuire, *The Cistercians in Denmark*, p. 169.
95. Christian Krötzl, *Pilger, Mirakel und Alltag: Formen des Verhaltens im Skandinavischen Mittelater (12.–15. Jahrhundert)*, Studia Historica 46 (Helsinki: Suomen Historiallinen Seura, 1994), pp. 129, 148–150; *Margareeta Pohjolan Rouva ja Valtias: Kalmarin unioni 600 vuotta* (Stockholm: Nationalmuseet, 1997), pp. 240–241.
96. David Bell, 'From Molesme to Cîteaux: The Earliest "Cistercian" "Spirituality"', *Cistercian Studies Quarterly* 34 (1999), p. 474.
97. *Codex Diplomaticus Brandenburgensis*, ed. Adolph Riedel (Berlin: Reiner, 1860), vol. 19, pp. 444–445.
98. Gerhard Jaritz, 'The Standard of Living in German and Austrian Cistercian Monasteries of the Later Middle Ages', in *Goad and Nail*, pp. 57–59; Peter McDonald, 'The Papacy and Monastic Observance in the Later Middle

Ages: The *Benedictina* in England', *Journal of Religious History* 14 (1986), p. 119.
99. Jane Geddes, 'Cistercian Metalwork in England', in *Cistercian Art and Architecture*, p. 258.
100. Glyn Coppack, 'The Planning of Cistercian Monasteries in the Later Middle Ages, the Evidence from Fountains, Rievaulx, Sawley and Rushen', in *The Religious Orders in Pre-Reformation England*, ed. James Clark (Woodbridge: Boydell and Brewer, 2002), pp. 197–209; David N. Bell, 'Cistercian Scriptoria in England: What They Were and Where They Were', *Cîteaux: Commentarii Cistercienses* 57 (2006), p. 65.
101. *Statuta*, vol. 3, 1287: 9, 1314: 4, 1323: 12, 1327: 3, David N. Bell, 'Chambers, Cells, and Cubicles: The Cistercian General Chapter and the Development of the Private Rooms', in *Perspective for an Architecture of Solitude*, pp. 188–189.
102. *Statuta*, vol. 3, 1335: 23.
103. *Statuta*, vol. 3, 1370: 2.
104. Bell, 'Chambers, Cells, and Cubicles', pp. 190–192.
105. Jean de la Croix Bouton, 'Nuns of Cîteaux', in *Hidden Springs: Cistercian Monastic Women, Medieval Religious Women*, vol. 1, ed. John A. Nichols and Lilian Thomas Shank (Kalamazoo, MI: Cistercian Publications, 1995), p. 21.
106. *Statuta*, vol. 5, 1476: 67, vol. 6, 1494: 45; Bell, 'Chambers, Cells, and Cubicles', pp. 192–193.
107. Harper-Bill, 'Cistercian Visitation', p. 106.
108. In the event only 4 marks went to brother Heinrich, the rest being taken by the abbey. It seems that Heinrich Westfal had performed unsatisfactorily when in charge of the abbey's court (estate) in Vogelsang and had left the abbey without permission – possibly fearing punishment. It was his inheritance of 16 marks a year that allowed Heinrich to return to the abbey, with the latter taking its share of it as a kind of compensation for the actual or perceived economic mismanagement. Andreas Niemeck, 'Kloster und Stadt. Die Personell-sozialen Beziehungen zwischen den Zisterzienserklöstern Neuenkamp und Hiddensee und der Stadt Stralsund', in *Klöster und monastische Kultur in Hansestädten: Beiträge des 4. wissenschaftlichen Kolloquiums Stralsund 12. bis 15. Dezember 2001*, ed. Claudia Kimminus-Schneider and Manfred Schneider (Rahden: Verlag Marie Leidorf, 2003), pp. 140–141 and n. 16.
109. *Diplomatarium Danicum*, series II, vol. 6, no 91; McGuire, *The Cistercians in Denmark*, p. 183.
110. Heinrich Grüger, 'Die Monastiche Disziplin der Schlesischen Zisterzienser im Späten Mittelalter', in *Cystersi w kulturze średniowiecznej Europy*, pp. 69–70.
111. Hermann Diruf, 'Zwischen Infirmerie und Schloß. Baugeschichtliche Beobachtungen im östlichen Bereich der Klosteranlage', in *Maulbronn*, pp. 401–405.
112. *Monasticism in Late Medieval England, c. 1300–1435*, ed. Martin Heale (Manchester: Manchester University Press, 2009), pp. 19–20.

113. Paweł Stróżyk, 'Symbole władzy opata w przestrzeni klasztoru cysterskiego', in *Ingenio et Humilitate: Studia z dziejów zakonu cystersów i kościoła na ziemiach polskich*, ed. A.M. Wyrwa (Katowice: Biblioteka Śląska 2007), pp. 46–48.
114. Claudia Mohn, *Mittelalterliche Klosteranlagen der Zisterzienserinnen. Architektur der Frauenklöster im Mitteldeutschen Raum* (Petersberg: Michael Imhof Verlag, 2006), pp. 81–82.
115. Marek Derwich, 'Rola opata w koronacjach królów polskich', in *Imagines Potestatis: Rytuały, Symbole i Konteksty Fabularne Władzy Zwierzchniej. Polska X–XV w. (z przykładem czeskim i ruskim)*, ed. Jacek Baszkiewicz (Warsaw: Wydawnictwo Instytutu Historii PAN, 1994), p. 39.
116. C. Fergusson, 'St Mary's Abbey, Holme Cultram', *Transactions of the Cumbrian and Westmorland Antiquarian and Archaeological Society*, old series, 1 (1874), pp. 263–275.
117. Wolfgang Lehner, *Die Zisterzienserabtei Fürstenfeld in der Reformationszeit 1496–1623*, Münchener Theologische Studien (Munich: Anton H. Konrad: 1999), pp. 254–255.
118. Stróżyk, 'Symbole władzy opata', pp. 50, 56.
119. Grüger, 'Die Monastiche Disziplin', p. 76; *Statuta*, vol. 6, 1502:17.
120. Marek Wójcik, 'Średniowieczne pieczęcie cystersów rudzkich', in *Cystersi w społeczeństwie Europy Środkowej*, ed. Andrzej Marek Wyrwa and Józef Dobosz (Poznań: Wydawnictwo Poznańskie, 2000), p. 412; Martin Heale, 'Mitres and Arms. Aspects of the Self-representation of the Monastic Superior in Late Medieval England', in *Self-Representation of Medieval Religious Communities: the British Isles in Context*, ed. Anne Müller and Karen Stöber (Münster: Lit Verlag, 2009), pp. 111–113.
121. Pavel R. Pokorný, 'Znaky klášterů v českých zemích', in *Klasztor w społeczeństwie średniowiecznym i nowożytnym*, ed. Marek Derwich and Anna Pobóg-Lenartowicz (Opole: LARHCOR, 1996), p. 260.
122. Heale, 'Mitres and Arms, p. 109.
123. Zofia Krzymuska-Fafius, 'Późnogotycki pentaptyk z kościoła pocysterskiego w Bukowie Morskim fundacji opata Henryka Kresse, *Nasza Przeszłość* 83 (1994), pp. 492–495.
124. Adam Wienand, 'Der Marienpsalter von Zinna', in *Die Cistercienser. Geschichte – Geist – Kunst*, ed. Ambrosius Schneider, Adam Wienand, Wolfgang Bickel and Ernst Coester (Cologne: Wienand Verlag, 1986), pp. 171, 176.
125. *Records of the Monastery of Kinloss with Illustrative Documents*, ed. John Stuart (Edinburgh: Clark, for the Society of Antiquaries of Scotland, 1872), vol. 2, p. 32.
126. Bell, 'Printed Books', p. 139.
127. Edgar Krausen, 'Generalkapitel außerhalb Cîteaux während des großen Schismas', *Cistercienser-Chronik* 63 (1956), pp. 7–10; Telesca, 'The Cistercian Dilemma at the Close of the Middle Ages', pp. 166, 169; Janet Burton, 'Homines sanctitatis eximiae, religionis consummatae: the Cistercians in England and Wales', *Archaeologia Cambrensis* 154 (2005), p. 39.

128. King, *The Finances of the Cistercian Order*, pp. 174–175.
129. Telesca, 'Problem of Commendatory Monasteries a', p. 167.
130. Kinder, *Cistercian Europe*, p. 38; Ian B. Cowan, *The Scottish Reformation: Church and Society in Sixteenth Century Scotland* (London: Weidenfeld and Nicolson, 1982), p. 30.
131. Kinder, *Cistercian Europe*, p. 38; Cowan, *The Scottish Reformation*, p. 30; Jolanta M. Marszalska, 'Opaci komendatoryjni wobec książki. Przyczynek do dziejów opactwa cystersów w Szczyrzycu', in *Klasztor w społeczeństwie średniowiecznym*, p. 351.
132. Telesca, 'The Problem of the Commendatory Monasteries', pp. 156–158.
133. Daniel S. Buczek, 'Medieval Taxation: The French Crown, The Papacy and the Cistercian Order, 1190–1320', *Annalecta Cisterciensia* 25 (1969), pp. 42–106.
134. Lekai, *The Cistercians*, p. 104.
135. Lekai, *The Cistercians*, p. 107.
136. Luchs, 'Alive and Well in Florence', pp. 114–115.
137. Jörg Oberste, *Die Dokumente der Klösterlichen Visitationen, Typologie des Sources du Moyen Âge Occidental 80* (Turnhout: Brepols, 1999), p. 35.
138. James France, *The Cistercians in Scandinavia* (Kalamazoo, MI: Cistercian Publications, 1992), p. 321.
139. *Auctoritate Papae: the Church Province of Uppsala and the Apostolic Penitentiary 1410–1526*, ed. Sara Risberg and Kirsi Salonen, Diplomatarium Suecanum Appendix II (Stockholm: the National Archives of Sweden, 2008), no. 436 (on p. 452).
140. Megan Cassidy-Welch, 'Incarceration and Liberation: Prisons in Cistercian Monasteries', *Viator* 32 (2001), p. 41.
141. F. Donald Logan, *Runaway Religious in Medieval England c. 1240–1540* (Cambridge: Cambridge University Press, 1996), pp. 54–57.
142. Lekai, *The Cistercians*, p. 97.
143. Michael Toepfer, *Die Konversen der Zisterzienser. Untersuchungen über ihren Beitrag zur mittelalterlichen Blüte des Ordens* (Berlin: Duncker & Humblot, 1983), pp. 54–62.
144. Jerzy Kłoczowski, 'Cystersi w Europie Środkowowschodniej wieków średnich', in *Cystersi w społeczeństwie Europy Środkowej*, pp. 44–48.
145. Lekai, *The Cistercians*, p. 97; Telesca, 'The Cistercian Dilemma', p. 168; King, *The Finances of the Cistercian Order*, p. 192.
146. *La Désolation des Églises, Monastères, Hopitaux en France vers le milieu du XVe siècle*, ed. Henri Denifle, vol. 1 (Macon: Protat Freères, 1897), nos. 274, 498, 513, 557, 726, 891, 891, 897.
147. Gerhard Jaritz, 'Cistercian Migrations in the Later Middle Ages', in *Goad and Nail*, pp. 194–195.
148. Unpublished *Chronica Monasterii Pelplinensis*, cited in Marek Radach, 'Najazdy na opactwo pelplińskie i jego posiadłości w czasie wojny trzynastoletniej w świetle korespondencji krzyżackiej', in *Kulturotwórcza rola cystersów na Kociewiu*, ed. Aleksander Dariusz Dekanski (Pelplin-Tczew: Bernardinum, 2002), p. 55.

149. La Corte, 'Pope Innocent IV's Role', pp. 292–293; Bruno Griesser, 'Registum Epistolarum Stephani de Lexington', *Analecta Cisterciensia* 2 (1946), pp. 93, 102.
150. Leokadia Grajkowska, 'Polonizacja klasztoru cystersów w Wągrowcu', in *Cystersi w kulturze średniowiecznej Europy*, pp. 113–121.
151. José Rabory, 'Documentos sobre la Congregación de Aragón de la Orden del Cister', *Cistercium* 12 (1960), p. 248; Peter Feige, 'Filiation und Landeshoheit. Die Entstehung der Zisterzienserkongregationen auf der iberischen Halbinsel', in *Zisterzienser-Studien*, vol. 1 (Berlin: Colloquium Verlag, 1975), p. 66.
152. William J. Telesca, 'Papal Reservations and Provisions of Cistercian Abbey at the End of the Middle Ages', *Citeaux: Commentarii Cistercienses* 26 (1975), p. 137.
153. Telesca, 'The Cistercian Dilemma', pp. 183–184.

CONCLUSION

Whereas traditional histories of religious orders have generally been written in terms of cycles of development – rise, decline and reform – the aim of this book has been to get away from the narrative approach and to focus instead on the structures of the Cistercian movement in the middle ages, both as a trans-European order centred on its General Chapter, and as a congeries of individual houses with very diverse experiences. How far can one draw general conclusions from the experiences of one abbey, region or country? How relevant were developments at the centre and in the trans-European networks to those at a local level? Is it even worth attempting to encapsulate the history of the medieval Cistercian order over several centuries in one simple thesis or one interpretational model? It seems, in fact, that there are a number of central features and themes that characterise the Cistercian experience, both at the level of individual communities and at the centre, and it is these that this book considers to constitute the essence of the history of the Cistercian movement in the middle ages.

Most important is the concept of reform – as not only providing the background from which the movement emerged in the late eleventh century, but exercising a lasting influence on it to the end of the middle ages and beyond. The concept of reform as a renewal and reversion to the roots linked the Cistercians to longstanding monastic traditions going back to the Desert Fathers. It also helped to formulate an approach to the changing world of the later middle ages, in which adjustment to the new conditions and adoption of novel ideas and practices regarding higher education, the relationship between community and the abbot, and the Order's finances could be accommodated in such a way that neither individual houses and nor the Order lost what they considered to be their Cistercian identity. By evoking the *Carta Caritatis* and reiterating the role of the observance, late medieval Cistercian monks could adapt to change because the rhetoric of reform as a return to the roots gave it a moral and spiritual legitimacy.

The powerful concept of identity is the second key element of medieval Cistercian history. The memory of each monastic community recorded in the chronicles, cartularies, foundation histories, commemorative lists, genealogies and many other types of texts were essential to create a sense of belonging to the community. It provided a narrative of overcoming difficulties and illuminated the surrounding social environment. Because individual stories of Cistercian houses borrowed topoi from *Exordium Parvum* and other early Cistercian texts, they helped to sustain a sense of belonging to a trans-European network of monasteries with a shared tradition. This brings us to a third key element of medieval Cistercian history: the fact that the white monks were organised in structures that reached beyond individual houses influenced not only the nature of their communities, but the church as a whole.

The Cistercian Order represented the first developed form of religious organisation that came into being in the central middle ages. They pioneered the system of centre and periphery (General Chapter and individual abbeys) connected by filiation bonds. This was subsequently adopted by other religious organisations, especially the mendicants and, with Pope Benedict XII's reform, by the Cluniacs, Benedictines and Augustinians, who became organised orders. The normative guidelines laid down at the centre were applied to the whole of the Cistercian Order and its representative assemblies to create large structures capable of supervising both affairs of individual Cistercian monasteries and the communications between them.

Even stronger than the Order-wide connection centred on the General Chapter was the bond between mother and daughter housees, the filiation. This may account for the relative scarcity of chronicles of the whole Order (in contrast to the profusion of Dominican and Franciscan chronicles) as opposed to the single-abbey chronicles typical of the Cistercians. The authority of the father-abbot often loomed large over the daughter houses. The connection with the mother house was all-important. It was the channel through which oral and written information travelled, as well as exerting influence over the abbatial appointments.[1]

The fourth factor shaping the history of Cistercians in the middle ages was their engagement with the outside world. The local evidence shows clearly that the Cistercians owed their success in establishing monasteries throughout Christendom to the value that the lay society attached to the religious foundations and the ability of the monastic communities to fulfil the spiritual, devotional, social and cultural needs of wide range of people – founders, patrons, benefactors; those who wished to become Cistercian monks and nuns; and those who wanted to be buried in the Cistercian house, to visit a shrine located in the abbey church or chapel, or to receive charity. Separation from the world, through the architectural structure of the precinct and the selective approach to burials and commemorations, did not represent a rejection of the world – after all, the white monks shared the fundamental principle of monasticism as intercessor for the laity – but simply a proper observance: an observance by which monks were separated from the rest of the world but still fulfilled their duty towards it.

Finally, there was from the very foundation of the Order an element of tension between the centre and periphery, which became very pronounced in the later middle ages. 'Surviving cartularies show that local or regional affairs, interests or threats dominated the existence of many religious houses irrespective of their wider organisational affiliations.'[2] The regionalisation of the Cistercian order in the fourteenth and fifteenth centuries was paralleled by the fragmentation occurring within the church as a whole. 'The Order was founded upon the security of papal protection..., monastic exemption fared well behind a shield of *Privileges*... But the old institutions of Christianity did not survive the challenges of the fourteenth century and the Schism.'[3] Meanwhile, the Order had to contend with centrifugal forces on the macro-scale, such as the emergence of new monarchies with their thirst for control and taxation, rigid borders and destructive wars, and also, on a micro-scale, internal centrifugal forces such as linguistic and cultural changes, which affected specific regions. Although academic study and learning was a rewarding feature of the Cistercian experience in the later middle ages, it was never the aim or core of the Cistercian vocation.[4] In some respects university education also weakened Cistercian unity as monks' choice of university became restricted to their particular linguistic areas. Even at the highest institutional level, there was always something of a dichotomy between the centre and the periphery. In the later middle ages, as the efficiency of the international network decreased and political, social and even linguistic barriers proliferated, and Cîteaux remained the symbolic centre of the Order, the most prominent houses in different regions took over the role of centre in their localities.

Historians of the Cistercian Order have traditionally focused most on its early history, and even monographs on individual houses usually pay more attention to the high middle ages than to the fourteenth and fifteenth centuries. Admittedly, the source material for Cistercian history in the later middle ages is distinctly more sparse for some parts of Europe than for others, but this cannot account for the concentration on the twelfth and thirteenth centuries. It is rather a consequence of a fairly entrenched assumption that as the Cistercian Order lost its vitality after 1300 and the white monks became just like any other rural religious community, they ceased to be an appropriate subject for a special study. In fact, however, examples of vitality and correct observance abound up to the very end of the middle ages, and even a catalogue of examples of 'corruption' only shows, in the context of other thriving or at least satisfactorily functioning monasteries, that the picture was altogether too complex to summarise in black or white terms. As David Bell has observed: 'adaptation is not necessarily decadence, though if the prurient wish to hunt for examples of decadence, they will undoubtedly find them'.[5]

Just as late medieval Cistercian history as a whole has been neglected, the role of Cistercian nuns has been marginal to the narrative of the male part of the order. For a long time, Cistercian nuns were believed to be late and reluctant arrivals in the Order, almost amounting to a 'problem' for the monks, although recent historiography has acknowledged the female presence in the movement from the very beginning. White nuns' life at community level are far less well documented than those of the monks. This is partly just a question of poor source survival, but is also linked to the complexity of associations that nunneries had with the Cistercian Order. Not all Cistercian nunneries were formally part of the order, but all of them shared Cistercian spirituality. This brings us to the important issue of the boundaries of the Order and the nature of Cistercian observance. Was being a Cistercian monastery – either male or female – primarily a matter of organisation, belonging to the specific structure, or a matter of sharing a particular ethos and spirituality? The example of female communities is particularly valuable as the Cistercian religiosity, the role of charity and emotive spirituality, is what drew nunneries to seek a place in the Cistercian Order.

The Cistercian Order beyond the Middle Ages

The Reformation, and the blows it inflicted on monastic life, did not, of course, end the history of the Cistercian Order. The impact of the Reformation varied greatly across Europe; in England communities of the white monks were suppressed together with all other religious houses in the 1530s, and their buildings, furnishings and lands were requisitioned by the crown and generally sold off. Although the Reformation only arrived in Scotland later, in the 1560s, it arrived in a Calvinist version that was even more destructive of the fabric of Cistercian monasteries. In Lutheran territories, in northern Germany and in Scandinavia, there was no uniformity in the handling of monastic houses: they were all subject to suppression to different degrees. In Denmark monasteries were not abolished, but their abbots had to swear an oath of loyalty to the new religion. After 1539 all Danish monasteries were obliged to provide religious education for protestant priests, and Cistercian libraries came to include works by Luther and other Protestant reformers.[6] It was a gradual process in which the Cistercian communities faded out, rather than a brutal closure. Similarly in Sweden, where monastic lands and valuables were confiscated and a ban on accepting novices was introduced in 1527, it took a few decades for monasticism to finally fade away. In northern Germany dukes and princes who turned to Lutheranism were perhaps more assiduous in suppressing monastic houses and taking over their properties: many abbeys became the centres of landed estates, with their buildings reconfigured as residences, administrative centres or hunting lodges.

Cistercian abbeys in the regions that remained Catholic – Italy, Spain, France, southern Germany, Austria and Poland – continued to function, but also underwent many changes. The progressive fragmentation of the trans-European Order strengthened the power of national chapters and the proliferation of separate congregations with the Order;[7] Cistercian churches were rebuilt or redecorated, but in the Baroque style typical of the Counter-Reformation. In other respects, many of the tendencies characteristic of late medieval monasticism continued: the problem of commendatory abbots remained to plague Cistercian communities, the elevated status of the abbatial office developed even further. In the seventeenth and eighteenth centuries many abbatial residences were rebuilt as elegant palaces with formal gardens, enriching still more the visual splendour of the office, while formal portraits of Cistercian abbots and abbesses presented them as powerful aristocrats and prelates. The influence of post-Tridentine innovations was felt in the Order, for example the establishment of schools in the Cistercian abbeys.

Meanwhile, the concept of reform and renewal, so important in the medieval history of the Order, continued to make an impact in the sixteenth and seventeenth centuries, most notably in the Trappist movement, founded by Armand Jean le Bouthillier de Rancéa, commendatory abbot of La Trappe Abbey in Normandy, after his spiritual conversion in 1664 leading to the formation of the reformed congregation within the Cistercian Order. Its essence was the strict and literal adherence to the Rule of Benedict and to the Cistercian observance as regards communal arrangements, austerity and the Divine Service. The role of manual labour was given far more prominence than in the 'traditional' Cistercian observance.

Whilst the French Revolution was a major blow to monasticism in France, with the physical destruction of the proto-mothers of the Order, and substantial losses of irreplaceable archival material and libraries, most of the Cistercian houses in central Europe, not only in Protestant Prussia but in territories under Catholic Habsburg and Wittelsbach control, were subject to suppression during the nineteenth century, with only a small number being able to survive without a break into the twentieth and twenty-first centuries. Already by 1891 the centuries-old Cistercian family had been formally divided into the two separate orders – Cistercians of Common Observance (O.Cist) and Trappists (OCSO) – which continue to maintain monastic houses on all continents to this day.[8]

Of course, as far as the middle ages are concerned, the Cistercians are widely regarded as one of the most successful religious orders. Yet there is no one agreed definition for measuring success: it might be defined as maintenance of the spiritual principles ascribed to the founders of the movement; or the ability to influence ecclesiastical and secular politics; or the engineering of economic prosperity that translates into impressive architecture; or even simply good administration.[9] Modern assessments of Cistercian success have always reflected the perspective, methodologies and assumption of the historians writing about them. In the hey-day of economic history in the 1960s and 1970s the study of Cistercian monasticism was dominated by analyses of the economic activity of the monasteries, which largely ignored any religious dimensions of the white monks' communities that were highly valued in the medieval society. Such a perspective was of a piece with assumptions about the declining role of Christianity at institutional and societal level in the twentieth century. For historians who liked to describe the Reformation as 'inevitable', the image of the moral decline and practical failure of the Cistercian Order fitted in very well with their view of the late medieval church. As the violent events of the present century have reminded us, however, religion can be a very powerful motor of human behaviour; and the experience of globalisation has perhaps given us a clearer appreciation of the importance of extensive networks than was vouchsafed to earlier historians. Ultimately, it is easier now to describe medieval Cistercian history as a multi-faceted one, which cannot be explained by one paradigm, model or linear narrative of development, success and decline.

Notes

1. Jens Röhrkasten, 'Regionalism and Locality as Factors in the Study of Religious Orders', in *Mittelalterliche Orden und Klöster im Vergleich: Methodische Ansätze und Perspektive*, ed. Gert Melville and Anna Müller, Vita Regularis 34 (Berlin: Lit Verlag, 2007), p. 253.
2. Röhrkasten, 'Regionalism and Locality', p. 255.
3. William J. Talesca, 'The Order of Cîteaux During the Council of Basel, 1431–1449', *Cîteaux: Commentarii Cistercienses* 32 (1981), p. 35.
4. David Bell, 'Printed Books in English Cistercian Monasteries', *Cîteaux: Commentarii Cistercienses* 53 (2002), p. 135.
5. Bell, 'Printed Books', p. 138.

6. Patrick Brian McGuire, *Conflict and Continuity at Øm Abbey: A Cistercian Experience in Medieval Denmark* (Copenhagen: Museum Tusculanum, 1976), p. 132.
7. These include, for example, 1567 Congregation of Portugal, 1616 Congregation of the Crown of Aragon, 1623 Roman Congregation, 1623 German Congregation, 1806 Helvetic Congregation and 1894 Swiss-German Congregation.
8. Their official websites are: www.ocso.org and www.ocist.org
9. Röhrkasten, 'Regionalism and Locality', p. 265.

GLOSSARY

Ambulatory: a semicircular passage in the east end of the church behind the sanctuary where the high altar is located.
Antiphonary: a liturgical book use by the choir during the mass.
Apse: the semicircular-shaped east end of the church.
Black monks: an informal name for Benedictine monks, alluding to the colours of their habits.
Blood-letting: removing a quantity of blood for curative or preventive reasons.
Bull: a formal papal letter authenticated by a lead seal know as a bulla.
Carthusians: a reformed congregation and later order established by St Bruno in 1084; each monastery is a collection of individual hermitages.
Cartulary: a collection of copies of document (in full or summaries) relating to the properties of a monastery.
Charter: a written record of property transaction, grant of assets or rights.
Chasuble: a highly decorated outer liturgical vestment worn by priests for the celebration of mass.
Chevet: a form of an east end of the church including sanctuary, ambulatory and radiating chapels
Church Fathers: a group of early theologians (between second and sixth centuries) whose works became a cornerstone of the medieval church's teaching. There was no fixed list of who was a Father and who was not, but the most important were Augustine, Ambrose, Jerome, Cassian and Pope Gregory the Great.
Cloister: an enclosed rectangle space at the centre of the monastery; usually the central open space (garth) was surrounded by covered galleries or walkways.
Cluny: a monastery founded in Burgundy in 909/10 by Duke William of Aquitaine, who granted it freedom from all external interference (including his own and that of his family), and placed it under the protection of the pope. Cluny's influence grew in the tenth and eleventh centuries and it came to stand at the head of a family of monasteries, and its practices were influential in monasteries that were not directly part of this family.
Coenobitic: a communal way of life of monastic communities, *see also* eremitic.

GLOSSARY

Collation: the daily meeting of the monks for reading in the north cloister walk.

Commendatory abbot: a person (lay or ecclesiastic) who has a right to draw revenue from a monastery, but does not perform the normal duties of the abbot. Usually a non-resident.

Confraternity: a form of association between a religious institution (monastery, cathedral or even a parish church); its prime role was to aid the salvation of the soul. The names of members of the confraternity were entered into the Books of Life (*Libri Vitae*).

Conversi (lay brothers): a distinct group of members of Cistercian communities who took simplified monastic vows, but whose prime role was manual labour. Their status was lower than that of the choir monks.

Corrody: a type of old-age pension guaranteeing board and upkeep of a lay person until death in a religious house. A person holding it was called a corriodian. Corrody could have been purchased with money or held by royal or episcopal appointment.

Cowl: a religious dress worn by monks. A long, loose robe with wide sleeves and a deep hood. Cistercian cowls were white or greyish-white.

Customary (pl. customaries, Latin *consuetudines*): a set of rules, norms and procedures governing life in a monastery. It was use to supplement general regulations of the Rule of Benedict. The Cistercian customary was *Ecclesiastica officia*.

Definitor (pl. *definitores*): literally 'the one who defines', a member of the executive committee of the General Chapter.

Desert Fathers: a group of third- and fourth-century monks and hermits who lived particularly ascetic life in the deserts of Egypt, Syria and Palestine. They were venerated as saints and their writing and hagiography became very influential in the medieval monasticism.

Devotio Moderna: a lay religious movement in the fourteenth and fifteenth century originating in the Netherlands and focusing of emotive piety, inner devotion and meditation.

Divine Office: a set of collective daily services performed by the monastic communities: Vigils, Lauds, Prime, Terce, Sext, None, Vespers and Compline.

Ecclesiastica Officia: a book of customs and practices followed by the Cistercian communities.

Eremitic: a secluded way of life of monks who do not form one community but live separately, sometimes in loose groupings.

Eucharist: literally the re-enactment of the Last Supper. During the mass, the bread and wine are transformed into the body and blood of Christ (this doctrine is known as transubstantiation). The Eucharist is the principal sacrament of the Christian church.

Exemplum (pl. *exempla*): a short story used in sermons to explain and illustrate a moral or doctrinal issue.

Feast of Purification of Mary (2 February): marking 40 days after the birth of Jesus, his presentation in the Temple and ritual purification of Mary. Its alternative name, Candlemas, refers to the tradition of blessing of candles.

Florilegium (pl. *florilegia*): literally a gathering of flowers, denoting a collection of extracts of various texts ('best of').

Galilee porch: a western porch of a church.

Gradual: a volume containing all sung parts of the mass.

Glossa: a commentary on Biblical passages.

Granges (Latin *grangium*): Cistercian farms ranging in size from 15 to 200 hectares managed by a master of the grange, usually a lay brother. Depending on the local conditions, granges could specialise in particular type of production (wool, cheese, wine, meat production, horse breeding, etc.) or general farming.

Great Schism: a split within the Latin Church between 1378 and 1417, when a succession of rival popes resided in Rome and Avignon, leading to a crisis of authority with the church.

Gregorian Reform: a series of reforms between *c.* 1050s and *c.* 1080s, culminating during the papacy of Gregory VII (1073–1085). Its main focus was on the moral reform of the clergy and strengthening of papal authority, but in its final stage it became a conflict between the papal and lay power over who had the right to appointment to the high church offices.

Hagiography: writing about saints, especially lives (holy biographies).

Hauskloster: a monastery established by a noble or royal founder to commemorate the family and secure burials for the subsequent generations. Often the patrons had significant control over the finances of such a monastery and influenced abbatial appointments.

Heresy: any kind of false belief about central articles of the Christian faith. For a belief to be heretical it is essential that the person holding it persists in doing so deliberately and obstinately even after it has been pointed out that it is wrong.

Horarium: a daily schedule of prayers and masses which members of a religious community follow.

Hundred Years War: a series of wars between France and England (1337–1453) over succession and control of a large part of French territory.

Hussites: a religious and political movement in fifteenth-century Bohemia originating in the teaching of Jan Hus (d. 1415), who was condemned as a heretic and burned at the Council of Constance.

GLOSSARY

Lent: a period in the liturgical year of 40 days from Ash Wednesday to Easter marked by fasting (especially abstinence from meat and animal fats), abstinence from sexual intercourse and in general from many kinds of secular activity, including fighting. For members of religious orders it was also marked by more intense penance and prayer.

Liturgy: in the broadest sense, the whole complex of official services, all the rites, ceremonies, prayers and sacraments of the church. More narrowly, it can also mean specific arrangements of the above used by a particular church (e.g. Roman Liturgy).

Monstrance: a liturgical vessel in which the Eucharistic host is displayed in the church during particular devotional services and also taken in the processions.

Nave: the central, largest and main part of the church where the congregation stands; it is located on the approach to the altar.

Novice: a person who has entered a religious order and is undertaking probation period, but has not yet taken final vows.

Oblate (child oblate): a child given to a monastery by its parents or guardians as a gift. They usually remained as a monk or a nun for the rest of their lives.

Observance: an act of practising and following a specific set of rituals and practices.

Opus Dei: literally the 'work of God', denoting services held by the monastic community at night and day, which form the centre of monastic life.

Order of Savigny: a reform religious congregation originating in the early twelfth century from France and merged with the Cistercians in 1147.

Orders, holy: the ranks of the clergy, divided into major orders (bishops, priests and deacons) and minor orders (various grades and titles). Entry into orders was marked by shaving the head (tonsure) and by the laying on of hands. Only bishops could confer orders, which (for priests and bishops) meant the power to administer sacraments.

Penance: the act of showing repentance for some sin or crime committed. Can involve abstaining from some food, undertaking a pilgrimage, or giving a donation the church.

Pietà: a depiction (usually sculptural) of the Virgin Mary holding the lifeless body of Christ taken from the cross. It developed as a type of popular devotional image in northern Europe in the early fourteenth century.

Pittance: a gift to the members of a religious community for masses in commemoration of the benefactors, consisting of an extra allowance of food or wine.

Pontificals: the vestments and insignia symbolising episcopal status.

Profession: becoming a permanent member of a religious community by taking vows.

Proto-abbots: in the Cistercian Order the abbots of the oldest communities of Cîteaux, La Ferté, Pontigny, Clairvaux and Morimond.

Psalter: a volume containing the Biblical Book of the Psalms, often bound together with other devotional texts such as the litany of the saints.

Quadrivium: the upper level of the medieval university curriculum, consisting of four subjects: arithmetic, geometry, music and astronomy.

Retable: the most common shape of a late medieval altarpiece.

Rule of Benedict (Benedictine Rule): the most widespread rule for monks; believed to be written by St Benedict in the sixth century.

Sacraments: the seven actions performed by the church: baptism, confirmation, the Eucharist, penance, extreme unction (anointing with holy oil at the point of death), holy orders and marriage.

Sempringham Order (Gilbertine Order): a branch of regular canons established *c.* 1130 by Gilbert of Sempringham, a Lincolnshire priest. It had both male and female branches and some of the Gilbertine houses were also double (two monasteries – one for canons the other for nuns – side by side).

Simony: the term was applied especially to direct payment for church office, but could also be used to denote any kind of favour or benefit offered to acquire a church office or a church sacrament.

Stall: a seating in the church for the members of religious community, located in the chancel.

Templars (Knights Templar): a religious military order combining elements of contemplative spirituality of Cistercians with an active role in defence of the church and Christianity. It was formed in the Holy Land after the First Crusade. The name of the order refers to the Temple of Solomon in Jerusalem, which was its first headquarters.

Tithes: the tenth part of profit from the land paid to the church.

Transept: in Romanesque and Gothic churches, a transverse section located across the nave. It can also denote either of the two lateral arms of such a part.

Transubstantiation: the theological concept of the change by which the substance, but not the appearance, of the bread and wine in the Eucharist is retransformed into Christ's body and blood (known as 'Real Presence'). It was first proclaimed by the church in the canons of the IV Latern Council in 1215.

Trivium: the basic school curriculum, comprising grammar, rhetoric and logic.

GLOSSARY

Tympanum (pl. Tympana): in Romanesque architecture, a semicircular area above the door and below the archway, usually decorated with sculptural relief.

Vita Apostolica: literally 'the way of the Apostles', a central concept of the reformed movements of the late eleventh and twelfth centuries. It was conceived of as a return to the values and forms of primitive Christianity, a simple life in common.

Vir Dolorum: literally 'the man of sorrow', a medieval iconographical motif depicting the resurrected Christ with a painful facial expression pointing to the wounds resulting from the crucifixion.

White monks: an informal name for Cistercian monks, because of the greyish-white colour of their habits (note in German that the term 'grey monks' is used).

INDEX

abbess, 133, 137–139, 141–142, 144, 146, 148, 149, 254, 258, 261, 263, 289
abbot, 8, 15, 16, 17, 18, 20, 27, 30, 31, 33, 34, 44–49, 51, 55–61, 63, 65–68, 72, 75, 77, 81, 82, 93–96, 102, 104, 106, 108, 113, 114, 116, 125, 129, 131, 133–136, 137, 138, 143, 146, 160, 161, 165, 166, 167, 168, 178, 188, 194, 209, 211–213, 218, 222–224, 238, 240, 241–243, 246, 247, 249–251, 263–265, 266 269, 272, 285, 286
  burial, 57, 63, 104, 162, 167
  coat of arms, 264, 265
  commendatory, 244–246, 251, 265, 267, 268, 289
  holy, 104, 162–163, 167, 220, 226, 257
  'privilege of pontifical', 264, 265
  residence, 57, 61, 171, 263
  seal, 242, 264
Abelard, 29, 31, 229
Acquafredda Abbey, 73, 276 n. 35
Adam of Perseigne, 55, 60, 114, 126, 142
Alain of Lille, 64, 67
Alberic of Trois-Fontaines Abbey, 226
Alexander III, pope, 20, 27, 34
altar, 48, 97, 160, 161, 201, 227, 225, 255, 258
  altarpiece, 99, 163, 172, 173, 174, 175, 178, 255, 263, 265
  high, 95, 104, 105, 106, 162, 174
  retable, 173

Altenberg Abbey, 106, 162, 174, 236 n. 75, 251, 256, 257, 270, 272, 276, n. 35
  Arnold von Monnikendam, abbot of, 251
Altenkamp Abbey, 30
Altzella Abbey, 143, 165, 192, 213
Alvastra Abbey, 69, 75, 143, 144
  Stefan, the first archbishop of Uppsala, monk of, 75
Amelungsborn Abbey, 65, 79
  Berno, monk of, 79
Anacletus, pope, 32
Anjou, 7
  Charles of, 113
antiphonary, 15, 143, 161, 176, 210
Aragon, 45, 197, 243
  Congregation of, 272
  James I, king of, 98
archive, 46, 61, 208, 215–217, 219, 223
Argensolles nunnery, 146
armarium – *see* library
Articuli Parisienses, 243, 244
Assisi, 259
Aubepierre Abbey, 45
Auberger, Jean-Baptiste, 24
Aubert, Marcel, 159
Augsburg, 198, 199
Augustinian Canons, 50, 53, 57, 80, 97, 100, 105, 135, 139, 242, 245, 286
Augustinian Hermits, 230
Aulne Abbey, 249
Aulps Abbey, 17
Austria, 5, 69, 104, 210, 256, 271, 289

INDEX

Autun, bishops of, 244
Auxerre, 146, 244
  Alain of, 34
  Geoffrey of, 28, 34
Avignon, 46, 147, 244, 266, 268
  Cistercian college in, 212
Axholm Priory, 256
Aywières nunnery, 127, 142
  Lutgard, nun of, 142, 149

Babenberg, 100
  Leopold VI, duke, 104
Balerne Abbey, 244
Balmerino Abbey, 223
Baltic, 43, 72, 74, 79, 80, 81, 159, 186, 193, 224, 271
Barbeau Abbey, 131
Baumgarten, 210, 254, 278 n. 66
  Nicolas Wydenbosch, abbot of, 253–254, 255
Baumgartenberg Abbey, 210
Beaulieu Abbey, 47, 48, 109, 114, 200
  Denis, abbot of, 48
  Hugh, abbot of, 47, 114
  John, abbot of, 114
Beaulieu Abbey (Cyprus), 74
Bebenhausen Abbey, 107, 167, 265
Begard Abbey, 49
beguines, 113, 127, 130, 140
Bell, David, 212, 288
Bellevaux Abbey, 30, 54
Belmont Abbey, 74
Benedict XII, pope, 242, 266, 286
Benedict, saint, 23, 99, 128, 163, 177
Benedictines, 2, 6, 7, 8, 13, 15, 16, 17, 18, 19, 21, 25, 26, 27, 29, 30, 34, 43, 46, 49, 51, 55, 57, 63, 64, 66, 74, 77, 93, 95, 97, 101, 102, 107, 108, 115, 126, 130, 134, 140, 157, 164, 168, 175, 176, 178, 184, 211, 220, 221, 222, 224, 226, 227, 242, 245, 246, 247, 267, 286
benefactor, 1, 6, 8, 18, 19, 52, 53, 60, 66, 92, 93, 94, 95–101, 104, 105, 107, 108, 111, 112, 113, 115, 116, 124, 125, 126, 131, 137, 144, 145, 148, 156, 163, 164, 172, 176, 177, 178, 184, 185, 189, 190, 194, 197, 200, 201, 203, 218, 219, 221, 231, 248, 255, 260, 264, 265, 266
Berdoues Abbey, 196
Bergen nunnery, 145, 146
Berman, Constance, 24–25, 49, 64, 128, 148, 187
Bernard of Clairvaux, 3, 7, 8, 13, 15, 16, 17, 18, 21, 23, 25, 26, 28–33, 35, 55, 58, 60, 72, 78, 79, 92, 99, 125, 126, 156, 157, 158, 162, 208, 209, 212, 215, 225, 227, 228, 229, 231, 252, 255
  Apologia ad Guillelmum, 25, 156
  'Bernardine Renaissance', 252
  cult, 158, 162, 163, 173, 174, 178, 246, 256
  De consideratione ad Eugenium Papam, 32
  letters of, 17, 28–29, 31, 125
  sermons, 208, 212, 225, 227, 229, 255
  visual representations, 173–174
  Vita Prima, 18, 21, 34
  Vita Secunda, 34
Bernstein nunnery, 258
Bethlehem, 259
Bible, 15, 169, 175, 176, 210, 212, 214, 252
  exegesis, 209, 212
  Psalms, 48, 62, 78, 98, 214, 269
  Song of Songs, 25, 174, 227, 228
bishops, 15, 27, 28, 29, 30, 31, 32, 47, 51, 52, 57, 61, 72, 80, 81, 101, 102, 105, 106, 107, 108, 112, 130, 131, 132, 133, 134, 135, 138, 139, 144, 166, 167, 177, 213, 217, 221, 226, 243, 253
  former Cistercian monks as, 28, 33, 34, 35, 68, 74, 79, 82, 114

· 299 ·

INDEX

Black Death, 64, 92, 175, 200, 269, 270
Bohemia, 22, 69, 75, 99, 103, 109, 114, 140, 162, 187, 188, 222, 247, 264, 271
  Elizabeth Richenza, queen of, 147
  Wenceslaus II, king of, 109, 114, 147
Bolonia, 249
Boniface VIII, pope, 140
Boniface IX, pope, 259, 266
Bonmont Abbey, 69, 276 n. 35
books, 48, 64, 96, 97, 208–211, 213, 214, 216, 248, 250, 253, 254, 262
  donation, 101, 143, 210, 250
  liturgical, 14, 16, 50, 81, 176, 208, 210, 253, 254
  printed, 214, 253, 254
  reading, 6, 20, 44, 62, 63, 165, 166, 167, 169, 208, 210, 215, 225, 231
  storage, 165, 212, 213–214
  vernacular, 141, 143, 214–215, 219, 255
  writing, 34, 209, 214, 218–224, 254
  see also library, manuscript, scriptorium
Boquen Abbey, 213
Bordesley Abbey, 190
Boston (Lincolnshire), 199
Bouchard, Constance, 24, 96, 184
Brandenburg, 54, 93, 143, 174, 210, 254, 258
breviar, 254
Bridgettine Order, 143
Brigitta, saint, 143–144
Brittany, 95, 98, 125
Buch Abbey, 260
Buckfastleigh Abbey, 61
Buildwas Abbey, 214, 216
bull, papal, 20, 45, 74, 126, 129, 140, 147, 217, 218, 231, 240, 241, 242, 243, 245, 250, 257, 261, 262, 264, 268

Burgundy, 13, 14, 28, 29, 49, 69, 74, 94, 97, 98, 107, 140, 178, 241, 244
  Charles the Bold, duke of, 244
  Odo I, duke of, 14
burial, 4, 21, 53, 94, 115
  of lay people, 99, 101–106, 109, 110, 113, 131, 132, 145–147, 200, 201, 222, 255, 259, 263, 274, 286
  of monks, 161
  tombs, 57, 63, 104, 105, 106, 145, 146, 162, 163, 167, 177, 201, 259
Burton, Janet, 9, 135
Byland Abbey, 52, 67, 114, 165, 192, 220, 223
  Historia Fundationis, 220, 223
Byszew Abbey, 48

Caesarius of Arles, 128
Caesarius of Heisterbach, *Dialogus miraculorum*, 60, 78, 126, 142, 175, 228, 257
Calatrava Order, 74
calendar, liturgical, 60, 76, 210, 219, 257
Calixtus II, pope, 20, 30
Camaldoli, 6, 7, 64
Cañas Abbey, 139
Canivez, Joseph, 24
canon law, 212, 213, 214, 251
canonisation, 23, 33, 34, 103, 144, 162, 163
Canterbury, 134, 243, 259
  Henry Chichele, archbishop of, 253
  Richard, archbishop of, 27
cantor, 48, 49, 56, 58, 78, 214, 257
Carlisle, 114, 200
Carta Caritatis, 8, 20–21, 22, 24, 25, 44, 157, 158, 241, 285
Carthusians, 6, 7, 64, 97, 113, 141, 245, 251, 256
cartulary, 49, 133, 217–218, 223, 231, 285, 287
Casamari Abbey, 32, 78

INDEX

Castile, 45, 69, 139, 243
   Alfonso VIII, king of, 113, 145
   Alfonso X, king of, 98
   Congregation of, 133, 268
   Eleanor, queen of, 133, 145
Catalonia, 45
cellarer, 56, 57, 58, 66, 67, 68, 186, 193, 215, 219, 261, 273
La Celle Abbey, 79
Cestello Abbey, 163–164, 246, 268
Chaalis Abbey, 192, 210
Châlon, 15, 27, 29, 244
Champagne, 28, 29, 73, 103, 137, 198, 200, 210
chantry, 105, 145, 201
chants, 15, 16, 22, 58, 62, 78, 105, 145, 161
chapter house, 57, 63, 93, 103, 104, 111, 132, 164, 166, 170, 172, 253
   burials, 102, 104, 107, 162, 167
   meetings, 63, 166
charity, 7, 16, 17, 20, 29, 55, 92, 136, 137, 148, 165, 170, 194, 227, 228, 248, 286, 288
Charles IV, emperor, 249, 267
Charles V, emperor, 133
charnel house, 161
charter, 2, 27, 47, 50, 52, 53, 94, 95, 96, 97, 103, 106, 109, 111, 112, 113, 146, 148, 196, 216, 217, 218, 219
Cherlieu Abbey, 241
Chiaravalle Abbey, 54, 69
Chorin Abbey, 167, 250
Christ, 5, 16, 33, 55, 79, 99, 108, 132, 137, 141, 142, 144, 158, 163, 172, 173, 174, 176, 178, 227, 228, 229, 248, 252, 255, 257, 258, 265
   crucifix, 148, 172, 174, 228, 229
   imitatio Christi, 55, 228, 252, 255
   Pietà, 173, 256
   Vir Dolorum, 176
Christian, bishop of Whithorn, 226

chronicle, 2, 16, 33, 35, 45, 61, 68, 79, 104, 107, 109, 132, 146, 209, 211, 218, 219, 220, 222, 223, 224, 231, 271, 285, 286
church, monastic, 51, 61, 99, 100, 101, 102, 103, 104, 105, 131, 132, 156, 157, 160, 162, 163, 166, 167, 194, 224, 255, 258, 259, 265
   chancel, 156, 158
   chapel, 99, 102, 104, 160, 161, 163, 164, 258
   chevet, 158, 160, 162
   choirs, 99, 104, 105, 106, 160, 161, 162, 163, 164, 166, 168, 173, 213, 263
   furnishings, 4, 146, 161, 168, 172, 174, 177, 178, 257, 265
   nave, 64, 101, 102, 158, 160, 161, 163, 164, 168, 170
   stalls, 161, 174, 263
   west porch, 104, 108
Church Fathers, 173, 209, 211, 224, 229
Cikádor Abbey, 69, 113
Cîteaux
   Abbey, 8, 13, 14, 15, 16, 20, 21, 23, 27, 28, 30, 34, 44, 45, 46, 49, 64, 67, 69, 107, 113, 126, 128, 135, 171, 175, 176, 186, 214, 218, 220, 221, 245, 247, 248, 254, 266, 270, 273, 287
   Alberic, abbot of, 8, 15
   Arnaud Amaury, abbot of, 78, 214
   Gerard de Buxières, abbot of, 78, 214
   Gui, abbot of, 78
   Jean de Cirey, abbot of, 175, 240, 243, 244, 245, 252, 257, 267
   John, abbot of, 135, 247
   Raynard de Bar, abbot of, 20, 21
   Stephen Harding, abbot of, 8, 15, 20, 21, 126, 128, 176
   William of Montague, abbot of, 209
Clairefontaine, 46, 73
Clairets nunnery, 126, 142

INDEX

Clairvaux
  Abbey, 19, 23, 26, 28, 29, 32, 33, 44, 49, 54, 69, 72, 73, 128, 156, 158, 161, 162, 171, 209, 211, 225, 226, 240, 241, 243, 254, 273
  Bernard of – *see* Bernard of Clairvaux
  church, 157–158
  Congregation of, 245
  Herbert of, 75, 76, 173, 226
  Jacques de Pontailler, abbot of, 254
  Jean Foucand, abbot of, 254
  Nicholas of, monk, 26
  Pierre de Virey, abbot of, 245, 254
  Stephen Lexington, abbot of, 77, 136, 240, 271, 272
Clement IV, pope, 45, 241
Clement VI, pope, 266
cloister, 58, 103, 104, 111, 138, 139, 156, 162, 164, 165, 166, 167, 168, 169, 170, 171, 172, 202, 213, 215
Cluniac communities, 14, 23, 25, 26, 74, 97, 101, 107, 156, 230, 286
Cluny, 6, 25, 26, 56, 97
  Peter the Venerable, abbot of, 21, 27
Colder Abbey, 224
Coldstream Abbey, 147
college – *see* university
Cologne, 198, 199, 245, 249, 250, 251, 256, 259
  Bruno, archbishop of, 31
  Friedrich II, bishop of, 106
  Seyne nunnery in, 246
colonisation, 54, 187
commemoration, 115, 145, 286
  laity, 4, 53, 97–101, 103, 255, 263
  liber vitae, 97
  monks, 63, 66, 97, 110, 167
  necrology, 66, 68, 98, 110, 214
  Office of the Dead, 34, 62
  patrons, 93, 97–101, 103, 131–132, 221–222
  visual, 99–100, 163–164, 172, 177, 201

conflict, 27, 44, 45, 47, 61, 72, 77, 94, 105, 111–113, 191, 229, 231, 246, 251, 272
  resolution of, 29, 47, 95, 112, 148
Constance nunnery, 134
conventual
  buildings, 160, 164–172, 222
  seal, 175, 242
conversi (lay brothers), 17, 30, 51, 56, 59, 63–64, 65, 93, 137, 160, 226
  accommodation, 7, 107, 108, 161, 162, 163, 164, 165, 169, 170
  decline, 65, 270
  duties, 7, 22, 51, 63–64, 138, 186–7
  numbers of, 65, 188
corrodian, 65, 110
council,
  Basel, 247, 248
  Fourth Lateran, 27, 230
  Lyon, 194
  Pisa, 27, 266
  Tours, 34
  Troyes, 33
  Vienne, 194
Coupar Angus Abbey, 223, 267
Croatia, 113, 200, 252
Croxden Abbey, 222
La Crête Abbey, 30
crucifix – *see* Christ
crusade, 43, 77–81, 103, 135, 136, 196, 197, 224, 241, 267
  Second, 29, 32, 33, 79
  Third, 33
  Fourth, 74, 33
custom, Cistercian, 16, 20, 21, 24, 25, 34, 47, 73, 74, 76, 134, 135, 138, 139
Cyprus, 45, 74

Daphni Abbey, 74
Dargun Abbey, 54, 72, 75
decline, concept of, 1–5, 183, 202, 227, 230, 239, 285, 290
Deer Abbey, 45, 68, 106, 223
Definitores, 45

INDEX

Degler-Spengler, Brigitte, 127, 128, 130
Denmark, 49, 69, 105, 131, 145
   Margaret I, queen of, 99, 104
   Margaret I, queen of Denmark Sweden and Norway, 259
   Olaf II, king of, 99
   Valdemar I, king of, 53, 79
   Valdemar IV Atterdag, king of, 98
desert, concept of, 18, 19, 54, 215, 221
Desert Fathers, 6, 16, 23, 55, 285
Devotio Moderna, 252, 255
Dijon, 14, 28, 93, 175, 176, 244, 270
Dimier, Anselm, 157
Dissolution, 3, 102, 252, 253
diurnal, 254
Doberan Abbey, 72, 75, 79, 102, 104, 161, 173, 174, 199, 201, 212, 257, 258
Dominicans, 81, 138, 141, 142, 144, 147, 230, 240, 245, 286
donation – *see* grant
donor – *see* benefactor
Donzelbacher, Peter, 79
Dore Abbey, 48, 106, 131, 258, 262
dormitory, 48, 106, 131, 208, 262, 51, 59, 64, 77, 161, 164, 165, 168, 170, 214, 217, 261, 263
Droiteval Abbey, 54
Dryburgh Abbey, 191
Dublin, Holy Cross Abbey, 246
Dünamünde Abbey, 80, 81
Dundrennan Abbey, 45, 67, 77, 106, 211, 223, 224, 247
Les Dunes Abbey, 69
Durham, 226

Easholt Abbey, 143
East-Central Europe, 2, 52, 69, 73, 75, 95, 112, 188, 270
Eaunes Abbey, 247
Eberbach Abbey, 23, 169, 199, 211, 247, 276 n. 35
   Conrad of, 23, 173, 255
   Herman abbot of, 247

Ebrach Abbey, 105, 177, 198, 219, 248, 260
   Conrad of, 251
Eccles nunnery, 147
Ecclesiastica Officia, 21, 22, 107, 168, 175, 215
Les Écharlis Abbey, 49
Egris Abbey, 76
Elba River, 43, 187, 193
Eldena Abbey, 199
Elm, Kaspar, 4
Empire, 72, 78, 266, 267
Engental nunnery, 252
England
   Edward I, king of, 98, 197, 218, 266
   Edward II, king of, 110
   Edward III, king of, 119, 200
   Henry I, king of, 31, 53
   Henry II, king of, 7
   Henry III, king of, 134, 135, 197
   Henry IV, king of, 110
   John, king of, 110, 114, 197, 224
   Richard I, king of, 98, 114, 197
   Stephen, king of, 53
Erfurt, 249, 250, 252
l'Escaladieu Abbey, 213
Esrum Abbey, 53, 72, 75, 95, 99, 131, 255, 259, 263
Esser, Karl Heinz, 156
Estonia, 79–81
Eucharist, 31, 141, 146, 228, 151, 257
   Eucharistic Mill, 173
   Holy Blood cult, 135, 174, 258, 259
Eugenius III, pope, 20, 32, 33, 82, 126
Eugenius IV, pope, 247
Evans, Gillian R., 31
Exordium Cistercii, 21, 22, 24, 73, 183, 220, 221
Exordium Magnum Cisterciense, 23, 173, 255
Exordium Parvum, 21, 23, 24, 27, 107, 157, 158, 220, 286

Falkenau Abbey, 81
Falleri Abbey, 78

INDEX

familiares, 56, 65, 66, 97, 98, 101, 102, 138, 162
fasting – *see* food
feast, liturgical, 60, 62, 64, 224, 225, 257
   of Annunciation, 141, 224
   of St Benedict, 14, 224
   of St Bernard, 246
   of *Corpus Christi*, 257
   of dedication, 131, 224, 258
   of Purification of Mary, 162, 224
   of Victor of Xanten, 76
   of St Eligius, 76
   of St John the Baptist, 59, 224
   of St Stephen, 76
Felbach nunnery, 134
La Ferté Abbey, 15, 28, 44, 49, 69, 74, 126, 209, 243
filiation, 1, 11, 26, 34, 43, 44, 47, 49, 66, 67, 68, 72, 77, 81, 128, 130, 133, 138, 140, 159, 174, 176, 210, 212, 217, 224, 225, 238, 242, 245, 256, 268, 269, 273, 286, 267
fisheries, 192
fishing, 52, 190
Fitero Abbey, 69
Flanders, 29, 33, 50, 98, 146, 148, 189, 195
   Philip, count of, 97
Flaxley Abbey, 195, 197
Florence, 163, 246, 255, 268
Florilegia, 209
Foigny Abbey, 225
Fontenay Abbey, 166
Fontevivo Abbey, 73
Fontfroide Abbey, 73
Fontmorigny Abbey, 45
Font-Vive Abbey, 73
food, 6, 17, 63, 169, 191, 198, 219, 242, 259, 260–262, 271, 273
   communal meal, 166, 168, 169, 215
   fasting, 108, 142, 166
   fish, 17, 63, 191, 192, 193, 260

meat, 17, 59, 63, 169, 191, 193, 242, 260, 261
pittances, 99, 145, 219, 260, 261, 263
spices, 17, 63
Forde Abbey, 105, 226
   Baldwin, abbot of, 228, 257
Fossanova Abbey, 32, 78
foundation, 1, 2, 13, 28, 31, 32, 44, 49–54, 72–75, 126, 128, 129, 130
   motivation for, 52–53
   narratives of, 1, 23, 54, 69, 73, 145–147, 186–187, 217, 218, 220, 221
   process, 50–51
founder, 35, 50–54, 72, 73, 77, 93, 94, 99, 100, 101, 102, 103, 107, 112, 115, 124, 125, 127, 130, 131, 143, 144, 145, 146, 147, 148, 163, 177, 186, 187, 200, 218, 219, 221, 222, 248, 248, 265, 286
   see also benefactor
Fountains, 109, 114, 135, 161, 195, 197, 218, 220, 224, 226, 250, 261, 269
   Marmaduke Huby, abbot of, 135, 136, 243, 253
   Richard, abbot of, 25
Fourteen Helpers-in-Need, 258
France, 78, 102, 103, 106, 113, 136, 137, 146, 148, 171, 188, 196, 197, 199, 211, 213, 214, 274, 226, 241, 243, 249, 262, 266, 267, 273, 289
   Blanche, queen of, 113, 145
   Louis VII, king of, 7, 32, 98, 131
   Louis IX, king of, 78, 103, 113, 136
   Louis XI, king of, 244
   Philip III, king of, 98, 136
   Philip IV, king of, 197
Franciscans, 31, 113, 138, 141, 230, 240, 242, 242, 245, 250, 286
Franconia, 198, 271, 257

· 304 ·

INDEX

Frankfurt-an-der-Oder, 250
fraternity, 97, 98, 108, 113, 201, 258
Frederick II, emperor, 142
Freeman, Elizabeth, 134, 209
Freiburg, 250
friendship
  between monks, 55, 126, 228
  between monks and nuns, 126, 142, 149
  De spiritali amicitia, 228
  with lay people, 28, 29, 95, 143
Frienisberg Abbey, 134
Frisia, 45
Fulda Abbey, 220
Fulgens sicut stella (*Benedictina*), papal bull, 242, 243, 250, 261
Furness Abbey, 106, 109, 223, 224
  Jocelin, monk of, 226
Fürstenfeld Abbey, 103, 190, 196, 198, 256
  St Leonard chapel in Inchenhofen, 256

Galicia, 44
Gascony, 187, 197, 241
gate, 51, 105, 108, 131, 160, 170, 171, 178, 185, 259
  chapel, 108
genealogy, 49, 218, 219, 221, 222, 285
General Chapter, 8, 18, 20, 22, 27, 43–44, 47, 48, 50, 57, 59, 61, 62, 64, 65, 76, 77, 78, 81, 93, 98, 101, 102, 107, 127, 129, 130, 131, 132, 134, 136, 139, 144, 156, 158, 194, 195, 209, 211, 212, 213, 238, 240, 241, 242, 244, 246, 249, 250, 251, 253, 254, 257, 258, 261, 262, 264, 266, 268, 269, 270, 272, 273, 285, 286
  meetings of, 20, 34, 44–47, 50, 133, 223, 242, 243, 266, 270
  statutes of, 22–24, 44, 46, 47, 50, 59, 63, 72, 101, 109, 125, 128, 129, 131, 134, 135, 166, 176, 177, 210, 217, 240, 250, 253, 261
  travel to, 44–45, 248, 266
Georgenthal Abbey, 252
Germany, 75, 80, 102, 130, 135, 141, 142, 171, 215, 226, 249, 257, 258, 288, 289
Gilbert of Hoyland, 158
Glasgow, William, bishop of, 106
Glenluce Abbey, 224
'Golden Age', concept of, 2, 3, 5, 115, 227
Gnadental nunnery, 246
Grace Dieu Abbey, 54
gradual, 137, 143, 176, 210
Grandmontines, 7
Grandselve Abbey, 248
grange, 64, 65, 66, 110, 112, 131, 140, 185, 187, 189, 198, 202, 259, 271
  creation of, 185–187, 189, 190
  home-grange, 57, 170, 185
  lease of, 188, 189, 194, 202
  management of, 138, 187, 190–191
  master of, 56, 188, 198
  records related to, 217, 219
grant, 15, 18, 27, 49, 50, 51, 52, 53, 78, 96, 100, 103, 109, 111, 112, 113, 183, 189, 190, 191, 201, 202
  ceremony, 94–95
  countergift, 94, 103, 110,
  foundation, 52, 185
  motivation for, 92–95, 115
  of object, 96, 177, 214
Greece, 2, 45, 46, 74
Gregory IX, pope, 240
Gregory X, pope, 54
Gregory the Great, Saint, *Moralia in Job*, 211, 229
Great Famine, 241
Greifswald, 199, 249
Grey Abbey, 223
Guerric of Igny, 28, 55, 79, 225
guest-master, 57, 107

INDEX

habit, 16, 17, 60, 63, 77, 137, 168, 174
  cowl, 17, 48, 60, 63
Habsburgs, 100, 289
hagiography, 65, 208, 225–227
  Golden Legend, 256
  Liber de Natalitiis, 226
  'Life of St Edward the Confessor', 226
  'Life of St Godric of Finchale', 226
  'Life of St Ninian', 226
  'Life of Waltheof', 226
Hadrian IV, pope, 27
Hailes Abbey, 106, 108, 213, 258
  John of Gloucester, abbot of, 131, 258
  Sagar, abbot of, 253
  William, abbot of, 61
Haina Abbey, 174
Hamburg, 193
  Hartvig, Archbishop of Hamburg-Bremen, 72
Hampole nunnery, 143
Hanseatic League, 192, 198
Hattula church, 259
Hautecombe Abbey, 103
Haute-Fontaine Abbey, 210
Les Hayes nunnery, 147
Heidelberg, 249, 250, 251, 252
  St Jacob College in, 251
Heiligengrabe nunnery, 258
Heiligenkreuz Abbey, 5, 22, 69, 100, 210
Heilsbronn Abbey, 161, 216, 257, 266
Heisterbach Abbey, 49, 68, 131, 190, 251, 258
  Caesarius of – *see* Caesarius of Heisterbach
  Christian II, abbot of, 245
  Peter von Jülich, monk of, 250
Helfta Abbey, 132, 141
  Gertrude of Hackeborn, abbess of, 141
Helmold of Bosau, chronicler, 79

Henry VI, emperor, 197
Henryków Abbey, 110, 192, 211, 214, 221, 236 n. 75, 258
  Book of, 221, 222
  Peter, abbot of, 222
Herckenrode nunnery, 146
heresy, 67, 77, 78, 82, 229, 230, 241
  Albigensian, 78, 142
  Hussite, 247, 251, 271
Herrevad Abbey, 69
Hessen, 174, 249
Hiddensee Abbey, 192, 201
Himmelpfort Abbey, 250
Himmelstädt Abbey, 250
Himmerod Abbey, 50, 138, 156, 198, 210, 254, 260
Hirschau Abbey, 64
historiography, 2, 5, 8, 18–20, 25, 78–79, 124–125, 127, 128, 133, 158, 288
Hohenstaufen, 103, 114
  Conrad III, 177
Holdsworth, Christopher, 79
Holm Cultram Abbey, 67, 200, 217, 223, 224, 264
  Robert Chamber, abbot of, 264
Holy Land, 2, 30, 33, 78, 79, 80, 103, 215, 224, 259
Honorius III, pope, 22
hospital *see* – infirmary
hospitality, 22, 45, 92, 94, 95, 96, 107–111, 115, 116, 131, 136, 148, 194, 263
  guests, 45, 56, 61, 66, 68, 102, 107–108, 110, 111, 137, 162, 163, 168, 171, 191, 263
  guest-house, 51, 107–108, 165, 168, 185
  guest-master, 56, 57, 107
Hovedøya Abbey, 73
Las Huelgas Abbey, 133, 134, 138, 145, 272
Hugh of St Victor, 55, 229
Humanism, 252, 254

INDEX

Hungary, 45, 69, 75, 76, 80, 113, 134, 270, 271
   Charles, king of, 147
   Gertrude, queen of, 103
hymn, 15, 62, 99, 257
hymnary, 210

Iberian peninsula, 2, 74, 106, 188, 272, 273
'Ideal and reality', concept of, 2, 4, 10 n. 9, 14, 24, 158, 183, 193, 274
Idung of Prüfening, 26
indulgence, 131, 219, 258, 259
infirmarian, 56, 58
infirmary, 58, 59, 61, 100, 109, 110, 167, 168, 169, 170, 171, 214, 261, 263
   see also medicine
Innocent II, pope, 27, 29, 32
Innocent III, pope, 74, 78, 80, 127, 146
Innocent IV, pope, 129, 240
Innocent VI, pope, 266
Innocent VIII, pope, 243, 245, 268
Instituta, 23, 24, 47
intercession, 98, 115, 132, 145, 255
Ireland, 43, 44, 48, 50, 69, 73, 76, 77, 246, 271
Isaac of Stella, 55, 228, 231
Italy, 6, 32, 48, 69, 106, 188, 226, 266, 267, 289
   Congregation of St Bernard in, 268

Jacques de Vitry, 130
Jan Štěkna, 251
Jędrzejów Abbey, 52, 69, 216
Jerusalem, 17, 125, 259
Jervaulx Abbey, 95, 106, 220, 223, 256, 261
   George Lazenby, monk of, 256
   Historia Fundationis, 223
Jews, 16, 78, 79, 258, 272
   anti-Semitism, 258
John XXII, pope, 241, 242, 262, 268
John Cassian, 6
John of Salisbury, 229
Jully nunnery, 126

Kaisheim Abbey, 254
Kamień Pomorski, 112
Kamieniec Abbey, 108, 258
Kamp Abbey, 65, 69, 76, 248, 256
Keldholme nunnery, 213
Kinder, Terryl, 9, 159, 177
Kinloss Abbey, 53, 68, 223, 267
   Thomas Crystall, abbot of, 265
Kirchheim Abbey, 215
Kirkham Priory, 105
Kirkstall Abbey, 134, 135, 195, 259
Kirkstead Abbey, 73, 106, 191
kitchen, 46, 65, 108, 167, 169, 170, 172, 193, 261
   building, 169, 261
   see also food, refectory
Klosterneuburg Priory, 100
Knowles, David, 2, 3, 35
Koblenz, 198
Kołbacz Abbey, 53, 72, 80, 95, 109, 112, 250
   Dietmar, abbot of, 95
Königsbronn Abbey, 73
Koszalin, Cistercian nunnery in, 256
Kraków
   Matthew, bishop of, 31
   University of, 249, 250, 251
Krzeszów Abbey, 258

Lackner, Bede, 7
Ląd Abbey, 99, 174, 256
   Simon, abbot of, 176
Lagny, 198
Langheim Abbey, 258, 271
language, 5, 95, 272
   French, 77, 271, 272
   German, 215, 219, 249, 270, 272
   Greek, 252
   Hebrew, 15, 252
   Latin, 16, 59, 141, 143, 144, 169, 201, 214, 215, 219, 225, 252, 272
   sign, 56
   vernacular, 106, 141, 143, 166, 169, 201, 214, 215, 219, 225, 255, 256, 271, 141, 256, 271

INDEX

Languedoc, 52, 78, 247, 248
latrine, 64, 168, 170, 172, 261
Laurence, abbot of Westminster, 226
Lausitz, 93
Leclercq, Jean, 79
Lehnin Abbey, 210, 250, 251
Leipzig, 214, 249
   Cistercian college of St Bernard in, 249
Lekai, Louis, 2–4, 34, 127
Łekno Abbey (later Wągrowiec Abbey), 73, 80, 256, 272
Lent, 62, 63, 166, 196, 215
Leo X, pope, 273
Leon, 45
Lester, Anne E., 136, 137
Libelli difinitionum, 44, 46
library, 31, 58, 143, 176, 208, 209, 210–216, 225, 226, 229, 231, 248, 250, 252, 253, 254, 271, 288, 289
   buildings, 165, 254
   catalogue, 209–210, 212–213, 216, 221
   librarian, 56, 58, 214
Liège, 127, 257
light, 99, 158, 162, 172, 191, 215, 258
Lilienfeld Abbey, 104
Lillienthal Abbey, 135
Lincolnshire, 135, 199
liturgy, 7, 16, 20, 22, 33, 47, 50, 57, 58, 61, 62, 63, 64, 76, 78, 81, 101, 116, 137, 142, 156, 159, 162, 170, 201, 224, 225, 229, 239, 242
   books, 14, 16, 50, 81, 96, 143, 176, 208, 210, 211, 215, 254
   see also antiphonary, breviary, diurnal, gradual, hymnary, martyrology, missal, psalter
   vessels, 96, 110, 157, 160, 172, 176, 177, 198, 271
   vestments, 96, 137, 157, 163, 172, 264
Livonia, 45, 79, 80, 81
Livonian Sword Brothers, 80, 81
Loccum Abbey, 80, 220
   Bertold, bishop of Livonia, abbot of, 80
Løgum Abbey, 190
Lombardy, 210
London, 106, 110, 200, 266
   St Mary Graces Abbey in, 106, 110, 226, 269
Loos Abbey, 97
Lorsch Abbey, 211
Louis IV, Emperor, 177
Louth Park Abbey, 190
Low Countries, 141, 245, 246, 257
Lübeck, 193, 198, 201
Lubiąż Abbey, 110, 176, 222
Lubusz Abbey, 146, 264
Lucelle Abbey, 247, 276, n. 35
Lund
   Absalon, archbishop of, 131
   Eskil, archbishop of, 29, 72
Lüneburg, 193, 201
Luxemburg, John of, 114
Le Lys nunnery, 113, 145
Lyse Abbey, 69, 73, 269

Maastricht, 246
McGuire, Brian Patrick, 25, 126, 142
Magdeburg, 141, 265
   Mehtild of, 141, 149
Malachy, archbishop of Armagh, 29, 73
manuscript, 18, 22, 24, 25, 28, 31, 34, 56, 137, 137, 143, 157, 173, 175, 176, 185, 210, 211, 212, 213, 214, 215, 216, 225, 226, 228, 252
   borrowing, 176, 211, 216, 226, 254, 212
   copying, 176, 208, 215–216, 225, 231
Margam Abbey, 54, 106
Marham nunnery, 134
Mariawald Abbey, 256
Marienfeld Abbey, 107, 165, 210
Mariengarten Abbey, 258
Marienstatt Abbey, 65, 260

INDEX

Marienstern nunnery, 143
Marienstuhl nunnery, 246
Mariental Abbey, 174
Marienwalde Abbey, 73, 250, 260
Marmosolio Abbey, 78
Martin Luther, 252, 254, 288
martyrology, 63, 143, 166
masons, 51, 52, 159
mass, 7, 18, 44, 62, 78, 97, 98, 99, 101, 105, 107, 131, 138, 145, 161, 162, 163, 170, 177, 191, 222, 229, 241, 250, 255, 257, 258, 263
Maubuisson Abbey, 113, 145
Maulbronn Abbey, 100, 101, 161, 167, 171, 172, 247, 248, 252, 263
    Albrecht IV von Ötisheim, abbot of, 263
    Berthold von Rosswag, abbot of, 100, 248
    Conrad Leontorius, monk of, 252
    John, abbot of, 247
    Peter von Gosmaringen, abbot of, 265
Meaux Abbey, 61, 65, 96, 109, 197, 213
    Alexander, abbot of, 213
    Thomas de Burton, bursar and abbot of, 61, 96
Mechthild of Hackeborn, 141, 149
Mecklenburg, 75, 79, 102, 161, 193, 201, 212, 257, 258
medicine, 58, 109, 212, 213
    blood-letting, 59, 167
    care, 58, 109, 130, 136
Meißen, 93, 249
Mellifont Abbey, 69, 73, 77, 246
    John Troy, abbot of, 246
Melrose Abbey, 53, 67, 68, 69, 102, 104, 105, 106, 110, 167, 171, 191, 200, 224, 226, 257, 267, 271
    Chronicle of, 45, 107, 211, 223, 224
    Ernald, abbot of, 67
    Jocelin, abbot of, 106, 168
    Patrick, abbot of, 226
    Waldeof, abbot of, 167

mercenarii, 188
Metz, 16, 249
Michaelstein Abbey, 65
Milan, 15, 69
miracles, 23, 34, 35, 76, 174, 210, 226, 256, 257, 258
missal, 210, 223, 254
Mogiła Abbey, 211, 249, 272
Molesme Abbey, 8, 13, 14, 15, 21, 25, 27, 126, 126
    Robert, abbot of, 8, 13, 14, 15, 16, 23
money, 66, 94, 113, 115, 185, 186, 193, 194–197, 202, 262
    credit, 193, 194, 195, 196, 197, 201, 211, 267
    debt, 46, 147, 188, 194, 195, 196, 197, 201, 244
    rent, 58, 137, 139, 140, 148, 192, 194, 196, 200, 242, 270
    tax, 46, 52, 114, 132, 136, 187, 191, 193, 196, 197, 216, 241, 242, 244, 264, 266, 267, 287
    usury, 194
monstrance, 146, 177, 265
Montpellier, 67, 243, 248
Moreruela Abbey, 69, 187
Morimond, 30–31, 44, 49, 65, 69, 74, 211, 243, 246, 249, 251
    Arnold, abbot of, 30
    Berthold, abbot of, 78
    Hugh, abbot of, 48
Morimondo Abbey, 210
Mormountier Abbey, 93
Mortemer Abbey, 60
Moselle Valley, 198, 210
mother house, 6, 20, 46, 49, 50, 51, 57, 68, 69, 72, 77, 105, 126, 133, 134, 138, 159, 210, 211, 224, 238, 266, 269, 286
Mount Grace Priory, 256
Munkeby Abbey, 76
Muslims, 79, 272, 273
    Islam, 31

INDEX

Naestved Abbey, 99
Navarre 45, 74, 243
   Blanche, countess of, 146
Neath Abbey, 54, 106
Neuberger Abbey, 210
Neuenkamp Abbey, 65, 146, 262
Neukloster Abbey, 256
Neuzelle Abbey, 250, 258
Newbattle Abbey, 53, 223
Newman, Martha, 25
Newminster Abbey, 67, 109, 224
Newnham Abbey, 129
Nicholas V, pope, 268
Normandy, 7, 114, 142, 211, 289
North Sea, 193, 199
Norway, 45, 69, 73, 259
Notre-Dame-des-Prés nunnery in Douai, 143
Novalia, 27–28
novice master, 56, 59, 60, 66, 67, 251
novices, 17, 21, 56, 59–60, 63, 64, 67, 137, 143, 161, 166, 168, 208, 209, 210, 213, 225, 231, 272, 289
nuns, 5, 9, 62, 65, 103, 109, 124–149, 156, 175, 200, 215, 226, 257, 261, 262, 270, 271, 288
   attitudes to, 124–132
   churches in nunneries, 163
   claustration, 116, 128, 136, 137, 138, 140, 143, 144, 148, 156, 163, 246, 247
   nunnery, 102–103, 113, 124, 126–149
   relationship to the male order, 132–136
   spiritual care of, 129, 138, 141, 252
   spirituality of, 132, 140–144, 230
Nuremberg, 266
Nydala Abbey, 69

Obazine, 50
oblates, 15, 59, 141, 142
Obłok nunnery, 103
Obra Abbey, 218, 256

Office, Divine (*horarium*), 6, 58, 158, 185, 253, 267, 269
Oliwa Abbey, 214, 250
Øm Abbey, 220
Opager nunnery, 147
Opus Dei, 62, 164, 169
Orderic Vitalis, 16
ordo, 15, 16, 17, 20, 24, 26, 29, 30, 50, 81, 126, 127, 131, 135, 138
Orthodox Church, 31, 74
Orval Abbey, 54
Otto of Freising, 33, 63
Ourscamp Abbey, 76
Owińska nunnery, 103
Oxford, 31, 240, 243, 249, 250
   Cistercian college of St Bernard in, 248, 253

pagans, 226
   in the Baltic, 33, 75, 79, 80, 145, 224
   Mongols, 223
Paradyż Abbey, 52, 250
   Jacob von Jueterbord, monk of, 251
Paris, 145, 148, 201, 211, 240, 243, 249, 251
   Cistercian college of St Bernard in, 230, 240, 242, 248, 249
   University of, 240, 250
parish, 92, 99, 102, 145
   church, 52, 105, 106, 108, 110, 140, 146, 160, 184, 259
parliament, 114, 244
Parvus fons (*Clementina*), papal bull, 45, 241
Paschal II, pope, 15, 27
patron, 1, 8, 52, 53, 72, 73, 77, 92–101, 104, 105, 106, 107, 109, 111, 113, 115, 116, 125, 131, 135, 137, 139, 144–148, 156, 158, 162, 163, 164, 172, 177, 178, 185, 186, 189, 191, 194, 218, 219, 221, 222, 224, 249, 255, 256, 264
peasants, 17, 43, 65, 103, 187, 270
Pelplin Abbey, 98, 211, 212, 271

INDEX

Peter of Castelnau, 78
Peter Lombard, 211, 212, 214, 229
Peter of Tarentaise, 35
Periculoso, papal bull, 140
Pforta Abbey, 211
Picardy, 76, 210, 225
pilgrimage, 15, 103, 108, 143, 256, 258, 259
pilgrims, 92, 125, 131, 132, 157, 167, 257, 258, 259
Pipewell Abbey, 111, 261
Plasy Abbey, 109, 114
Poblet Abbey, 133
Pohled nunnery, 140
Poland, 48, 69, 75, 186, 193, 216, 218, 267, 272, 289
   Greater Poland, 52, 99, 174, 176, 187, 211
   Mieszko the Elder, duke of, 176
Pomerania, 53, 54, 79, 95, 98, 109, 112, 173, 186, 211, 214, 249, 271
Pontigny, 61
poor, 92, 97, 108, 109, 110, 116, 132, 136, 137, 165, 170, 200, 241, 248, 259
Poor Clares, 130 141
Portugal, 44, 46, 130, 243
   Mafalda, infanta, 146
   Sancha, infanta, 146
   Sancho I, king of, 146
   Teresa, infanta, 146
poverty, 5, 6, 7, 16, 17, 132, 137, 148, 157, 167, 183, 241, 247, 264
Prague, 109
   Bethlehem Chapel in, 251
   Cistercian college of St Bernard in, 249
   University of, 249, 251
prayers, 6, 7, 8, 16, 18, 22, 44, 52, 53, 55, 62, 64, 66, 78, 92, 93, 94, 97, 98, 100, 105, 108, 115, 133, 137, 141, 142, 143, 144, 145, 158, 161, 165, 168, 169, 173, 178, 185, 208, 215, 221, 255, 256, 260, 274

communal, 16, 137, 159
individual, 98, 185, 143, 144, 161
preaching, 29, 32, 33, 37, 78, 79, 81, 145, 166, 208, 214, 224–225, 227, 230, 231, 256
   exempla, 225, 226, 254
   sermons, 44, 60, 79, 208, 209, 212, 213, 224–225, 227, 229, 230, 255
Přemyslid dynasty, 109, 114, 162
prior, 56, 57, 61, 66, 67, 68, 75, 106, 143, 144, 166, 167, 209, 219, 267, 268
prison, 167, 169
property, 7, 18, 31, 50, 52, 57, 65, 92, 94, 95, 103, 110, 112, 115, 138, 139, 140, 148, 183, 184, 188, 191, 195, 196, 198, 199, 200, 202, 216, 217, 218, 243, 246, 262–263, 270, 289
   arable, 190–192
   exchange, 94, 96, 112, 183, 189, 190, 199, 201, 202
   forest, 52, 53, 109, 190, 191, 192
   lease, 188, 189, 194, 200, 254
   pasture, 52, 94, 111, 112, 185, 190, 191, 192
   purchase, 27, 112, 183, 189, 194, 196, 199, 197, 202
   sale, 190, 200, 242, 267
   serfs, 14, 21, 184, 187, 188, 194, 200
   see also grant
Prussia, 79, 80, 271, 289
psalter, 143, 161, 210, 214, 254, 265
punishment, 58, 63, 95, 125, 166, 169, 194, 249

Quadrivium, 137
Quanta in Dei Ecclesia, papal bull, 243
Quarr Abbey, 240

Raitenhaslach Abbey, 258, 260
Realvalle Abbey, 113
receptores, 46
Reconquista, 43, 74, 272

INDEX

refectory, 51, 63, 64, 164, 165, 168, 169, 170, 172, 185, 193, 215, 261
reform, 1, 5, 6, 7, 13, 14, 16, 21, 23, 25, 28, 29, 30, 31, 45, 50, 51, 64, 68, 69, 73, 76, 77, 82, 128, 133, 163, 209, 227, 230, 239, 240, 241, 242, 243, 245, 246, 247, 268, 273, 285, 286, 289
Reformation, 1, 102, 146, 241, 253, 267, 288, 290
Regensburg, 199
regionalisation, process of, 202, 287, 49, 238, 240, 246, 248, 266, 272, 273
Reigny Abbey, 49, 94
relics, 33, 101, 163, 174, 258
reliquary, 99, 177
Revesby, 67, 223
Rhineland, 33, 69, 79, 142, 190, 198, 199, 210, 211, 226, 245, 246, 251, 257, 272
Richard Rolle, 143
Rievaulx Abbey, 53, 55, 58, 66, 67, 105, 110, 111, 112, 114, 166, 167, 168, 171, 195, 197, 211, 212, 223, 224, 264
  Ailred, abbot of, 55, 58, 59, 60, 65, 66, 79, 92, 158, 166, 225, 226, 228, 257
  Matthew, cantor of, 257
  William, abbot of, 104, 67
Riga, 80, 81, 198
Robert of Poule, 229
Roche Abbey, 256
Rodez Abbey, 247
Roger of Sicily, 32
Rome, 15, 32, 61, 78, 144, 241, 259
Romuald, saint, 6, 7
Rosenthal Abbey, 54
Roskilde, 76
  nunnery in, 131, 145, 148, 259
  Peder, bishop of, 102
Rostock, 75, 198, 199, 249
  Holy Cross nunnery in, 174
  University of, 249, 251
Royaumont Abbey, 113

Ruda Abbey, 211
Rufford Abbey, 191, 223
Rügen, 79, 146
  Jaromir, prince of, 145
  Pribisław, prince of, 75
  Wisław I, prince of, 146
Rule of Benedict, 6, 14, 15, 16, 17, 20, 21, 22, 23, 34, 44, 57, 59, 60, 63, 74, 76, 92, 107, 108, 127, 166, 168, 170, 171, 177, 210, 224, 225, 244, 245, 272, 289
Rulle Abbey, 137
Ryd Abbey, 72

saint, 99, 101, 132, 137, 164, 173, 174, 221, 226, 256
  cult, 76, 142, 162, 226, 227, 256, 257
  shrine, 104, 162, 163, 167, 172, 256, 258, 259, 286
  see also feast
Saint-Antoine-des-Champs nunnery, 113, 145, 148, 201
  Gile, abbess of, 148
St Michael's Stamford nunnery, 135
Salamanca, 243
Salem Abbey, 134, 198, 254, 257
  Eberhard of Rohrdorf, abbot of, 134
salt, 56, 193
  consumption, 193
  production, 192, 193, 199, 201, 202
  trade, 193, 198, 199
Salvatio Abbey, 74
Sambucina Abbey, 32
San Martino Abbey, 78
Santes Creus Abbey, 166
Santiago de Campostela, 143, 259
Savigny, 50, 136, 211, 240
Savoy, 103, 247
Sawley Abbey, 67, 224
  Stephen of, 55, 67
Saxony, 141, 192, 211, 246, 249, 258, 260, 271
  Henry the Lion, duke of, 79
  Lower, 79, 135, 174, 220, 258

INDEX

Scandinavia, 2, 43, 46, 72, 75, 173, 288
Schism, 29, 32, 245
  Great, 92, 239, 249, 266, 270, 273, 287
Schönau Abbey, 103
Schönthal Abbey, 54
Scotland, 31, 43, 44, 45, 67, 69, 76, 77, 102, 105, 106, 171, 190, 191, 192, 223, 224, 241, 246, 247, 265, 267, 288
  Alexander II, king of, 224
  David I, king of, 53, 66, 104, 191
  Robert I, king of, 105
scriptorium, 67, 167, 176, 208, 211, 215–216, 225
  master of, 56
sculpture, 104, 106, 157, 172, 173, 174
Sedlec Abbey, 69, 114
  Heydenreich, abbot of, 114
'self-sufficiency', concept of, 17, 129, 136, 183, 185, 193
Sempringham Order, 50
Sénanque Abbey, 166, 212
Sept-Fons Abbey, 73
sermon – *see* preaching
Settino Abbey, 246
Sezemice nunnery, 140
Sibculo, Congregation of, 245
Sicily, 32, 44, 98
silence, 6, 7, 17, 55, 56, 59, 63, 158, 172
Silesia, 103, 110, 128, 176, 187, 192, 211, 221, 222, 258, 264, 271
  Bolesław, duke of, 222
  Hedwig, duchess of, saint, 103, 163
  Henry the Bearded, 103, 146
  Henry II the Pious, duke of, 223
Silvanès Abbey, 49
Simony, 241
Sinningthwaite Priory, 143
Sixtus IV, pope, 245, 251

Slangerup nunnery, 131, 139
Sorø Abbey, 49, 72, 99, 102, 105, 131, 147, 259
Southern, Richard W., 127
Spain, 43, 48, 103, 133, 171, 187, 190, 247, 289
  Isabel, queen of, 247
  Ferdinand, king of, 247
spirituality, 1, 3, 4, 6, 16, 33, 50, 67, 81, 114, 127, 132, 140, 141, 142, 143, 147, 148, 149, 158, 159, 163, 172, 173, 174, 178, 208, 227–230, 252, 255, 256, 257, 274, 288
Staffarda Abbey, 210
stained glass, 157, 163, 173
Stanley Abbey, 240
Staré Brno nunnery, 147
Stephen of Lexington – *see* Clairvaux
Stična Abbey, 58, 211, 254
St Gallen Abbey, 221
Stralsund, 192, 201, 262
Strata Florida Abbey, 106, 110
Stratford Langthorne Abbey, 211, 250, 269
  Herman, abbot of, 108
Styria, 45, 210
Sulejów Abbey, 48, 216, 218
Swabia, 134
Sweden, 69, 75, 259, 260, 288
  Sverker I, king of, 75
Swine Priory, 146
Syria, 45
Szczecin, 198
Szpetal Abbey, 48

Tamié Abbey, 247
Tarouca Abbey, 69
Tarrant nunnery, 129, 134
Tart Abbey, 126, 138
Tautra Abbey, 73, 76
Templars (Knights Templar), 33
Ter Duine Abbey, 189
Teutonic Knights, 80, 81, 271
Thame Abbey, 197

· 313 ·

INDEX

theology, 6, 67, 158, 208, 213, 214, 227–230, 240, 250, 251, 252
Thuringia, 141, 249, 252
Tintern Abbey, 54
Tironensians, 53
tithes, 17, 19, 21, 27, 52, 135, 140, 184, 252
Toplica Abbey, 113, 200
Toulouse, 243
   Cistercian college of St Bernard in, 248
town, 74, 81, 130, 147, 193, 198–201, 246, 249, 256, 270
   bastides, 188
   granges in, 198–201
Tre Fontane Abbey, 32
Le Trésor Abbey, 113
Trier, 198
Trivium, 137, 212
Trondheim, 76, 259
Troyes, 33, 198, 199
Trzebnica nunnery, 103, 128, 146, 163
   Gertrude, abbess of, 103
Turks, 270, 271

uniformity, 15, 16, 20, 22, 43, 47, 49, 68, 77, 81, 102, 144, 210, 239, 240, 242, 254
university, 46, 214, 230, 240, 250, 252, 287
   Cistercian colleges, 113, 212, 240–243, 248, 249, 250, 251, 253
   monks as faculty, 251
   monks studying, 214, 230, 241, 250, 251, 254, 267, 274
   role of higher education, 143, 208, 214, 230, 231, 243, 248, 250, 251, 252, 273, 287
   subjects, 58, 212, 229, 230, 250
Untermann, Matthias, 4
Urban II, pope, 15
Urban VI, pope
Ursula, saint, 174, 256
Usus Conversorum, 22, 175

Vadstena Abbey, 144, 259
Val-Bressieux, 147
Val-des-Vignes nunnery, 114
Val-Dieu Abbey, 68
Valasse Abbey, 211
Vale Royal Abbey, 54, 218
   'Ledger Book of', 218
Vallbona Abbey, 54
Valle Crucis Abbey, 77, 105
Vallombrosans, 7, 64
Valmagne Abbey, 52, 54, 248
Valois, 92
Varnhem Abbey, 75, 143
Vauluisant Abbey, 171
Vaux-de-Cerney Abbey, 210
Vézelay, 32
Vienna, 249, 266
Villers Abbey, 60, 101, 171
   Charles, abbot of, 60
Villiers-to-Nonnains nunnery, 147
violence, 53, 66, 76, 112, 188, 271
Virgin Mary, 125, 256
   cult, 14, 126, 141–142, 145, 174, 175, 178, 229, 242, 256
   intercessory role, 175
   liturgy, 98, 99, 224, 229
   Mater Misericordiae, 175–176
   visual representations, 173, 174, 175, 248, 256, 265
visitation, 22, 27, 44, 47, 48, 58, 61, 68, 77, 108, 131, 133, 136, 138, 139, 213, 240, 241, 243, 250, 251, 257, 258, 262, 268, 269
   De forma visitationis, 22
Vita Apostolica, 6, 34
Vitskøl Abbey, 72, 226
Vittoria Abbey, 114
Volkenroda Abbey, 65
Vyšší Bród Abbey, 99, 161, 177

Wąchock Abbey, 48, 193, 218
Waddell, Chrysogonus, 11 n. 15, 20, 21, 22, 24
Walberberg nunnery, 246
Waldsassen Abbey, 258

INDEX

Wales, 50, 54, 105, 114, 195, 196, 197, 241, 246
Walkenried Abbey, 51, 65
war, 33, 53, 110, 112, 197, 239, 241, 266, 267, 270, 271, 274, 287
   Hundred Years, 270
   Hussite Wars, 271
   Thirteen Years, 271
   Wars of Independence (Scotland), 271
Ward, Benedicta, 18
Warden Abbey, 109, 114, 191, 223
Wasserleben Abbey, 258
water, 17, 54, 56, 93, 190, 191, 192, 199
   lavabo, 165, 172
   mandatum, 172
   mill, 171, 186, 190
   provision of, 73, 164–165, 169–170, 172
   symbolism, 229
   waste, 168, 172
Waverley Abbey, 69, 190
Westphalia, 249
Wettingen Abbey, 134
Wienhausen nunnery, 137, 145, 258
wilderness, concept of, 14, 18, 54, 73, 198, 220
William of Conches, 212
William Giffard, bishop of, Winchester, 51
William of Saint Thierry, 19, 21, 25, 26, 28, 31, 34, 55, 158, 212, 228, 231
Wilsnack, 259
Wismar, 198
Wittelsbach, 103, 289

women, 1, 5, 124, 125, 126, 127, 128, 143, 170
   access to the monastic spaces by, 125, 131–132, 258–259
   lay, 51, 66, 101, 102, 104, 106, 110, 125, 131, 132, 146–148
   see also nuns
wool, 16, 17, 190, 197
   production, 192, 195, 199
   trade, 192, 195, 202
work, 3, 6, 7, 14, 17, 61, 64, 65, 138, 165, 184, 185, 188, 208, 255
Worms, 266
Wrocław, 221
   Henry, bishop of, 108
Wulfric of Haselbury, 226, 227
Würzburg, 177
   Bertold von Sterneberg, bishop of, 105
   Cistercian college in, 248

York, 199, 256
   Corbridge, archbishop of, 213
   St Mary's Abbey, 25
Yorkshire, 53, 54, 67, 94, 95, 103, 105, 135, 143, 146, 192, 199, 213, 220

Zagreb, 200
Zbraslav Abbey, 109, 162, 249
   Conrad, abbot of, 114
Žd'ár Abbey, 222, 264
   Cronica domus Sarensis, 222
Zehdenick nunnery, 258
Zinna Abbey, 174, 199, 250, 254, 265
Zlatá Koruna, 187
Zwettl Abbey, 18, 210, 218, 260
   Liber Fundatorum, 218

Main

AUG 0 6 2014

WITHDRAWN

PORTLAND PUBLIC LIBRARY SYSTEM
5 MONUMENT SQUARE
PORTLAND, ME 04101

04/28/2014 $39.95